Routledge Handbook of African Media and Communication Studies

This handbook comprises fresh and incisive research focusing on African media, culture and communication. The chapters from a cross-section of scholars dissect the forces shaping the field within a changing African context. It adds critical corpora of African scholarship and theory that places the everyday worlds, needs and uses of Africans first.

The book goes beyond critiques of the marginality of African approaches in media and communication studies to offer scholars the theoretical and empirical toolkit needed to start building critical corpora of African scholarship and theory that places the everyday worlds, needs and uses of Africans first. Decoloniality demands new epistemological interventions in African media, culture and communication, and this book is an important interlocutor in this space. In a globally interconnected world, changing patterns of authority and power pose new challenges to the ways in which media institutions are constituted and managed, as well as how communication and media policy is negotiated and the manner in which citizens engage with increasing media opportunities. The handbook focuses on the interrelationships of the local and the global and the concomitant consequences for media practice, education and citizen engagement in today's Africa. Altogether, the book foregrounds convivial epistemologies relevant for locating African media and communication in the pluriverse.

This handbook is an essential read for critical media, communications, cultural studies and journalism scholars.

Winston Mano is a Reader and a member of the University of Westminster's top-rated Communication and Media Research Institute (CAMRI). He is also a Course Leader for the MA in Media and Development and the Founder/Editor-in-Chief of the *Journal of African Media Studies*. Mano is also a Senior Research Fellow at the University of Johannesburg, South Africa.

viola c. milton is a Professor in the Department of Communication Science at the University of South Africa.

Routledge Handbook of African Media and Communication Studies

Edited by Winston Mano and viola c. milton

LONDON AND NEW YORK

First published 2021
by Routledge
2 Park Square, Milton Park, Abingdon, Oxon OX14 4RN

and by Routledge
52 Vanderbilt Avenue, New York, NY 10017

Routledge is an imprint of the Taylor & Francis Group, an informa business

© 2021 selection and editorial matter, Winston Mano and viola c. milton; individual chapters, the contributors

The right of Winston Mano and viola c. milton to be identified as the authors of the editorial material, and of the authors for their individual chapters, has been asserted in accordance with sections 77 and 78 of the Copyright, Designs and Patents Act 1988.

All rights reserved. No part of this book may be reprinted or reproduced or utilised in any form or by any electronic, mechanical, or other means, now known or hereafter invented, including photocopying and recording, or in any information storage or retrieval system, without permission in writing from the publishers.

Trademark notice: Product or corporate names may be trademarks or registered trademarks, and are used only for identification and explanation without intent to infringe.

British Library Cataloguing-in-Publication Data
A catalogue record for this book is available from the British Library

Library of Congress Cataloging-in-Publication Data
A catalog record for this book has been requested

ISBN: 978-1-138-57477-9 (hbk)
ISBN: 978-1-351-27320-6 (ebk)

Typeset in Bembo
by Apex CoVantage, LLC

No one is without knowledge, except the one who asks no questions.
Those who ask questions can never lose their way.
African Proverb

This book is for those who questioned before us, and for all those who will continue to ask questions.

Contents

List of contributors	ix
Acknowledgments	xiv

1 Decoloniality and the push for African media and communication studies: an introduction
  Winston Mano and viola c. milton — 1

2 Afrokology of media and communication studies: theorising from the margins
  Winston Mano and viola c. milton — 19

3 Frantz Fanon, Ngũgĩ wa Thiong'o, and African media and communication studies
  Pier Paolo Frassinelli — 43

4 Rethinking African strategic communication: towards a new violence
  Colin Chasi — 54

5 Afrokology and organisational culture: why employees are not behaving as predicted
  Elnerine W.J. Greeff — 68

6 To be or not to be: decolonizing African media/communications
  Kehbuma Langmia — 81

7 Communicating the idea of South Africa in the age of decoloniality
  Blessed Ngwenya — 91

8 Decolonising media and communication studies: an exploratory survey on global curricula transformation debates
  Ylva Rodny-Gumede and Colin Chasi — 107

Contents

9   Africa on demand: the production and distribution of African narratives through podcasting   126
Rachel Lara van der Merwe

10   The African novel and its global communicative potential: africa's soft power   141
Mary-Jean Nleya

11   Citizen journalism and conflict transformation: exploring netizens' digitized shaping of political crises in Kenya   155
Toyin Ajao

12   Ghetto 'wall-standing': counterhegemonic graffiti in Zimbabwe   166
Hugh Mangeya

13   "Arab Spring" or Arab Winter: social media and the 21st-century slave trade in Libya   181
Ashley Lewis, Shamilla Amulega, and Kehbuma Langmia

14   On community radio and African interest broadcasting: the case of Vukani Community Radio (VCR)   192
Siyasanga M. Tyali

15   Not just a benevolent bystander: the corrosive role of private sector media on the sustainability of the South African Broadcasting Corporation   205
Kate Skinner

16   Health communication in Africa   217
Elizabeth Lubinga and Karabo Sitto

17   The politics of identity, trauma, memory and decolonisation in Neill Blomkamp's *Chappie* (2015)   234
Beschara Karam

18   Nollywood as decoloniality   245
Ikechukwu Obiaya

19   Afrokology as a transdisciplinary approach to media and communication studies   256
viola c. milton and Winston Mano

Index   *276*

Contributors

Toyin Ajao is Peace and Conflict Doctoral Fellow at the University of Pretoria where she was Assistant Lecturer from 2014 until 2016 teaching international relations. She is an alumna and an associate of the Africa Leadership Centre (ALC) at King's College, London and Nairobi. She is also an alumna of the Obafemi Awolowo University, Ile-Ife, Nigeria. Ajao was a Social Science Research Council (SSRC) 2015–2016 Next Generation Social Sciences in Africa Doctoral Dissertation Research Fellow and a Fellow of the Andrew Mellon grant under the Peace and Security research theme at the University of Pretoria. In 2017, she received additional grants for Dissertation Completion Fellowship of the SSRC and the ALC. Her research foci include human security, peace processes, African peace mechanism, cultures of peace, conflict transformation, social media activism, new media technology, citizen journalism, visionary feminism and gender, and sexual rights.

Shamilla Amulega is a third-year doctoral student in the Communication, Culture and Media Studies Department at Howard University in Washington, DC. She is also pursuing a certificate in women's studies. Amulega earned a BA in journalism, electronic media (TV/radio/print/film) with a minor in psychology and public relations at Daystar University, Nairobi, Kenya in 2003. She graduated from Bethel University, St. Paul, Minnesota, with a MA in communications in 2006 and a post-graduate certificate in teaching in 2009. Her communication research areas of interest are global communications, new technologies as they relate to Africa in world affairs, media advocacy and international development.

Colin Chasi is Professor of Communication Studies at the University of the Free State (UFS) and the Director of the Unit for Institutional Change and Social Justice at UFS. He is the former Head of the Department of Communication Studies at the same university, a position he also held at the University of Johannesburg. He works in various aspects of the philosophy of communication and has written extensively on aspects of media, communication and the decolonization of the discipline. He is currently occupied in the development of what has been called participation studies – an attempt at presenting a quintessentially African approach to the field. This work follows from his efforts to put forward an existential approach to HIV/AIDS communication. His latest research is focused on the transformation of higher education, in view of the contemporary decolonization debate. He has authored and co-authored dozens of articles and book chapters, as well as written and edited several books in the fields of communication and media studies. He was the deputy President of Sacomm, and subsequently President from 2016 to 2018. He is rated as a nationally recognised researcher (C3) by the National Research Foundation of South Africa.

Contributors

Pier Paolo Frassinelli is Associate Professor in the Department of Communication Studies at the University of Johannesburg. He has published widely in the fields of critical theory, postcolonial and decolonial studies, communication and media studies, and African cinemas. He is the Book and Film Reviews Editor of the *Journal of African Cinemas*.

Elnerine W. J. Greeff is Associate Professor in Organisational Communication at the University of South Africa (UNISA) where she co-coordinates the advanced research project module for honours students and teaches organisational communication theory, marketing communication, advertising and public relations. For her tuition work, Greeff received UNISA's Excellence in Teaching award in 2016. Greeff is an internationally published researcher whose research interests hinge principally on internal organisational communication, specifically as it pertains to diversity in employee populations. Her research in the mining and construction industries of South Africa, specifically, sees her engage acutely with the social and economic issues that accompany internal safety communication. On the back of this, Greeff received National Research Foundation (NRF) rating in 2017. Her research culminated in various research reports, policy documents and safety system documentation for top-ranking organisations within these industries, as well as accredited research publications. She has been a member of SACOMM since 2008 and a senior member of the Academy of World Business, Marketing and Management Development since 2016. She is the current President of the South African Communication Association.

Beschara Karam is Associate Professor in the Department of Communication Science, at the University of South Africa (UNISA) and teaches political communication and film studies. Beschara co-wrote the white paper on film in 1996 that served as the basis for the conceptualisation and implementation for the National Film and Video Foundation. She has published on censorship and film, representation and the media, gender and the media, trauma, counter-memory, post-memory and the artist William Kentridge. Karam is on the editorial board of the accredited journal *Image/Text*. She is the co-founder of the community engagement project Landscapes of Cinema: Hearing Our Voices, Screening Our Cultures, which screens and presents seminars about African trauma, memory and post-colonialism. Karam was an anti-apartheid activist in Imbali, Pietermaritzburg and its surroundings at the height of the state of emergency, in the middle of the civil war in KwaZulu-Natal (then Natal). She also served on the Executive Committee of the Black Sash during that time. Karam also wrote and introduced the first South African undergraduate political communication module in 2001.

Kehbuma Langmia is Fulbright Scholar/Professor and Chair in the Department of Strategic, Legal and Management Communication, School of Communications, Howard University. A graduate from the Mass Communication and Media Studies Program at Howard University in 2006, Kehbuma has extensive knowledge and expertise in information communication technology (ICT), intercultural/international communication and social media. Since earning his PhD in mass communications and media studies from Howard University in 2006, he has published 11 books, 14 book chapters and 9 peer-reviewed journal articles nationally and internationally. His most recent books include *Globalization and Cyberculture: An Afrocentric Perspective* (2016) and *Social Media: Culture and Identity* (2017).

Ashley Lewis is a Doctoral Candidate at Howard University in Washington, DC. A student in the Communication, Culture, Media Studies Department, Ashley's research interests include but are not limited to subcultural studies, critical discourse studies and areas related to race and inequality. Her passions also lie in human communication studies, rhetoric and teaching pedagogy. Lewis holds a BA in human communication studies, with minors in ethnic studies and Spanish, from Shippensburg University of Pennsylvania, and an MA in media studies from Howard University. She is a member of Lambda Pi Eta National Communication Honor Society and is published in the *Howard Journal of Communication*, with her work more recently being included in an edited volume.

Elizabeth Lubinga holds a doctoral degree and is Senior Lecturer in the Department of Strategic Communication at the University of Johannesburg. Her teaching experience spans across various communication subjects at both undergraduate and postgraduate levels. She has published peer-reviewed journal articles and book chapters and has presented papers at various national and international conferences.

Hugh Mangeya is a Lecturer in the English and Communication Department at the Midlands State University, Zimbabwe. He is currently teaching discourse analysis, trends in linguistics and linguistic theories. His major research interests lie in the exposition and explication of discursive practices in graffiti.

Winston Mano is a Reader and Director of the Africa Media Centre at the University of Westminster, UK. He is also a Course Leader of the MA in Media and Development and the Founder/Editor-in-Chief of the *Journal of African Media Studies*, published by Intellect Ltd. He joined the University of Westminster's Communication and Media Research Institute (CAMRI) from the University of Zimbabwe in 2000. He has studied in Zimbabwe, Norway and Britain. He is Senior Research Fellow at the University of Johannesburg, South Africa. Mano has published in peer-reviewed journals and published books that include *Racism, Ethnicity and the Media in Africa* (edited), *Everyday Media Culture in Africa: Audiences and Users* (co-edited with W. Willems) and *Social Media and Elections in Africa, Vol 1 and Vol 2* (co-edited with M.N. Ndlela).

viola c. milton is a Professor in the Department of Communication Science at the University of South Africa. She is Editor-in-Chief of *Communicatio: South African Journal for Communication Theory and Research*. Her research focuses on the negotiation of media policy in South Africa as well as issues of media, citizenship and identity. She has authored and co-authored dozens of articles and book chapters in the fields of communication and media studies. She most recently co-authored *New Voices Over the Air: The Transformation of the South African Broadcasting Corporation in a Changing South Africa* (2012) with P. Eric Louw.

Blessed Ngwenya is a Lecturer in the Department of Communication Science at the University of South Africa. He holds a DPhil in socio-legal studies from the University of Oxford. His current research interests are on global coloniality and its impact on local histories in Africa. His most recent projects examine the role of the media in mediating and consolidating political power. Ngwenya is the author of *Media Power and Hegemony in South Africa: The Myth of Independence* (Routledge 2020).

Mary-Jean Nleya is the Founder and Editor of *The Global Communiqué*, a current affairs digital magazine. She is a visiting fellow at the OCP Policy Center, a Moroccan think tank and research institution, and an Associate Fellow for the Royal Commonwealth Society. Previously, she was the Senior Editor for Op-Eds at the Harvard *Africa Policy Journal* and was an intern (and later a contractor) at the International Criminal Court, The Hague. Nleya holds a LL.M. from Harvard Law School and a LL.B. (cum laude) from the University of Pretoria. In 2016,

Mary-Jean was awarded the Excellence in Media Award by the African Media Initiative for the AU Agenda 2063 reporting category. She has a keen interest in analysing media narratives and is fascinated by the intersection between law, media, international development and public policy.

Ikechukwu Obiaya is the Dean of the School of Media and Communication, Pan-Atlantic University. He has a background in English, having studied it at both the undergraduate and the master's levels. His PhD engaged with the Nigerian film industry, analysing the impact of state intervention, through the NFVCB. His current research includes case studies on the audience of the Nigerian video film as well as workers in the Nollywood industry. Obiaya has practical experience working in the Nigerian media, both in broadcasting and publishing.

Ylva Rodny-Gumede is the Head of the Division for Internationalisation and a Professor in the School of Communication at the University of Johannesburg. She is also a senior associate researcher with the Stanhope Centre for International Communications Policy Research at the London School of Economics. She holds a PhD from the School of Oriental and African Studies (SOAS), London University, as well as an MA in politics from the University of Witwatersrand in South Africa and an MA in journalism from Cardiff University in the UK. Rodny-Gumede has worked in journalism, marketing and PR and has consulted for several government, private and academic institutions in Europe and Southern Africa, including the United Nations Development Programme (UNDP), the United Nations Educational, Scientific and Cultural Organisation (UNESCO) and the Swedish National Agency for Higher Education. She has also worked as a researcher and project officer for the U.S. National Democratic Institute (NDI) and the SADC Parliamentary Forum. She holds a C3 rating from the South African National Research Foundation (NRF).

Karabo Sitto is a Lecturer and PhD Candidate in the Department of Strategic Communication, Faculty of Humanities at the University of Johannesburg. Her research areas of interest include online communication, identity and social representations, as well as teaching and learning.

Kate Skinner is the Executive Director at South African National Editors' Forum (SANEF). Skinner has a long and outstanding track record of media freedom advocacy. For the past two decades she has done work for various organizations and watchdogs dedicated to promoting fair, quality and ethical journalism, to defend the right of journalists to report without fear or favour. Skinner has over 20 years' experience in the media industry, including chairing the board of the Freedom of Expression Institute (FXI), as a director of Kagiso educational television and most recently founding the Save Our SABC (SOS) coalition. In 2017, she received her PhD from Wits University on public service broadcasting in the digital age.

Siyasanga M. Tyali is Associate Professor and Chair of the Department of Communication Science at the University of South Africa (UNISA), Pretoria. He holds a PhD from the University of the Witwatersrand (South Africa). His research interests are in political communication, health communication, African media systems and cultural studies.

Rachel Lara van der Merwe is an Assistant Professor in the Centre for Media and Journalism Studies at the University of Groningen in the Netherlands, but she is originally from Cape

Town, South Africa. She received a PhD in Media Research and Practice from the University of Colorado Boulder, where she remains as a research fellow at the Center for Media, Religion and Culture. She has an MA in cultural studies, with a concentration in media studies, from Claremont Graduate University. Rachel's research explores the intersection of digital and screen media, national identity and coloniality – particularly within South Africa and the global South. Her recent publications include "Imperial Play" (published in *Communication, Culture and Critique*), an examination of colonial frameworks and procedural rhetoric in digital games.

Acknowledgments

Many people helped to make this volume possible. First of all we would like to thank the contributors of the individual chapters whose thought-provoking submissions helped to sharpen our own thinking on African media and communication. We also owe a special debt to the anonymous peer-reviewers for their careful, thoughtful and often sharp perspectives that helped the book take shape. For professional reasons, they will not be named. We are thankful to colleagues at the University of Westminster and the University of South Africa, for they are part of this dialogue to enrich learning in our field. We also appreciate the role of our students who often challenge us to contribute to African theories. We believe the book contributes to scholarship which centers African theories in media and communication studies. We would also like to thank Routledge, and especially Leanne Hinves, Henry Strange and Rose Anderson for professional publishing support. In editing the book, Ganesh Pawan Kumar Agoor and his team have been an invaluable resource. Finally, the continued sacrifice, assistance and support of our families and friends kept us on track. We are indebted to all of them. The book embodies scholarly conviviality in its collective approach towards centering Afrokology and all previously marginalised perspectives in media and communication studies.

1
Decoloniality and the push for African media and communication studies

An introduction

Winston Mano and viola c. milton

Media and communication are integral to politics, culture, economies, societies and everyday life. The teaching and research of media and communication involves making sense of the ways in which we communicate as well as accounting for the impact of media and technology on society. It entails investigating how people, communities and institutions influence the media and how media and communication technologies themselves shape social relations. As a result, media and communication are implicated in the constitution of power relations and exercise of power. Media power and political power, for example, combine in ways that, amongst other things, shape and direct geopolitical contestations informing politics, culture and knowledge in the academy. It can thus be noted that media and communication are implicated in specific agendas that can result in the marginalisation of those without power. The media are an important means for understanding centers of power that must be questioned and challenged.

From an academic point of view, the area of media and communication can be an entry into contemporary debates about marginalised and silenced epistemologies and ontologies. This academic injustice is a mobilising force for the academic quarrel underpinning this volume. The volume is, in the first place, a recognition of the structural violence imposed by asymmetrical power relations between trajectories of media and communication in the academy, and secondly a call to action for centering African approaches which have thus far been understated or ignored as legitimate knowledge. The study of Africa without Africa has become a dangerous pattern not only in Western universities but within Africa itself. This is evident in the extent to which African universities and scholarship at large have developed media and communication as a discipline without engaging knowledge, praxis and theories from the continent. The systematic imposition of theories and ideas from the global North in communication and media research, syllabi and curricula across the continent led some to question whether we have African universities or universities in Africa (Nabudere 2006; Ndlovu-Gatsheni 2013; Nyamnjoh 2016; Asante 2016). The quest for establishing truly *African* universities, aligned to continental exigencies, finds resonance in a context where voices from the global South are loudly claiming their space and positioning within the academic pluriverse. In this context, the *Routledge Handbook of African Media and Communication Studies* is claiming space for *African* media and communication studies.[1]

African media and communication is a formative intellectual field whose core focus and shared concepts are arguably not yet clearly identifiable, nor adequately represented in academic discourses. This volume addresses this gap at a time of decoloniality and renewed questioning of knowledge about Africa that misrepresent, essentialise or marginalise the continent. African perspectives are being mobilised to reimagine the field of media and communication in tandem with lived experiences of Africans. To this end, African media and communication studies reclaims power to unapologetically explore the manifestations of media and communication *in* Africa, *from* Africa and *by* Africans. This is not meant to signal an ethnic preoccupation, but is instead about relevance, voice and power. Media and communication have been implicated in the manifestation of power in Africa, from the precolonial through to the contemporary era. We argue for the need to "make intelligible" the emerging field of African media and communication.

Contributions to this volume recognise that knowledge production in Africa has emerged from colonised spaces occupied by those with power, and hence there is an urgent need to disrupt and undo the marginalisation, silencing and disidentification of efforts by the continent's scholars. It is an attempt to stir scholars writing in and on African media and communication more towards reflecting on the politics of polemicising, to relexicalise the language and space within which their roles and status in the academy are debated. The academic stance implied here is meant to boldly advance a pluriverse of knowledge and enlightenment. The chapters in this volume lay out a critique against the notion of "universal" knowledge as well as the nuances of a pluriverse of knowledge. The academic quarrel centers on the lack of ontological pluralism in media and communication studies. The quarrel, born out of systemic biases, unequivocally advocates a new trajectory that reimagines prevailing narratives of Africa and its positioning in new academic fields such as media and communication. The narratives in question are shaped by colonial institutions, colonial texts and anthropological ethnographies and are now urgently being reread or replaced to restore the epistemological dignity of Africans. It is a necessary response to bring into conversation input from African scholars that has over the years been consigned to obscurity. It connects with how scholars in different disciplines have rightly questioned blind reliance on the legacy of colonial scholarship that has failed to respond to and capture the realities in Africa and the global South. They critique how the continent has been undermined by Western representations that both consciously and unconsciously ignore or misrepresent the African condition.

The theorisations and practice from an unacknowledged center have made it difficult for Africans to have a voice in the academy. This practice results in marginalisation and even erasure of the African epistemological and ontological realities in academic life. African scholars have justifiably recognised the need to disrupt, reshape and reject such forms of ideological domination by others. They have declared that a wrong exists and signalled their intent to disrupt the accepted processes of knowledge creation about Africa, its communications and its people.

The fulcrum of the coloniality/modernity/decoloniality nexus in universities is the Falls movements of 2015, which signalled a collective stand against coloniality by Africans, echoed by other marginalised groups across the globe. While the creative force of resistance and re-existence that emerged from the Falls movement certainly provides rich ground for understanding and exploring the dynamics of intellectual dissent and disruption, this volume argues that the questioning of knowledge about Africa that misrepresents, essentialises or marginalises it is not a new concern. Concerns about Africa's representation have been raised by scholars ranging from Frantz Fanon (1925–1961), Steve Biko (1946–1977) to Ngũgĩ wa Thiong'o (1938–), to give but a few examples. More recent contributions include key texts such as *The Invention of Africa: Gnosis, Philosophy and the Order of Knowledge* (Mudimbe 1989); *On the Postcolony* (Mbembe

2001); *Coloniality of Power in Postcolonial Africa: Myths of Decolonization* (Ndlovu-Gatsheni 2013); *Afrikology, Philosophy and Wholeness* (Nabudere 2011); and *Afrikology and Transdisciplinary* (Nabudere 2012). These texts by African scholars represent indomitable efforts at the forefront of questioning the colonial frameworks and contributing to the decolonising perspective. The overriding concern of these works is not only to expose the politics of knowledge within colonial and postcolonial contexts but to also suggest new narratives that speak to realities in Africa. The critiques raised by voices from the South and their clarion call for knowledge equity also resonated in the findings of the UNESCO-funded McBride Report (UNESCO 1980), which, spurred by decolonisation (if not decoloniality), called for equity in global communication and the removal of structural imbalances in the field of communications. From an academic perspective, this volume adds to the rebalancing needed in this area, but with a much stronger focus on the insights from decoloniality discourses in the global South.

In media and communication studies, the growth of African scholarship is signalled by the emergence of scholarly journals related to communication, media and journalism studies, such as *Communicatio: South African Journal for Communication Theory and Research* (1974); *Ecquid Novi: African Journalism Studies* (1979); *Critical Arts: A Journal of South-North Cultural and Media Studies* (1980); *Communicare: Journal for Communication Sciences in Southern Africa* (1981); *African Media Review* (1986); *Communitas: Journal for Community Communication and Information Impact* (1995); *African Communication Research* (1997); and *Journal of African Media Studies* (2009). While all of the journals proclaim a situatedness in Africa, Mano's (2009) inaugural editorial for the *Journal of African Media Studies*, aptly entitled "Repositioning African Media Studies", criticised how academic journals have remained decidedly "Northern". Mano's provocative editorial served as a clarion call for thinking Africa from the African metropolis rather than alongside it. To this end, *Communicatio* 38(2) in 2012 was a themed issue on "African Communication and Media Theory". The publications added to efforts by individual academics, such as Francis Nyamnjoh, anthropologist cum communication scholar, who has long been among those advocating for rethinking how we do communication studies in African contexts. CODESRIA's *Africa Media Review* (especially prominent between 1986 and 1997) was also a precursor to many of the discussions about decolonising and/or Africanising communication studies today. Even earlier, the late Professor Fancis Kasoma had been arguing for "Afriethics", by which he called for journalism ethics aligned to continental ethical roots to provide more relevance for the profession in Africa as well as frameworks that could actually teach the rest of the world journalistic manners (Kasoma 1996; Banda 2009). But, in the context of a changing Africa and shifting geopolitics, it is worth asking once more if the study of Africa can walk more in tandem with the lived realities of African people and their intellectual, sociopolitical and economic trajectories.

It is widely accepted that those who produce knowledge about a discipline, wield considerable power over it. The silencing of African stories and the lack of the African in African studies is an ongoing and concerning matter. This epistemological and ontological gap has prompted a notable response from Africans. African scholars have sought to redraw epistemological, methodological and theoretical approaches to the study of Africa, from an African perspective, that is with Africans as authoritative subjects rather than objects of history. Yet, in spite of the disruptive challenges to knowledge production about Africa, the 54 countries that constitute Africa have yet to be appreciated, not just in their own terms, but as part of a connected and vibrant continent with rich histories and shared, yet diverse, lived experiences. Africans have always produced knowledge about their continent and their condition and the provocative demand instigated by the call for contributions to this volume is that Africans can and should be the most authoritative voice on Africa. The disruption of knowledge hierarchies opens up new domains of inquiry by highlighting the contingency of established ways of engaging with and making sense of Africa. Some argue that critiques of Africa's misrecognition is not based on sufficient evidence. For Scott (2015, 193), "It is a myth that we know how Africa is covered in the US and UK media . . . [because] the comprehensiveness of existing research has been maintained through certain citation practices and interpretations of evidence". His main point here is that such assumptions are implicated within multiple political and commercial agendas. Nothias (2018, 1153) responds to Scott's article through analysis of news presentations of Africa in foreign newspapers. He found that, while there may indeed be instances of change in how Africa is being represented, a more nuanced reading of the empirical evidence suggests continuity in terms of how African contexts are framed and discussed, even when attempts are made to be more representative. This includes the emergence of an Africa-rising narrative which projects an overly positive media image of Africa to promote investments as part of a broader neoliberal agenda (Bunce et al. 2016).

The effect of misrecognition of the continent is seen, for example, in U.S. president Donald Trump's outrageous claim that "once immigrants from Nigeria had seen the U.S., they would never 'go back to their huts' in Africa" as reported by *The New York Times* at the time (2017, n.p). During an immigration meeting in April 2018, he added to this uninformed view of Africa by allegedly refering to several African countries as "shithole countries". Thus, the assertion that research on misrecognition and misrepresentation of Africa might be misguided, is undermined by the so-called leader of the free world. His utterances clearly play into existing racist tropes about the continent and its people in ways that have implications for power relations in international policy and investments in Africa. It also signals that the destructive epistemologies that guided knowledge about and representations of Africa are far from disappearing, hence the urgent need to confront them head on. Disruptive intervention is needed to fundamentally change existing intellectual engagement with the sociopolitical and economic realities of everyday life in African contexts.

The chapters included in this volume make clear the contestations and resignification struggles over a more genuine connection with being African, in ways that do not only disrupt the remnants of coloniality but also promote emancipation and enlightenment (Cabral 1973). Media and communication is widely understood to be conduits of the narratives through which we come to understand the social, political, ideological and economic conditions of our existence. In fact, one could argue that narratives are key to how we imagine and understand the world we live in. Yet, the "single story" (Adichie 2009) that often arises from the way African stories are told and how media in and about Africa is being positioned and studied, often leads to oversimplistic and sometimes even false perceptions about the continent and its people. Single stories impact our own identities, how we view others and the choices we make. Narratives about Africa and knowledge creation about Africa matter. How these narratives unfold often reveals structural inequalities that tend to negate or disempower African voices, knowledges and experiences, while valorising voices and perceptions of Africa from outside. We witness this not only in the ways in which Africans and those from African descent are treated in the North, but even through images and narratives filtering through from sociopolitical and economic partners in the global South. The present moment thus calls for a fundamental disruption of conventional hierarchies of knowledge production. It holds that we should question how we research and teach communication and media studies in African universities. It acknowledges that what we know or think we know as scholars and intellectuals invested in African studies, acquire meaning and become intelligible through familiarity and repetition of previously articulated ideas, representations and ideologies from our own context. The ideas, representations and ideologies available for citation are shaped by existing orders and structures of power, with Africanist perspectives striving for space.

The contributions in this volume bring past and present African scholars in the discipline of media and communication in conversation in order to build on and be shaped by attempts at redressing asymmetries in the global knowledge hierarchy. The scholarship represents notable contributions to overcome limits and gaps in our empirical and theoretical engagement with media and communications in Africa. Collectively and incrementally, they lay bare new aspirations and upscale what can be achieved and claimed by those previously excluded from the conversation. While past efforts might today be seen as "not going far enough" or even failing in terms of disrupting the status quo, they provide important context and reference points in the process of changing and reshaping the intelligibility of media and communication studies in Africa. As an interventionist project, the underlying ethos of this volume is to argue for media and communication studies that places Africa at the center.

Doing media and communication as a single story, in the context of this volume, means writing about it primarily from Euro-North-America–centric perspectives. Take for example, how some of the early texts on mass media in Africa were largely written by researchers from outside the continent and with some motivated by colonial agendas. These works include Leonard W. Doobs's *Communication in Africa: A Search for Boundaries* (1961), which was partly funded by the US army. Other notable efforts include British scholar Graham Mytton's *Mass Communication in Africa* (1983), American scholar Louise M. Bourgault's *Mass Media in Sub-Saharan Africa* (1995) and French scholar André-Jean Tudesq's *Feuilles d'Afrique: Étude de la presse de l'Afrique subsaharienne* (1995). While important, these efforts also reinforced the influence of Anglo-American and French theories and methodologies in the discipline. Some of these works were later criticised for their limited insights on indigenous African communications. This observation gels with Downing's (1996, x) observation that the bulk of work in media theory is "based upon data from just two spots, Britain and the United States, which have . . . remarkably similar leitmotifs in their cultural, economic and political history that mark them out from other nations on the planet".

Arguably, evidence and theories from the global North continue to be the default setting in media and communication. Yet the situatedness of theoretical concepts in both historical and geographical contexts calls into question the relevance and accuracy of the ways in which media and communication is conceived in distinctly non-Western, postcolonial settings (De Valck and Teurlings 2013, 10–11). For our purpose, it means that the discipline of media and communication must continue to reflect on its grand theories and cannons, especially in response to knowledge from the global South and as part of decolonising the academy. Scholars from the South are not alone in questioning the relevance of theories for specific contexts and/or groups. Critiques of Habermas' (1989) public sphere, Siebert et al.'s (1956) normative media theories and Hallin and Mancini's (2004) media systems theories abound in media, communication and cultural studies. Such questioning of accepted knowledge and paradigms is a necessary part of learning and theoretical development.

Theoretical explanations of something or sets of guiding principles are neither natural nor universal; people do them. For example, the aforementioned theories attempting to operationalise (Western) frameworks for universal application continue to change when met by critiques against such notions of universalism. The resulting revisions aim to broaden their scope and focus to include, for example, contributions from previously marginalised groups and geographical spaces. The theoretical contributions of what we today refer to as "theories from the North" are without doubt contextually important, and their contributions to mapping the discipline are acknowledged, yet their focus on primarily Northern/Western concerns leaves a gap about the contributions from the South, including those by Africans. The mobility of theories, "be it from person to person, from situation to situation, from one period to another, needs to be understood fully within the context of the political and cultural affiliations of the theory from whence it originated, and the conditions of its creation and writing" (Said 1991, 226–227). In other words, great care must be taken when one pulls a concept from one sphere or region to another – it cannot be done with a sense of borrowing or adapting, else there is a very real chance of such a concept/theory becoming a relatively tame academic substitute (ibid). Said's (1991) stance is an important element of addressing the academic quarrel between the dominant global centers of knowledge and the underrepresented and marginalised global South, so-called academic peripheries. The circulation of concepts, theories and evidence from the South to the North and vice versa can help liberate the discipline of media and communication from "theoretical travelogue", i.e. unnecessary intellectual and cultural theoretical fashions that function as dogma or traps (New Formations 1987, 4).

Theories without context have resulted in disconnections; concepts have become obsolete, inadequate or merely redundant as technology, media and contexts change (de Valck and Teurlings 2013, 9). This, for us, forms the basis of the quarrel within the discipline of media and communication. It has implanted theories from the global North and underplayed knowledge from the African context. As early as 1997, Nordenstreng (1997) lamented the paucity of efforts aimed at media theorisation from Africa, citing lack of relevance and poor connection with local situations. Early work from Africans that attempted to offer an alternative perspective include Francis B. Nyamnjoh's (2005) *Africa's Media: Democracy and the Politics of Belonging* and Kwasi Ansu-Kyeremeh's (2005) *Indigenous Communication in Africa: Concept, Application, and Prospects*. Even though theorising about African media has been changing, critics such as Ebo (1994) and Nyamnjoh (2005) note the continued problem of dominance of media theory inherited from discourses of modernisation and liberal democracy. This in spite of the unsuitability of such theories for the lived reality of journalists and media workers in African contexts (Wasserman 2010). This observation gels with the emphasis that critics such as Blankenberg (1999) place on the inappropriateness of using Western theoretical and philosophical constructs without scrutinising their suitability within the African context. Hence, a multitheoretical approach – acknowledging the multifaceted nature of the continent as well as its situatedness in a global context – should take heed to interrogate African theories alongside their Western counterparts (Banda 2007; Wasserman and Rao 2008). In this regard, Mbigi (1995, 6) notes that, "people who free themselves from foreign domination will not be actually free unless, without underestimating the importance of positive contributions from the oppressors' culture and other cultures, they return to the upward paths of their own culture". Berger (2002, 21–22) similarly cautions against "lifting concepts like media and democracy from western conditions and applying them unthinkingly to Africa", noting that what is needed is to explain what *did* happen in African theory and practice, rather than what did not.

Certainly, transformation by imitation or mimicry of theories from other contexts is doomed to failure. In the context of decolonisation, so-called universal concepts cannot be left unchallenged. The pluriverse requires that we take serious input from other regions and contexts. Without such reconsideration, "the most often mistaken impression that the Western text and Western ways of making meaning are universal, and, therefore, to be copied by academics the world over" continues unabated (Nyamnjoh 1999, 17–18). Nyamnjoh's observation is not based on mere academic revisionism but rather a call for serious innovation and dialogue in our field. More broadly in our field, Waisbord's *The Communication Manifesto* (2019) demonstrates the value of such dialogue between particularity and so-called universality within a pluriversal context. Drawing on his knowledge of Latin American scholarship and his work outside academia, Waisbord's clarion call argues for communication scholarship (with rich intersections between theory and practice, Northern and Southern insights) that shuns single narratives and connects intellectual work to the causes of solidarity, humanity and social justice. This *Routledge Handbook of African Media and Communication Studies* similarly moves away from a single story about media and communication in Africa towards a pluriversal account of a rapidly developing multilayered discipline in a diverse and ever-evolving context. It is an activist, political and counter-hegemonic project that both foregrounds and mainstreams ideas and theories from the African context.

The *Routledge Handbook of African Media and Communication Studies* offers a critical examination of the ontological, epistemological and pedagogical rewards and risks of doing *African* media and communication studies. It is a response to the scornful disregard and policing of particularity, central to the academic quarrel about Africanising and decolonising communication studies which has so far informed the unwritten segregation of international and local knowledge production. Following Burawoy (2015), the approach in this volume argues for Southern theories to travel north without losing their radical edge or "becoming domesticated in the jaws" of the knowledge powerhouses of the global North. What we are proposing is African-driven approaches that are recognisable as such.

As should be discernible from our deliberation thus far, the tension arises from perceptions about theoretical particularism as opposed to universality. If one is inclined to pay close attention to the academic debates around Africanising and decolonising communication research, it becomes evident that, much like debates in other Southern contexts that question the application of particularity, there are at least three issues at stake (cf. Jia et al. 2016). First, this involves the inclusion of intellectual efforts that engage with local knowledge, experiences, cultures and philosophy such as Ma'at and Ubuntu (cf. Asante 1980). Secondly, the debate involves the importance of particularity in rethinking theory in ways that challenge the notion of universality, including global North dominance and bias in media and communication theory. Thirdly, particularity emphasises solution-based scholarship which attempts to recommend policy and practical applications to local contexts (Mano and milton 2020). Warnings against particularity also abound in African scholarship. The most often heard critique at regional conferences is that there is no concrete theorisation, supported by empirical evidence, that is African. In addition, concerns are raised that Africanisation might result in reverse essentialism, extreme subjectivism and a narrowing of universality (Tomasselli 2003). Often, African universities with an outward-facing decolonisation objective encourage scholars to consider global relevance above particularity. Hence, African media and communication continues to be misrecognised, marginalised and in some cases completely absent at universities and centers of knowledge and power in the global North. In fact, Adejubmobi (2016, 125) notes that

> A number of institutionally configured firewalls perpetuate continuing marginalization of African media studies . . . [and] has consequences for African media studies worldwide since the marginality inflicted upon African media scholarship at the center is often exported to supposedly peripheral locations.

This tension between particularity and universality has been a major constraint in moving the theorisation of African media and communication studies forward. As a result, the status of African media and communication studies remain undecided. This ambivalence in part underpins the timeliness of this intervention.

Two perspectives guide our entry into the current status and debate about African media and communication. One view is that the field of African media and communication has evolved as an alternative or counterforce for the liberation of African epistemology and as a space for combative reflection and meditation. This view assumes a common agenda or "the existence, or at least the possibility, of consensus on the substance, type and parameters of media and communication research to be pursued by scholars working in and on Africa" (Lugalambi 2009, 210). Such an approach could speak to the continent's communicative diversity as well as the multiple strands of the field. The other view is that this space does not as yet exist and will need to be first established as a coherent theoretical, practical and empirical space that can unapologetically claim its place in the context of global media and communication. While sympathetic to the first view, this volume argues that the organising framework for African media and communication is what needs to be identified. What is needed is a narrative about its manifestations, especially in an historic and academic sense. It is necessary to locate African media and communication as part of the mainstream without undermining its epistemological and ontological agendas, within its formative field of inquiry. African media and communication, presented as this, is not necessarily just a realm of oppositional academic struggle but also a space for reclaiming capacity to envision the new and to push back against academic marginalisation. It is an attempt to envision a new trajectory that shapes the narrative of media and communication as a transformative field of inquiry which itself is a place of struggle. It necessitates accounting for gaps in the dialectic between metropolitan centres of knowledge production and so-called peripheries, including Africa (Tomaselli 2009). Whether or not scholars of Africa have lived up to this mandate is worth examining across academic disciplines. Nonetheless, this approach recognises that Africans have always produced knowledge about Africa but that their contributions have been consciously and unconsciously silenced by others. The immediate task includes a concise rendering of the nuances within media and communication contexts arising from the shared geographies, histories and experiences of Africa that constitute this emerging academic space. For us this quest is more urgent in the area of African media, communication and cultural studies. We are keen to unpack the rationale behind existing theories and practice. We explore how this has resonated with what constitutes "African" in today's world. These are central questions in the quest to rethink and unthink the academic discipline of African media and communication.

The task of positioning African communication and media is urgent given the growing number of courses, publications and scholarship speaking to this area. For this volume, defining African media and communication is not merely about glorifying particular publications, experts and specialisms, but more so locating it within relevant historical, social and cultural practices and academic disciplines in relation to other areas of study. It is noted here that "redressing the marginalization of scholarship on African media will require interventions and activism on many fronts" (Adejubmobi 2016, 137). The volume argues that shaping African media and communication entails establishing conceptual frameworks on which meanings and cultures are shared and formed among African media and communication scholars in this emerging area of study, not just about cultural and geographical reorientation. It is about disrupting and forging alternative avenues of approaching the discipline. As pointed out throughout this introduction, the idea of African media and communication studies is not new, and has been debated in numerous articles, conferences and other spaces, yet, what remains missing from these debates is a way to move forward, to imagine our way to a place that, in Halldian terms "is becoming" (Hall 1990). In our view, African media and communication studies is characterised by this liminality, hence the contributions to this volume were generated by an open call for papers which stated in part that

> In focussing on African Media, Culture and Communication, this book will be an important interlocutor in this space, offering scholars the theoretical and empirical toolkit needed to start building critical corpora of African scholarship and theory that places the everyday

worlds, needs and uses of Africans first. Unlike the majority of existing literature which is steeped in Euro-American centric paradigms, this book promotes engagement with an African perspective as it attempts to situate African media, culture and communication studies in an historical as well as within contemporary cultural and global contexts.

We received 30 abstract proposals, considered 20 as relevant, out of which 11 full chapters were eventually accepted after a rigorous external double-blind peer-review process. We commissioned and subjected to external peer review an additional five chapters to address gaps identified in the first round of peer reviewing. We detail these contributions in the following paragraphs. Before we do so however, it is important to first mention that this volume is, in the first place, an attempt to map the contours of the study of African media, culture and communication in order to redefine and document the shift from (pre)colonial to so-called postcolonial and indeed decolonial forms of communication and mass media in Africa. Africa's colonial history had an impact on the contributions received through the open call which was published in various spaces on the continent and beyond. As will become clear, the contributions in this volume focus primarily on Anglophone regions of Africa. We argue that this is consistent with the historical legacy and hegemony of colonialism's impact on the socioeconomic, political and cultural trajectories of the different regions in Africa. The partition of Africa which began with the Berlin Conference of 1884–1885 did not only create Africa's borders but also segregated the continent linguistically. To this day, European languages or colonial languages remain the official lingua franca in most African countries, even though most Africans continue to speak indiginous languages as a first language. In many African countries the language of instruction in schools as well as the official language of government and business remains these so-called colonial languages. This ethnolinguistic fragmentation and polarization impact on the ways in which knowledge in and about the continent is produced and circulated. The scholarship from the global North left Africa with a parcelised regional approach to practice and research of media and communication. In this respect, it has been observed that existing scholarship across disciplines (produced inside and outside the continent) tend to be predominantly from the English-speaking regions of Africa, and in these contexts contributions are primarily in English and less in local languages, such as Swahili. On the other hand, scholarship from Francophone, Lusophone and the Maghreb tend to be published primarily in either French, Portuguese or Arabic respectively, with few or no translations. As a result, familiarity with communication scholarship across the different linguistic regions of Africa tends to be restricted within and across continental regions. Since many of the works tend to be distributed in the foreign language publications spoken in the different regions, their distribution outside of the continent is also limited, while linguistic difficulties make pan-African writing and reading of scholarship extremely difficult. Hence access to scholarship outside Anglophone Africa regions remains invisible to all except those within the specified linguistic regions. Equally, publishing within an English-language publication continues to be restricted to scholars able to produce work in that language. Suffice to say media practice is equally affected, with countries such as South Africa, Nigeria, Ghana and Kenya serving as the key hubs for research and praxis. This special situation makes it difficult for researchers from other regions to gather primary data and to keep abreast with the research trends across the continent. While we were hopeful that an open call distributed to all linguistic regions would disrupt this trend, we still ended up with a majority of submissions (and eventual contributions) from English-speaking regions of Africa whose empirical foci are also specific to these regions. This situation notwithstanding, the volume's focus on coloniality of knowledge, coloniality of being and coloniality of power is relevant to the entire continent.

As a text meant to move the conversation forward, the volume approaches communication and forms of media as harbingers of African sociopolitical and economic transformations in Africa. As such, it presents some theses on the philosophy of media, culture and communication in the context of intensified calls for Africanisation and decolonisation of the media in Africa. It argues that in a globally interconnected world, changing patterns of authority and power pose new challenges to the ways in which media institutions are constituted and managed, as well as how communication and media policy is negotiated and the manner in which citizens engage with the increasing media opportunities. Opting to take a "vertical view" the volume focuses on the interrelationships of the local and the global and the concomitant consequences for media practice, education and citizen engagement in today's Africa. This requires taking seriously academic geopolitics and the very circumstances which have given rise to it, including its characteristics and structured programme of action. It is about positioning African media and communication within the historical and contemporary conditions which are behind its development on the continent. The academic trajectory emanates from a changing African context where media and communication institutions and practices are rooted. Precolonialism, colonialism and postcolonialism have bequeathed socioeconomic conditions that underpin the field, leaving shared, similar and yet different histories and experiences. The volume reflects the extent to which there is a shared agenda that mobilises the efforts of individuals working within such diverse social, cultural, historical and institutional formations. It questions the extent to which there is unity of focus in efforts by individuals working independently in this nascent field. The volume considers whether African media and communication is identifiable as a coherent academic discipline/field premised on historical, contextual and other factors that shape its development. The focus is not only on the academic but also on the social, political, economic, regulatory, media and communication institutions that have common, but different origins.

To this end, the authors in this volume are committed to three prevailing lines of inquiry: theory, social justice and decoloniality. Reflecting the burgeoning academic interest in Africanisation and decoloniality and the intersection thereof with social justice concerns, the *Routledge Handbook of African Media and Communication* unpacks these concepts and concerns. The authors denounce the use of a single perspective, theory or method in their interpretations, critiques and understanding of media and communication. The volume similarly questions an overreliance on irrelevant theoretical models and templates, especially developed by those unfamiliar with Africa, which have so far undermined local approaches in African media and communication. Put simply, the volume champions the possibility and promotes the need of mainstream, continental, African-derived theories that serve as more relevant heuristic lenses in their own terms. The rethinking and unthinking of theoretical positions in media and communication from an African perspective is urgent given the politics of knowledge that has long silenced and/or negated ideas from the continent. We draw from a range of perspectives to build an African heuristic tool which is both convivial and transformative (Nyamnjoh 2017; Nabudere 2006; Asante 1980). Following Nabudere's early work, the concept of Afrokology (2006), later presented as Afrikology[2] (2011, 2012), is put forward as a decolonial heuristic tool for African media and communication studies. For Asante (1990, 2005, 2016) and Nabudere (2011, 2012) Africology/Afrikology is the name of a discipline they advanced in order to center Afrocentric thought in the study of Africa and her people. Throughout this volume, we use the terms Africology and Afrikology interchangeably to refer to the disciplinary use of the concepts as outlined by Asante, Van Horne and Nabudere (Asante 2005; Van Horne 2014; Nabudere 2011, 2012). As will become clear in Chapter 2, our decolonial heuristic tool for the study of African media and communication centers on Afrokology and draws from Africology/Afrikology as well as Nyamnjoh's concept of "convivial scholarship and epistemologies". To note, "Conviviality is a popular concept across and even beyond the social sciences, with authors employing it to depict diversity, tolerance, trust, equality, inclusiveness, cohabitation, coexistence, mutual accommodation, interaction, interdependence, getting along, generosity, hospitality, congeniality, festivity, civility and privileging peace over conflict, among other forms of sociality" (Nyamnjoh 2017, 263). As such, invoking the concept allows us to unpack the links between a range of disciplines, theories and ideologies that have constructed and made meaning of Africa and the impacts thereof on the construction of Africa in media and communication studies.

In intellectual terms, the evolving and exciting turn to Africa in the academy has spurned many terms and concepts, methods and approaches. As outlined in the final chapter of this volume, we are not after establishing a new term or discipline, but are instead adopting the tenets of Afrocentrism and Afrikology to develop a connected heuristic tool based on self-standing and transformative African perspectives. For Asante, what he originally termed Africalogy is

> Centrism, the groundedness of observation and behavior in one's own historical experiences, shapes the concepts, paradigms, theories, and methods of Africalogy. In this way, Africalogy secures its place alongside the other centric pluralism without hierarchy and by a commitment to centering the study of African phenomena and events in the particular cultural voice of the composite African people. Furthermore, it opens the door for interpretations of reality based on evidence and data secured by reference to the African world voice.
>
> *(1990, 12)*

Afrikology, Nabudere adds, is a restorative African epistemology that

> recognises all sources of knowledge as valid within their historical, cultural or social contexts and seeks to engage them into a dialogue that can lead to better knowledge for all. It recognises peoples' traditions as a fundamental pillar in the creation of such cross-cultural understandings. . . . [Afrikology] is not a closed system but an open-ended one, demonstrating once more the accommodative character of African.
>
> *(2011, 125)*

Nyamnjoh (2017, 269) builds on these ideas with an emphasis on "epistemological conviviality and interconnectedness" which involves amongst others "the integration of sidestepped popular epistemologies informed by popular universes and ideas of reality." Based on these ideas we propose Afrokology as a transdisciplinary heuristic tool that takes into account the decolonial turn from the vantage point of African epistemologies.

The prevailing lines of inquiry in this volume, therefore, commit to fostering a critical (inter)national engagement with the theory, practice and politics of African media and communication studies. To this end, the contributions in the volume deploy critical, interpretive methodologies to deal with social justice and decoloniality issues within and outside media. It scaffolds African media and communication studies within changing socioeconomic conditions on the continent.

This volume contains contributions which collectively (re)define and argue for a space for African media and communication. The first set of contributions not only challenge the marginalisation and silencing of African perspectives but unpack the theoretical arguments for a self-contained theorisation of African media and communication. To begin, Mano and milton introduce Afrokology as a heuristic tool to rethink and reposition communication and media studies in Africa in a manner that meaningfully engages with past and future realities of life on the continent. Afrokology, in their view, is a mode of intellectual inquiry which, much like the concepts "cultural studies" and "postcolonial studies" constitute an analytical framework that allows for multiple entry points, nuanced explanatory concepts as well as transdisciplinary vantage points to inform the object of study, in this case, African media and communication studies. An Afrokology approach allows these nuances to unfold in our reading, writing and explications of media and communication. Pier Paolo Frassinelli's "Return to the source: Frantz Fanon, Ngũgĩ wa Thiong'o, and African media and communication studies" responds to Mano and milton's efforts to carve a future trajectory that is routed in transdisciplinary conversations between past, present and future, through rethinking the history of African media and communication studies. It does so through focusing on two authors who are often referenced in debates on decolonisation but are not usually included in the field of media and communication studies. Frassinelli's contribution presents an introduction to Frantz Fanon and Ngũgĩ wa Thiong'o, and argues for more relevance of their work to African media and communication studies. Frassinelli's chapter introduces possibilities opened up by Fanon and Ngũgĩ's writings for historicising African media and communication studies. Chasi similarly responds to the call to carve out space for African theories for the discipline. In "Rethinking African strategic communication: towards a new violence", Chasi presents the moral philosophy of ubuntu as a viable approach in the area of strategic communication. In his chapter, Chasi asks if strategic communication can be separated from violence and warfare, and draws implications utilizing ubuntu as an approach for African strategic practice. For Chasi, communication is violence. Chasi's reworked definition of both ubuntu and strategic communication culminates in a new perspective: Africans cannot avoid fighting since human practices are characterised by violence. Rethinking approaches to strategic communication is also the focus of Elnerine W.J. Greeff's chapter, "Afrokology and organisational culture: why employees are not behaving as predicted." Greeff argues that it is problematic that corporate communication theories (especially those that are deemed "seminal") mainly originate and speak from Western/Euro, particularly American, perspectives. Greeff then uses *Fanagalo* to explicate how management strategies born from Western/Euro-American ideologies are not equipped for handling or understanding an African workplace reality. Her chapter concludes that corporate communicators need to filter theories and their applications through an Afrokological understanding. It is only once this is done that a true understanding of African organisations, their cultures and members will be gleaned. This call towards Africanising approaches towards media and communication is supported by Langmia's chapter which similarly calls for decolonising communications in Africa. In "To be or not to be: decolonising African media/communications", he argues that language is the vehicle of culture and laments that local forms and languages are still at the margins and have yet to be decolonised. For Langmia, if Africa is to truly decolonise its media and communication systems, there is a need for a paradigm shift towards one operated and managed by Africans. His decolonising approach is premised on language, independence and culture. Throughout the first section of the volume, these three can be seen as the pillars of a decolonising Africanisation approach that foregrounds the humanity of others without erasing difference. The approach to justice is explored in depth in the second section of the volume.

Ngwenya's "Communicating the idea of South Africa", analyses postapartheid South African contestations of the role of mainstream media, both print and broadcast, as well as the construction of nation and citizenship after 1994. Using the decolonial epistemic lens, the chapter discusses traditional methodological and theoretical strands, particularly political economy's limitations in discussing power relations in contemporary South Africa. On a similar note, Rodny-Gumede and Chasi's "Decolonising communication and media studies: An exploratory reading of views on curricula from around the world" questions the process and impact of decolonising in the educational sphere. It specifically questions if there is a genuine shift towards a truly global media and communication curricula that is also decolonised and relevant to the global South. Thus, Rodny-Gumede and Chasi seek to engage with how decolonisation is understood and what constitutes the elements of decolonisation of the curriculum in differing contexts, as well as the challenges that confront efforts to decolonise the curriculum. Decolonisation is necessary for informing the shifting narratives and practices in media and communication. van der Merwe's "Africa on demand: The production and distribution of African narratives through podcasting" discusses how the digital medium of the podcast is a socially transformative force by which African communities are sharing their stories at regional, national and international levels. Podcasting has allowed for innovative sharing of multiple stories across such for varied audiences. She argues that podcasts challenge the static and monolithic narratives that have traditionally been recounted about the continent and that are produced by hegemonic forces domestically and abroad. Podcasts can help Africans amplify their voice and experiment with new tools for decolonising knowledge. Close to decolonisation via podcast is the need to decolonise the book industry given its immense power as a global cultural medium. In her chapter "The African novel and its global communicative potential: Africa's soft power", Nleya examines the role of African literary works in reshaping African narratives. She examines three African novelists whose literary works have received international critical acclaim: Chinua Achebe, Wole Soyinka and Chimamanda Ngozi Adichie. The works of the aforesaid novelists are analysed in relation to epistemological decolonisation in global discourses. Nleya concludes with the finding that the postcolonial African novel is a vehicle through which Africa's soft power can be realised in the global political economy. Like podcasts, novels can be the basis of decolonising cultural representation, and this is important for decoloniality in media and communication.

New technologies are also significant in the process of decolonisation. Ajao's chapter, "Citizen journalism and conflict transformation in Africa: Kenyan netizens' digitized shaping of Kenya's political crises", analyses postconflict nonviolent technological interventions by Ushahidi, Sisi ni Amani, Mzalendo, Map Kiberia, Afroes and the Twitter Chief. What is stake is the technological uptake together with their transformative influence on Kenya in 2008. The chapter discusses how the open sourcing of information by the Ushahidi Platform emerged to fill a void as a result of the ban of live broadcasts by the Kenyan government.

Technological and popular culture disruptions in postcolonial Africa are illustrative of the key areas that drive social change in today's Africa. Popular culture in Africa is implicated in decolonial narratives linked to change and resistance to authoritarianism. In "Ghetto 'wall-standing': counterhegemonic graffiti in Zimbabwe", Mangeya demonstrates how graffiti discursive practices in Zimbabwe's urban areas are implicated in African ideological notions of governance and serve as a confluence of public spaces and political discourses. Analysis of the inscriptions in Zimbabwe reveals how writers employ graffiti to construct political identities, call for leadership change and disseminate hate speech as part of resistance and change in postcolonial conditions.

Uprisings in Africa, whether motivated by local or external factors, have not always resulted in positive social change but they are important building blocks for transformation. In the chapter, "'Arab Spring' or Arab Winter: social media and the 21st-century slave trade in Libya", it is argued that the protests that forced the removal of Colonel Muammar Gadaffi from power in Libya were followed by untold chaos, which has, amongst other developments, resulted in Black Africans being sold to Arab merchants. This crisis has recently gained national attention and sparked conversation among everyday global citizens, while developed Northern countries choose to remain silent on the matter. Through discourse analysis, the chapter examines the emergence of "social media abolitionism" by studying Facebook groups that address the modern-day slavery crisis in Libya, and the voices that have emerged though new technology. The approach creates new awareness and promotes a counter-discourse that challenges the hegemonic structures that normalise and enable modern slavery practices to thrive.

Radio in Africa has been at the forefront of reshaping and restoring African identity. In "On community radio and African interest broadcasting: the case of Vukani Community Radio (VCR)", Tyali explores the decolonising role of a community radio platform in "postcolonial" South Africa. The chapter employs a case study approach to theorise the decolonisation role of the community radio sector by understanding its cultural "liberatory" role in relation to the history and memory of a particularised African community. Tyali asks how a community radio station such as Vukani Community Radio (VCR) adapts its broadcasting content to suit the everyday needs of the African community it serves. He unpacks the manifestation of African memory on the airwaves of a media institution and the making and the remaking of "previously" colonised "spaces" into African interest–driven spaces. The chapter demonstrates how radio as an institution plays an identifiable decolonisation role through reflecting on the subliminal and overt means of resistance by an African community against the vestiges of colonialism, coloniality and Western imperialism. While radio is significant, the existing postcolonial broadcasting policy environments in Africa have remained fragile. There is a problem with how national broadcasters in Africa have handled competition and rivalry from private broadcasters. In "Not just benevolent bystanders: The corrosive role of private sector media on the sustainability of public service broadcasting in South Africa", Skinner explores the private sector impact on public service broadcasting using the South African case study of the SABC and the subscription broadcaster, MultiChoice. The focus is specifically on television. Broadcasting policy debates in South Africa – over the last decade – have been focused particularly on television transformation and the digital migration from analogue to digital terrestrial television (DTT). The chapter can be read in terms of the broader efforts and barriers in postcolonial transformation and indigenisation of public service media institutions.

Health communication in Africa has seen debates about the suitability of existing methods and frameworks. In "Health communication in Africa", Lubinga and Sitto argue that communicating health in Africa is further compounded by some unique continental challenges such as homogenous health messages communicated to publics that are often heterogeneous. The challenges include illiteracy and impoverished rural settings with poor infrastructure and lack of access to resources. This adds to other common divides behind cultural communication barriers. The chapter discusses communicative challenges from different parts of Africa, questions the applicability of Western theories and highlights the important elements in the African context which are useful for rethinking approaches to media and communication.

African experiences and social justice is also at the forefront of how film engages with change as part of decolonisation in Africa. Karam's chapter, "The politics of identity, trauma, memory, and decolonisation in Neill Blomkamp's *Chappie* (2015)", explores identity, trauma and memory in the South African film *Chappie* (2015). The film speaks to social change and transformation issues in South Africa as a postapartheid, postcolonial and democratising society. Karam argues that the film is a metaphor and an "allegory" for the quest for identity by South Africa. For Karam, *Chappie* is also a significant entry into discourses of decolonisation and neocolonization within South Africa's context, using frameworks that include trauma and memory studies; film studies; and decolonisation studies. Further afield, Nigerian films have been at the forefront of production of African narratives that are popular with Africans and also challenge the monopoly of the film producers in the global North. In "Nollywood as Decolonisation", Obiaya shows how film in Nigeria is part of larger processes of decoloniality. He argues that Nollywood's upturning of the old order did not take the Fanonian path of physical violence but rather was achieved by disrupting the established system to attain real cultural independence. From a media economics approach, Obiaya identifies and analyses three key areas in which Nollywood has caused a disruption, namely distribution, audience acceptance and funding. In the final chapter, having assessed the emerging work on African media and communication studies outlined in this volume, as well as in African journals of media and communication, milton and Mano return to the notion of Afrokology. In this final chapter, they operationalise Afrokology as a transdisciplinary theoretical perspective for doing African media and communication studies. Drawing on models of Africanisation, decoloniality and methodologies of the oppressed, the chapter argues for African media and communication studies that "matter". The chapter advocates for theoretical and methodological approaches that embrace the African experience together with an understanding that the knowledge produced must be liberating. The chapter operationalises what it might mean for research and teaching praxis to include approaches that meet people where they live and thrive. In essence, the chapter moves away from an outward-facing decoloniality that "ticks all the right boxes" towards charting a path that reconfigures and even replaces the "master's tools" (Lorde 1984) in order to recontour the discipline of media and communication. The argument is for an African approach that encompasses relevant perspectives, theories and methodologies cognisant of African realities and recognised as such within an international or global context.

Conclusion

The volume contributes to the ongoing academic quarrel manifest in the grappling and tension between particularity and universality in our field. It unapologetically and unequivocally argues for African approaches in media and communication. This decolonial task, we argue, is shared and applicable to other previously marginalised contexts such as Asia, Latin America the Middle East and also within broader subaltern scholarship arguing for increased voice. The main issue is to critically develop approaches which are more relevant, driven by indigenous worldviews, cultural values and language that is applicable to the contexts within which theories emerge and apply. Navigating between the particular and so-called universal approaches to our field requires a starting point that goes beyond critique of universalism and concentrates efforts on articulating the narratives of those struggling to retain or create diverse ways of life against the hegemony of mainstream debates. This volume gives voice to transformative alternatives to the currently dominant processes of knowledge making, teaching and research in the discipline of media and communication. In a pluriverse account of media and communication, the so-called peripheries will not just sit side by side with those from the dominant North but will be in conversation that promotes intellectual knowledge. Such connected intellectual interventions, within a pluriverse of media and communication, are without doubt contextually important, but the idea is to project a multifaceted intellectual conversation in the discipline which does not leave a gap about the contributions from the South, including those by Africans. The time is ripe to amplify transformative alternatives to a wider scholarly network, and to facilitate bridges while respecting their geopolitical and epistemic specificities. The volume argues for a grounded African media and communication studies that is self-defined, continent-facing, relevant and situated within the politics of decoloniality as part of an Afrokology theory, which we outline in Chapter 2. We strongly believe that such an African approach to our field can enrich the pluriverse of media and communication which has so far been not only too Northern but also incomplete in both its theorisation and exemplification. The book constitutes the first part of a project that seeks to bring Afrokology as a necessary theoretical bedrock for weaving together the emerging frameworks for African media and communication. It argues why there is a need for an African approach in conversation with itself as well as with other strands of media and communication in the pluriverse. The second project will be the collection *Key Thinkers in African Media and Communication* (milton and Mano forthcoming), and the third project will be the monograph *Afrokology of Media and Communication* that together consolidates the genesis and structure of the nascent field of African media and communication.

Notes

1 According to Najam (2005, 111), the North as a distinct category includes the developed and industrialized economies of the global North as contrasted with the global South which refers to the lesser developed countries that form the membership of the Group of 77 (G77). The North is generally referred to as those countries comprising membership in the Organisation for Economic Co-operation and Development (OECD). While the terms "North" and "South" were originally devised in reference to political entities, the border has become blurred. Today, the terminology of the "South" is increasingly being understood as an ideological expression representing a range of concerns that developing countries are facing. The term acts as a mobilising symbol uniting diverse developing countries towards a strategy for organising relations with the more powerful industrialised states in the North via decision-making groups such as the NAM and G77 (Alden et al. 2010, 3).

2 The concept of "Afriocology" was ostensibly first coined by Uzong (1969) and has evolved, with Asante (1980) using it in the American context to underpin an Africology informed by Afrocentricity (Flemming 2017). For South Africa's Afrikology Institute and Koka (2002), Afrikology is in essence the study of Afrika in its totality based on a multidisciplinary and integrated methodology. In this volume we are especially motivated by the late Nabudere (2006, 2011, 2012), a key thinker of Afrikology, who articulated Afrikology as a versatile epistemological and philosophical restorative African lens that engages other knowledge forms into a dialogue. This volume will deploy Afroikology as a relevant decolonial heuristic tool to think through African media and communication (Mano 2010, 2017; milton 2019).

References

Adejubmobi, M. 2016. African media studies and marginality at the center. *Black Camera*, 7(2): 125–139. Published by Indiana University Press. DOI:10.2979/blackcamera.7.2.125.

Adichie, C. 2009. The danger of a single story. In *Technology, Entertainment, Design*. Oxford: Keble College, TED Talk, 23 July.

Alden, C., Morphet, S. and Vieira, M. 2010. *The South in World Politics*. New York: Palgrave Macmillan.

Ansu-Kyeremeh, K. 2005. *Indigenous Communication in Africa: Concept, Applications, and Prospects*. Accra: Ghana Universities Press.

Asante, M.K. 1980. *Afrocentricity, the Theory of Social Change*. Buffalo, NY: Amulefi Pub.

Asante, M.K. 1990. *Kemet: Afrocentricity and Knowledge*. Trenton, NJ: Africa World Press, Inc.

Asante, M.K. 2005. The discipline of africology at the crossroads: Toward an Eshuean response to intellectual dilemma. *The Black Scholar*, 35(2): 37–49.

Asante, M.K. 2016. Decolonizing the universities in Africa: An approach to transformation. In Asante, Molefi Kete and Ledbetter, Clyde E., eds. *Contemporary Critical Thought in Africology and Africana Studies*. Lanham, MD: Lexington Books, 1–14.

Banda, F. 2007. An appraisal of development journalism in the context of public service broadcasting (psb). *Communicatio: South African Journal for Communication Theory and Research*, 33(2): 154–170.

Banda, F. 2009. Kasoma Afriethics: A reappraisal. *The International Communication Gazette*, 71(4): 227–242.

Berger, G. 2002. Theorizing the media – democracy relationship in Southern Africa. *Gazette: The International Journal for Communication Studies*, 64(1): 21–45.

Blankenberg, N. 1999. In search of real freedom: Ubuntu and the media. *Critical Arts*, 13(2): 42–65.

Bourgault, L.M. 1995. *Mass Media in Sub-Saharan Africa*. Bloomington: Indiana University Press.

Bunce, M., Franks, S. and Paterson, C. 2016. *Africa's Media Image in the 21st Century: From the 'Heart of Darkness' to 'Africa Rising'*. New York: Routledge.

Burawoy, M. 2015. Travelling theory. *Open Democracy/ISA RC-47: Open Movements*, 21 March. https://opendemocracy.net/michael-burawoy/travelling-theory.

Cabral, A. 1973. *Return to the Source*. New York and London: Monthly Review Press.

Connell, R. 2007. *Southern Theory*. Ann Arbor: Polity.

De Valck, M. and Teurlings, J. 2013. *After the Break: Television Theory Today*. Amsterdam: Amsterdam University Press, 7–17.

Doobs, L.W. 1961. *Communication in Africa: A Search for Boundaries*. New Haven: Yale University Press.

Downing, J. 1996. *Internationalizing Media Theory Transition, Power, Culture*. London: Sage.

Ebo, E. 1994. The ethical dilemma of African journalists: A Nigerian perspective. *Journal of Mass Media Ethics*, 9(2): 84–93.

Fanon, F. 2004 [1961]. *The Wretched of the Earth*, trans. Philcox, R. New York: Grove Press.

Flemming, T.K. 2017. Africology: An introductory descriptive review of disciplinary ancestry. *Journal of Pan African Studies*, 11(1): 319–387.

Habermas, J. 1989. *The Structural Transformation of the Public Sphere: An Inquiry into a Category of Bourgeois Society*, trans. Burger, T. Cambridge: Polity Press, Blackwell Publishers.

Hall, S. 1990. Cultural identity and diaspora. In Rutherford, J., ed. *Identity: Community, Culture, Difference*. London: Lawrence and Wishart, 222–237.

Hallin, D.C. and Mancini, P. 2004. *Comparing Media Systems: Three Models of Media and Politics*. Cambridge: Cambridge University Press.

Jia, H., Miao, W., Zhang, Z. and Cao, Y. 2016. Road to international publications: An empirical study of Chinese communication scholars. *Asian Journal of Communication*, 1–2. DOI:10.1080/01292986.2016.1242020.

Kasoma, F.P. 1996. The foundations of African Ethics (Afriethics) and the professional practice of journalism: The case of society-centered media morality. *Africa Media Review*, 10(2): 93–116.

Koka, K. 2002. *Afrikology: The Logical Study of Afrika (in Its Totality)*. Johannesburg: Institute of Afrikology.

Lorde, A. 1984 [2007]. The master's tools will never dismantle the master's house. In Lorde, A., ed. *Sister Outsider: Essays and Speeches*. Berkeley, CA: Crossing Press, 110–114.

Lugalambi, G. 2009. Building an agenda for media and communication research in Africa. *Nordicom Review*, 209–216, June, 30 Jubilee.

Mano, W. 2009. Positioning African media studies. *Journal of African Media Studies*, 1(1): 3–7.

Mano, W. 2010. Communication: An African perspective. In Allan, S., ed. *Rethinking Communication: Keywords in Communication Research*. Cresskill, NJ: Hampton Press.

Mano, W. and milton, v.c. 2020. Civil society coalitions as pathways to PSB reform in Southern Africa. *Interactions*, 11(2): 135–158.

Mbembe, J.A. 2001 *On the Postcolony*. Berkeley: University of California Press.

Mbigi, L. 1995. *Ubuntu: A Rainbow Celebration of Cultural Diversity*. Pretoria: Ubuntu School of Philosophy.

milton, v.c. 2019. Kind of blue: Can communication research matter? *Critical Arts*, 33(3): 30–45.

milton, v.c. and Mano, W. Forthcoming. *Key Thinkers in African Media and Communication Studies*. London: Routledge.

Mudimbe, V.Y. 1989. *The Invention of Africa: Gnosis, Philosophy, and the Order of Knowledge*. Bloomington: Indiana University Press.

Mytton, G. 1983. *Mass Communication in Africa*. London: Edward Arnold.

Nabudere, D.W. 2006. Towards an Afrokology of knowledge production and African regeneration. *International Journal of African Renaissance Studies*, 1(1): 7–32.

Nabudere, D.W. 2011. *Afrikology, Philosophy, and Wholeness: An Epistemology*. Pretoria: Africa Institute for South Africa.

Nabudere, D.W. 2012. *Afrikology and Transdisciplinarity: A Restorative Epistemology*. Pretoria: Africa Institute for South Africa.

Najam, A. 2005. Why environmental politics looks different from the South. In Dauvergne, P., ed. *Handbook of Global Environmental Politics*. Cheltenham: Edward Elgar Publishing Inc.

Ndlovu-Gatsheni, S. 2013. *Coloniality of Power in Postcolonial Africa: Myths of Decolonization*. Dakar: Codesria.

New Formations. 1987. Introduction: Travelling theory. *New Formation*, 3: 3–4.

The New York Times. 2017. Trump's way: Stoking fears, Trump Defied bureaucracy to advance immigration agenda. *The New York Times*. www.nytimes.com/2017/12/23/us/politics/trump-immigration.html?hp&action=click&pgtype=Homepage&clickSource=story-heading&module=first-column-region&region=top-news&WT.nav=top-news (Accessed 15 January 2020).

Nordenstreng, K. 1997. Beyond the four theories of the press. In Servaes, J. and Lie, R., ed. *Media and Politics in Transition: Cultural Identity in the Age of Globalization*. Amersfoort: Uitgeverij.

Nothias, T. 2018. How Western journalists actually write about Africa: Reassessing the myth of representations of Africa. *Journalism Studies*, 19(8): 1138–1159.

Nyamnjoh, F.B. 1999. African cultural studies, cultural studies in Africa: How to make a useful difference. *Critical Arts*, 13(1): 15–39.

Nyamnjoh, F.B. 2005. *Africa's Media: Democracy, and the Politics of Belonging*. London and Pretoria: UNISA Press.

Nyamnjoh, F.B. 2016. *#RhodesMustFall: Nibbling at Resilient Colonialism in South Africa*. Bamenda: Langaa RPCIG.

Nyamnjoh, F.B. 2017. Incompleteness: Frontier Africa and the currency of conviviality. *Journal of Asian and African Studies*, 52(3): 253–270.

Said, E. 1991. Travelling theory. In *The World, the Text and the Critic*. London: Vintage, 226–247.

Scott, M. 2015. The myth of representations of Africa. *Journalism Studies*, 18(2): 191–210.

Siebert, S.F., Peterson, T. and Schramm, W. 1956. *Four Theories of the Press*. Chicago: University of Illinois.

Tomasselli, G.K. 2003. 'Our culture' vs. 'foreign culture': An essay on ontological and professional issues in African journalism. *International Communication Gazette*, 65(6): 427–441. http://gaz/sagepub.com/cgi/content/abstract/65/6/427 (Accessed 22 October 2009).

Tomaselli, K.G. 2009. Repositioning African media studies: Thoughts and provocations. *Journal of African Media Studies*, 1(1): 9–21.

Tudesq, A.J. 1995. *Feuilles d'Afrique: Étude de la presse de l'Afrique subsaharienne*. Pessac: Maison des Sciences de l'Homme d'Aquitaine.

UNESCO. 1980. *Many Voices, One World: Report of the International Commission for the Study of Communication Problems*. Paris: UNESCO.

Uzong, E. 1969. *Africology*. The Union Academic Council Series, African Studies. London: Union Academic Council for African Studies, vol. 1.

Van Horne, W. 2014. Africology: A theory of forces. *The Journal of Pan African Studies*, 7(3): 3–47, September.

Waisbord, S. 2019. *The Communication Manifesto*. Cambridge: Polity Press.

Wasserman, H. 2010. *Tabloid Journalism in South Africa*. Bloomington: Indiana University Press.

Wasserman, H. and Rao, S. 2008. The glocalization of journalism ethics. *Journalism*, 9(2): 163–181.

2

Afrokology of media and communication studies

Theorising from the margins

Winston Mano and viola c. milton

This chapter constitutes a quarrel from the margins, an explication of Afrokology and an introduction to its counter-hegemonic heuristic approach in media and communication studies. The chapter goes beyond critiques of the marginality of African approaches in media and communication studies to position Afrokology as a decolonial heuristic tool that is collaborative, convivial and transdisciplinary in its conversation with other forms of knowledge. It argues that the marginalisation of African epistemologies from theoretical debates in media and communication studies parallels the routine sociocultural, political and economic disempowerment and exclusion of the continent's people from global processes. This is similar to how other previously colonised regions such as Asia, the Middle East and Latin America have been epistemologically marginalised in spite of growing evidence of the depth and scope of their scholarly contributions. The discipline of media and communication studies has remained captive to theoretical and methodological approaches from the global North, especially European and American perspectives. The marginalisation of media and communication staff, texts, theories, methods and scholarship from the global South has become routine within top academic institutions in the "powerful" global North and, ironically, also in the global South (cf. Mano and milton 2021). In this use, margin makes evident both the position and place of being constrained, but importantly, it also kindles potential for resistance, relexicalising and realignment. Thus, we argue, living on the margins does not entail giving up or surrendering to a powerful unofficial center, as the margin can offer the "possibility of radical perspective from which to see and create, to imagine alternatives, new worlds" (hooks 1989, 20). This radical reorientation is central to the approach in this chapter as we view marginality as a pivotal location for the production of counter-hegemonic discourse as well as a new location from which to articulate our sense of the world as Africans. In doing so, we propose a way forward that in our view avoids the pitfalls of using marginalisation in ways that might impose a paralysing and false homogeneity upon African epistemes, cultures and people. In fact, the chapter works to wrest the notion of the margin from one whose existence and meaning is only dependent on the construction of a unified, empowered and privileged center (Howitt 1993, 2).

In spite of attempts to police the discipline's core theories, epistemologies and research foci, media and communication studies in the global North has itself been subject to questioning of its academic standing. While the discipline has remained popular among employers and students (Quin-Jarvis 2014, n.p), recurrent debates by politicians and academia alike continue to question media studies' relevance, rigour and quality threshold. As such it has been described variously as "vacuous", "quasi academic", soft, pointless and "a mickey mouse course" (Luckhurst 2006, n.p; Quin-Jarvis 2014, n.p). Therefore, this chapter argues that where media and communication studies is concerned, the center itself is a construction that is precariously positioned. Media and communication studies as a whole must recognise its incompleteness as well as its debts and indebtedness to epistemes from the global South. Such recognition holds potential for a media and communication studies that is more open to critiques of its rationale, methods and theories, thereby allowing itself to engage seriously with the reconstitution and multidirectional flows of the discipline in ways that surpass the superficial embrace of difference through mere "accommodation" (Nyamnjoh 2020). Epistemological conviviality is necessary if the discipline is to overcome tokenistic inclusions, engage historic absences and be fully responsive to initiatives that include centering work from the margins. The concept "conviviality" gained traction in the humanities since it was first raised by Ivan Illich in 1973 who viewed convivial life as synonymous with emancipation (Costa 2019, 23). He argued that choosing "conviviality" was meant to

> designate the opposite of industrial productivity. I intend it to mean autonomous and creative intercourse among persons, and the intercourse of persons with their environment; and this in contrast with the conditioned response of persons to the demands made upon them by others, and by a man-made environment.
>
> *(Illich 1973, 11)*

In Illich's explication, we note how the concept "conviviality" already points to the significance of informal epistemes and transdisciplinarity, which in recent years have gained "conceptual and practical traction for its transformative value in accounting for the complex challenges besetting humankind, including social relations and natural ecosystems" (Du Plessis et al. 2014, Location 10 of 252). Echoes of transdisciplinarity can also be seen in Paul Gilroy's (2005, Location 160 0f 3943) explication, which draws on and enriches Illich's arguments, by looking at conviviality to refer to "the processes of cohabitation and interaction that have made multiculture an ordinary feature of social life". For Gilroy, the radical openness that brings conviviality alive, "makes a nonsense of closed, fixed and reified identity and turns attention toward the always unpredictable mechanisms of identification" (ibid, Location 168 of 3943). In fact, he sees it as a gateway to "cosmopolitanism from below", articulated in the negotiations of daily coexistence with and in difference (Gilroy 2004, 2013). Nyamnjoh's (2017, 2020) views on incompleteness and epistemological conviviality as applied within the context of African epistemes and knowledge asymmetry, aligns with Illich's decolonial and radical humanist approaches of conviviality. It also chimes with Gilroy's explication of the various analytical and theoretical positions in the interpretation of the limits and contexts of meaning in which differences are articulated (Costa 2019, 23). As will become clear, conviviality and incompleteness are key to how we repurpose Afrokology.

The continued hegemony of global North–centric theories is no longer viable, given that such singular engagement with exogenous epistemologies leaves societies, especially those in the decolonising global South, vulnerable and without credible solutions to modern problems (Ndlovu-Gatsheni 2015). In this regard, Ndlovu-Gatsheni (2015, 485) specifically argues that global North–centric theories and knowledge frameworks "have become exhausted if not obstacles in understanding contemporary human issues". The reclaiming of epistemologies and ontologies from the margins is therefore a necessary liberatory stance for centering African intellectual thought. The quest for a self-evident *African* media and communication studies comes from a site entirely marginal to the Anglo-American centers of this academic discipline. This relationship inevitably gives rise to ideological tensions and epistemological contestations that feed the capacity to resist and change in African epistemologies. We propose Afrokology as an approach to media and communication that can affirm the resilience and counterpower of previously colonised people in the "margin".

In this chapter, we foreground a heuristic tool, rooted in Afrokology, for understanding the peculiarities, nuances and intersections of an African approach to media and communication studies, both as an entity in and of itself, but also as part of the larger body of work that exists in a global context. At issue is how to connect and give meaning to the seemingly disparate empirical and theoretical work within the nascent field of African media and communication studies. It has been pointed out by many that neither African media studies nor African communication studies exist in academia either as trajectories with a shared definition nor in clearly identifiable terms operating within specific institutions (Tomaselli 2009; Skjerdal 2012; Blankenberg 1999). In addition to this observation, we argue that African media and communication scholarship has not been adequately informed by the cultural contexts and circumstances within Africa. A key question to ask in this regard is what work the disciplines do to reinforce or undermine unequal power relations (Jansen 2018). The need to challenge and redress epistemological asymmetries is a key mobilising factor behind this chapter. The transformative power of the margin should be explored as a conceptual site from which to imagine the dialogue between particularity and universality within a pluriversal context. As argued in Chapter 1, what is at stake in such dialoguing is creating space for African-driven theories and approaches to travel without losing their radical edge or "becoming domesticated in the jaws" of the knowledge powerhouses of the global North (Burawoy 2015). What we are proposing is African-driven approaches that are recognisable as such.

To harness Afrokology's transformative potential we thus begin by questioning whether African media and communication studies already exist as a discipline rooted in continental history, knowledge and experience. It is without question that education in Africa, in general, has not always been informed by the reality on the ground. In the decolonial moment, we argue that we need to do better to aid the overall drive towards epistemological emancipation. Afrokology in this sense provides a radical possibility for unsilencing that creates new ways of seeing and knowing. In this decolonisation space, the African(ist) intellectual can become the creative balancer in the dialogue between critical particularity and universality within a pluriversal context. As hooks (1989, 23) reminds us: "This is an intervention from that space in the margins that is a site of creativity and power, that inclusive space where we recover ourselves, where we move in solidarity to erase the category of colonised/coloniser". Afrokology for us is therefore a pathway to liberation which seeks to open a dialogue, a form of writing and speaking from a "particular place and time, from a history and culture which is specific" (Hall 1989, 68).

We deliberately start our writing about African media and communication in an unapologetically positioned and contextual manner. This is in tacit acknowledgment of how academic trajectories in Africa were manipulated by colonial knowledge bearers and that the resultant distortion of knowledge has left Africans with a hegemonic structure that constructs the global North as the unofficial "center" of media and communication studies. This chapter contributes to work needed to create alternative pathways towards Africanising and/or decolonising knowledge. Here, we do not use Africanisation and decolonisation interchangeably. While we view the project of Africanisation to be multifaceted and specific to the continent, we argue that decolonisation goes further in that it connects Africa to other postcolonial and regional initiatives that place indigenous knowledge at the center. The debate has become increasingly intense across the humanities, notably also in the terrain of media and communication studies. Suffice to note that continued coloniality remains a wider problem in economic, political and social spheres in Africa after decolonisation because of structural and ideological continuities.

The trend towards a pluriversal approach to media and communication studies as reflected in calls to decentralise, de-Westernise and differentiate the field, have gathered momentum. In essence, it is argued that there is a need to focus on indigenous thinking, the local, national and continental contexts as well as the entire endogenous cultural dynamic, while avoiding the pitfalls of Anglo-Saxon parochialism. Yet, the outcomes of the various attempts towards Africanising media and communication theory have been decidedly mixed.

On the one hand, there are those for whom the viability of African approaches to media and communication studies triggers debates about lowering of standards (Van der Zee and Boogaart 2020, 36). Others vilify it for what they consider to be the vulnerability of moral philosophy (which they argue underpins African approaches towards media and communication) to political misuse (Fourie 2008). Yet others are simply sceptical and cannot immediately grasp the purpose, context and need for the new theoretical efforts from Africa, expressing instead a lack of interest in ideological "mouthfuls" or "neologisms" (response from the editor of a well-respected journal on our use of the concept "Afrokology" – this in spite of the concept's lengthy history!).

On the other hand, there are growing demands by students in Africa and elsewhere for the decolonisation of curricula. Students for example argue that studying "white philosophers" should be only " 'if required', and even then their work should be taught solely from "a critical standpoint" (Petre 2017, n.p). African (studies) students specifically call for revised curricula that acknowledge the colonial context. This clarion call for genuinely diverse and inclusive academic education is best exemplified in the Falls movement that started in South Africa in 2015, but soon spread to universities across the globe. While the quest for recognition was dismissed by some academics and institutional authorities as "ignorant", "rather ridiculous", pandering to what is "fashionable", "dangerous political correctness" and attempts to "rewrite history", more recent Black Lives Matter (BLM) protests have forced the debates into sharp relief (ibid). In light of the BLM protests, some universities in the global North are now reconsidering their resistance towards scholarly engagement and gearing up for decolonisation (Mohdin et al. 2020). This turn towards decoloniality notwithstanding, approaches to decolonise curricula in both Southern and Northern contexts are wide ranging, offering no blueprint for the actual act of decolonising.

Although scholars are starting to realise that theories from the global South have value, they do not always recognise that these theories can work independently. Some, for example, argue that the epistemes from the global South have value only "because of their grounding in the cultural and historical conditions of the West" (Rao and Wasserman 2007, 31). Rao and Wasserman argue in this respect that, even though Western values are capable of transcending the cultural, geographic or religious experiences in which they originate, there is room for them to "fit", "insert" or "incorporate" other concepts from the global South. The attempts to "find a theoretical space" for alternative concepts and values could benefit Western and non-Western professionals and "result in true theoretical syncretism and engagement" (ibid, 47). Their call for theoretical syncretism and engagement is attractive, but it remains problematic precisely because their suggested framework continues to position African (and other global South) approaches as appendages or mere corollaries. As is noted by Olukushi (cited in Oluyemi-Kusa 2016, n.p), the attempts to fit in with existing global North standards undermines Africa's original contributions. He notes that "We have an opportunity to establish a much more nuanced and considered definition of ambition that speaks to our context" (ibid, n.p). Such an approach is central to our chapter.

Thus, we argue that what is needed instead is for global South approaches to be considered as independent and meaningful categories on their own terms that produce an epistemic shift based on African lived experiences and vantage points. Such an approach should avoid the pitfalls of binary thinking. Here, as will be seen, Afrokology can be a key interlocutor to transcend dichotomous thinking and the traps of essentialism. Instead, Afrokology encourages a critical engagement with all settled knowledge. Its embrace of incompleteness and epistemological conviviality makes way for understanding knowledge as entangled, rather than purely dichotomous. At issue is a transformational goal to produce knowledge and graduates who are engaged citizens working for social justice.

The problem of global North hegemonic and ideological knowledge positions as previously outlined, could, both consciously and unconsciously, easily constrain the "choice" of discourse for marginalised academics and silence their voices. However, there has been, and remains to be, great interest from African scholars in turning to alternative mechanisms for explicating media and communication in tandem with the lived realities of Africa's people. This chapter suggests that Afrokology can be a starting point to address this lacuna. To accomplish this task we review and build on past and current attempts to rethink new frameworks for African media and communication (Blankenberg 1999; Banda 2007, 2010; Mano 2009, 2010; Mano and Meribe 2017; Nyamnjoh 2011; milton 2019).

We enter the Afrokological discussion with an understanding that we cannot assume or imply that a unified subject called "African media and communication studies" is currently operative. Instead, studies in and about media and communication in Africa "span centres, departments, institutes and campuses, and are located in disciplines as diverse as [literature, anthropology, psychology, philosophy, political science, business] and so on. They are situated within diverse politics, languages, theories and methodologies" (Cooper and Steyn 1996, 7). This chapter proposes Afrokology as a heuristic tool that can help to resolve the theoretical impasse and bring nuance to our perspective on the emerging field of African media and communication. A question that we are often asked is why this insistence on introducing more theories or concepts – or, even more suspiciously, why the insistence to differentiate an African media and communication studies? Prof Colin Chasi (2018) explains that such labeling is necessary for shaping the emerging frameworks, building a recognisable identity, ensuring sustainability thereof and reaching a critical epistemological mass. We believe this is both necessary and facilitative: "Give name to the nameless so it can be thought" (Audre Lorde, cited in Sandoval 2000, Location 1 of 243). So, in essence then, what a label does in this instance is to acknowledge that a critical dialogue about media and communication *in* Africa, *from* Africa and *about* Africa is underway in multiple spaces and disciplines and hence an urgent need to recognise that these dialogues represent a canonical shift that requires connected epistemic perspectives that can respond to both hegemonic and marginal fundamentalisms (Grosfoguel 2011, 4).

Crucially, this task involves "de-provincialisation", defined here as "an enlargement of frames of reference that emphasizes broader connections and conceptualizations – not to substitute, but to counterbalance established practices" (Ahenakew et al. 2014, 217). Used in this way, the concept "de-provincialization" redirects our understanding of earlier calls to universalise African approaches while provincialising "Western" approaches to media and communication towards the thematic concerns raised by scholars in relation to the past and the restrictions placed on knowledge production which has so far denied room to other frameworks (Chakrabarty 2000; Mano 2009; Willems 2014; Willems and Mano 2016). Importantly, 'de-provincialising' [indigenous epistemes] underscores the decolonial objective of 'de-universalising' knowledge.

De-provincialising, unlike provincialising, frees us from the obligation to "remain within [Western/global North] language, epistemology and ontology [while claiming] to be doing the opposite" (Ahenakew et al. 2014, 217). Counterbalancing established practices requires an understanding that formal education and research is but one actor in a participatory civil society and thus places emphasis on transdisciplinarity that encourages amongst others the inclusion of so-called scientific and nonscientific stakeholders. One of the most significant barriers to the widespread adoption of proposed epistemic shifts in institutional culture is a reticence on the part of the academy to let go of its own privileged position as the "rightful" and sole home of knowledge production and dissemination (Paphitis and Kelland 2016, 202). In this regard, and as stated in Chapter 1, epistemological conviviality and interconnectedness (Nyamnjoh 2020) are core to our repurposing of Afrokology as a necessary heuristic tool to conceptualise and center African media and communication studies. Afrokology, as employed here draws on some of the key tenets of Africology/Afrikology (Asante 2015; Nabudere 2011, 2012), and thus "has the ability to deploy a transdisciplinary theoretical perspective to address the interconnected global dimensions of African" media and communication studies (Zulu 2017, 1). This aligns with Nabudere's (2006) initial explication of Afrokology as not relativistic to Africa.

We redefine the Afrokological approach to critically engage the multidimensional and multidirectional knowledge processes and experiences in response to changing African agendas. Afrokology, for us, is a mode of intellectual inquiry which, much like the concepts "cultural studies" and "postcolonial studies", constitute an analytical framework that allows for multiple entry points, nuanced explanatory concepts as well as transdisciplinary vantage points to inform the study of African media and communication. In this sense, we redeploy Afrokology as a decolonial heuristic tool that tactically mobilises African heritage such as *ubuntu, ujaama, humanism, maat, sankofa* to uncover epistemological frameworks as part of a strategic turn to the core preoccupation with what it means to be African and human today. As we will argue later in this chapter, such a tactical use of heritage differentiates Afrokology from the disciplines of Africology/Afrikology as proposed by Asante and Nabudere, as it signals a move away from the often more romanticised invocations of the past, evident in their explications. Afrokology moves beyond "nostalgic desires" to uncritically renovate and appropriate past African civilisational achievements that tend to view African culture as a lost object which needs to be recovered in its "pure form", in order to redeem the "unified, true and unmediated voice" of the people (Spivak 1988). We instead argue for a more critical, subtle line in strategies of representation and in the mediation of African identities. Such a revised approach concurs with what Butler (2006) refers to as "new humanism" through which alternative experiences and conceptualisations of "personhood" are brought into view, alongside the diverse modes of representation that "being human" takes.

For Nabudere (2006, 8), this requires a dual process of historical deconstruction and consciousness-raising to reconstruct our "understanding of ourselves as Africans and how our relationships with the rest of humanity has led us where we are in the context of a global historical process". Seen in this way, Afrokology embraces Masoga's (2017) notion of an *Afro-sensed* approach, which he describes as different from an *Afrocentric* approach, as it refers to one's innate awareness, a so-called sense of one's identity, that is, being African, without making it "centric", at the exclusion of all else and thereby implicating oneself in another hierarchical regime structure where one is better than another. Afrokology does, however, acknowledge that a failure to be responsive to lifeworlds "not yet visible" within current framings of media and communication studies would leave the field in "ignorance of the majority of humankind" and, as such, it would be a redundant force (Chakrabarty 2000, 29). As Said also argues, we need to eviscerate the field of the oppressive filter of "Western" liberalism, and embrace a "new humanism" which is not only capable of critically apprehending alternative conceptualizations of "otherness" and "othering" but which is responsive to the "besieged subject" (Said 2003). Employing Afrokology as a decolonial heuristic tool thus situates it within a nexus that defines and places related key theoretical and philosophical concepts at the center of our understanding of African media and communication.

Afrokology allows us to unpack locally grounded knowledge with a clear understanding that while such knowledge is likely to vary in kind, recognising the differences in local contexts is an important first step in defining the trajectory of African media and communication studies. Its commitment towards ontological and epistemological pluralism is evident in its rejection of abstract global designs in favour of intercultural dialogue amongst multiple people(s), including peoples who deem collective and nonhuman entities to be of fundamental moral importance. In addition, Afrokology rejects universality in favour of 'pluriversality'. We anchor our explication of the Afrokology approach in Nyamnjoh's (2017) notion of incompleteness. It is only by coming to terms with one's incompleteness that one would be able to connect, reconnect and build the new. Nyamnjoh argues that incompleteness is a quintessential human condition which should be seen not in the negative but as an enabler of possibilities. His argument primarily centers on the necessity for a more "equal" treatment of alternative forms of knowing and humaneness within the knowledge paradigm as a way to bridge divides and facilitate interconnections. For Nyamnjoh (2017),

> In a context of recognised and well-represented incompleteness, there is a shared imperative for harmony and collective success, as everyone intuitively recognises the relevance and importance of interdependence.
>
> *(263)*

Building on this notion of "incompleteness", this chapter unpacks the arguments for Afrokology as a heuristic tool for African media and communication studies based on existing scholarship and praxis. It is our view that a dialogical approach to life experiences and intellectual work can help foster greater self-reflection, connections, knowledge and relational accountability that can inform incompleteness in epistemologies.

Given the diversity of cultural experience on the continent and the professional practice and academic work taking shape in our field, a heuristic approach which emphasises relational accountability and decoloniality is necessary to understand and theorise the work that is being done. Researchers engaged in shared concepts of theory could generate conversations in a transdisciplinary context, across diverse examples and locales. It contributes to ongoing efforts in the "construction of new theories and methodologies in communication research that would appropriately fit the African context" (Obeng-Quaidoo 1986, 89). It allows the widening of epistemologies and their interdependence with practice. Associating and dissociating past, existing and emerging approaches could be nourishing and more productive.

Towards an African media and communication studies

There have been many attempts to construct a distinct African media and communication studies paradigm (cf. Ugboajah 1985; Obonyo 2011; *Journal of African Media Studies* (JAMS) 2009; *Communicatio* 2012, Issue 38). Notably, this has been done predominantly within the framework of film studies and film theory (where a proliferation of conferences, journals, journal articles and books speak to the distinctiveness of African cinema) and journalism (where media ethics was the driving force behind various attempts at constructing a distinct African journalism paradigm from as early as the 1960s). Skjerdal (2012, 637), however, notes that a close look at the history of African media studies shows that there is no consensus on a distinct African journalism paradigm that stands out as an agreed alternative to a Western or Northern paradigm. Although there have been bold attempts to present *ubuntu* and other similar perspectives as grand theories for general application in media and communication studies, our approach is sceptical of the idea that there is a need for a *singular* grand African media or journalism paradigm and/or associated theory which have broad applicability. In the same way that no single theoretical system can possibly ask all the interesting questions or provide all the satisfying answers, a singular paradigm might not necessarily yield explanations that can speak to a diverse continent. There is no 'grand theory' that can explain Africa. As will be clear below, our Afrokological tool unmasks the incompleteness of grand theories and instead pushes for interconnectedness of epistemologies.

Africanisation debates have been at the center of constructing frameworks for African media and communication studies. Africanisation is employed in a dizzying variety of ways in social science and political theory/thought. In short, it could be argued that Africanisation is a "reverse discourse: if colonialism rode on the crest of wanting to 'Europeanise' or 'civilise' Africans, Africanisation is the African response to a colonising genre" (Zegeye and Vambe 2009, 126). Forming part of postcolonial discourse, Africanisation is thus often described as a renewed focus on Africa which entails, amongst others, salvaging what has been stripped from the continent. Others point out that a singular focus on the past might not adequately account for the complexities in Africa within the context of contemporary geopolitical concerns (Zegeye and Vambe 2009; Ngcaweni et al. 2013, 44). A focus that negates the relevance of the current and emerging needs of Africans, and that steers towards a collective authorship of African knowledge, misrecognises individual creativity. In doing so, it relegates individuals as passive receivers of others' imagination (ibid). We therefore contend that calls for a blind return to a pristine past cannot adequately do justice to Africa's diversity, multiple experiences, dialectics and geographies. Some rightly attempt to broaden the scope by arguing that Africanisation is not about excluding Europeans and their cultures, but about affirming the African culture and its identity in a world community; however, this realisation is often accompanied by a narrow identification of who is African (Makgoba 1997). There are also implicit contradictions in how external cultures are seen to be plural and diverse, yet Africa is seen as a singular "culture". Such monolithic, insular and fixed approaches to Africanity belie the changing mosaic of cultures on the continent. It is therefore necessary to carefully consider questions about who gets to decide what was "good and respected in African culture" or even how to define and interpret African identity and culture(s).

Given the diversity of existing approaches, Africanisation ought to be examined through a critical lens. This requires close scrutiny of efforts that continue to underpin Africanisation debates. Clearly, efforts towards Africanisation have been ongoing, with much of the focus centered on African ideas of belonging. Past efforts have emphasised non individuality of the African as a core value boundary, but this is not without problem. For instance, former presidents Kwame Nkrumah (Ghana/Gold Coast, 1952–1966) and Julius Nyerere (Tanganyika/Tanzania, 1961–1985) placed emphasis on "non individuality" as the basis of their advocacy for collectivism *consciencism* and *villagisation* which they perceived to be key tenets of Africanity (Bell 2002). Former president Joseph-Désiré Mobutu's (1965–1997) "deculturation" programme built on these efforts, and argued that it was "necessary to 'deculturate' [the Zairese] to get rid of the scars the colonial culture had left in him . . . returning to the thousand year old wisdom of our ancestors, to rediscover ourselves again" (Sese Seko and Remilleux 1989, 107). His interventions included, most notably, the renaming of the country from the Republic of the Congo to Zaire. Similar changes were evidenced in how former president Robert Mugabe renamed Rhodesia to Zimbabwe as well as the above referenced renaming of Ghana and Tanzania. These attempts at positioning Africans as central to their own destinies are not without merit, but they raise many questions about narrow prescription, relevance, authenticity and their overall approaches to defining African identity. In essence, one should avoid the blind romanticism of African life that often accompanies calls towards inward looking indigenisation and Africanisation. Cultures – including African cultures – are not static, nor would we want them to be. Hence, efforts towards Africanisation should avoid treating cultures and peoples as fixated on the past with little to no interest in the present and future.

This task demands foregrounding of innovative approaches that would enhance African media and communication studies. In this sense, some African (studies) scholars have started looking at ways in which "African peoples, cultures, institutions and communication environments impede or facilitate social research" (Obeng-Quaidoo 1986, 89). From this African self-introspection developed indigenous efforts in the construction of new theories and methodologies in communication research that would appropriately fit the context of development on the continent. For Obeng-Quaidoo (1986) being African involves identifying

> four key areas which. . . , come closer to the core value boundaries of African culture. These are: (1) the role of the supreme God/Allah and lesser gods in the daily life of the African; (2) the African concept of time and its influence on him/her; (3) the African's concept of work and its relationship to how he/she perceives his/her own relationship to nature; (4) the non-individuality of the African and how this affects his/her worldview.
>
> *(ibid, 89)*

These perceived core value boundaries of the areas were seen to help explicate the implications for communication research and methodological development in the African context. The early debates in *Africa Media Review* go further explaining the problem of centering African thought as not only one of conceptualization but also of social research processes and administration. Contributors registered "a general dissatisfaction with African social research based on foreign theoretical and methodological assumptions" (Ugboajah 1987, 1). Ugboajah (ibid, 9) notes in this regard that fieldwork in Africa can be hampered by the use of recording devices and even pen and paper, as it militates against the assurance of confidentiality in contexts where this can be abused. This observation is as relevant in today's African contexts as it was in the 1980s as can be seen in the ways in which governments continue to harass and even jail journalists for failing to disclose their sources (cf. Right2Know 2016). Ugboajah therefore suggests the need to question *what* kind of approaches, distinctly African, will aid in minimising the disenchantment of interviewees and avoid the contamination of the responses. The main solution is seen as going "back to our roots", including modifying methodologies for the African rural areas to better understand African societies. Taylor and Nwosu (2001, 300) name a few of the studies that have offered glimpses into what we do not know about how Africans communicate:

- The difficulty of applying Western-derived concepts and empirical approaches to African communication research.
- The failure of the dominant paradigm of communication and national development.
- Acceptance that the transfer of technology brings particular value systems that may create conflicts with existing indigenous systems.
- The futility of cultural dependency on national development.

- The notion that African media philosophies are antithetical to Western media principles.
- The value of integrating folk media into Western mass media, including the concept of oramedia.
- The suggestion that Western intervention efforts in Africa have, in some ways, been the source of the problem.
- The need for indigenous communications systems to be part of the global conversation on communication.

Thus, it can be ascertained that for some African scholars an African approach is not necessarily anathema to approaches from the global North. Wiredu (1995, 2004) argues in this respect for combining Western and African knowledge systems, especially when this can do the Africans good. As we stressed earlier in this chapter, however, syncretism at the expense of mutual respect for African thought first and foremost in its own right should be avoided. African knowledge should never be merely as a suppressed category or appendage in its relation with other worldviews.

Africanising media and communication research is thus faced with two interrelated challenges. The first is the search for methodologies which are not driven by blind assertion of African ideas and concepts as mere replacements for Western terms. Instead, critical reflection is needed to identify, filter, provide and apply factual and data-related protocols based on an integrated indigenous knowledge system (Mutema 2003, 81). The second challenge is to craft research methodologies that are fit for purpose. As will be seen below, we posit that Afrokology can help overcome narrow and prescriptive models of Africanising media and communication.

Afrokology: explicating and positioning an African approach

The many divergent views of Afrokology necessitate an explication of its formation and etymology when one wishes to invoke its intellectual purchase. Genealogically, Afrokology is related to "Africology", a concept coined by Uzong in 1969 (Flemming 2017). Since then, there have been intense academic efforts, most notably by Winston Van Horne and Molefe K Asante, to define the concept adequately and achieve analytical clarity. Central to the work of both Van Horne and Asante, is a commitment to establish a new discipline or field based on the centrality of African knowledge and experience as articulated by Asante's theory of Afrocentricity (Flemming 2017). Afrocentrism served, and continues to serve, as a framework for "Africological" studies with clearly delineated ideological and intellectual goals, political purpose and a set of commonly understood methods and theories that serve as an important resource for African scholarship engaged in various projects of decolonisation (Okafor 2014; Chawane 2016; Flemming 2017). Yet, for some, the "conception of the primary rootedness of the discipline in the African American initiative and experience and the Black Freedom Movement and its emancipator thrust" (Karenga 2009) was troubling. Hence efforts to theorise *for* the African continent *from* the African continent gained momentum.

In 2005, at the International Conference on African Renaissance Studies: Multi-, Inter- and Transdisciplinary Paradigms, Ugandan scholar Dani Nabudere contributed *Afrokology* to the conversation, clearly delineating it as a scientific approach not only for "investigating historical phenomena in which African achievements are properly recognised" but also for creating the "basis for articulating an African agenda for knowledge production that is relevant to African conditions and beyond" (Nabudere 2006, 8–9). Nabudere offered his input as an original African intervention, emanating from Africa rather than the Euro-American space.

He later gave a formal conceptual and analytical identity to his approach, which he renamed Afrikology, and situated it as "a new science/discipline", different from Afrocentricity and its associated Africology (2011, 162). For Nabudere (ibid) Afrikology, because of its location and place of origin, is best suited to address African problems arising from the colonial and postcolonial experience and to identify tools that can resolve those problems and contradictions in a positive manner. His assessment of Afrocentricity is echoed by Ngcaweni et al. (2013, 44) who argue that such intellectual–political approaches are "largely reactive in orientation and confined to an essentialism that does not appreciate the complexity of today's influences like globalisation, multi-polarity, ecological concerns, and polycentric technological phenomena". In spite of Nabudere's critiques of Africology, and the associated theory of Afrocentricity, we have argued elsewhere that his expanded theorisation of the concept of Afrikology in actual fact overlaps with the American Africology in terms of its key tenets and underlying assumptions. Later in the chapter we will briefly outline Nabudere's later (2011, 2012) arguments and explain how our chapter adopts an approach that reworks his original *Afro*kology from a decolonial perspective, underpinned by epistemological interconnectedness and conviviality.

In delineating Afrikology, Nabudere (2011, 164) draws on Kershaw (1998) to identify the three types of knowledge he considers as necessary for the emancipation of Africa, i.e. *practical knowledge, technical knowledge* and *participation in action*. This, we contend, is not dissimilar to what Karenga (2009, 61) describes as Afrocentricity's "triple mission of cultural grounding, academic excellence, and social responsibility and the critical, corrective, and multidimensional task it calls for and compels". Yet, for Nabudere, Afrikology's open-ended and all-inclusive nature makes it better suited than any other approach to accomplish this disciplinary task. Of course, a close reading of Africology (i.e. the so-called American intellectual branch of the discipline) shows that there are many similarities and overlaps with Nabudere's Afrikology. A common denominator for both Africology and Afrikology is, for example, a core concern to build upon and expand multi-, inter- and transdisciplinary perspectives focused on "an African-centered, structured, and critical exploration, analysis and synthesis of the historical evolution and contemporary nature of the global black experience" (Okafor 2014, 219). Still, lines of demarcation continue to exist in the field based on

- Subject-matter approaches to the definition of the discipline.
- Disciplinary permeability.
- Epistemological perspective or worldview approaches to the definition of the discipline.
- The centrality of the African American experience.
- Diasporic visions of the discipline.
- Global visions of the discipline.
- Outsiders' versus insiders' perceptions of the scope of the discipline.
- Disciplinary marketability or viability as a gateway to both intellectual development and job opportunities (Okafor 2014, 209).

We consider these nuances as evidence of the dynamic nature of the intellectual debates around centering Africanity, rather than a rejection of the core objectives of Africology/Afrikology. Thus, as Levi (2012) notes,

> Whether we want to call it African-Centered Studies, Afrocentric Studies, or Africana Studies, the most important part of these nomenclatures is that we start with Africa as our

> center and that the focus of Africana Studies has its location in the Nile Valley, where the first cultural highway served as the womb for so much of African culture.
>
> *(180)*

What is needed therefore is not to dismiss existing interventions, but to bring African interventions into conversation with each other as well as with scholarship in the broader global South and the global North contexts – hence a coalescing heuristic tool.

We propose Afrokology as a heuristic tool for African media and communication. Our approach to Afrokology inevitably involves relixicalising the field in a way that centers African knowledges. Relexicalising often relies on building compound-noun concepts comprising several terms, in this case:

> Afro [linking to and situated in Africa] + (K) [acknowledging the epistemic disobedience it embodies] + ology [referring to a subject of study, or a branch of knowledge]

First, it is "Afro" as opposed to "Afri", to signal at once the interconnectedness with aspects of the theoretical project of *Afro*centricity, as well as its emancipatory roots wrested from the lived experiences of Africans in Africa and the diaspora. "Afro" in Afrokology is suitable for us also because it links to alternative and subaltern discourses of black identity which for example saw the Afro hairstyle become an important symbol of struggle, identity and agency during the civil rights movements in the 1960s and in the struggles for liberation in Africa. The Afro, in spite of disputes about its African roots, has been and continues to be, symbolic of black pride and empowerment. While having an Afro is not automatically political, the "Afro" links our use of the concept to the interconnectedness of black identity struggles while it also signals Afrokology's indebtedness to *Afro*centric theory. This commitment to an emancipatory and activist stance in pursuit of epistemological justice, is further affirmed by our preference for Nabudere's "k" rather than a "c" (2006, 2011, 2012). To paraphrase Madhubuti (1994), in the spelling of Afrokology, a "k" is used rather than a "c", because many public intellectuals and activists use the "k" specifically to represent an acknowledgement that "K" is germane to Afrika (cf. Abif 1998, 44; Koka 2002; Nabudere 2006). Most vernacular or traditional languages on the continent spell Afrika with a "K". When one, therefore, speaks of AfriKa, they're bringing an Afrikan-centered view to the meaning of the word (Madhubuti 1994). "K" in this sense embodies "epistemic disobedience" called for in this chapter, as it gives visual affirmation to the clarion call for excavating the African voices silenced by colonialism/universalism, thereby asserting epistemic rights from the margin. Therefore, Afrokology spelt with a 'k' for us represents a redefined and potentially different starting point – one that engages more directly with realities and lived experiences on the African continent. Having now outlined the reasoning behind our preferred spelling, it is necessary to distinguish, in more detail, how our use of Afrokology diverges from Africology/Afrikology.

For us, the key element of differentiation can be found in Nabudere's earliest definition of "Afrokology" as:

> a universal scientific epistemology that is not necessarily African-centric or Afrocentric . . . that goes beyond Eurocentrism, or other ethnocentrisms. It recognises all sources of knowledge as valid within their historical, cultural or social contexts and seeks to engage them into a dialogue that can lead to better knowledge for all. . . . This task does not, however, need Africans to develop their own "centricism" to achieve it.
>
> *(Nabudere 2006, 9, 13)*

In this sense, Nabudere's initial approach emphasises Afrokology as a dialogical approach. It therefore invites a self-reflective approach to think about Africanity in a broader sense. The fact that Nabudere's first AfroKology does not require Africans to develop their own centrism is an important distinction from (the American) Africology, as we argue that such centrist approaches remain caught up within the confines of a hegemonic division of knowledge. Our approach, however, attempts to also overcome contradictions in Nabudere's articulations of Afrokology (Nabudere 2006), as well as its successor, Afrikology (Nabudere 2011, 2012).

The first point of difference is highlighted by Zegeye and Vambe's (2009) critique of Nabudere's explication of Afrokology's focus on a singular tradition, rather than traditions (thereby ignoring diversity of sources and traditions). They note that Nabudere speaks of "African knowledge" without ever naming it in the plural, nor giving it concrete form and, especially so it seems, the idea that African knowledge derives from "a unified whole that has emerged from collective authorship". This echoes Osha's (2018, 126) observation that "Nabudere's project adopts the same kind of posture and intent as the universalists of science that he opposes". We are sympathetic to Zegeye and Vambe's (2009, 130) view that an "Africanisation programme that does not value individual creativity and initiatives, as is the case with [Nabudere's] Afrokological assumptions, can only undermine the efforts that ordinary people display when they want to make Western modernity work for themselves".

We submit that Zegeye and Vambe's (2009) reading of Nabudere's explication of Afrokology points to a contradiction in terms of the concept's explicit commitment to the recognition of other sources of knowledge. In the first place, Nabudere's focus on a singular source of knowledge production (i.e. "tradition" and "African knowledge") negates diversity. Secondly, his focus on the collective authorship of African knowledge, at the expense of individual creativity, is tantamount to evoking images of Africa's "glorious" past and "uncritically projecting them as the basis of a viable Africanisation . . . agenda in contemporary Africa" (ibid).

These insights are echoed in Sanya Osha's (2018) critique of Nabudere's later Afrikology (2011, 2012) as "epistemological totalitarianism". Osha (2018, 125) posits that Nabudere's Afrikology is presented as an

> "all-encompassing epistemology" able to transcend the perceived fallacy and shortcomings of Cartesianism, able to engender true justice in social relations, able to act as an emancipatory program for oppressed peoples, and finally, able to restore the injured dignity of the black race.

In addition, Nabudere's uncritical and romanticised embrace of the African past, at times sits uneasily with his advocacy for openness and plurality of knowledge. It displays "a marked racial agenda on the side of blackness" (ibid). We are opposed to the implied notion of a homogenous African culture as presented in Nabudere's work. Our understanding of culture as dynamic and complex also conflicts with the notion of an African culture that is frozen, static and waiting to be renovated. Instead, we put a premium on African cultural diversity and interconnections. Contradictions in Nabudere's approach and associated narrow view of Africanity could be read as a throwback to nativism. Nativism is a concept Said (1994) used to refer to a general trend in the late 1980s and early 1990s to "reclaim one's past". For Said, it is important to move beyond the confines of such local identities which claim, for example, that only the Irish are Irish, or the Africans African – as can be seen in Nabudere's continued quest for revival and preservation of a black African past. We agree that Nabudere's characterisation of "ancient of Africa" is at times too romanticised and lacking adequate insight of the diverse experiences on the continent, outside Egypt. Afrikology, in his later works, while seen as synonymous with "transdisciplinarity" (2011, 99), also looks at the world in terms of universality and sameness, thereby negating difference and pluriversality. The task for us therefore is to disrupt this universalism by recognising that both Western and African epistemologies are equally situated in historical and contemporary social realities.

Osha (2018) therefore questions the viability of Afrikology as an epistemological approach. For Osha what is least convincing is Nabudere's (2011) call to return to an "ethos of wholeness and interconnectedness" of an African past based on the use of languages without addressing the logistical requirements for attaining such a goal. Osha also notes how Nabudere is "silent" about which African language is applicable for this task, noting the need for more "evidence" before one grounds Nabudere's Afrikology as a "paradigm of oppositionality" (Nabudere 2011, 103). Nabudere (2011, 125) ostensibly saw Afrikology as demonstrative of the accommodative character of African knowledge systems. In reality however, Nabudere's "Afrikology" appears to not only have a relatively closed reading of Africa, but could also be read as dismissive of existing African approaches, such as *maat*, *ubuntu* and *sankofa*, describing these as either "political manifestos and ideologies for ruling elites faced with problems of mobilisation and political organisation" or constructions meant to "meet the needs of academic consumption, [or] created to engender debate" (Nabudere 2011, 126). Such characterisations are illustrative of Nabudere's perfunctory and closed approach to the broader community of African scholarship and ideas. It is a marked difference from our convivial embrace of intellectual scaffolding in African thought. Convivial scholarship, in our view, is important if one is to engage with decoloniality in media and communication studies. While the highlighted criticisms of Nabudere's work are legitimate, we maintain that we invoke Afrokology differently. Importantly, both Africology and Afrikology are defined by their proponents as either a new science and/or a new discipline, and as pointed out earlier, both are imbued with essentialist attributes. To overcome this theoretical impotency we propose to repurpose and innovatively mobilise Nabudere's original "Afrokology" as a coalescing heuristic tool. It is our view that Afrokology used in this way can be a significant signpost in understanding the relationship between the media and society. Like Afrikology, its philosophical undercurrent is defined by African ideals, but unlike Afrikology, it is not meant to force a false unity between Africans. Instead, Afrokology is cognizant of the fact that Africa is a continent consisting of at least 54 countries, each with its own idiosyncrasies.

Our reappraisal of Afrokology is premised on decolonial epistemological conviviality through which African knowledges can enter into purposeful and critical dialogues with other sources of knowledge. Decolonial thinking is underpinned by tactical strategies, mobilisations and hegemonic reconceptualisation that create new spaces. Our vision for Afrokology recognises that the basic tenets of Western knowledge – i.e. Cartesian – rationality, teleological (focusing on a foreseeable end goal) and universal reasoning (the idea of only one possible rationality) – are historically situated, and potentially restrictive if universalised throughout, and as such they prevent the imagination of other possibilities (Andreotti and Ahenakew 2013). Unlike Nabudere, our use of Afrokology operates more within the context of decoloniality. We are not in search of universality, opting instead for pluriversality which is viewed as "a need to consider how different worlds can coexist, not submitted in one reality, but in incommensurability" (cf. Querejazu 2016, 2).

The emphasis on pluriversality is a key aspect of Afrokology's connectedness to decoloniality which include conscious acts of reclamation and validation. This manifests in a double gesture: first, Afrokology demands a critical engagement with the inadequacy of existing epistemologies and their linkages with coloniality, but it also, secondly, demands delinking oneself from these knowledge systems and reimagining present-futures of African media and communication (Grosfoguel 2008, 1). In this sense, our use of Afrokology aims to move discussions away from the uncritical and wholesale embrace or complete rejection of modernity. In adopting the tenets of decoloniality, it similarly asks "Can we produce knowledges beyond Third World and Eurocentric fundamentalisms? . . . and . . . How can we overcome Eurocentric modernity without throwing away the best of modernity as many Third World fundamentalists do?" (ibid). These remain important questions for us as they identify the incompleteness of dominant global North paradigms together with a need to move beyond a mere superficial engagement with hitherto underrepresented epistemologies from the global South.

We are persuaded by the insights put forward by Nyamnjoh's (2017, 2020) explication of scholarly conviviality grounded in incompleteness. For Nyamnjoh, incompleteness is neither an inadequacy nor something to feel inferior about, but rather a gateway to relational epistemologies through which we can bring historical ethnography into conversation with the ethnographic present (2020, 13). He argues against throwing away the Western (knowledge) baby with the bathwater. It is within this context that we invoke the intellectual currency of Afrokology. Afrokology in this sense acknowledges that the shift from colonialism to the present has produced a duality of life which cannot be avoided – one has to engage with it and the urgent question is *how* to do so. Africa has to reimagine its place in a postcolonial, postmodern, decolonised and globalised world where the very notion of identity has become mired in ambiguity and controversy. Appiah's (1992) assertion that "'the colonial' is not dead, since it lives on in its 'after-effects'" is especially apropos here (Appiah 1992, 71). Colonization was not only a process of cultural and political domination and oppression, but also a process of cultural hybridisation which is best understood as a transculturation process which sees the creation of a new mixed cultural order whereby both coloniser and colonised become transformed (Bhabha 1994, 33). It is necessary therefore for both the global South and the global North to lean into this duality at the core of the colonial experience. In Zeleza's (2005) words, Afrokology therefore sees the urgent task for media and communication scholars to be the radical rethinking of how we engage with media and communication theory and research both in Africa and elsewhere.

Afrokology's groundedness in incompleteness and scholarly conviviality invites us to place a premium on dialogue between, and respect for, various points of view. It also emphasises the importance of acknowledging and valuing different experiences. This, we argue, could create added impetus for conversations with alternative voices, not just on the periphery, but in the center. Afrokology's embrace of duality further foregrounds the importance of historical intersectionality in our explications of the roles and contributions to knowledge production by marginalised voices.

Clearly, Nyamnjoh's accommodative stance and gesture of compassion to disabuse and save the "western [knowledge] baby" is one that would compel the global North, as well as the global South, to be more open to other ontologies and epistemologies. Using the metaphor of eating and being eaten, Nyamnjoh (2018, 40–41) also argues that

> In the game of life characterised by unequal encounters between individuals and cultures compelled to share places and spaces like scorpions in a lidded basket, it would appear that the question is not so much whether cannibalism is possible but rather who is eating whom, how and why, and the power relations that render such eating or being eaten visible and invisible in particular ways and contexts.

In other words, this is about addressing asymmetrical power relations and creating "spaces and opportunities for mutually edifying conversations across various divides, hierarchies and inequalities" (Nyamnjoh 2017, 266). In regards to this, we propose Afrokology as a heuristic toolkit rather than a discipline or a unified set of premises that rigidly guide African intellectual thought in media and communication studies. An Afrokological approach offers conceptual and practical tools for repositioning African media and communication in ways that are in conversation with other approaches.

Centering a convivial Afrokological heuristic tool

Afrokology, as a heuristic tool, is open and creative in its embrace of emerging ideas, concepts and connections as resources for new thinking and relexicalising the discipline of media and communication studies. We do not propose an Afrokological position that is insular or defensive of Africanity. Instead we repurpose Afrokology, freeing it from Nabudere's (2011, 2012) essentialist tendencies, and steering it to align more with Nyamnjoh's (2017, 2020) explication of incompleteness and scholarly conviviality. This approach, we argue, acknowledges that the duality that results from colonialism and the inevitable realities of encounters and interactions between coloniser and colonised, result in inextricable interconnections and fluidities. For this reason, Afrokology considers colonial importation and the decolonisation of media and communication studies, not as steps in a linear move towards African emancipation but rather as entangled and perhaps even inextricable. Afrokology therefore does not merely imply an effort to revive a desired and idealised past, as it is aware that blind constructions of past values and traditions cannot be uncritically superimposed on contemporary issues. Deploying Afrokology as a heuristic tool instead presents a necessary corrective against uncritical particularity that inhibits critical dialogues in African media and communication. As presented in Chapter 1, what needs to be avoided is an insular particularity that leads to essentialisms. We propose *critical* particularity which, in our view, is necessary for rethinking theory in ways that challenge the notions of universality, including global North dominance in media and communication (cf. Chapter 1). Considering Afrokology against this backdrop, it could be at once a *clarion call* for a continued African resistance to domination and exploitation of Africans as well as *a decolonial hermeneutic tool* through which Africans can manifest their sense of identity and independence in all their diversity. Centering a convivial Afrokology in media and communication highlights possibilities in the African past that have a bearing upon the present and would entail critically reflecting upon Africanist roots. It can therefore be applied in ways that carefully renovate and excavate those resources that add to the lived experiences of contemporary Africans. Such excavation, we argue, allows us to negotiate African intellectual interventions that center the margin. Taking seriously past African knowledges, which have been silenced by unexamined universality, and placing them in conversation with emergent African and global epistemologies thus become part of the ecology of Afrokology. Renovating history in this sense signals that African knowledge systems are not novel as they have been in existence for some time, even if that existence has been marginalised, silenced and ignored. Hence, to excavate and renovate African knowledges does not mean that one is "stuck in the past"; instead, it advocates for a *strategic* return to the source, i.e. looking backwards to find those resources that can aide so one can go forward with strength (Sweeting 2017, 1). To excavate and renovate therefore is not a stagnate or retrograde "looking backwards", rather it is an important precondition for understanding the context from which you come and to utilize the source as a place of intellectual awakening, renaissance and reformation (Sweeting 2017, 2). In this regard, an Afrokological approach is more accommodative in its centering of an African heuristic tool in the mainstream. It underscores Africa's role in renovating and fostering an inclusive global citizenship and recognises that the past is in the present in as much as the present defines the past.

Afrokology, as deployed here, is attuned to African knowledges, comfortable with difference and embraces change and new ideas even as it invites a critical evaluation of the status quo. It resists efforts to weaponise fear of the unfamiliar, arguing instead that academic theory and political practice need to be grounded in particular identities while recognising the intersectionality of difference (Dei 2000). Our use of Afrokology is characterised by what Maxwell (2011, 27) and others describe as a distributive view of culture, which sees societies as united to large extent by the interaction and complementarity of diverse views, rather than solely by sharing or commonalities. Afrokology argues that the "taken-for-grantedness" of imported knowledge about Africa should be questioned. It equally posits that any "return to the source" should be done with a critical lens firmly intact. Drawing on Gilroy's *The Black Atlantic: Modernity and Double Consciousness* (1993) it argues that the critical potential of black thought and culture is often more readily found in the cultural artefacts that speak directly to the African experiences of dislocation. Nigerian Afrobeat creator Fela Kuti's music for example addresses the scourge of colonialism as the root cause of the socioeconomic and political problems that plague the African people. His open critiques of corruption as one of the worst political problems facing Africa, arguably reveal more about the contingencies of modernity than any attempt to reassemble a lost African past or forge a future from a European present. Dei (2000, 42) argues in this respect that "the critical educator [needs] to wrest 'theory' from lived realities and feelings in order to connect human responses and feelings to dominant systems of meaning and social action". He invokes Stuart Hall to argue that we need to see the challenge of difference as ensuring that all peoples have the

> resources to be productive, creative, to explore their own histories, to tell their own stories and to develop their own identities in the future . . . understanding the axis of difference is to examine the linkage between material forces and social ideologies in producing difference.
>
> *(ibid)*

Afrokology's dialectical stance advocates for research foci that do exactly that, but which avoid the misfires from earlier work on Africanising media and communication.

Afrokology extends Africanisation (with its inward-facing continental objective) to include also a decoloniality objective (which is broader in scope as it connects African [hi]stories to those of the so-called global South as well as the colonial encounter). In this sense, Afrokology aligns with Said's (1993) cross-cultural, cross-national, cross-hemispheric vision of decoloniality which takes into account complex ambivalence and hybridity in order to engender a more generous and pluralistic vision of the world. This challenges scholars to explore ways of thinking in which "things, words, deeds and beings are always incomplete, not because of absences but because of their possibilities" (Nyamnjoh 2017, 256). In our version, Afrokology acknowledges the incompleteness of epistemologies in *both* the global North *as well as* the global South. If we accept this hypothesis, it would come with a concomitant task to continuously reassess existing academic approaches, cognisant of the multiple possibilities of interconnections which can overcome obvious epistemological inadequacies. What is crucial here, as Nyamnjoh (2017, 257) argues, is a recognition of "Being and becoming as works in progress [which] require borrowings and enhancements to render them beautiful and acceptable. It is this capacity to enable and disable simultaneously that makes absence present and presence absent in certain places and spaces, private and public alike". We perceive this recognition as a crucial precursor to questioning epistemological claims. The Afrokological heuristic tool unlocks possibilities for questioning, distinguishing and revalidating knowledges relevant for media and communication.

For us, connecting past and present epistemologies, creates a bridge with the epistemic disobedience called for in Mignolo's (2009) view of decoloniality. Epistemic disobedience in this sense requires careful attention to the silences of Western epistemologies, the excavation of those silences and an affirmation of the epistemic rights of the margins (Mignolo's 2009, 2). This view of epistemic disobedience, as pointed out earlier, is at odds with scholars such as Rao and Wasserman (2007) – who argue for "inserting" theories from the global South into Western values – as it goes over and beyond their attempts to append concepts from the global South. Merely appending global South concepts to existing frameworks in the global North could deepen rather than overcome existing epistemic traps through which struggles of resistance become captured in a grammar of oppression. The resultant epistemic blindness undermines struggles for inclusion as it prevents scholars from listening to possibilities that, for example, are not framed by Cartesian, teleological and universal reasoning (Andreotti and Ahenakew 2013). As Comaroff and Comaroff (2012, 115) also remind us, the consequence of such attempts is that the South is rarely seen as a source of theory and explanation for world historical events as it "continues to be the suppressed underside of the North". While Afrokology holds that the knowledge and cultural capital of African epistemologies are valid in their own right, it is not blind to hermeneutical injustice which has so far misrecognised other knowledges, especially from the global South.

Afrokology as a heuristic tool is driven by the need to build bridges across theoretical chasms and to create strategies for centering African media and communication from the margins. It is an appreciative conversation underscored by epistemological conviviality and incompleteness (Nyamnjoh 2017). In appreciative conversations, there are no correct answers, but value is derived from an ability to initiate dialogue across chasms and divides. Here it is useful to remind the reader of Nyamnjoh's (2017, 258) argument of academic discipline approaches as incomplete, "constantly in need of activation, potency and enhancement through relationships with incomplete others". For him Africans have already been at the forefront of convivial approaches which embrace incompleteness:

> Frontier Africans are those who contest taken-for-granted and often institutionalised and bounded ideas and practices of being, becoming, belonging, places and spaces. *They are interested in conversations not conversions.*
>
> *(ibid, our emphasis)*

Deploying Afrokology as a heuristic tool serves to engender and mobilise efforts of frontier Africans.

In this view, Afrokology is a transformative approach which encourages epistemological recognition and conviviality and, as such, holds great potential for engendering shifts in perspectives. It invokes what Sandoval refers to as "differential consciousness", described by Davis in her foreword to Sandoval (2000, Location 80 of 6280) as "a self-conscious flexibility of identity and political action and for the development of competent critiques of the movement of power along axes of race, gender, class and sexuality, that could in turn serve as ingredients for a new methodology of liberation". In this respect then, an Afrokology of media and communication studies draws on Sandoval's *Methodology of the Oppressed* in its attempt to:

- Advance a series of methods, not only for analyzing texts, but for creating identities that are capable of speaking to, against and through power.
- Cultivate theory and method of oppositional consciousness in postcolonial Africa and the African diaspora.
- Resituate and reinterpret the work of Euro-American theorists in relation to the insights of those African experiences that insist on international solidarity and resistance to all forms of prejudice and bias (Davis in Sandoval 2000, Location 80–81 of 6280).

Hence, Afrokology is a decolonizing heuristic tool that facilitates oppositional consciousness. It recognises skewed power relations and gives voice to those previously marginalised. In doing so, it opens a space to relexicalise and construct new vocabularies that can help to decolonise epistemological imagination. This approach draws on the participation studies framework developed at a preconference on participation studies at the 2015 International Association of Media and Communication Research (IAMCR) conference.

From a media and communication studies perspective, Afrokology engenders an understanding that technologies as well as socioeconomic and political changes are impacting and altering communities across Africa in unique ways. There is no one theory that can explain everything for everyone; rather, Afrokology acknowledges that shaping Africa's geopolitical future will come from the experimentation and social change that individuals, families, communities and cities embark on as they try to navigate their way through this highly volatile environment. It only asks that such experimentation avoids the intellectual violence imposed by negating African knowledges and that it is done with a clear understanding of the usefulness of decriminalising difference. This is in line with the African proverb that states that wisdom is like a baobab tree, no one individual can embrace it.

In the ultimate, the convivial Afrokological turn for media and communication studies is one that refutes the claims that the global North is the normal order, complete with all theoretical and methodological solutions. The heuristic tool exposes the fallacy of such claims of "completeness" in the academy and brings the reality of epistemological incompleteness to the fore.

Concluding reflections

The chapter effectively introduced and contextualised Afrokology as a heuristic toolkit that mobilises and speaks to issues of decolonising, Africanising, internationalising, indigenising media and communication studies. In so doing, it advocates for centering *African* media and communication studies. Borrowing from Shome (2019, 198), we argue that our centering of Afrokology goes beyond de-Westernizing or internationalizing media and communication:

> Dewesternization or Internationalization does not necessarily lead us into the Global South. One can dewesternize but still remain within the privileged spheres of the Global North with its capitalist excesses and geopolitical privileges.

Thus, while it can undoubtedly feed into those gestures, Afrokology is unapologetically South-centered, engendering relational ways of seeing the world through *walking* decoloniality. Afrokology deployed in this way explores how the field of media and communication studies can embrace a relational theoretical and methodological episteme. Such an epistemological turn would make explicit the issue of praxis, i.e. listening and learning from others in any development towards meaningful engagement with realities in Africa. This is what gives "shape, movement, meaning and form to decoloniality" (Walsh 2018, Location 460 of 7946 Kindle). What is at stake here is initial "complicated conversations" that do not "conform to predetermined outcomes, but produce something new and transform those engaged in the conversation of Africanisation and decoloniality" (Le Grange 2018, 6). In so doing, Afrokology explores that which might be revealed if we place seemingly disparate ways of knowing in conversation, particularly emphasising and centering "the perspectives and points of view of those whose very existence is questioned and produced as indispensable and insignificant" (Walsh 2018, Location 451 of 7946 Kindle). Herein lies perhaps the most provocative aspect of this tool: it allows for a transdisciplinary approach for media and communication studies which can inform theory from below. As such, Afrokology "allows for the empowerment of the individual and group alike, not the marginalisation of one by or for the other" (Nyamnjoh 2017, 262). This, we argue, allows for new dialogue and conversation that can deepen intellectual thought undergirding academic work in media and communication.

Following from the foregoing, our explication of Afrokology as a heuristic toolkit is itself an example of the approach we put forth. We are borrowing particular ideas from different authors and perspectives in an attempt towards building a toolkit that can be useful in thinking about *African* media and communication studies. As discussed in this chapter, the questioning of epistemological frameworks in relation to contemporary challenges is gathering pace at an international level. Afrokology is therefore to be seen as part of these intellectual interventions and disruptions. As Misra (2018, n.p) rightly points out, decoloniality and we would add, Africanity, implies an urgent need to "disrupt the accepted status quo and rupture the 'comfortable ignorance' of those immune to the ramifications of race, [class and gender]. It is high-time that marginalised communities and their histories claim their rightful space, albeit at the expense of white and European discomfort".

We maintain that Afrokology, with its explicit emphasis on and commitment to research guided by the lived experiences of the researched, provides a pathway towards enfolding research with praxis. This, in our view, is important for empowerment of marginalised/silenced communities to challenge their oppression. Afrokology can awaken relational accountability that promotes respectful representation, reciprocity and rights of the researched. Afrokology is a novel way to *think about the thinking on* African media and communication in a more relevant and engaged manner. We appreciate that there are no shortcuts to the top of Mount Kilimanjaro, as it is an undertaking that needs serious planning, preparations and decisions, with the choice of route to the summit having implications. This to say that our choice of Afrokology does not portend to bring answers to the questions of how cultural relations between the North and the South *ought to* be conducted or even *whether* they need to be formulated at all. However, in the tradition of theories from the South, we assert that movement forward lies in the way we put the questions:

> Truth lies in the road (maybe in ambush), for how can we prejudge the contours of the destination that will be shaped by our getting there? Traveling creates its own landscapes, and that goes for the migration of ideas as well. The reassuring thing is that one does always end up with a destination. Naturally, on the way out, as maverick mortals [we'd] be inclined to say "we *must*", "we *ought* to"; [we'd] even be inclined to stitch [our] own speculative "truths" as patchwork lining inside the dark and suffocating coat of Certainty, if only to use as secret maps.
>
> (Breytenbach 2009, 2–3)

Thus, we can conclude that our centering of Afrokology as a heuristic is part of a journey, a trajectory that maps and reclaims African intellectual thought applicable to knowing and doing media and communication. Here, it is not our intention to provide a digested theory for the reader – instead, we wrote this chapter as an introductory deliberation first of all for ourselves and for other writers in this emergent tradition to try to articulate what we are doing and to explore both the continuities and breaks we represent with the earlier history of media and communication studies with, in and about Africa. Altogether, Afrokology of media and communication studies is a call towards engaged listening and collaboration. In the final chapter of this volume, we operationalise the heuristic tool in order to underpin it as an Afrokological transdisciplinary approach for African media and communication. We submit that Afrokology as heuristic tool allows for more sensitive and imaginative theoretical interpretations of African contexts and identities to emerge.

We conclude on a hopeful note: "[We] beg you. . . . Have patience . . . try to love the questions themselves. Live the questions now. Perhaps then, someday far in the future, you will gradually, without even noticing it, live your way into the answer" (Rilke 1903, n.p).

References

Abif, K.K. 1998. At work in the children's room. In Venturella, K.M., ed. *Poor People and Library Services*. Jefferson, NC: McFarland & Company, 44–61.

African communication/media theory. 2012. *Communication: South African Journal for Communication Theory and Research*, 38 (1–2). Pretoria: Taylor and Francis.

Ahenakew, C., Andreotti, V., Cooper, G. and Hireme, H. 2014. Beyond epistemic provincialism: Deprovincializing indigenous resistance. *Alternative: An International Journal of Indigenous Peoples*, 10(3): 216–231.

Andreotti, V. and Ahenakew, C. 2013. Educating. In Matthewman, S., West-Newman, C. and Curtis, B., eds. *Being Sociological*. New York: Palgrave Macmillan, 3rd ed., 233–250.

Appiah, K. 1992. *In My Father's House: Africa in the Philosophy of Culture*. New York: Oxford University Press.

Asante, M.K. 2015. Molefi Kete Asante: Why Afrocentricity? Interview by George Yancy. *The New York Times*, 7 May. https://opinionator.blogs.nytimes.com/2015/05/07/molefi-kete-asante-why-afrocentricity/.

Banda, F. 2007. An appraisal of development journalism in the context of public-service broadcasting. *Communicatio: South African Journal for Communication Theory and Research*, 33(2): 154–170.

Banda, F. 2010. African political thought as an epistemic framework for understanding African. *Equid Novi*, 12(1): 79–99.

Bell, R.H. 2002. *Understanding African Philosophy: A Cross in Cultural Approach to Classical and Contemporary Issues*. New York: Routledge.

Bhabha, H.K. 1994 [2004]. Dissemination: Time narrative and the margins of the modern nation. In Bhabha, H. K., ed. *The Location of Culture*. London: Routledge, 199–244.

Blankenberg, N. 1999. In search of real freedom: Ubuntu and the media. *Critical Arts*, 13(2): 42–65.

Breytenbach, B. 2009. *Notes from the Middle World*. Chicago: Haymarket Books.

Burawoy, M. 2015. *Travelling Theory*. Open Democracy/ISA RC-47: Open Movements, 21 March. https://opendemocracy.net/michael-burawoy/travelling-theory.

Butler, B. 2006. Heritage and the present past. In Tilley, C., Keuchler, S., Rowlands, eds. *Handbook of Material Culture*. London: Sage Publications, 463–479.

Chakrabarty, D. 2000. *Provincializing Europe: Postcolonial Thought and Historical Difference*. Princeton, NJ: Princeton University Press.

Chasi, Colin T. 2018. Interview by v.c. milton and W. Mano, Johannesburg, 5 May.

Chawane, M. 2016. The development of Afrocentricity: A historical survey. *Yesterday & Today*, 16: 78–99.

Comaroff, J. and Comaroff, J.L. 2012. Theory from the South: Or, how Euro-America is evolving toward Africa. *Anthropological Forum*, 22(2): 113–131.

Cooper, B. and Steyn, A., eds. 1996. Introduction. In Cooper, B. and Steyn, A., eds. *Transgressing Boundaries: New Directions in the Study of Culture in Africa*. Rondebosch: UCT Press.

Costa, S. 2019. The neglected nexus between conviviality and inequality. *Novos Estudos: CEBRAP*, 38(1), 15–32, 6 May.

Dei, G.J.S. 2000. Recasting anti-racism and the axis of difference: Beyond the question of theory. *Race, Gender & Class*, 7(2): 38–56.

Du Plessis, H., Sehume, J., and Martin, L. 2014. *The Concept and Application of Transdisciplinarity in Intellectual Discourse and Research*. Johannesburg: Real African Publishers, kindle ed.

Flemming, T.K. 2017. Africology: An introductory descriptive review of disciplinary ancestry. *Journal of Pan African Studies*, 11(1): 319–387.

Fourie, P.J. 2008. Ubuntuism as framework for South African media practice and performance: Can it work? *Communicatio: South African Journal for Communication Theory and Research*, 34(1): 53–79.

Gilroy, P. 1993. *The Black Atlantic Modernity and Double-Consciousness*. London and New York: Verso.

Gilroy, P. 2004. *After Empire: Melancholia or Convivial Cultures*. London and New York: Routledge.

Gilroy, P. 2005. *Postcolonial Melancholia* (The Wellek Library Lectures). New York: Columbia University Press, kindle ed.

Gilroy, P. 2013. Postcolonialism and cosmopolitanism: Towards a worldly understanding of fascism and Europe's colonial crimes. In Braidotti, Rosi et al., eds. *After Cosmopolitanism*. London and New York: Routledge, 111–131.

Grosfoguel, R. 2008. Transmodernity, border thinking, and global coloniality: Decolonizing political economy and postcolonial studies. *Revista Critica de Ciencias Sociais*, 80: 1–23.

Grosfoguel, R. 2011. Decolonizing post-colonial studies and paradigms of political-economy: Transmodernity, decolonial thinking, and global coloniality. *Journal of Peripheral Cultural Production of the Luso-Hispanic World*, 1(1): 1–38. http://escholarship.org/uc/item/21k6t3fq.

Hall, S. 1989. Cultural identity and cinematic representation. *Framework: The Journal of Cinema and Media*, 36: 68–81.

hooks, b. 1989. Choosing the margin as a space of radical openness. *Framework: The Journal of Cinema and Media*, 36: 15–23.

Howitt, R., ed. 1993. Marginalisation in theory and practice: A brief conceptual introduction. In Howitt, R., ed. *Marginalisation in Theory and Practice*. Sydney: University of Sydney. Economic and Regional Restructuring Research Unit (Series: ERRRU Working Paper; 12).

Illich, I. 1973. *Tools for Conviviality*. New York: Harper & Row.

Jansen, J. 2018. The future prospects of South African universities policy and funding options. *Viewpoints*, 1: 1–7.

JAMS. 2009. *Journal of African Media Studies*, Issue 1 onwards.

Karenga, M. 2009. Names and notions of black studies: Issues of roots, range, and relevance. *Journal of Black Studies*, 40(1): 41–46.

Kershaw, T. 1998. Afrocentrism and the Afrocentric method. In Hamlet, J.D., ed. *Afrocentric Visions: Studies in Culture and Communication*. London: Sage.

Koka, K. 2002. *Afrikology: The Logical Study of Afrika (in Its Totality)*. Johannesburg: Institute of Afrikology.

Le Grange, L. 2018. Decolonising, Africanising, indigenising, and internationalising curriculum studies: Opportunities to (re)imagine the field. *Journal of Education*, (74): 4–18.

Levi, J.B. 2012. The intellectual warfare of Dr. Jacob H. Carruthers and the battle for ancient Nubia as a foundational paradigm in Africana studies: Thoughts and reflections. *The Journal of Pan African Studies*, 5(4): 178–195.

Luckhurst, T. 2006. What is the point of media studies? *The Independent*, 27 August. www.independent.co.uk/news/media/what-is-the-point-of-media-studies-413472.html (Accessed 20 June 2020).

Madhubuti, H.K. 1994. From plan to planet: Life studies – the need for Afrikan minds and institutions. In *"Four Reasons for Using 'K' in Afrika," The Nubian Message*, 2(9): 3, 27 January. Digitized by the Special Collections Research Center, North Carolina State University, Raleigh, NC. https://soh.omeka.chass.ncsu.edu/items/show/692.

Makgoba, M. 1997. *Mokoko: The Makgoba Affair – A Reflection on Transformation*. Florida: Vivlia Press.

Mano, W. 2009. Re-conceptualizing media studies in Africa. In Thussu, D.K., ed. *Internationalizing Media Studies*. Abingdon: Routledge, 277–293.

Mano, W. 2010. Communication: An African perspective. In Allan, S., ed. *Rethinking Communication: Keywords in Communication Research*. Cresskill, NJ: Hampton Press.

Mano, W. and Meribe, N. 2017. African communication modes. *The International Encyclopedia of Intercultural Communication*, 1–10.

Mano, W. and milton v.c. (2021). *Decoloniality and the push for African media and communication studies: An introduction*. London and New York: Routledge. pp. 1–18.

Masoga, M.A. 2017. Critical reflections on selected local narratives of contextual South African indigenous knowledge. In Ngulube, P., ed. *Handbook of Research on Theoretical Perspectives on Indigenous Knowledge Systems in Developing Countries*. Hershey, PA: IGI Global, 310–331.

Maxwell, J.A. 2011. Paradigms or toolkits? Philosophical and methodological positions as heuristics for mixed methods research. *Mid-Western Educational Researcher*, 24(2): 27–30.

Mignolo, W.D. 2009. Epistemic disobedience, independent thought and decolonial freedom. *Theory, Culture & Society*, 26(7–8): 159–181.

milton, v.c. 2019. Kind of blue: Can communication research matter? *Critical Arts*, 33(3): 30–45.

Misra, A. 2018. Decoloniality, 'diversity', and discomfort: Transforming the academy. *Medium*. https://medium.com/@anamikamisra_23692/decoloniality-diversity-and-discomfort-transforming-the-academy-a751541741c1 (Accessed 14 July 2020).

Mohdin, A., Adams, R. and Quinn, B. 2020. *Oxford College Backs Removal of Cecil Rhodes Statue*, 17 June. www.theguardian.com/education/2020/jun/17/end-of-the-rhodes-cecil-oxford-college-ditches-controversial-statue (Accessed 14 July 2020).

Mutema, G. 2003. Phenomenology, hermeneutics and the study of indigenous knowledge. *Indilinga: African Journal of Indigenous Knowledge Systems*, 2(1): 81–88.

Nabudere, D.W. 2006. Towards an Afrokology of knowledge production and African regeneration. *International Journal of African Renaissance Studies*, 1(1): 7–32.

Nabudere, D.W. 2011. *Afrikology, Philosophy, and Wholeness: An Epistemology*. Pretoria: Africa Institute for South Africa.

Nabudere, D. W. 2012. *Afrikology and Transdisciplinarity: A Restorative Epistemology*. Pretoria: Africa Institute for South Africa.

Ndlovu-Gatsheni, S. 2015. Decoloniality as the future of Africa. *History Compass*, 13(10): 485–496.

Ngcaweni, B., Sehume, J. and Motaung, D. 2013. In the works of Masilela, Black people are given history and the potential to re-member their humanity and their very being: The archive as testament to living heritage a tribute to Ntongela Masilela politics. *The Thinker*, 57: 43–45.

Nyamnjoh, F.B. 2011. Cameroonian bushfalling: Negotiation of identity and belonging in fiction and ethnography. *American Ethnologist*, 38(4): 701–713.

Nyamnjoh, F.B. 2016. *#RhodesMustFall. Nibbling at Resilient Colonialism in South Africa*. Bamenda, Cameroon: Langaa Publishing.

Nyamnjoh, F.B. 2017. Incompleteness: Frontier Africa and the currency of conviviality. *Journal of Asian and African Studies*, 52(3): 253–270.

Nyamnjoh, F.B. 2018. Introduction: Cannibalism as food for thought. In Nyamnjoh, B., ed. *Eating and Being Eaten: Cannibalism as Food for Thought*. Bamenda: Langaa.

Nyamnjoh, F.B. 2020. *Decolonising the Academy: A Case for Convial Scholarship*. Basel: Basler Afrika Bibliographien (Namibia Resource Centre & Southern Africa).

Obeng-Quaidoo, I. 1986. A proposal for new communication research methodologies in Africa. *Africa Media Review*, 1(1): 89–98.

Obonyo, L. 2011. Towards a theory of communication for Africa: The challenges of emerging democracies. *Communicatio: South African Journal for Communication Theory and Research*, 37(1): 1–20.

Okafor, V.O. 2014. Africology, Black studies, African American studies, Africana Studies, or African world studies? What's so important about a given name? *The Journal of Pan African Studies*, 6(7): 319–388.

Oluyemi-Kusa, D. 2016. *What African Universities Must Do to Remain Relevant*, 14 June. http://dayokusa.blogspot.com/2016/06/ (Accessed 24 July 2020).

Osha, S. 2018. *Dani Nabudere's Afrikology: A Quest for Holism*. Dakar: Council for the Development of Social Science Research in Africa.

Paphitis, S.A. and Kelland, L. 2016. Transformation: Developing civic-minded graduates at South African institutions through an epistemic shift in institutional culture. *Education as Change*, 20(2): 184–203.

Petre, J. 2017. Plato and Descartes be dropped from university syllabus. *The Mail on Sunday*, 8–11 January. www.dailymail.co.uk/news/article-4098332/They-Kant-PC-students-demand-white-philosophers-including-Plato-Descartes-dropped-university-syllabus.html (Accessed 20 July 2020).

Querejazu, A. 2016. Encountering the pluriverse: Looking for alternatives in other worlds. *Revista Brasileira de Política Internacional*, 59(2).

Quin-Jarvis, E. 2014. Media studies: It's not a "mickey mouse" degree. *The Guardian*. www.theguardian.com/education/mortarboard/2014/feb/03/why-study-media-studies-students (Accessed 22 July 2020).

Rao, S. and Wasserman, H. 2007. Global media ethics revisited: A postcolonial critique. *Global Media and Communication*, 3(1): 29–50.

Right2Know. 2016. Africa Day: Call for AU to protect journalists. *Bizcommunity*, 25 May. www.bizcommunity.africa/Article/410/15/145233.html (Accessed 23 July 2020).

Rilke, R.M. 1903. *Letters to a Young Poet*. Bremen: Worpswede, 16 July. www.carrothers.com/rilke4.htm (Accessed 27 July 2020).

Said, E.W. 1993. *Culture and Imperialism*. New York: Vintage BooksKnopf.

Said, E.W. 2003. *Orientalism*. London: Penguin Books.

Sandoval, C. 2000. *Methodology of the Oppressed*. Minnesota: University of Minnesota Press.

Sese Seko, M. and Remilleux, J.L. 1989. *Dignity for Africa*. Paris: Albin Michel.

Shome, R. 2019. Thinking culture and cultural studies – from/ of the global South. *Communication and Critical/Cultural Studies*, 16(3): 196–218.

Skjerdal, T. 2012. The three alternative journalisms of Africa. *International Communication Gazette*, 74(7): 636–654.

Spivak, G.C. 1988. Can the subaltern speak? In Nelson, C. and Grossberg, L., eds. *Marxism and the Interpretation of Culture*. Urbana and Chicago: University of Illinois Press, 271–313.

Sweeting, D. 2017. Inaugural address: Ad Fontes, back to the sources. *Centennial Review*, 9(5): 1–4.

Taylor, D.S. and Nwosu, P.O. 2001. Afrocentric empiricism: A model for communication research in Africa. In Milhouse, V.H., Asante, M.K. and Nwosu, P.O., eds. *Transcultural Realities: Interdisciplinary Perspectives on Cross-Cultural Relations*. Thousand Oaks: Sage.

Tomaselli, K.G. 2009. Repositioning African media studies: Thoughts and provocations. *Journal of African Media Studies*, 1(1): 9–21.

Ugboajah, F.O. 1985. 'Oramedia' in Africa. In Ugboajah, F.O., ed. *Mass Communication, Culture and Society in West Africa*. München: Hans Zell, 165–176.

Ugboajah, F.O. 1987. Current debates in the field of mass communication research: An African viewpoint. *Africa Media Review*, 1(2): 1–17.

Uzong, E. 1969. *Africology. The Union Academic Council Series, African Studies Volume 1*. London: The Union Academic Council for African Studies.

Van der Zee, K. and Boogaart, B. 2020. Assessing the readiness of universities for diversity: Application of a diversity scan. In Crul, M., Dick, L., Ghorashi, H. and Valenzuela, A., eds. *Scholarly Engagement and Decolonisation: Views from South Africa, The Netherlands and the United States*. Stellenbosch: African Sun Media.

Walsh, C.E. 2018. The decolonial for: Resurgences, shifts and movements. In Mignolo, D. and Walsh, C.E., eds. *On Decoloniality: Concepts. Analytics. Praxis*. Durham: Duke University Press, kindle ed.

Willems, W. 2014. Beyond normative dewesternization: Examining media culture from the vantage point of the global South. *The Global South*, 8(1): 7–23.

Willems, W. and Mano, W. 2016. Decolonizing and provincializing audience and internet studies: Contextual approaches from African vantage points. In Willems, W. and Mano, W., eds. *Everyday Media Culture in Africa: Audiences and Users*. London: Routledge.

Wiredu, K. 1995. *Conceptual Decolonization in African Philosophy*. Ibadan: Hope Publications.

Wiredu, K. 2004. Prolegomena to African philosophy of education. *South African Journal of Higher Education*, 18(3): 11–26.

Zegeye, A. and Vambe, M. 2009. *Close to the Sources: Essays on Contemporary African Culture, Politics and Academy*. Pretoria: University of South Africa, UNISA Press.

Zeleza, P.T. 2005. *Banishing the silences: Towards the globalization of African history*. Unpublished Paper Presented at the 11th CODESRIA General Assembly Conference, Maputo, Mozambique, 6–10 December.

Zulu, I.M. 2017. Transdisciplinarity in Africology: Demonstrating elasticity and durability. *Africology: The Journal of Pan African Studies*, 10(5): 1–2.

3

Frantz Fanon, Ngũgĩ wa Thiong'o, and African media and communication studies

Pier Paolo Frassinelli

Introduction

This chapter aims to contribute to writing a decolonial history of African media and communication studies by focusing on two authors, Frantz Fanon and Ngũgĩ wa Thiong'o, who are often referenced in debates on decolonisation but are not normally seen as part of this field. This inclusion will help to historicise African communication and media as social and cultural practices and fields of study, rather than academic disciplines whose histories glorify experts and specialists. After all, Fanon worked as a journalist and editor, wrote on media and communication, and was acutely aware of the role of communication in political struggle, while Ngũgĩ has written extensively on language, communication, and popular culture, and his involvement in popular theatre was dictated by the need to develop new communicative practices.

Jürgen Habermas and Marshall McLuhan, two of the most widely cited media and communication theorists, were, respectively, a social theorist and philosopher and a literary-trained interdisciplinary scholar. I see no reason why Fanon and Ngũgĩ cannot also be inserted into the genealogy of media and communication studies on the African continent.

Needless to say, in the brief space of this chapter I will only be able to sketch, in the barest outline, a basic introduction to some aspects of Fanon's and Ngũgĩ's work that are especially relevant to this volume. Readers who want to pursue this line of research are encouraged to consult and read the texts included in the bibliography – beginning, of course, with Fanon's and Ngũgĩ's own writings.

Frantz Fanon

More than 50 years after his death, Fanon's thought and politics are still a point of reference and source of inspiration for many of the popular movements and struggles that take on socioeconomic inequalities and the power of postcolonial elites across the African continent. Fanon's name was one of the most frequently evoked by student activists during the #RhodesMustFall and #FeesMustFall protests that spread across South African campuses in 2015 and 2016 (see Gibson 2017). As South African scholar Richard Pithouse wrote during the protests, "Fanon offers compelling accounts of the pathologies of both the colony and the postcolony – spaces that some of the young people at the fore of the new ferment in South Africa feel they must inhabit simultaneously" (Pithouse 2016a).

Frantz Fanon, who was born on the Caribbean island of Martinique in 1925, had trained as a psychiatrist in Paris before moving to Algeria, where in 1953 he took the position of head of the psychiatry department at Blida-Joinville hospital, only to resign three years later to join the *Front de Liberatión Nationale* (FLN) in the Algerian war of liberation. He was expelled from Algeria in 1957 and worked first in Tunisia as an editor of the FLN newspaper, *El Moudjahid*, and then as FLN ambassador to Ghana and Mali. He would die of leukaemia in 1961, at the age of 36, just one year before Algeria gained independence.[1] Fanon's main role in the FLN was to supply material for its international political campaigns and newspaper. He wrote political pieces for *El Moudjahid* as well as for several other reviews and magazines. Four books authored by Fanon have been translated from French and published in English. They are: *Black Skin, White Masks* – originally published as *Peau noire, masques blancs* (1952); *A Dying Colonialism* – originally published as *L'an V de la révolution algérienne* (1959), or *Year Five of the Algerian Revolution*; *The Wretched of the Earth* – first published in France under the title of *Les damnés de la terre* (1961), or *The Damned of the Earth*; and *Toward the African revolution* (1964) – a collection of articles, essays, and letters that spans the period between *Black Skin, White Masks* and *The Wretched of the Earth*.

Fanon's first book, *Black Skin, White Masks*, was written when he was a 27-year-old student in medicine, originally as his thesis, titled "Essay on the disalienation of the black", which was not approved by his supervisor, and Fanon ended up replacing with another study more in line with academic conventions. In this text, written in a plurality of voices and mixing anecdotal and autobiographical narratives with theoretical elaboration, Fanon sets out to outline a "psychoanalytical interpretation of the black problem" (Fanon 1986, 12). Fanon's focus is the combination of psychological, existential, and cultural effects of colonial violence and oppression. He describes this approach and the object of knowledge it produces as "sociogeny" (Fanon 1986, 13), a term that draws attention to the social, intersubjective, cultural, historical, and economic factors responsible for the origin and development of a person and her or his pathologies. In the English translation of Fanon's words, "the black man's alienation is not an individual question" (Fanon 1986, 13). It is the product of the structure and manifestations of a colonial and racist order. Fanon's key interests in this context are embodied forms of alienation and the objectifying racist gaze that annihilates the black subject's desire to freely inhabit the world and find meaning in it: "I came into the world imbued with the will to find a meaning in things, my spirit filled with the desire to attain to the source of the world, and then I found that I was an object in the midst of other objects" (Fanon 1986, 109).

Fanon elaborates a theory of disalienation that starts by accounting for the psychological harm done by colonialism on both the colonised and the colonisers. His project is to transform psychically pathologised subjects and their circumstances in a world dominated by the psychosexual oppression and racism engendered by the colonial order and racialized capitalism. Built into this project there is an exposure of the limits of psychiatry's individualisation of psychic pathologies: "There will be an authentic disalienation only to the degree to which things, in the most materialistic meaning of the word, will have been restored to their proper places" (Fanon 1986, 13–14). The "solution", Fanon writes, "implies a restructuring the world" (Fanon 1986, 82).

This restructuring passes through the recognition of black subjectivity – "What does the black man want?" (Fanon 1986, 10) – negated by the colonial world. Fanon's "response to the impossibility of a dialectic of recognition", however, "is not to give up on the aspiration for a world of mutuality, of universal humanism" (Pithouse 2016b, 126) – even though Fanon recognises that this aspiration can only be brought into being through a commitment to struggle and action. Significantly, at the end of the book, Fanon's humanism, his hopeful commitment to a "human world", is expressed as an invitation to both the "Negro" and the "white man", both of whom "[are] not", to "turn their backs on the inhuman voices which were those of their respective ancestors in order that authentic communication be possible. Before we can adopt a positive voice, freedom requires an effort at disalienation" (Fanon 1986, 231).

I have guided the reader through some aspects of Fanon's elaboration in *Black Skin, White Masks* to show how opening up possibilities for "authentic communication" across the racial divide that dehumanises all human beings plays into Fanon's vision of a disalienated world. As we will see, contra caricatures of Fanon as a theorist and apologist of violence (for a refutation of this view, see Gibson and Beneduce 2017, 4–8; Pithouse 2016a), this is a theme that will recur throughout Fanon's writing, all the way to his last book, *The Wretched of the Earth*, where Fanon argues that the "consciousness of self is not the closing of a door to communication" (Fanon 1965a, 179).

Fanon's second book, *A Dying Colonialism*, was written and published after Fanon had resigned from his post as a psychiatrist on the ground that he could not psychiatrically cure the psychic wounds inflicted by colonialism. As he stated in his resignation letter, if "psychiatry is the medical technique that aims to enable man no longer to be a stranger to his environment, I owe it to myself to affirm that the Arab, permanently an alien in his own country, lives in a state of absolute depersonalization" (Fanon 1967, 55).

A Dying Colonialism chronicles the progress made by the Algerian revolution in its first five years. Of particular interest to media and communication scholars are the first two chapters, "Algeria unveiled" and "This is the voice of Algeria", where Fanon analyses the veil and the radio as communication devices embedded in historical and social relations.

"Algeria unveiled" presents a historical semiotic analysis of how the veil, "one of the elements of the traditional Algerian garb, was to become the bone of contention on a grandiose battle" between the colonial occupying forces and the Algerian people (Fanon 1965, 36). For Fanon, French colonial power had waged a war on Algerian culture and identity by portraying the veil as an instrument of oppression and subjugation: "Converting the woman, winning her over to the foreign values, wrenching her free from her status, was at the same time achieving a real power over the man and attaining a practical, effective means of destructuring Algerian culture" (Fanon 1965, 39). Fanon's account divides this battle of the veil into distinct phases. By trying to "save" and unveil the Algerian woman, the colonising forces had hoped to subjugate and domesticate Algerian society. The colonised responded by defending the veil as a symbol and instrument of resistance. At first they reacted to French cultural imperialism by defensively protecting the traditional cultural and religious value of the veil and turning it into a "cult" (Fanon 1965, 47). But when women became involved in the Algerian revolution the symbolism of the veil became part of the combat in new, semiotically subversive ways. Algerian women recruited into the liberation army unveiled. The unveiled woman entered the European areas of the city to carry out military attacks together with men. She took advantage of European perceptions of Arab unveiled women:

> Carrying revolvers, grenades, hundreds of false identity cards or bombs, the unveiled Algerian woman moves like a fish in the Western waters. The soldiers, the French patrols, smile to her as she passes, compliments on her looks are heard here and there, but no one suspects that her suitcases contain the automatic pistol which will presently mow down four or five members of one of the patrols.
>
> *(Fanon 1965, 58)*

Pier Paolo Frassinelli

When the occupying forces found out and Europeans joined the liberation struggle a change of tactics was required, and so the veil was now turned into a protective garb to hide weapons and other material to be smuggled into the European city: "Removed and reassumed again and again, the veil has been manipulated, transformed into a technique of camouflage, into a means of struggle" (Fanon 1965, 61). The veil was now donned and embraced as an instrument of material and symbolic resistance. It was resignified, its traditional connotations altered. Fanon concludes that there "is a historic dynamism of the veil that is very concretely perceptible in the development of colonization in Algeria" (Fanon 1965, 63).

In the documentary *Black Skin, White Masks* (1998), Stuart Hall subjects Fanon's chapter to a typically perceptive analysis. Hall unpacks how Fanon semiotises and historicises the veil and its communicative function:

> I think the essay on the veil . . . represents a real insight of Fanon, which is that you can't abstract the cultural sign from its context, and that no cultural sign is fixed in its meaning. So you can't say just because the veil has functioned in the relation between men and women in Islamic societies in this way in the past that is going to be exactly the same forever more. It always will be. . . . The veil is a sort of bar, but it doesn't actually prevent something being seen. Women sometimes, involved in the armed struggle, appropriated the veil as a way of taking arms from one place to another, of delivering explosive. And that is because they could depend on the reactionary reading by the French! They would say of course, a woman in the veil is a dependent woman who would never be brave enough to act. So, in a sense, they could turn the veil against its meaning, return the look in the opposite way.

At the same time, Hall reminds us of the complex positionality of Fanon in Algeria, which is revealed by Fanon's silence on religion and his blindness to the "way in which this is going to impact on the revolution" (Hall in Julien and Nash 1996).[2]

The second chapter of *A Dying Colonialism*, "This is the voice of Algeria", follows a similar historical path. Fanon traces the changes of attitude of Algerians towards the radio. He looks at the social and political dimensions of the use and appropriation of what he calls "a technical instrument" (Fanon 1965, 69). Fanon starts with Algerian people's resistance to this medium, when it was used to disseminate French propaganda via Radio Alger and the great majority of receiving sets were owned by Europeans. In this initial phase, while for Europeans settlers the radio represented a link to "civilisation", for the native population the refusal to listen to the radio was, according to Fanon's reconstruction, originally motivated by traditions of respectability. The radio was perceived as a tool in the hands of the occupying power, a symbol of French presence in Algeria, which did not fulfil any need for the native population. The radio broadcasts were a closed semiotic system from which the colonised felt excluded.

Things however radically changed with the beginning of the war of liberation, when Algerians began to feel "the compelling and vital need to be informed" and enter the "network of news" (Fanon 1965, 75). Algerians first turned to the democratic French press but it was when the *Voice of Free Algeria* broadcasts were publicised among the local population in 1956 that the radio became a vital means of communication and access to news. Fanon recounts that the entire Algerian stock of radio sets was bought up in less than 20 days (Fanon 1965, 82–83). As the war of liberation progressed, the function of the radio changed. From a means of accessing news, the radio became a tool to stay in touch with the revolution. The technical instrument was politicised. It was enmeshed in new social relations and political struggles. French censorship tried to clamp down on this revolutionary use of the radio by prohibiting its sales and jamming the sound waves, which became a battleground. Listening to the radio was now to clandestinely participate in the revolution. Fanon writes that after the beginning of the revolution "the radio assumed totally new meanings": from an extraneous and hostile device into an instrument and technique of the liberation struggle (Fanon 1965, 89).

"This is the voice of Algeria" invites us to pay attention to the interactions between media, social and political actors, communicative practices, and the political and social role media play in specific political and social contexts and circumstances. More broadly, in the two chapters that I have discussed, Fanon shows how semiotic and historical readings of communication and culture can be used as a critical tool to analyse the reification of identity and culture in situations marked by the cultural and epistemic violence that go hand in hand with colonial oppression and its legacies.

Fanon's last book was *The Wretched of the Earth*, which he completed in ten weeks as he was struggling with leukaemia. The French edition was published and confiscated in the same week that Fanon died. A reflection on the Algerian war of liberation, *The Wretched of the Earth* describes not only the resistance to colonialism, but also how this emancipatory struggle "brings a natural rhythm into existence, introduced by new men, and with it a new language and a new humanity. Decolonization," Fanon sums up, "is the veritable creation of new men" (Fanon 1965a, 36).

Throughout the book, Fanon's qualities as a political writer and communicator shine not only in the incisiveness and clarity with which he outlines his political arguments, often delivered in the modality of critique, but also at the level of the individual sentence or dictum:

> Decolonization, which sets out to change the order of the world, is, obviously, a program of complete disorder.
>
> *(Fanon 1965a, 36)*

> "The last shall be first and the first last". Decolonization is the putting into practice of this sentence.
>
> *(Fanon 1965a, 37)*

> [C]olonialism is not a thinking machine, nor a body endowed with reasoning faculties. It is violence in its natural state, and it will only yield when confronted with greater violence.
>
> *(Fanon 1965a, 61)*

> Each generation must out of relative obscurity discover its mission, fulfil it, or betray it.
>
> *(Fanon 1965a, 206)*

This selection of oft-quoted phrases is not meant to suggest that Fanon was adept at sloganeering. But he was alert to the power of language in political communication. Perhaps nowhere does the haunting quality of Fanon's prose come alive more vividly than in Göran Hugo Olsson's documentary film *Concerning Violence* (2014), where Fanon's words, excerpted from the first chapter and the conclusion of *The Wretched of the Earth*, are recited by African American singer and rapper Lauryn Hill as a narrative accompaniment to the film's historical footage of chilling colonial brutality and anti-imperialist resistance across the African continent.

Although it has been read as a celebration of violence, *The Wretched of the Earth* in fact champions a popular politics based on democratic and participatory forms of communication. Fanon insists on the role of community and its participation in inclusive and democratic meetings not only as the organisational and political foundation of the liberation struggle, but also as a humanising practice. He describes branch and committee meetings as opportunities for people to come together to

> discuss, propose, . . . receive directions. . . , and to put forward new ideas. . . . They are privileged occasions given to a human being to listen and to speak. At each meeting, the brain increases its means of participation and the eye discovers a landscape more and more in keeping with human dignity.
>
> *(Fanon 1965a, 195)*

This extends to participatory forms of communication, such as those taking place in production and consumption committees in which peasants become "experts" and "theoreticians", so as to undo the historically sedimented compartmentalisation of intellectual and manual labour:

> We did not have any technicians or planners coming from big Western universities; but in these liberated regions, the daily ration went up to the hitherto unheard-of figure of 3,200 calories. The people were not content with coming triumphant out of this test. They started asking themselves theoretical questions: for example, why did certain districts never see an orange before the war of liberation, while thousands of tons are exported every year abroad? Why were grapes unknown to a great many Algerians whereas the European peoples enjoyed them by the million? Today, the people have a very clear notion of what belongs to them.
>
> *(Fanon 1965a, 192)*

The Wretched of the Earth, like the other writings that Fanon produced during the period of his involvement with the Algerian liberation struggle, is a political intervention in the world and struggles from which it originates. As Stuart Hall comments, it "is very much a text of a moment – the moment the rising tide of national liberation movements, and of decolonisation – and it addresses problems and questions which all the national liberation movements have to face" (Hall in Julien and Nash 1996). This is surely so, but the enduring relevance of Fanon's texts shows that decolonisation remains on the agenda long after national independence. Fanon's works provide us with still significant ideas and concepts about colonialism, postcoloniality, and the politics of decolonial revolutionary humanism. As I have briefly outlined, they also offer important insights for African media and communication studies. These include the relation between alienation, disalienation, and communication in a racist world; how the cultural sign is fixed by colonial and neocolonial epistemic violence and can be unfixed and subverted by emancipatory struggles; and the role of inclusive, democratic, and participatory communication in emancipatory forms of struggle and organisation.

Ngũgĩ wa Thiong'o

Ngũgĩ wa Thiong'o was born in Kamiriithu, Kenya, in 1938, and baptised James Ngũgĩ. He graduated in English from Makerere University College in 1963. His career as a writer is mainly associated with his work as a novelist. Ngũgĩ's debut novel *Weep Not, Child*, published in 1964, was the first novel in the English language by a writer from East Africa. His second novel, *The River Between*, came out the following year. Ngũgĩ subsequently changed his name to Ngũgĩ wa Thiong'o and started writing in Gĩkũyũ and Kiswahili. Among his other critically acclaimed novels are *A Grain of Wheat* (1967); *Caitaani mũtharaba-inĩ* (1980) – translated into English as *Devil on the Cross* (1982) – the first modern novel in Gĩkũyũ, originally written on prison-issued toilet paper during a period of detention resulting from his activities as a dissident community theatre practitioner; *Matigari* (1986b), translated from the original in Gĩkũyũ by Wangũi wa Goro; and *Wizard of the Crow* (2006), translated into English from Gĩkũyũ by the author. In addition to his novels, Ngũgĩ wrote many essays on African and postcolonial writing, politics, and culture. They are collected in *Decolonising the Mind: The Politics of African Language and Literature* (1986a); *Writers in Politics: A Re-engagement with Issues of Literature and Society* (1981); *Moving the Centre: The Struggle for Cultural Freedoms* (1993); and *Globalectics: Theory and the Politics of Knowing* (2012).

Among these, *Decolonising the Mind* remains one of the most widely read and discussed documents of the African debate on decolonisation. Ngũgĩ's main focus in this text is the issue of language in postcolonial African societies, which he frames in terms of the conflict between the neocolonial mindset embodied by African writers' use of European languages – or what Ngũgĩ calls "Afro-European literature" – and the adoption of "African languages" that by "addressing themselves to the lives of the people become the enemy of a neo-colonial state" (Ngũgĩ 1981, 30). Ngũgĩ's text, which he announces in an opening statement as his last in the English language (Ngũgĩ, xiii), argues for the use of African languages in African literary and cultural production. To express the rationale of his critique of African writers who write in colonial and formerly colonial languages, Ngũgĩ uses an economic metaphor. He argues that by representing and conveying local realities, idioms, and cultures in Western languages African writers enrich these languages while African languages get nothing back. As he writes in *Moving the Centre*:

> In the area of economics and geography, it is the raw materials of gold, diamonds, coffee, tea, which are taken from Africa and processed in Europe and then resold to Africa. In the area of culture, the raw material of African orature and histories developed by African languages are taken, repackaged through English or French or Portuguese and then resold back to Africa.
>
> *(Ngũgĩ 1993, 38)*

By contrast:

> It is revitalised African languages rooting themselves in the traditions of orature and of written African literature, inspired by the deepest aspirations of the African people for a meaningful social change, which will also be best placed to give and receive from the wealth of our common culture on an equal basis.
>
> *(Ngũgĩ 1993, 41)*

Ngũgĩ has a dual view of language as a means of communication and as a carrier of culture. He describes the communicative function of language as an expression and mediation of human relations. Language not only represents life but produces sociality through communication (Ngũgĩ 1993, 11–14). This communicative function is the basis of culture, which embodies the moral, ethical, and aesthetic values of a society and is carried by language. Languages define people's cultural identities – their particularities as members of the human species (Ngũgĩ 1993, 15). It follows that colonial imposition and postcolonial self-imposition of the languages of the colonisers alter colonised people's perceptions of themselves and their world. They alienate colonised and neocolonised people from their environments and cultures and make them see the world through someone else's eyes.

In a more recent contribution – "The politics of translation: Notes towards an African language policy" (2018) – Ngũgĩ returns to his lifelong concern with power relations between colonial and indigenous African languages to underscore how language choices on the African continent still bear the imprint of the legacy of colonialism: what "began in the colonial era, the delegitimization of African languages as credible sources and basis of knowledge, was completed and normalized in the post-colonial era" (Ngũgĩ 2018, 125). Just as the colonial state can be theorised as an imperfect replica or translated copy of an original, so, too, does a postcolonial one that continues to deploy Western languages to mediate its linguistic diversity. In these circumstances, the relation between local and global languages is the site of an unequal exchange that hampers the radical potential of translation, the "language of languages", and mutlilingualism for "enabling mutuality of being and becoming even within a plurality of languages" (Ngũgĩ 2018, 131). For Ngũgĩ, this potential is today displayed by language use among "border communities" that operate across a variety of languages in a "networkingly" rather than hierarchical relationship. Among the communication strategies adopted by these communities are practices of translation and multilingualism that include developing a shared lingua franca that coexists with their other languages without displacing them (Ngũgĩ 2018, 127–128).

Conversely, instead of valorising their linguistic diversity, many postcolonial African states have explicitly or implicitly adopted a monolingual norm, often based on privileging the former colonial language. Ngũgĩ describes this norm as "the fundamentalism of monolingualism". This is the view that a "nation is not really a nation without a common language to go with the commonality of territory, economy and culture". As a result, the different African languages used by people who live in the same nation are seen as a threat to the integrity of the nation: "Monolingualism is seen as the centripetal answer to the centrifugal anarchy of multiplicity of languages. European languages are seen as coming to the rescue of a cohesive Africa, otherwise threatened by its own languages". But in reality, "there are very few, if any, monolingual nations in the world. What most have is an officially imposed language as the national language: the language of power" (Ngũgĩ 2018, 125).

In *Decolonising the Mind*, Ngũgĩ also underscores how in Africa language hierarchies correspond to hierarchies of expressive forms. Colonial languages are the languages of elitist forms of literary expression, but along with them there are popular arts, such as drama, oral storytelling, song and dance that are part of the cultural tradition of African languages and that came under attack from missionaries and colonial administrations in the colonial period. Ngũgĩ's turn to popular theatre in Gĩkũyũ with the Kamiriithu Community Education and Cultural Centre in the 1970s, which he describes in the second chapter of the book, "The language of African theatre", was both a rediscovery of these traditions and an attempt to create a popular and participatory form of cultural expression for the postcolonial moment. This was a theatre that created a rural African public sphere (Tomaselli and Mboti 2013, 525–526). It is worth reading Ngũgĩ's evocative description of that experiment to get a sense of how this innovative African public sphere came about:

> there was an actual empty space at Kamiriithu. The four acres reserved for the Youth Centre had at that time, in 1977, only a falling-apart mud-walled barrack of four rooms which we used for adult literacy. The rest was grass. Nothing more. It was the peasants and workers from the village who built the stage: just a raised semicircular platform backed by a semi-circular bamboo wall behind which was a small three-roomed house which served as the store and changing room. The stage and the auditorium – fixed long wooden seats arranged like stairs – were almost an extension of each other. It had no roof. It was an open air theatre with large empty spaces surrounding the stage and the auditorium. The flow of actors and people between the auditorium and the stage, and around the stage and the entire auditorium was uninhibited: Behind the auditorium were some tall eucalyptus

trees. Birds could watch performances from these or from the top of the outer bamboo fence. And during one performance some actors, unrehearsed, had the idea of climbing up the trees and joining the singing from up there. They were performing not only to those seated before them, but to whoever could row see them and hear them – the entire village of 10,000 people was their audience.

(Ngũgĩ 1986a, 42)

In a subsequent interview, Ngũgĩ would remark that he was drawn to theatre because it represented a "communal effort" and because of "its capacity for immediate communication" (Ngũgĩ 2006, 201).

The issue of language, and specifically of the hierarchy between colonial and indigenous languages, for Ngũgĩ is linked to broader questions to do with epistemic, sociopolitical, economic, and cultural inequality. One of the phrases he uses for challenging and undoing these systemic inequalities is "moving the centre". If under colonialism Europe and the West were assumed to be the centre of the world, we must now abandon this idea and reimagine a world with a multiplicity of centres. This is what Ngũgĩ describes as creating a world enriched by linguistic and cultural diversity: "The wealth of a common global culture will then be expressed in the particularities of our different languages and cultures very much like a universal garden of many-coloured flowers" (Ngũgĩ 1993, 42). In fact, Ngũgĩ's phrase "moving the centre" does not refer only to the geography of knowledge production, nor is it just a metaphor. It also points to the need to challenge the hierarchies of race, class, gender, language, and culture that still structure postcolonial societies.

In *Globalectics: Theory and the Politics of Knowing* (2012), Ngũgĩ turns to the opportunities offered by cyberspace and digital media's convergence of modes and expressive forms for African cultural production. He highlights the challenge cyberspace poses to the "aesthetic feudalism" that in modern Western culture and its colonial outposts established a hierarchy between the written and the oral whereby the latter, "even when viewed as being 'more' authentic or closer to the natural, is treated as bondsman to the writing master. With orality taken as the source for the written and orature as the raw material for literature, both were certainly placed on a lower rung in the ladder of achievement and civilization" (Ngũgĩ 2012, 63).

Ngũgĩ argues that the multimodal and transmedia forms of expression and communication we encounter online interrupt the hegemony of writing the West imposed on African cultural forms and open up new possibilities for its hybridisation with the oral and other expressive modes:

The lines between the written and the orally transmitted are being blurred in the age of internet and cyberspace. This has been going on for some years with the writing down of the orally transmitted; the electronic transmissions of the written as spoken through the radio and television; or simply the radio as a medium of speech. But it has surely accelerated with all corners of the globe becoming neighborhoods in cyberspace. Through technology, people can speak in real time face to face. The language of texting and emailing and access to everything including pictures and music in real time is producing a phenomenon that is neither pure speech nor pure writing. The language of cyberspace may borrow the language of orality, twitter, chat rooms, we-have-been-talking when they mean we-have-been-texting, or chatting through writing emails, but it is orality mediated by writing. It is neither one nor the other. It's both. It's cyborality.

(Ngũgĩ 2012, 84)

From his coinage of the term cyborality, Ngũgĩ derives "cyborature" to name the permutations of orature and literature in the age of internet and cyberspace (Ngũgĩ, 85). Digital media have offered a platform for the production, circulation, and reception of diverse texts and performances through modes of delivery that make them travel outside of the literary establishment and its canonical forms. From there, Ngũgĩ predicts, will emerge forms of cultural expression born from a new synthesis of the written and the oral, literature and orature:

> writing and orality are realizing anew the natural alliance they have always had in reality, despite attempts to make the alliance invisible or antagonistic. I hope that this means that no cultures and communities need be denied history because they had not developed a writing system; that the oral and the written are not and have never been real antagonists. Certainly, the powers of their products, orature and literature, will continually be harnessed to enrich creativity in the age of internet and cyberspace. The problem has not been the fact of the oral or the written, but their placement in a hierarchy. Network, not hierarchy, will free the richness of the aesthetic, oral or literary.
>
> *(Ngũgĩ, 85)*

It thus seems fitting to conclude this section with an initiative by *Jalada Africa*, an online journal out of Nairobi that published a short story originally written in an African language and subsequently translated into 30 other African languages. Titled "Ituĩka rĩa mũrũngarũ: Kana kĩrĩa gĩtũmaga andũ mathiĩ marũngiĩ", and authored by Ngũgĩ wa Thiong'o, the story was published in March 2016 in Gĩkũyũ and translated into English by the author as "The upright revolution: Or why humans walk upright". According to its publishers, this is the African language story most translated into other African languages (see Flood 2016).

Conclusion

This chapter has provided a brief introduction to Frantz Fanon and Ngũgĩ wa Thiong'o and argued for their relevance to African media and communication studies. I have show that there are significant aspects of their work that are pertinent both to the field and, more specifically, to current calls for its decolonisation. In this spirit, I hope to have provided a useful rough guide to some of Fanon's and Ngũgĩ's work that will invite African media and communication scholars to a closer and more sustained engagement with these authors.

Notes

1 For a biography of Fanon, see Macey 2012.
2 Fanon's chapter also needs to be read in light of Fanon's position within FLN internal politics – see Gibson 2012; Macey 2012, 262–264, 297–298 for more details.

References

Fanon, F. 1965 [1959]. *A Dying Colonialism*, trans. Chevalier, Haakon. New York: Grove Press.
Fanon, F. 1965 [1961]. *The Wretched of the Earth*, trans. Farrington, Constance. New York: Grove Press.
Fanon, F. 1967 [1964]. *Toward the African Revolution: Political Essays*, trans. Chevalier, Haakon. New York: Grove Press.
Fanon, F. 1986 [1952]. *Black Skin, White Masks*, trans. Markmann, Charles Lam. London: Pluto Press.
Flood, A. 2016. Short story by Ngũgĩ wa Thiong'o translated into over 30 languages in one publication. *The Guardian*, 29 March. www.theguardian.com/books/2016/mar/29/jalada-africa-short-story-ngugi-wa-thiongo-translated-over-30-languages-publication (Accessed 6 August 2018).

Gibson, N. 2012. Thinking Fanon, 50 years later: Fanonian translations in and beyond 'Fanon studies'. *Pambazuka News*, 14 March. www.pambazuka.org/governance/thinking-fanon-50-years-later (Accessed 5 August 2018).

Gibson, N. 2017. The specter of Fanon: The student movements and the rationality of revolt in South Africa. *Social Identities: Journal for the Study of Race, Nation and Culture*, 23(5): 579–599.

Gibson, N. and Beneduce, R. 2017. *Frantz Fanon, Psychiatry and Politics*. Johannesburg: Wits University Press.

Julien, I. and Nash, M. 1996. *Black Skin, White Masks*. London: Arts Council of England.

Macey, D. 2012. *Frantz Fanon: A Biography*. London: Verso, 2nd ed.

Ngũgĩ, J. 1964. *Weep Not, Child*. London and Ibadan: Heinemann.

Ngũgĩ, J. 1965. *The River Between*. London: Heinemann.

Ngũgĩ wa Thiong'o 1967. *A Grain of Wheat*. London: Heinemann.

Ngũgĩ wa Thiong'o 1980. *Caitaani mũtharaba-inĩ*. Nairobi: Heinemann (Translated as *Devil on the Cross*. London: Heinemann, 1982).

Ngũgĩ wa Thiong'o 1981. *Writers in Politics: A Re-Engagement with Issues of Literature & Society*. Oxford: James Currey.

Ngũgĩ wa Thiong'o 1986a. *Decolonising the Mind: The Politics of Language in African Literature*. London: James Currey.

Ngũgĩ wa Thiong'o 1986b. *Matigari ma njiruungi*. Nairobi: Heinemann (Translated as *Matigari*. Oxford: Heinemann, 1989).

Ngũgĩ wa Thiong'o 1993. *Moving the Centre: The Struggle for Cultural Freedoms*. London: James Currey.

Ngũgĩ wa Thiong'o 2006a. *Ngũgĩ wa Thiong'o Speaks. Interviews Edited by Reinhard Sanders and Bernth Lindfors*. Oxford: James Currey.

Ngũgĩ wa Thiong'o 2006b. *Wizard of the Crow*. Nairobi: Harvill Secker.

Ngũgĩ wa Thiong'o 2012. *Globalectics: Theory and the Politics of Knowing*. New York: Columbia University Press.

Ngũgĩ wa Thiong'o 2018. The politics of translation: Notes towards an African language policy. *Journal of African Cultural Studies*, 30(2): 124–132.

Olsson, G.H., dir. 2014. *Concerning Violence: Nine Scenes from the Anti-Imperialistic Resistance*. Sweden: Dogwood 85 min.

Pithouse, R. 2016a. Violence: What Fanon really said. *Mail and Guardian*, 8 April. https://mg.co.za/article/2016-04-07-violence-what-fanon-really-said (Accessed 10 June 2018).

Pithouse, R. 2016b. Frantz Fanon: Philosophy, praxis, and the occult zone. *Journal of French and Francophone Philosophy – Revue de la philosophie française et de langue française*, 24(1): 116–138.

Tomaselli, K.G. and Mboti, N. 2013. Doing cultural studies: What is literacy in the age of the post? *International Journal of Cultural Studies*, 16(5): 521–537.

4
Rethinking African strategic communication
Towards a new violence

Colin Chasi

Introduction

With just over a billion people and significant growth prospects, Africa is an exciting frontier for those interested in investing in emerging markets. However, beyond narrow claims that Africans value harmony and therefore also reconciliation – even in business – little is known about what an African strategic approach entails. This chapter asks: If strategic communication cannot be separated from violence and warfare, what are the implications for African strategic practice?

It is evident that Africans are not all followers of the same moral philosophy. Less obvious is that there are many different thematic variations to interpretation of ubuntu. However, it is widely held that it is possible and useful to speak of ubuntu as an African moral philosophy – others such as Metz (2007) and Kamwangamulu (1999) have made this point elsewhere. Gade (2011) has located indigenous and scholarly discourses on ubuntu in historical developments in Zimbabwe and South Africa.

In this chapter I present new insights on how the many Bantu language–speaking Africans who live in sub-Saharan Africa and who articulate the moral philosophy of ubuntu may approach the violence of strategic communication. The intention is not to refute the idea that Africans value harmony. It is to advance new insights into ubuntu that take into account the fact of violence in the world. In this way, I hope to extend rather than reduce the conceptual appeal of ubuntu, i.e. I hope to advance an avenue for thinking about this quintessentially African moral philosophy that reveals ubuntu to be even more capacious than may have been otherwise thought – because it even has valuable things to say about strategic practices that are associated with violence and war.

I do this in the understanding that communication is violent (Vince and Mazen 2014; Zizek 2008; Burke 1969, 19–23), human existence is characterised by violence (Schopenhauer 2004; Benatar 2006) and that strategy is hence inextricably violent. Strangely, as far as I can tell from extensive reading of the literature, Africans have been described as peoples who value harmony but without consideration of the inherence of violence in their existence. This chapter addresses this omission by drawing out some implications for strategy that arise from the study of how the quintessentially African moral philosophy of ubuntu may be acted out with violent communication in a violent world. The idea is to conclude with a new perspective on ubuntu and the African perspective that says (1) for Africans there is nothing alien about using violence and warfare; and (2) the challenge is to strategically use violence and warfare to advance development and democracy.

Human communication is violent

The world is violent. It is not fundamentally harmonious as some scholars of ubuntu have rendered it (Ramose 1999). Acknowledging this violence, some pessimists have gone so far as to say that there is so much pain and harm in the world that it is better to never have been born (Schopenhauer 2004; Benatar 2006). Consistent with this pessimistic view, which describes the harsh realities of how people seek meaningfulness and pleasure amidst inevitable lack, suffering and death – this chapter takes the perspective that the communication that expresses human modes of existence in the world is fundamentally violent; it is about warfare in various guises and modalities (Sonderling 2013).

Human communication is rooted in the unique ability to use and respond to linguistic signs in ways that induce cooperation (Burke 1969, 43; Tomasello 2010). Use of communication introduces a violent process that denies that the self and the other have unique biographically determined perspectives (Schutz 1971, 323). This is to say that attempts to co-substantially act together are inherently characterised by identification and conflict. The "human substances" involved in communication are fundamentally separate and distinct in such ways that any efforts at co-substantiation involve violent contestations for space, autonomy and integrity (Burke 1969, 19–23). Often the violent acts of domination and symbolic violence by which individual and collective identities are achieved are removed from scrutiny by acts of fantasy and other such forms of violent innocence that sustain practical attitudes (Vince and Mazen 2014; Zizek 2008).

Even the shared intentionality that characterises human communication and cooperation is achieved with violence. Attainment of shared meaning, cooperation, organisation and harmony involves symbolic processes that inevitably crush, distort and harm what those who partake in them would grasp. Communication entails colonising or otherwise manufacturing conceptual grounds on which meanings and cultures are shared and formed. It involves changing the states of being of those who receive the meaning of intended communicators (Grice 1957; Sperber and Wilson 1995). Even the qualities of promoting shared meaning, cooperation, organisation and harmony with which communication is associated can be understood as mechanisms by which people have waged war against nature and each other in order to create colonies in which they hope to live well. Where human cultures, organisations and civilisation have formed, this has been done with various degrees of violence inflicted to control nature and people, while denying individual humans the capacity to maximise gains in all instances (Bastiat 2001; Foucault 2004; Freud 1950; Coase 1937).

In nature, some animals are stronger or physically more dangerous than Homo sapiens. To overcome and control dangers posed by nature, humans have evolved cooperative strategies that enable them to survive and thrive as arguably the top predators on earth. This same human capacity for cooperative action is the basis for the formation of companies. The words "company" and "cooperation" invite recognition of how those involved in the formation of these bodies come together co-substantially in what Goffman (1959) has enabled us to term "everyday strategic communicative" acts to cultivate a "firm" with its common consensual grounds for human cooperative action. Strategy is an important means by which companies seek to maximise their chances of survival in a dangerous world (Henderson 1989).

Prima facie the view that Africans have developed a moral philosophy which values and normalises harmony (Metz 2007; Ramose 1999; Shutte 2001; Mbigi 2005) conflicts with the understanding that strategic communication entails violence and warfare. I ask: If strategic communication cannot be separated from violence and warfare, what are the implications for African organisational practice? I proceed by first discussing organisational strategy and in particular corporate communication strategy as practices that are intrinsically and variously violent.

Strategy – that old military term

The continued dominance in contemporary business scholarship of that old military term "strategy" (Audebrand 2010) reveals how companies are commonly conceptualised as being involved in the business of fighting for resources, markets and survival (Henderson 1989; Kim and Mauburgne 2009; Ghemawat 2002; Klein 1999); this often entails colonising the life-worlds of people (Deetz 1992; Boyle 2003).

Etymologically, "strategy" (from the Greek word *strategos* – the art of the general) speaks of an art and of an actor whose mode of expression cannot be separated from the business of violence. In this "military" sense, strategy implies an idea of planning and acting towards victory in what are generally win-lose situations in which actors often fearsomely use all means available to achieve intended goals, even in situations of general uncertainty. Strategic communication involves violence and warfare to secure the firm grounds on which business corporations take root. A primary requirement for strategic organisational action is to regiment people in such ways that individuals work to their prescribed roles. Strategic communication practices are machinations of the warfare by which organisations seek to deny individual difference and uniqueness in order to control individuals (MacIntyre 1999; Nord and Fox 1996), or to generally manufacture the consent of others (Herman and Chomsky 1988; Carey 1995) by colonising their life-worlds (Deetz 1992) as a management function that aims to intentionally and rationally make decisions and take actions towards the achievement of organisational goals (Verčic and Grunig 2000; Sandhu 2009; Swerling and Sen 2009; Grunig and Grunig 2008). Thus construed, strategic communication deploys innumerable means of war to ensure that organisations achieve their goals, with orchestrators being mindful of both fathomable and unfathomable risks posed not only by today's competitors but also by customers, suppliers, potential entrants and substitute products (Porter 1996, 25).

Organisational strategists ask: "What is our business and what will it be in the future?" Alternatively: "What is our mission and what is our vision?" (Puth 2002, 183). They often ask this while scanning through what Kim and Mauborgne (2002, 78) call a muddle of engrossing and often conflicting masses of data that are incapable of giving certainty to strategic action. In these conditions of fundamental uncertainty (Simon 1993, 134) strategists are lauded for developing powerful and decisive missions and visions (Machiavelli 1925, 136–138) with due regard to alternatives.

While strategists repeatedly refer to the past with pride, the rationality of their actions is only indicative of the retrospective valorisation of their actions that is fought for, won and lost in organisational sense-making processes. Strategic thinkers are always involved in a fight to gain and maintain legitimation. Good strategic planning enables the actor to review experiences so that each such plan determines how one views the past (Weick 1969, 102).

Judgements about the quality of a strategic plan are ultimately dependent on stories dumped upon society by those who control the means to tell the dominant stories. Given that patterns of dominance and processing of acquisition and deployment of news are variable, it is worth observing that what you get out of an organisation depends on what has been put in and also upon the specific time and place you reach into the "garbage can" (Marion 1999,

170–213; Cohen et al. 1972). Knowing this, organisations have increasingly come to prioritise the recruitment of individuals who are able to learn and to create knowledge. Such individuals are able to make the discretionary decisions that organisations need to make, in order not to live in the past and despite past memories (Ballard and Seibold 2003), but also so that they can thrive in the here and now. These and all other individuals have to recognise that institutional facts and practices are increasingly so fluid that for years now it has become common to observe that for managers the "greatest problem with rules is that organisations and their environments change faster than the rules. Most bad rules were once good, designed for a situation that no longer exists" (Perrow 1986, 26). In this flux, *strategy is constantly evaluated and reviewed to orchestrate effective and efficient social arrangements and practices aimed at the putative raison d'être of the organisation*. Yet it has long been known that organisations seemingly often take on goals of their own (Etzioni 1964, 5); organisations are battlefields in which multiple competing goals of individuals and collectives are negotiated, put down, pulled up, cut apart and variously wielded (Ahrne 1990).

Marshalling strategic organisational action is at best an inexact art of managing risk (Bernstein 1998; Machiavelli 1925, 154–155) where it is a creative challenge to even formulate the problem itself (Hatchuel 2001, 262). This is to say that in the face of the limited information available for decision making, organisational strategists inevitably act with discretion acquired from prior experiences when they choose courses of action (Perrow 1986, 22–23; March and Simon 1965, 148). The violent, discretionary character of strategic decision making is easily brushed aside in favour of rationalistic normative assertions.

Strategic communication management of risks associated with arbitrary individual action seeks to deny individuals the agency to "do arbitrary things". Strategy represents a distinctly management voice, the violence-laced silencing of discordant voices and the denial of the individual (Deetz 1992) who tends, in fact, to disappear in organisational study (Nord and Fox 1996). The organisational capacity to control rules, individuals and resources is implied by the idea that strategy involves the drawing up of strategic plans which are then to be implemented by members. There is a close relationship between "what legislators do and what managers do. Both groups construct reality through authority acts. When people enact laws, they take undefined space, time and action and draw lines, establish categories, and coin labels that create new features of the environment that did not exist before" (Weick 1995, 30–31). What is significant is that just as any application of the law involves violent acts that limit people's freedom of expression (Bastiat 2001), so, too, the application of organisational legal authority and the associated imposition of organisation rules involve the diminution of individual freedoms of expression, even if the organisations that are thus formed are thereby enabled to be more powerful and sustainable bodies (Coase 1960, 1937).

Communication functions in corporations to organise the behaviors of individuals towards achievement of outcomes: "The ultimate goal of the communicator is to alter his hearer's thoughts, and that is why he engages in communication at all" (Tanaka 1994, 18). In this specific sense the communicator is a coloniser who precisely aims to cut himself apart, take ownership of a territory and remake others in his image (Van Rinsum 2001). This raises ethical concerns regarding the choice and freedom of who are "communicated to". As a consequence, being strategic involves designing or coming up with solutions for problems that are impermanently and contingently dependent upon people's ends and the strategic means devised to achieve them. Purely strategic individuals are limited to focusing on strategic goals in such ways that they are constrained from being concerned with all other issues that legitimately bear upon or otherwise concern them. As such a strategist has no real relations with others; her relations are limited and determined by calculations of their use-value so that, ironically, such a person is lost also to herself because, subjectively, the way to the experience of self is lost to her (Buber 1987, 68).

In the context of the strategic organisation, the aim of identifying oneself and others is not to get to know the worker; rather the aim is to achieve a kind of domination of the organisational battleground to attain management's goals (Weick 1995; Deetz 1992). Carey's (1995) critique of the "manufacturing of consent" exposes the ongoing role of communication professionals in taking the risk out of democracy, by denying the individual choice and freedom of those who are managed. A norm is produced which supports the system of dominance construction. Strategic communication serves a conservative agenda in that it is constructed on models or knowledges which prioritise an underlying logic of large numbers, prioritising what is known in such ways it is claimed that the future is driven to repeat the known norm in ways that advantage those who have previously lost while disadvantaging those who have previously won (Bernstein 1998, 335).

Strategic communication is always marked with the possibility of creating master/slave and other such systems of relations built on difference, separation, "other-ing" and control, domination, violence and warfare (Olivier 2004, 85; Tomkins et al. 1975; Grunig and Grunig 2008). In the organisation, the hierarchy sets management apart from workers; the manager does not work but rather manages. Yet it is in the practice of managing that the manager localises and becomes indispensable to the description of the workplace and to the prescription of work.

When two men collaborate in an enterprise to which they contribute different kinds of services and from which they derive different amounts and kinds of profit, who is to say just where "cooperation" ends and a partner's "exploitation" of the other begins? (Burke 1969, 25).

What is curious is that organisational "hierarchy is complete only when each rank accepts the *principle of gradation itself*" (Burke 1969, 138; emphasis in original). This unusual state of affairs is achieved by means of myths that blame the victim through mythically apportioning guilt to those who are mysteriously located at the bottom of social hierarchies. According to Burke, mystery is, in this case, the "corresponding condition" of hierarchy, as mysteries arise socially "from different modes of life. The king will be a mystery to the peasant, and vice versa" (Tomkins et al. 1975, 136). In this case mystery has the quality of making the abnormal hierarchical organisational division of privileges and burdens justifiable and strangely normal. In the grips of the mysterious communion by which organisational roles and positions "occupy" people, there is *strange* estrangement (Tomkins et al. 1975, 137) that enables people to inflict harm bureaucratically, routinely and even as though it were a virtue (MacIntyre 1999).

Ubuntu and the vital force of the African strategist

It has been said that strategic communication cannot be separated from violence and warfare. It is now useful to go further and argue that the African moral philosophy of ubuntu, which values and normalises harmony (Metz 2007; Ramose, 1999; Shutte, 2001; Mbigi, 2005), can be reconciled with the understanding that strategic communication entails violence and warfare. This can be argued by pointing out that African cosmology values the vital force of individuals. This vital force cannot be understood without addressing the irrepressible possibility of violence in human existence.

Unfortunately, scientific racialism has laid the groundwork for claims that Africans are a form of Homo sapiens less capable of rational planning, learning and, controlling nature by forming civilised and generally forming culturally sophisticated societies (Dubow, 1995, 1993). In this context, many Africans have taken on the view that Africans value community and the well-being of others in ways that are inimical of Western competitiveness and its violence (Murove

2008). Drawing on the understanding that a person can only be a person through others, it is widely said that African leadership values human solidarity and interdependence, aiming at persuading and encouraging self-disciplining behaviours that involve empathic practices, listening and healing (Mbigi 2005, 218–219).

However, there are dissenting voices that point out that Africans are stereotyped when they are presented as incapable of finding, giving and extracting value from individual independence and even from tension in relations with others. One of these, Ngũgĩ (2009, 50), has tellingly argued that the isiZulu aphorism most associated with ubuntu, *umuntu ngumuntu ngabantu* (a person is a person with other persons), should not be read as a mere proverb. He contends it is not just a common expression of truths shared by a community. Rather, this saying reflexively engages with the non-viability of human existence without others and poses a complex antinomy; a thesis, antithesis and synthesis to elucidate that without others a person cannot be a person with the vital force to achieve a meaningful life. To reduce this complex aphorism to a mere proverb is to deny the complexity of African moral cultures and to deny that for Africans who often live in the harshest of circumstances, as for all humans "culture is struggle" (Ngũgĩ 2009, 52).

Africans cannot avoid fighting since because human practices are characterised by violence. African cosmology finds that human beings are fundamentally characterised by vital force and by agency which is an expression of power. This power impacts violently upon the world – for the good as well as for the bad. In African cosmology, agency is what is often described as the vital force that humans and other forms of existence embody in different measure (Tempels 1959). In African religious cosmology this vital force is said to be have been distributed in varying measures when God created a hierarchical world of beings and things. The concern among Africans is not so much to avoid the use of force, but to the use of force towards destructive ends.

It is not new to say that Africans have traditionally expressed interest in ensuring that vital force is used well. For example, there is much interest among Africans in the relationship between witches and the mysterious beasts called familiars, which carry out their horrid deeds. From research conducted in South Africa, Niehaus (1995, 515) says: "Witches are identified with familiars, have the attributes of animals, and actually metamorph into familiars. This duality lies at the heart of the conception of witchcraft as a dangerous, superhuman, power". His broad suggestion is that witchcraft happens in liminal spaces between human community (human settlements) and nature (forests), threatening the distinction between the two. I have no interest in questions regarding the mystical power ascribed to witchcraft. My point is that Africans have historically been interested in how vital force can be used in ways that preserve and advance human community from the harms that nature can inflict. From this, I wish to draw attention to the important observation that when African interest in how power is used or misused is not well theorised, practices that are unjust are likely to proliferate with punishing consequences for development. This is well documented in widespread attacks on women who are often unjustly accused of witchcraft when they challenge male patriarchal orders, with negative implications for development, particularly among women (Federici 2008).

Africans are not the only ones who have recognised that things in the world possess agency. French sociologist Bruno Latour (2000) has famously observed that contexts, in multifarious forms, also possess agency. The tools, buildings and other structural matter that define contexts are curiously identified agents that Latour (2000) has wonderfully addressed as "the silent masses" because their agentic roles are so often neglected. Latour's case for saying the context has agency involves suggesting that tools display intentionality. In contrast, Gidden's (1986) structuration approach makes intentionality unnecessary to the enunciation of agency. In saying this, the context itself is understood to be produced and reproduced through, in and by the intended and unintended consequences of the actions of human agents.

With vital force, people display the agency to act upon the world, to organise or to refrain from doing so with varying degrees of success and failure. Decoupling human agency from intentionality distinguishes it from classical considerations of rationality according to which the actions of the individual would have needed to be demonstrated as directed towards a goal before the agentic character of the act could be given. This decoupling makes possible an ethical standpoint according to which the capacity of the human being to act is itself respected. A key consequence is that people are granted dignity merely because of their "privileged ontological status as creator[s], maintainer[s] and destroyer[s] of worlds . . . in this fundamental way that is beyond our intention, human . . ." (Christians 1997, 13).

Tempels (1959) finds that Africans traditionally believe that people are imbued with more vital force than other forms of existence and that the closer one gets to God the more vital force one has. For example, elders and ancestors are understood to be imbued with greater amounts of vital force than younger people and those still living, respectively. This African notion of vital force does not depend on ascription of intention for one to be considered as having agency.

Without seeking to challenge the religious view of African vital force, I assume a secular view in terms of which human agency creatively and violently crafts social life. In doing this, I hold that people and other beings variously express vital force in all the ways in which they communicate.

Human beings are social actors who know a great deal about their conditions and the consequences of what they do; they know that they can change things and also that their agency is bounded (Banks and Riley 1993, 171). To the extent that this is so, it is viable to argue that the moral philosophy of ubuntu raises questions that arise because Africans recognise that social forms, culture and organisational structures are – as observed by scholars such as McPhee (1985, 164), Giddens (1986, 24), and Banks and Riley (1993, 173) – recursively achieved in social systems which are instantiated, coordinated and made sense of by agents whose actions are in turn enacted in time and space. More broadly, it also suggests that African moral thought is concerned with the view – which is well articulated by Tomasello (2010, 2009) – that people are unique among other animals in the world because we communicate and cooperate. Indeed, that Africans are cooperative beings is often addressed by speaking of Africans valuing collective or communal relations (Ikuenobe 2006; Ramose 1999). However, a more fundamental and much less noted point is that Africans recognise that living with others is a problem that requires the exercising of moral thought and guidance (Menkiti 2002).

It is widely noted that Africans value harmony in community relations (Ikuenobe 2006; Ramose 1999; Shutte 2001; Metz 2007). This has led many to erroneously conclude that Africans do not value individuals (Diagne 2009; Eze, 2008) even though human co-substantiality is inherently based on denial of the fact that human individuals are different or unique one from another (Burke, 1969, 19–23). The great enterprise of human culture that is enabled by communication is a falsehood that masks human selfishness, aggression and violence (Becker, 1973; Elias, 1978).

To understand why Africans cooperate requires recognising the utilitarian motivations or incentives that people have for doing so (Connell, 2007; Césaire, 2000; Kenyatta 1953). People, including Africans, organise, establish laws, norms, social contracts and morals in order to reduce what Nobel laureate Ronald Coase (1960, 1937) refers to as marketing or transaction costs related to organising. However, this requires that people acquiesce to getting only what their social contracts and related mores dictate. This acquiescence entails that people are in some sense violently denied rational maximum economic gains that are available in transactions

(Coase 1960, 1937). The altruism on the basis of which individuals, including Africans, sacrifice such gains is foundational to how people orchestrate cultures that productively reduce transaction costs so that over time humans have ratcheted up their advantage over other animals lacking this attribute (Tomasello 2009).

Human culture, civility and the related notions of productivity are founded on violent control and denial of the most violent and selfish interests of individuals. This may be illustrated with reference to Elias (1978), whose study of the birth of manners shows that violence is never abolished in human affairs: the strategic choices that peoples make to avoid external violence merely lead to internalisation in various symbolic forms. In pre-colonial Africa, it has been said that societal forms and societal laws regulating communal ownership of land, for example, illustrate how violent contestation and conquest were never far off and how the law and notions of morality were deployed to enforce order and peace (Kenyatta 1953). The law is a form of violence that has been repressed, internalised and otherwise appropriated to control and harness societal violence for the gain of those impose the law (Bastiat 2001; Foucault 2004; Freud 1950). In appreciation of this, performances of African moral philosophies of law are geared towards attainment of a living African law which seeks to overcome these limitations, and perpetuate and restore justice rather than to merely pursue what is defined as legal (Woodman 2011).

The strategic choices that individuals make in crafting their performances of self are strategic (Goffman 1959). Human beings take up different roles and also act differently, depending on the situation and the goals at stake. Interactions are variously well mannered or obscene and overtly violent depending upon these contingencies (Elias 1978); it is therefore not necessarily true that Africans are always convivial in their interactions, as Nyamnjoh (2009) may be misinterpreted to infer. Nyamnjoh (2010, 80) is cognisant of the fact that societies which aspire for very narrowly conceived notions of belonging and democracy are bound to implode as the human concern to be humane in relations with others and material or utilitarian concerns rather favour those who perfect the arts of using interdependence and conviviality for one's own good and for the good of others. People act in generally tactful ways in order to minimise the existential anxiety and other such factors which may otherwise compromise productive cooperative interaction (Giddens 1986, 156). The dramaturgical role-apparent nature of human strategic interaction violently levels everything to an obscene sameness when people's life circumstances, perspectives and performances are ever unique (Goffman 1959, 254–255).

The problem is not that human action should cease to be strategic. It is rather that people should be enjoined to be concerned about the issues that bear on them (Gordon 1995, 19) and to act with the fullness of their consciousness. I say this in the realisation that, as an example, ubuntu has often been misused to legitimate claims that Africans are conformists and communalists who can be easily led for nationalistic purposes, making it suitable for the purposes of many African dictatorships (Marx 2002) and also realising that ubuntu has been abused as a cognitive map to blunt the moral sensitivities of individuals in communities that have on occasion been whipped up to brutally kill those deemed to be "traitors" (Blankenberg 1999).

Too often people have been misanthropically made into zombies with no viable concerns of their own, nullifying achievable possibilities for productive social life (Nyamnjoh 2005) and even for democracy itself (Mbembe 1992). The point is that if the freedom and capacities associated with development are to be gained (Sen 2010) person by person, Africans must be encouraged to break free from the yoke of what Fanon (2004, 145) labelled "relative obscurity" in order to discover and fulfil the mission of being the most that each can be.

Nowhere are people totally free. Notwithstanding the efforts of demagogues, dictators and others intent on controlling others, ubuntu remains to a great extent an oral and fluid moral philosophy which gains meaning in action contexts where those involved in relevant practices are charged with the responsibility to find and enact the good. Because ubuntu has not historically had strong, immutable written prescripts, its performance remains to a great extent available for improvisation and contestation. Those who care for making ubuntu a moral philosophy which frees Africans to communicate strategically in ways that manage violence should be willing to fight for it.

Conclusion

Africans know a great deal about violence. In its various guises, it is an inordinate feature of African existence. It would be strange to think that it is not important for Africans to think about violence, about how to overcome its negative consequences and how to make the good, great and beautiful with it. In the manner that Homo sapiens grapples with energy in all its guises, understanding it can occasion harm and that it is fundamental to achieving the desirable.

In much the same way that one who would use fire wisely has to appreciate the fundamentally harm-inflicting potential of fire, one must appreciate the potential harms associated with the vital force of each person and of human cooperative interaction if one is to invest in using this force well. We miss a vital insight if our discussions of African cooperative action simply overlook the role of thinking about avoiding harmful violence and using violence towards the attainment of (all things considered) desirable outcomes, by (all things considered) desirable means (since violence cannot be avoided).

The essence of *good* strategic thinking is precisely that it attempts to account for all stakeholders from a wide scope of bottom lines, recognizing that it is not possible to avoid violence. This key essence can be traced in contemporary fields of study, including just war (DiMeglio 2005), ethical business practices (Brewer 1997; Menestrel et al. 2002) and ethical strategic communication (Muhr and Rehn 2014). This lesson of *good* strategic thinking is lost to Africans to the extent that violence is not adequately thought about. This chapter is a bold step in this direction.

Given that the world is violent, the moral philosophies of peoples are an expression of how they value the cultivation of cultures by which they may flourish. African cosmology shows concern for how people use their vital force. Attainment of community, organisational and other such forms of strategic cooperation can enable each individual to make the most of her vital force. At the same time, in the never-ending war against the many hazards that characterise human existence, failure to invest in cooperation is likely to leave individuals defenceless and vulnerable.

A consequence of the arguments I have presented is that we can say that to have a culture is to fight. Africans fight. The moral questions that are arise concern why, for what, where, with whom and how they should fight. I have not attempted to address all these moral questions. Instead I have been content to speak to the first philosophical preposition that human, and hence African existence, is characterised by violence.

Among the consequences of recognising that human existence is characterised by violence is that we can see that even cooperation comes with impositions. In other words, those who choose to cooperate in a bid for the fruits of cooperation take on obligations and constraints that are not necessarily chosen and that can hence be described as evincing violence. This is well described by the Shona saying: *kuwanda kwakanaka. Kwakangoshatira pupedza muto* (getting people together is good. It is only problematic in that the multitudes need to be fed). Indeed, the formation of communities requires the establishment of vital systems that ensure their sustenance. The quality of life of a society can to a large extent be understood in terms of the ways in which they put in place strategic arrangements to enable and regulate communal practices that yield the proverbial bread required for survival. What we do know is that such measures should address the requirements for enabling children to grow into responsible adulthood while advancing freedoms and reducing barriers to the self-expression by which people can make the most of their vital force.

There is nothing alien to Africans about organisational practices, rules and strategies to garner and harness resources, energies or forces to produce productive orders. Africans who act in freedom to enact economically competitive recurrent structures arise as warriors for development and democracy. Even when playing sport with all the ubuntu one can imagine, there is nothing alien about Africans fighting for gold!

References

Ahrne, G. 1990. *Agency and Organisation: Towards an Organisational Theory of Society*. London: Sage.
Audebrand, L. 2010. Sustainability in strategic management education: The quest for new root metaphors. *Academy of Management Learning & Education*, 9(3): 413–428.
Ballard, D. and Seibold, D. 2003. Communicating and organising in time: A meso-level model of organisational temporalilty. *Management Communication Quarterly*, 16(3): 380–415.
Banks, S. and Riley, P. 1993. Structuration theory as an ontology for communication research. *Communication Yearbook*, 16: 167–196.
Bastiat, F. 2001. *Bastiat's the Law*. London: Institute of Economic Affairs.
Becker, E. 1973. *The Denial of Death*. New York: The Free Press.
Benatar, D. 2006. *Better Never to Have Been: The Harm of Coming into Existence*. Cape Town: Oxford University Press.
Bernstein, P. 1998. *Against the Gods: The Remarkable Story of Risk*. New York: John Wiley and Sons.
Bewaji, J. and Ramose, M. 2013. The Bewaji, Van Binsbergen and Ramose debate on Ubuntu. *South African Journal of Philosophy*, 22(4): 378–415.
Blankenberg, N. 1999. In search of a real freedom: Ubuntu and the media. *Critical Arts*, 13(2): 42–65.
Boyle, D. 2003. *Authenticity*. London: Flamingo.
Brewer, M. and Chen, Y.R. 2007. Where (who) are the collectivists in collectivism? Towards conceptual clarification of individualism and collectivism. *Pscyhological Review*, 114(1): 133–151.
Brewer, K. 1997. Management as a practice: A response to Alasdair MacIntyre. *Journal of Business Ethics*, 16: 825–833.
Broch-Due, V. 2005. Violence and belonging: Analytical reflections. In Broch-Due, V., ed. *Violence and Belonging: The Quest for Identity in Post-Colonial South Africa*. New York: Routledge, 1–40.
Buber, M. 1987. *I and Thou*, trans. Smith, R. New York: Collier.
Burke, K. 1969. *A Rhetoric of Motives*. Berkeley: University of California Press.
Camus, A. 1955. Myth of Sisyphus. In Camus, A., ed. *The Myth of Sisyphus*. London: Hamish Hamilton, 96–99.
Carey, A. 1995. *Taking the Risk Out of Democracy: Corporate Propaganda Versus Freedom and Liberty*, ed. Lohrey, A. Urbana: University of Indiana Press.
Césaire, A. 2000. *Discourse on Colonialism*. New York: Monthly Review Press.
Chabal, P. 2009. *Africa: The Politics of Suffering and Smiling*. Scottsville: University of KwaZulu-Natal Press.
Chanock, M. 2004. *The Making of South African Legal Culture 1902–1936: Fear, Favour and Prejudice*. New York: Cambridge University Press.
Chasi, C. 2011. *Hard Words on Communication on HIV/AIDS*. Johannesburg: Real African Publishers.
Chipkin, I. 2007. *Do South Africans Exist? Nationalism, Democracy and the Identity of 'the People'*. Johannesbug: Wits University Press.
Christians, C. 1997. The ethics of being in a communication context. In Christians, C. and Traber, M., eds. *Communication Ethics and Universal Values*. London: Sage.
Cilliers, J. 2014. *South African Futures 2030: How Bafana Bafana made Mandela Magic*. Johannesburg: Institute for Security Studies.

Coase, R. 1937. The nature of the firm. *Economica*, 4: 384–400.
Coase, R. 1960. The problem of social cost. *Journal of Law and Economics*, 3: 1–44.
Cohen, M., March, J. and Olsen, J. 1972. A garbage can model of organizational choice. *Administrative Science Quarterly*, 17(1): 1–25.
Connell, R. 2007. *Southern Theory*. Cambridge: Polity Press.
Deetz, S. 1992. *Democracy in an Age of Corporate Colonization: Developments in Communication and the Politics of Everyday Life*. New York: State University of New York.
Diagne, S.B. 2009. Individual, community, and human rights. *Transition*, 101: 8–15.
DiMeglio, R.P. 2005. The evolution of the just war tradition: Defining just post bellum. *Military Law Review*, 186: 116–163.
Dubow, S. 1993. Wulf Sachs's Black Hamlet: A case of 'psychic vivisection'? *African Affairs*, 92(369): 519–556.
Dubow, S. 1995. *Scientific Racism in South Africa*. Johannesburg: Witswatersrand University.
Elias, N. 1978. *The Civilizing Process*. Oxford: Blackwell.
Emirbayer, M. and Mische, A. 1998. What is Agency? *American Journal of Sociology*, 103(4): 962–1023.
Etzioni, A. 1964. *Modern Organisations*. Englewood Cliffs: Prentice-Hall.
Eze, M. 2008. What is African communitarianism? Against consensus as a regulative ideal. *South African Journal of Philosophy*, 27(4): 386–399.
Fanon, F. 2004. *The Wretched of the Earth*, trans. Philcox, R. New York: Grove Press.
Fassin, D. 2007. *When Bodies Remember: Experiences and Politics of AIDS in South Africa*. Berkeley: University of California Press.
Federici, S. 2008. Witch-hunting, globalization, and feminist solidarity in Africa today. *Journal of International Women's Studies*, 10(1): 21–35. http://vc.bridgew.edu/jiws/vol10/iss1/3 (Accessed 27 April 2014).
Foucault, M. 2004. *Abnormal: Lectures at the Collège de France, 1974–1975*, eds. Marchetti, V. and Salomoni, A., trans. Burchell, G. London: Picador.
Freud, S. 1950. *Totem and Taboo*, trans. Strachey, S. New York: Routledge and Kegan Paul.
Gade, C. 2011. The historical development of the written discourses on ubuntu. *South African Journal of Philosophy*, 30(3): 303–329.
Ghemawat, P. 2002. Competition and business strategy in historical perspective. *Business History Review*, 76, 37–74.
Giddens, A. 1986. *The Constitution of Society: Outline of the Theory of Structuration*. Oxford: Polity Press.
Goffman, E. 1959. *The Presentation of Self in Everyday Life*. New York: Doubleday and Company.
Gordon, L. 1995. *Fanon and the Crisis of European Man: An Essay on Philosophy and the Human Sciences*. New York: Routledge.
Grice, H. 1957. Meaning. *Philosophical Review*, 377–388.
Grunig, J. and Grunig, L. 2008. Excellence theory in public relations: Past, present and future. In Zerffass, A., van Ruler, B. and Sriramesh, K., eds. *Public Relations Research*. Wiesbaden: VS Verlag fur Sozialwissenschften, 327–347.
Hatchuel, A. 2001. Towards design theory and expandable rationality: The unfinished program of Herbert. *Journal of Management & Governance*, 5(3–4): 260–273.
Henderson, B. 1989. The origin of strategy. *Harvard Business Review*, 67(6): 139–143.
Herman, E.S. and Chomsky, N. 1988. *Manufacturing Consent: The Political Economy of the Mass Media*. New York: Pantheon Books.
Himonga, C., Taylor, M. and Pope, A. 2013. Reflections on judicial views of Ubuntu. *Potchefstroom Electronic Law Journal*, 16(5): 372–428.
Ikuenobe, P. 2006. *Philosophical Perspectives on Commnualism and Morality in African Traditions*. Lanham: Lexington Books.
Jansen, J. 2011. *We Need to Talk*. Northcliff: Palgrave Macmillan.
Kabede, M. 2001. The rehabilitation of violence and the violence of rehabilitation: Fanon and colonialism. *Journal of Black Studies*, 31(5): 539–562.

Kamwangamulu, N. 1999. Ubuntu in South Africa: A sociolinguistic perspective to a Pan-African concept. *Critical Arts: A South-North Journal of Cultural & Media Studies*, 13(2): 18–24.

Kaunda, K.D. 1980. *Kaunda on Violence*. London: William Collins Sons & Company.

Kenyatta, J. 1953. *Facing Mount Kenya: The Tribal Life of the Gikuyu*. London: Secker and Warburg.

Kierkegaard, S. 1947. *A Kierkegaard Anthology*, ed. Bretall, R. Princeton, NJ: Princeton University Press.

Kim, W. and Mauborgne, R. 2002. Charting your company's future. *Harvard Business Review*, 76–83, June.

Kim, W. and Mauburgne, R. 2009. How strategy shapes structure. *Harvard Business Review*, 2–10, September.

Klein, N. 1999. *No Logo: Taking Aim at the Brand Bullies*. New York: Picador.

Latour, B. 2000. Where are the missing masses? The sociology of a few mundane artefacts. In Bijker, W. and Law, J., eds. *Shaping Technology/Building Society: Studies in Sociotechnical Change*. Cambridge, MA: MIT Press.

Li, C. 2006. The confucian ideal of harmony. *Philosophy East and West*, 56(4): 583–603.

Machiavelli, N. 1925. *The Prince*. London: Philip Allan & Co.

MacIntyre, A. 1999. Social structures and their threats to moral agency. *Philosophy*, 74: 311–329.

Mamdani, M. 2012. *Define and Rule: Native as Political Identity*. Cambridge: Harvard University Press.

March, J. and Simon, H. 1965. *Organizations*. New York: Wiley.

Marion, R. 1999. *The edge of organization: Chaos and complexity theories of formal social systems*. London: Sage.

Marx, C. 2002. Ubu and Ubuntu: On the dialectics of apartheid and nation building. *Politikon: South African Journal of Political Studies*, 49–69.

Mazrui, A.A. 1977a. The warrior tradition and the masculinity of war. *Journal of Asian and* Mbembe, A. 1992. Provisional notes on the postcolony. *Journal of the International African Institute*, 62(1): 3–37.

Mazrui, A.A. 1977b. Armed Kinsmen and the origins of the state: An essay in philosophical anthropology. *Journal of Asian and African Studies*, 12(1–4): 7–19; 13(1–4): 69–81.

Mazrui, A. 2008. Conflict in Africa: An overview. In Nhema, A. and Zeleza, P., eds. *The Roots of African Conflicts: The Causes and Costs*. Pretoria: UNISA Press, 36–50.

Mbigi, L. 2005. *The Spirit of African Leadership*. Randburg: Knowres Publishing.

Mbiti, J. 1970. *Concepts of God in Afrrica*. London: SPCK.

McPhee, R. 1985. Formal structure and organizational communication. In McPhee, R. and Tomkins, P., eds. *Organizational Communication: Traditional Themes and New Directions*. London: Sage, 149–176.

Menestrel, M., Van den Hove, S. and De Bettignies, H. 2002. Processes and consequences in business ethical dilemmas: The oil industry and climate change. *Journal of Business Ethics*, 41(3): 251–266.

Menkiti, I.A. 2002. Philosophy and the state in Africa: Some Ralwsian considerations. *Philosophia Africana*, 5(2): 35–51.

Metz, T. 2007. Towards an African theory. *The Journal of Political Philosophy*, 321–341.

Metz, T. and Gaie, J.B. 2010. The African ethic of Ubuntu/Botho: Implications for research on morality. *Journal of Moral Education*, 273–290.

Mkandawire, T. 2013. *Neopatrimonialism and the Political Economy of Economic Performance in Africa: Critical Reflections*. Stockholm: Institute for Future Studies.

Mouffe, C. 2000. Deliberative democracy or agonistic pluralism. *Political Science Series*, 70: 1–17. Vienna: Institute for Advanced Studies.

Mouffe, C. 2013. *Agonistics: Thinking the World Politically*. New York: Verso.

Muhr, S. and Rehn, A. 2014. Theorizing and researching the dark side of organization. *Organization Studies*, 35(2): 209–231, 1 February. DOI:10.1177/0170840613511925.

Murove, F. 2008. On African ethics and the appropriation of Western Capitalism: Cultural and moral constraints to the evolution of capitalism in post-colonial Africa. In Nicolson, R., trans. *Persons in Community: African Ethics in a Global Culture*. Kwa-Zulu Natal: University of Kwa-Zulu Natal, 85–110.

Nagel, T. 1970. *The Possibility of Altruism*. Oxford: Clarendon Press.

Ngũgĩ, W. 2009. Africa is not a proverb. *World Literature Today*, 83(1): 48–52, January–February.

Niehaus, I. 1995. Witches of the Transvaal Lowveld and their familiars: Conceptions of duality, power and desire. *Cahiers d'études africaines*, 35(138–139): 513–540.

Nord, W. and Fox, S. 1996. The individual in organisational studies: The great disappearing act? In Clegg, S., Hardy, C. and Nord, W., eds. *Handbook of Organisational Studies*. London: Sage, 148–175.

Norman, R. 2006. War, humanitarianism, intervention and human rights. In Sorabji, R. and Rodin, D., eds. *The Ethics of War: Shared Problems in Different Traditions*. Aldershot: Ashgate Publishing, 191–207.

Nussbaum, M. 2001. *The Fragility of Goodness: Luck and Ethics in Greek Tragedy and Philosophy*. Cape Town: Oxford University Press.

Nyamnjoh, F. 2005. Madams and maids in Southern Africa: Coping with uncertainties, and the art of mutual zombification. *Africa Spectrum*, 40(2): 181–196.

Nyamnjoh, F. 2009. *Africa's Media: Between Professional Ethics and Cultural Belonging*. Windoek: Friederich-Ebert-Stiftung.

Nyamnjoh, F. 2010. Racism, ethnicity and the media in Africa: Reflections inspired by studies of xenophobia in Cameroon and South Africa. *Africa Spectrum*, 45(1): 57–93.

Olivier, B. 2004. The (im)possibility of communication. *Communicarel*, 23(1): 79–91.

Perrow, C. 1986. *Complex Organisations: A Critical Essay*. London: McGraw-Hill, 3rd ed.

Porter, M. 1996. The five competitive forces that shape strategy. *Harvard Business Review*, 23–41, November–December.

Puth, G. 2002. *The Communicating Leader: The Key to Strategic Alignment*. Pretoria: Van Schaick.

Ramose, M. 1999. *African Philosophy Through Ubuntu*. Harare: Mond Books.

Ranger, T.O. 1968. Connexions between 'primary resistance' movements and modern mass nationalism in East and Central Africa: Part I. *The Journal of African History*, 9(3): 437–453.

Robespierre, M. 2007. *Virtue and Terror*. London: Verso.

Rousseau, J. 1997. *The Social Contract and Other Later Political Writings*. Cambridge: Cambridge University Press.

Sandhu, S. 2009. Strategic communication: An institutional perspective. *International Journal of Strategic Communication*, 72–101.

Schopenhauer, A. 2004. On the sufferings of the world. In Benatar, D., ed. *Life, Death & Meaning: Key Philosophical Readings on the Big Questions*. Lanham: Rowman & Littlefield Publishers, 393–402.

Schutz, A. 1971. *Collected Papers 1: The Problem of Social Reality*, ed. Natanson, M. The Hague: Martinus Nijhoff.

Sen, A. 2010. *The Idea of Justice*. London: Penguin Books.

Shutte, A. 2001. *Ubuntu: An Ethic for a New South Africa*. Pietermaritzburg: Cluster Publications.

Simon, H. 1993. Strategy and organisational evolution. *Strategic Management Journal*, 14(Special issue): 131–142.

Sonderling, S. 2013. To speak is to fight: War as structure of thought in Lyotard's postmodern condition. *Communicare: Journal for Communication Sciences in Southern Africa*, 32(2): 1–19.

Sperber, D. and Wilson, D. 1995. *Relevance: Communication and Cognition*. Cambridge: Blackwell.

Swerling, J. and Sen, C. 2009. The institutionalization of the strategic communication function in the United States. *International Journal of Strategic Communication*, 131–146.

Tanaka, K. 1994. *Advertising Language: A Pragmatic Approach to Advertisements in Britain and Japan*. London: Routledge.

Tempels, P. 1959. *Bantu Philosophy*. Paris: Presence Africaine.

Tomasello, M. 2009. *Why We Cooperate*. London: MIT Press.

Tomasello, M. 2010. *Origins of Human Communication*. London: MIT Press.

Tomkins, P., Fisher, J., Infante, D. and Tomkins, E. 1975. Kenneth Burke and the inherent characteristics of formal organisations: A field study. *Speech Monographs*, 42: 137–147, June.

Van Rinsum, H. 2001. *Slaves of Definition: In Quest of the Unbeliever and the Ignoramus*. Maastricht: Shaker Publishing.

Verčic, D. and Grunig, J. 2000. The origins of public relations theory in economics and strategic management. In Moss, D., Verčic, D. and Warnaby, G., eds. *Perspectives on Public Relations Research*. London: Routledge, 9–58.

Vince, R. and Mazen, A. 2014. Violent innocence: A contradiction at the heart of leadership. *Organization Studies*, 1–19, 22 January. DOI:10.1177/0170840613511924.

Vincent, L. 2006. Virginity testing in South Africa: Retraditioning the postcolony. *Culture, Heath & Sexuality*, 8(1): 17–30.

Wasserman, H. 2013. The Marikana aftermath: The language of listening. *Rhodes Journalism Review*, 111–113.

Webel, C. 2004. *Terror, Terrorism, and the Human Condition*. New York: Palgrave Macmillan.

Weick, K. 1969. *The Social Psychology of Organizing*. London: Addison-Wesley.

Weick, K. 1995. *Sensemaking in Organizations*. London: Sage.

Whyte, S.R. 1997. *Questioning Misfortune: The Pragmatics of Uncertainty in Eastern Uganda*. Cambridge: Cambridge Univesity Press.

Wilson, O. 1999. The heterogeneous sound ideal in African-American music. In Capori, G.D., ed. *Signifyin[G], Sanctifyin[g], & Slam Dunking: A Reader in African American Expressive Culture*. Manchester: The University of Massachusettes Press, 157–171.

Woodman, G. 2011. A survey of customary laws in Africa in search of lessons for the future. In Fenrich, J., Galizzi, P. and Higgins, T., eds. *The Future of African Customary Law*. New York: Cambridge University Press, 9–30.

Xaba, S., Hanekom, T., Mbada, M., Mbatha, S., Memela, S., Mthimkhulu, P. and Netshitenzhe, J. 2012. *Working Together to Create a Caring and Proud Society: A National Social Cohesion Summit Report. Walter Sisulu Square of Dedication, Kliptown, Soweto, 4–5 July 2012*. Pretoria: Department of Arts and Culture.

Yuan-kang, W. 2011. *Culture and Chinese Power Politics*. New York: Columbia University Press.

Zizek, S. 2008. *Violence: Six Sideways Reflections*. New York: Picador.

5
Afrokology and organisational culture
Why employees are not behaving as predicted

Elnerine W.J. Greeff

Introduction

The discussions put forward in the different chapters of this volume make it clear how Western/Euro-American ideas and ideologies saturate the theories of communication that have long been hailed as the principle ones of the discipline. The field of corporate communication is no different. Corporate communication theories (especially those that are deemed 'seminal') mainly originate and speak from Western/Euro-, particularly American perspectives. As Watson and L'Etang (2008, 328) state: 'scholars have always tended to assume that [corporate communication was] invented by Americans and then exported elsewhere'.

Authors such as Nabudere (2006) warn about the implications of applying theories with Western/Euro-American ideologies in African contexts. By virtue of their nature, such theories have a colonisation underpinning that thinks of taking control, exploiting and subordinating individuals towards a common goal. In corporate communication these common goals are that of the organisation and its capitalistic pursuit of profit and corporate survival.

This chapter focusses on the construct of culture in an organisational setting. It outlines the ways in which a colonisation mindset and legacy is evident in the theories for managing organisational culture. I argue that these theories are not sufficient for understanding the scope and depth of African organisations' culture or managing them. In order to demonstrate this stance, I make use of Fanagalo as industrial pidgin of the mining industry of South Africa. Fanagalo – as a language – was supposed to be phased out by all mining organisations in the country. In the face of formal management strategies to this effect, the language persists. Examining Fanagalo offers a useful example of how management strategies born from Western/Euro-American ideologies are not equipped for handling or understanding an African reality. Indeed, in this case, it could even lead to the industrywide implementation of an inapplicable policy on organisational culture and employees behaving in unanticipated or unpredicted ways.

To avoid this, corporate communicators need to filter theories and their applications through an Afrokological understanding. It is only once this is done that a true understanding of African organisations, their cultures and members will be gleaned.

In the following section, the Afrokological stance and understanding used in this chapter is outlined. This is followed by an explication of the construct of organisational culture and a review of the case example. The methodology used in empirically exploring the case example is then discussed, before the findings are finally presented.

Afroganisations

Afrokology and its tenets, as per the focus and considerations of this book, is discussed in detail in Chapter 1. In this chapter, I use Afrokology in two ways. First, it is used as a lens to view and evaluate specific applications of Western/Euro-American theories on organisational culture. Secondly, theoretical tenets born from the Afrokological tradition are used to address the concerns and voids left by Western/Euro-American theories, when applied to African organisations. In this way, I do not use Afrokology as a means of rejecting Western/Euro-American theories on organisational culture management wholesale. Rather, I use it to critically re-evaluate the theories and their main tenets of application. After Buntu (2013), I use Afrokology as a solution – a solution to the problems and voids left by the sole application of Western/Euro-American theories. Specifically, the Afrokological concept of ontology is used alongside the concepts of pluralism and multiplicity to offer a framework from which to understand the culture of African organisations. Such a framework makes it clear that context is of paramount importance and that culture is perhaps not as easily managed as Western/Euro-American would have them be.

Further to this, Mano and Meribe's (2017) concept of endogenous institutional communication is used to explicate the unanticipated or unpredicted behaviour of employees as it relates to Fanagalo, which has defied sufficient explanation, up and to this point. In the following section, the concept of organisational culture is outlined, making it clear why Fanagalo should be viewed as an element of the mining culture of South Africa.

Whose culture is it anyway?

Culture – used as a concept to describe the collective behaviours, beliefs, values, endeavours and agency of a group of individuals – has a rich scholarly history spanning well over a hundred years. At first, the concept was used to just denote societies, nations and populaces. In time, the quest to refine the specific lines by which a 'culture' is demarcated led to a broadening of the term. It was established that any grouping of three or more individuals had the potential to produce a culture (Alvesson and Berg 1992; Turner 2014). Armed with the idea of organisations being nothing more than an intentional grouping of individuals, some communication scholars started to aim their inquiries at the cultures of organisations. Organisational culture, as a concept in its own right, reached the zenith of its popularity in the 1980s when many scholars tried to distinguish organisational cultures from other types of cultures and show how an organisation's culture distinguishes it from other organisations.

At this time, scholars such as Schein (1984) turned to the field of anthropology, which has busied itself with the study of culture for much longer, to uncover exactly what organisational culture is. Building on the work of Keesing (1974), Schein (1984) came up with a typology that classified the observable elements of culture and shared meanings of members on three different levels. This typology became one of the defining seminal works on organisational culture. On the first, top level, Schein places the basic assumptions shared by organisational culture members. Below that, values are placed, as values are informed by basic assumptions. On the last

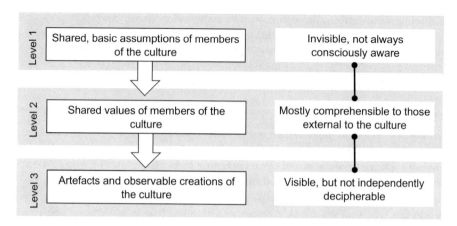

Figure 5.1 Schein's (1984) typology – the elements of organisational culture
Sources: Adapted from Schein (1984) and Ott (1989).

level, artefacts and creations of the culture – the observed manifestation of the culture's shared values and basic assumptions – are located.

What is clear from Figure 5.1 is that, although organisational culture manifests in different ways, no one element is independent from all others. The basic assumptions of cultural members inform their shared values, which in turn models the artefacts and tangible elements found in the organisation.

Viewing this seminal work from an Afrokological perspective, however, makes it clear that the typology does not offer the whole picture. The basic assumptions of the members of an organisation are not plucked out of thin air. Arguably one of the biggest tenets of the perspective is that behaviour and thought is a product of specific ontologies (cf. Anadolu-Okur et al. 2015; Chilisa 2012; Lincoln and González 2007; Smith 2012). These ontologies must be understood if thought and behaviour are to be understood. Indeed, by this way of thinking, artefacts are a direct manifestation of not only an organisation's culture, but also its ontology. Metaphorically, artefacts can be seen as the fruit by which the tree is known. They are more than just manifestations of the culture of an organisation; they are organisational ontological objects.

Artefacts as ontological objects

One would be hard-pressed to find an author writing on Afrokology who does not grapple with the issue of ontology. Simply, ontology deals with what it means to exist – the essential characteristics of existence (Chilisa 2012; Lincoln and González 2007; Smith 2012). In terms of organisations, this relates specifically to the way that organisations exist in society – the way that they position themselves therein. The field of corporate communication as a whole has a meta-ontology which it has yet to articulate. Here, Chilisa's (2012) relational ontology might step into the breach. The thrust of discussions on relational ontology, per Chilisa (2012, 20), hinges on the notion that 'among indigenous people, in the colonized and former colonized societies, people are beings with many relations and many connections'. Purely ontologically, it can tersely be stated that 'reality implies a set of relationships' (Chilisa 2012, 20).

For organisational contexts this is specifically apposite. The field espouses, foremost, an emphasis on relationships – for example with stakeholders (see: stakeholder relationship theory),

Afrokology and organisational culture

with the environment and its resources (see: resource dependence theory), with other organisations (see: competition literature). Still, very often in corporate communication literature, the commercial or non-commercial nature of an organisation is likened or equated to its ontology. It is understood or taken for granted that highly commercial, corporate organisations will have one kind of ontology, while non-profit organisations will have another. Accepting that the degree of commercialisation uncovers an organisation's ontology is a superficial rendering of the truth. An organisation's degree of commercialisation hinges on its ontological stance, but it does not define it.

Rather, using a relational ontology as a kind of 'meta-ontology' for the field offers the means by which to uncover organisations' established reality and the nature of their existence – their own distinct, organisational ontology. Put differently, looking at the ways that organisations position themselves in society by uncovering how they relate to individuals, other organisations and themselves gives a truer reflection of their distinct ontologies as organisations.

This ontology, which shapes an organisation's culture (through basic assumptions, beliefs and values), manifests as relationships. This is observably demonstrated through the behaviour of organisational members, the organisation's outputs, patterns of communication, written and spoken language, and the like. The artefacts of its culture, in other words. Figure 5.2 adapts Schein's (1984) model to reflect this argument.

In contemplating this figure, one major piece of critique becomes almost immediately apparent. One organisation has many different individuals in it, and they will not necessarily (more likely never) all share the same ontological stance. This is why it is important to look at ontology

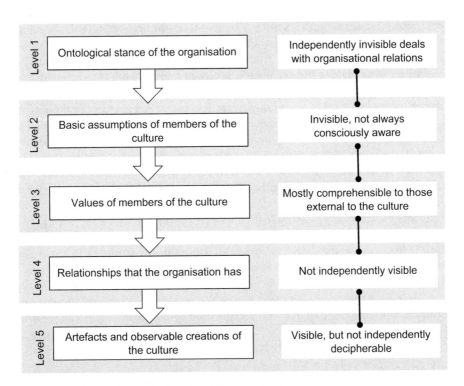

Figure 5.2 Typology of organisational ontology and culture

Sources: Adapted from Schein (1984) and Ott (1989).

71

as it manifests *through* organisational culture. It opens up avenues for exploring how and why this ontology permeated through the organisational culture and its artefacts. This brings to the fore questions around power and management and just how 'shared' the shared meaning and culture really is.

In corporate communication culture literature there is a dearth in terms of exploring this. Martin (2002, 17) explains:

> researchers usually define culture as that which is shared . . . studies that do focus on the shared often do so because they have tautologically justified excluding, via their definition of culture, any aspect of their data that is not shared by many or most people in the organisation.

She explains further that cultural elements should not be seen to be either clearly consistent or clearly inconsistent. Culture might sometimes be, but is not necessarily always one single, unitary, shared, demarcated entity. Although this might not be a novel idea for many fields working with culture, it is indeed a contested aspect within the field of corporate communication. This is largely due to the concept of cultural engineering which grew in prominence in the 1980s, endures and even thrives contemporarily. Flamholtz and Randle (2011, 9), for example, state that: 'Companies where there is a clearly defined culture, where time is invested in communicating and reinforcing this culture, and where all employees are behaving in ways consistent with this culture are defined as having a strong culture'. Martin (2002, 8) explains that the 'strong' culture argument sometimes even goes further to offer organisations 'the holy grail: If an organization could build a sufficiently "strong" culture, improved productivity and profitability would result'.

Those who subscribe to this idea make 'a business case' for 'reinforcing' a single culture. It subscribes to the 'monolith metaphor' wherein organisational culture is seen to be that which is consistent and represents consensus. Culture is a solid, single structure that looks to be the same no matter what angle or vantage point it is viewed from. A weak culture, by this way of thinking, is one where there is diversity in thinking and acting. The ontological stance that underlies this is very much Western/Euro-American in nature and goes against the acceptance of pluralism and multiplicity as put forward in the Afrokological paradigm (Chilisa 2012; Dastile 2013; Smith 2012). In contexts where diversity is present, this single, unitary culture will soon be contested. Referring back to Figure 5.2, ontological multiplicity (as is inherent in contexts with diversity) means that organisational members are starting off in different places, and this will manifest differences in organisational culture. This diversity is not only natural, but it can also be beneficial to the organisation.

In this way, the tenets of the Afrokological perspective will help shed light (perhaps, within this context, settle) the debate of managed-versus-emergent organisational cultures that has raged on in corporate communication literature. This stance is unpacked in the following sections. Furthermore, the persistence of the language (when it is meant to affront the very members that ensures its survival) will be explained by means of the Afrokological concept of endogenous institutional communication. Before this is done, the following section offers a contextualisation of the case example and an explication of the research methodology that lead to its exploration.

Is that an (arte)fact?

The nature of mining and the circumstances under which it was established as a commercial endeavour (its flouting of the 'digger's democracy' etc.) is fertile ground for discussions that centre around colonisation and its impact on individuals through commerce and economics. Although these are interesting and important topics to explore, the focus of this chapter revolves around the fact that this industry was diverse enough to establish its own language – Fanagalo – in order to facilitate communication between organisational members.

The exact origins of Fanagalo (also spelled Fanakalo or Fanekalo) is not known, although many authors have tried to establish its genesis (Mesthrie 1989; MQA 2011; Pewa 2001). What these authors agree on is that Fanagalo is a mainly Zulu-based pidgin (the only pidgin in the world that draws its structure from a non-colonial language (Monocle 2011)) that became widely used in southern Africa at the time of mining exploration.

By and by, Fanagalo became synonymous with mining and a clear element of mining culture (Greeff 2020). Organisational languages are inherently cultural, symbolising to members all aspects of organisational life and belonging to it. In that sense, Fanagalo is no different. One way in which it is different to other organisational languages is that it is an actual, literal language created within and for an organisational context. In other organisational contexts, language (as artefact of its culture) means to imply a special dialect, jargon, differences in syntax, vocabulary or structure of an existing language. It is a testament to the diversity of the mining industry and mining organisations that no one single language could be singled out and adopted for use by all. Instead, an amalgamation of languages was seen to be the most sensible solution.

The democratisation of South Africa in the mid-1990s saw the introduction of wider language policies, and a change from official bilingualism to multilingualism. As part of these policies, the Mining Qualifications Authority (MQA) was tasked in the early 2000s with phasing Fanagalo out of existence. The two main reasons cited for the phasing out was that Fanagalo was deemed to be inherently racist and too simplistic for use within the industry. Per the Leon Commission report (Leon 1995), which largely informed phasing out policies:

> The Commission considers [the use of Fanagalo] to be very unsatisfactory, because the language has a very limited vocabulary and is unable to convey subtle meaning. . . . Another problem concerning the use of Fanagalo was illustrated by Mr Zokwana. Although he spoke English and Afrikaans he was required and obliged to speak in Fanagalo when he took up work at the mines. Instead of addressing persons or mine officials as Mr or Meneer, he was required to use the Fanagalo expression 'Baas'. Workers find this offensive as does the Commission. The COMMISSION RECOMMENDS that having due regard to the complexity of the language issue all workers be given basic education and training in English.

The introduction of phasing out policies sees Fanagalo be removed from all official corporate communications, including the training of Fanagalo that used to be mandatory. Still, the use of Fanagalo, nearly 20 years after policy rollout, has diminished but not ceased. By the MQA's (2011, xv) own admission, '[t]he implementation of this [phasing out] policy has proved more complex and conflictual than envisaged'. Indeed, in some mines, Fanagalo is very much still the *de facto* language (Ravyse 2018; Greeff 2011).

Through empirical exploration, it became clear that the reasons for the persistence of Fanagalo as mining language cannot be understood when only Western/Euro-American theories are employed towards this end. Employing Afrokological concepts firstly shows that those who were tasked with phasing Fanagalo out of existence both overestimated and underestimated artefacts as ontological objects. Secondly, the nature of language artefacts in organisational culture was misjudged by not factoring the concept of endogenous institutional communication into the equation.

Tell me about it – the empirical exploration

For the purposes of empirically exploring the case of Fanagalo in the mining industry of South Africa, an interpretive qualitative approach with semi-structured interviews materialised. As always, this stemmed from the researcher's own ontological and epistemological stance, but also from the fact that cultural phenomena are best explored and understood when employing methodologies that allow for deeper reflection and freer expression on the part of research participants (Alvesson and Berg 1992; Turner 2014).

For the sampling of participants, a two-tiered process was followed. Firstly, the Southern African Institute for Mining and Metallurgy (SAIMM) published an invitation in their monthly journal for their members to participate in the research. The second tier comprised a chain-referral, or snowball, sampling technique. Research participants were asked to enlist further participants. The primary impetus behind the utilisation of this technique is the potential for a 'hidden population'. Due to the fact that many organisations officially do not make use of Fanagalo, it is nearly impossible to create or obtain a sampling framework of organisations where the language is still employed, and due to fear of prejudice even more difficult to obtain names of potential participants (cf. Atkinson and Flint 2001).

The sampling yielded a response rate of 18 interviews. Of these, 15 were black males, one was a white female and two were white males. The participants were employed on South Africa's mines in a range between 5 and 42 years. One participant asked that it be made clear that he is a shop steward of one of the major labour unions of the mining industry.

The data gathered by means of the 18 semi-structured interviews were grouped and transcribed per theme by means of a thematic content analysis (Keyton 2006; David and Sutton 2004).

Discussions: show me your ontology and I'll show you mine

The thematic content analysis of participant discussions in the interviews yielded five categories, which were grouped into two main themes.

Theme 1: language as artefact and ontological object

Earlier, an excerpt was offered of the Leon Commission Report (Leon 1995). This report was of critical importance and informed many policy decisions made by mining regulatory bodies. Its recommendations around Fanagalo were almost directly echoed in the MQA's phasing out reports and strategies, just as the Leon Commission Report itself echoes the sentiments of many reports on Fanagalo that went before it (e.g. Hanekom 1988). Even by just reading the excerpt it is clear that this report was written from a very particular ontology. As an example; this report only mentions two languages (Afrikaans and English) when discussing the language proficiency of one of its research subjects whose proficiency undoubtedly stretches far beyond that. Just so the fact that it cites an example of a racist Fanagalo word ('Baas') and proposes the 'better' alternatives of 'Mister' (English) or 'Meneer' (Afrikaans), as if the word 'Baas' is not itself from the Afrikaans language and English equals were not used contemporarily.

Viewing this report (an artefact itself) and its outcomes from a relational ontological frame makes it clear that the underlying problem was the relationships between people, not the language that they were relating in. Having said this, the report itself is not the focus of this study (however telling it might be). What is of value is the main recommendation made by the report and all others that follow it (without exception), including the MQA's. The recommendation of English as alternative to Fanagalo and as the new *lingua franca* of the mines.

Afrokology and organisational culture

The previous discussions make clear that language is an artefact of culture. As such, it is influenced by the values, beliefs and basic assumptions of organisational members and – as I propose in this chapter – by the overriding ontology of the organisation. From this vantage point, the policies to phase Fanagalo out of existence simultaneously overestimated and underestimated the power of language as artefact. A truer estimation of the language can be gotten when viewing it vis-à-vis the Afrokological understanding of ontology.

That's above my paygrade – overestimating the power of language

As can be seen in Figure 5.2 (depicted by the arrows), the influence scale of ontology and culture is predominantly downward directed. For the most part, those levels 'lower down' on the scale are influenced by those higher up. Largely, the ontology shapes all levels below it right down to the artefacts of the organisation. The inverse does not happen to the same degree. Artefacts do not have as much influence on ontology as ontology has on artefacts. The research participants touched on this. Said one participant: 'you can speak any language racistly if you yourself are a racist'. Another stated that, when it comes to Fanagalo, 'it's not words that are racist. It is a person'. Although the racist nature of a language is a complex issue, the point that is being made here is that getting rid of a 'racist' language does not do away with the problem of racism. Understanding organisational culture from an Afrokological perspective and thereby including ontology as a concept makes it clear that culture is much more complex than that. Changing the language of an organisation will not necessarily change the overriding ontology of the organisation.

One participant further indicated that Fanagalo is used as a 'scapegoat' by management. Another elaborated and asked: 'what is an easy way to show that you are doing something about [racism] in an industry that has a lot of [racism]? You pick something, make it out to be [racist] and show how you overcame it'. Whether this was done intentionally by management to sidestep a much more thorny issue, or whether it was done due to misunderstanding the nature of language in relation to ontology, the fact remains that viewing Fanagalo in isolation and as a 'perpetrator without backing' is overestimating it as an ontological object.

Don't count me out yet – underestimating the power of language

When writing about language – especially within the context of this volume – one would be remiss to leave matters at the previous point. Viewing language from a relational ontology makes it clear that language is also much more than just a functional feature of communication. It does not operate in isolation; it symbolically conveys the cultural and ontological natures of the organisation (Alvesson and Berg 1992). When asked about English as the official proposed alternative to Fanagalo, the responses of 16 of the 18 participants pointed to this proposal valuing Western/Euro-American ideals and agency above African ones. The two remaining respondents (who did not see a problem with implementing English as an alternative) where white males.

One of the participants who did not think English was a viable alternative explained his stance by exclaiming: 'Can you think! English? English? What? Maybe 20 percent, max, people on the mines are not African. Why would you ever ask 80 percent of people to change for 20 percent? It's because those 20 are the white 20'. Another participant expressed a similar view and stated that the reason why English is being introduced as alternative to Fanagalo is 'because whites can speak English, hey? No, no no. If they want people in mining to learn a new language that is not Fanagalo, why don't they get the whites to learn [an African language]?'.

What is being made clear here is that the same discriminatory Western/Euro-American ontology that was singled out as the problem of Fanagalo is still extant in the alternatives proposed for it. This links back to the previous section. It also shows how artefacts (i.e. the language being phased out, the one replacing it and the policies around it) are objects of the ontology of the mining industry. It does not matter how noble the impetus behind phasing out Fanagalo is. If it is done from the same Western/Euro-American ontology it will yield the same outcomes as before (or worse).

Furthermore, English as a language has many connotations associated with it, and those connotations should not be underestimated. Sixteen of the 18 participants to this study felt that introducing English as alternative to Fanagalo is a step in the wrong direction – that it would further the racism that they experience as mine workers, not improve it. Over and above that, they felt that it takes 'the mines further away from Africans' and imposes a certain identity on mine workers that is foreign to them in more ways than one. Fanagalo, for all its flaws, does not do this. Per one participant, with Fanagalo 'I am not asking you to talk in my language, and you, you are also not asking me to talk in your language. We are talking in a language that is not yours or mine, but that is yours and mine'. The 'shared' and communal nature of Fanagalo as amalgamation of languages ensures this.

Mind your language – identity and kinship

As it further relates to identity, the participants to this study felt that Fanagalo as language is central to their identity as mine workers. To these participants, Fanagalo symbolises 'the language of a hard worker'. Indeed, Fanagalo is the yardstick by which 'belonging' to the 'real' mining culture can be measured. The participants draw a distinction, culturally, between underground mine workers and those who 'work in the offices, and not with the people'. To their way of thinking, a person working 'in the offices' (administrative, so-called professional staff members, and management) 'might as well go work at a bank. It's the same thing'. They are not 'real' members of the mining culture, and this is signified by the extent to which they are fluent in Fanagalo. Said one participant: 'how good someone speaks [Fanagalo] tells you how long he have worked on the mines and if they were part of the real work'. The MQA (2011, xviii) report itself states that so-called professional staff learn Fanagalo in order to be 'accepted by the workers'.

The phasing out policies that saw to the official removal of Fanagalo in all corporate communications might have also inadvertently spurred on the transmission of the language between members of this culture. This removal ensured that the only way to learn the language is through *social* transmission. Two participants, specifically, gave insight into the way that this practically happens. One indicated that there was an older *Madala* who took him under his wing when he started on the mines. They lived in the same house at that time, and the older man told the younger that 'they will never take you seriously if you cannot speak Fanagalo. You can just tell them that you learned it because you can work'. The other participant stated that when he started work on the mines his opinion on Fanagalo was neither here nor there. The fact is his team supervisor – who happened to share a home language with this participant – would stop him every time he spoke in their mutual mother-tongue. When he did, he would say 'here, we speak what everyone understands'.

Ending the formal (organisational) transmission of the language only succeeded in strengthening the cultural nature of it. When a cultural element is shared or transmitted socially and relationally, all that it represents is also shared. This includes all underlying values, beliefs and representations of the language. Refer back to the participant being advised that he should tell others he speaks Fanagalo 'because [he] can work'. Hard physical work being a fundamental value of mining culture is reinforced through these kinds of transmissions. This is not necessarily the case when a language is transmitted in a classroom or organisational training situation.

Further to this, the Afrokological concept of endogenous institutional communication also explains why being fluent in this language is equated to belonging to the 'real' culture of the industry. Per Mano and Meribe (2017, 1):

> Institutional communication occurs when traditional or cultural institutions are used in communicating symbolically. Secret societies, masquerades, shrines, marriage, chieftaincy are some of the important institutions in African traditional societies. The rituals and rites of passage into or out of these institutions are ways of communicating not just the significance of life transitions but ideologies and philosophies.

In this way, Fanagalo is a rite of passage in belonging to this culture, this society. The importance of that within an African organisation should not be underestimated. The fact that the values of the language are shaped and transmitted socially through cultural members also means that the values – like the language – are more fluid than stagnant. It is within the power of organisational members themselves to change the associated meanings of the language. One participant gave voice to it in this way: 'if people speaking [Fanagalo] know that it is wrong to be racist, they will not use the racist way of speaking it. You can see it with the new ones. The old ones speak it maybe in an old way. But the new ones are better'. The management of meaning being in the hands of organisational members themselves is something that is central to the second theme of the findings.

Theme 2: the nature of culture and ontology – manage versus emerge

The phasing out policies of Fanagalo are in essence very managerialistic, stemming from a very rationalistic Western/Euro-American perspective. These policies prescribed the removal of Fanagalo from all official corporate communication of mining organisations (with almost immediate effect). To this way of thinking, the predictable outcome would be that the language would cease to exist. Nabudere's (2006) view on Western/Euro-American theories and their colonisation fundament expects this way of thinking. It is, after all, an underwriting philosophy of colonisation that a language can be phased out of existence by disallowing or banning it. Furthermore, the absence of the banned language would give over to new behaviours set out by those who are responsible of banning the language.

Reality did not reflect these 'predictable' outcomes of policy makers. The MQA (2011, xv) itself concedes that the outcome was not as 'envisaged'. In Western/Euro-American–dominated corporate communication literature, the appropriateness of taking a rational, managerial stance to organisational culture and its artefacts (such as language) is a topic of debate. Many scholars are of the view that the wholesale management of culture is, not only possible, but advisable. These scholars prescribe to the cultural pragmatist view, or the cultural engineering approach. On the other side of the debate are those who feel that culture cannot be managed, as it emerges from the collective inputs of its members to endow organisational experience with meaning.

Whichever side of the debate one falls, the reality of Fanagalo's continued existence cannot be ignored. The Afrokological understanding of relational ontology offers an explanation for it. When regarding the situation from this ontology, the focus is not on what the organisation or its management wants but the relationships that form within the organisation. From the interviews it is clear that organisational members – not management – saw to the transmission and endurance of Fanagalo through relationships. These relationships, by virtue of their nature, are not homogenous. Culture, by extension, is therefore also not homogenous. The monolith metaphor becomes outdated, and culture can no longer be seen as shared *meanings*. The shared *relationships* that allow for meaning creation is the essence of culture.

Does this imply a hands-off approach to the management of culture? I do not think that it does. If organisational managers place more trust in the emergent nature of cultures, they would need to understand that this entails dissonance. Organisational members will have different ideas and meanings attached to organisational culture and its artefacts. The dissonance will play out in various ways, for example through conflict in the relationships between members. It falls to management to manage this dissonance – not the culture (cf. Greeff 2020). As to how this dissonance should be managed, Afrokological literature stresses firstly understanding and accepting multiversality, and seeing universality for the fallacy that it is (Chilisa 2012; Dastile 2013; Smith 2012). This is especially true when ontology is factored into the equation. In the interviews, participants expressed the idea that Fanagalo has different meanings attached to it: 'some can see that it is racist', while others do not. In fact, many participants have, in themselves, conflicting ideas around Fanagalo. One participant spoke about how Fanagalo can simultaneously refer to and symbolise a sense of belonging or kinship as well as disassociation or objectivity (as in the sense of denial of subjectivity) in the following way:

> Fanagalo is a language for working, and we are here to work. To provide for our families. We are not here to be . . . we are here to work, not to play games. All of us. You see? But . . . but . . . but . . . the problem with this is that the idea is there that you only want to talk to people if you want them to work. . . . You are only talking if you are talking work. You are only telling them what to do and not talking to the person for, for the person.

The point here is that dissonance and conflicting meaning can co-exist – Fanagalo can be part of the culture of mining organisations even if members do not agree on its meaning. Cultural collectivism does not necessarily mean consensus. For managers, this implies a mind shift away from the idea of managing culture so that it is 'something that everyone can define' (Flamholtz and Randle 2011). Rather, management should revolve around the idea of culture being something that is *everyone's* to define.

This stance will allow for a more multiversal construction of organisational culture. Instead of representing just the stance of management, the diversity of organisational culture members should be mirrored. In this way, the Afrokological understanding of multiplicity and multiversality offers a truer understanding of culture as it emerges through its members and transmits through endogenous institutional communication. A relational ontology helps to understand how this takes place and what its 'management' should entail.

Conclusion

In this chapter, the various ways in which organisational culture, ontology and artefacts intersect were showcased by making use of the South African mining industry's industrial pidgin Fanagalo as case example. Admittedly, these intersections are convoluted but what is clear is that concepts born from Afrokological perspectives help to disentangle the various strands and in so doing offers an understanding of why the organisational reality does not always mirror managerial intent in South Africa. Firstly; the field of corporate communication can gain from admitting – like Afrokological and decolonisation literature proposes – that there is no such thing as ontological neutrality. In this chapter, it was revealed that this is as much true for an organisation as it is for an individual. The link between ontology and culture was also overtly established, and discussions showed how ontology permeates through culture to visibly manifest as artefacts. Artefacts are therefore in themselves objects of the ontology of the organisation. Secondly, through the Afrokological concept of multiversality, the chapter discussed the reality of differing ontologies and the ways in which it manifests in culture. This understanding lastly led to a new way of thinking about culture and a new way of defining it, making use of relational ontology as a meta-framework. Holding true to the relational ontology also opens up approaches for managing artefacts that are more trusting of their emergent natures, as cultural elements.

In these ways, the concepts from the Afrokological tradition offered clarity and understanding of empirical organisational phenomena, where it could not otherwise be gotten. The theoretical base from these traditions are still very much under-utilised and in certain cases under-appreciated. As is shown in this chapter, however, we will increasingly have to make use of these theories and concepts as corporate communicators if we want to truly understand what is being presented to us in our organisations – in Africa and beyond.

As it relates to ontology, culture and artefacts specifically, much further research is still needed. This chapter is rife with gaps that should form the basis for recommended further research. For example, I touch on the aspect of identity, but do not fully unpack it. The specific focus of this research is also not on the ways that power plays out and manifests in the shaping or emergence of organisational culture and the (pre)dominance of certain ontologies above others. A study devoted to this would be thought-provoking. One making use of Afrokological concepts towards this end will be comprehensive and profound.

References

Alvesson, M. and Berg, O.P. 1992. *Corporate Culture and Organizational Symbolism*. Berlin: de Gruyter.

Anadolu-Okur, N., Harris, D.B. and Tillotson, M. 2015. *Contemporary Critical Thought in Africology and Africana Studies*. New York: Rowman & Littlefield.

Atkinson, R. and Flint, J. 2001. Accessing hidden and hard-to-reach populations: Snowball research strategies. *Social Research Update*, 33(1): 1–4.

Buntu, B.A. 2013. Claiming self; the role of Afrikology in social transformation. *Scriptura: International Journal of Bible, Religion and Theology in Southern Africa*, 112(1): 1–12.

Chilisa, B. 2012. *Indigenous Research Methodologies*. Thousand Oaks, CA: Sage.

Dastile, N.P. 2013. Beyond Euro-Western dominance: An African-centred decolonial paradigm. *Africanus*, 43(2): 93–104.

David, M. and Sutton, C.D. 2004. *Social Research: The Basics*. London: Sage.

Flamholtz, E. and Randle, Y. 2011. *Corporate Culture: The Ultimate Strategic Asset*. Stanford: Stanford University Press.

Greeff, W.J. 2011. Different salves for different sores: International research remedies for a South African communication context. *Communitas*, 16: 113–130.

Greeff, W.J. 2020. Managing contestation in organizational culture: Lessons learned from the South African mining Pidgin Fanagalo. *The International Journal of Knowledge, Culture, and Change Management: Annual Review*, forthcoming.

Hanekom, E. 1988. *Die funksionele waarde van Fanagalo (Afrikaans)*. Pretoria: Raad vir Geesteswetenskaplike navorsing.

Keesing, R.M. 1974. Theories of culture. *Annual Review of Anthropology*, 3(1): 73–97.

Keyton, J. 2006. *Communication Research: Asking Questions, Finding Answers*. Boston, MA: McGraw-Hill.

Leon, S. 1995. Report of the Commission of Inquiry into Safety and Health in the Mining Industry: Volume 1. *Department of Minerals and Energy*. http://www.dmr.gov.za/Portals/0/Resource%20Center/Reports%20and%20Other%20Documents/2003_Leon%20Commission_Volume%201.pdf?ver=2018-03-13-020431-270 (Accessed 20 April 2020).

Lincoln, Y.S. and González y González, E.M. 2007. The search for emerging decolonizing methodologies in qualitative research: Further strategies for liberatory and democratic inquiry. *Qualitative Inquiry*, 14(5): 784–805.

Mano, W. and Meribe, N. 2017. Communication modes, African. *The International Encyclopedia of Intercultural Communication*, 1–10.

Martin, J. 2002. *Organizational Culture: Mapping the Terrain*. Thousand Oaks: Sage.

Mesthrie, R. 1989. The origins of Fanagalo. *Journal of Pidgin and Creole Languages*, 4(2): 211–240.

Monocle. 2011. *Monocolumn: Mine Your Language*. www.psfk.com/2011/02/monocolumn-mine-your-language.html (Accessed 20 April 2017).

MQA. Mining Qualifications Authority. 2011. *Research into the Implementation of the MQA's Language Policy with Specific Reference to the Phasing Out of Fanagalo*. Report submitted by EE Research focus (PTY) LTD to the mining qualifications authority.

Nabudere, D.W. 2006. Towards an Afrokology of knowledge production and African regeneration. *International Journal of African Renaissance Studies*, 1(1): 7–32.

Ott, J.S. 1989. *The Organizational Culture Perspective*. Pacific Grove, CA: Brooks, Cole.

Pewa, N.C. 2001. *Fanagalo in South Africa: An Overview*. MA Thesis. University of Zululand, 2001.

Ravyse, N. 2018. Against all odds: The survival of Fanagalo in South African mines. *Language Matters*, 49(1): 3–24.

Schein, E.H. 1984. Coming to a new awareness of organizational culture. *Sloan Management Review*, 25(2): 3–16.

Smith, L.T. 2012. *Decolonising Methodologies, Research, and Indigenous Peoples*. London: Zed Books, 2nd ed.

Turner, B.A., ed. 2014. *Organizational Symbolism*. New York: Walter de Gruyter GmbH & Co KG, vol. 19.

Watson, T. and L'Etang, J. 2008. Writing PR history: Issues, methods and politics. *Journal of Communication Management*, 12(4): 319–335.

6

To be or not to be

Decolonizing African media/communications

Kehbuma Langmia

Introduction

In June 2009, Facebook Swahili was launched by Swahili scholars in the west (BBC News 2009). This marked a major step towards decolonizing media dissemination and consumption in the horn of Africa from the claws of western domineering languages (English, French and Portuguese). If Cheikh Anta Diop is reputed to have said "no nation ever developed using the language of another people" (Asante 2007a, 13) then this is a major step in the right direction. This decolonized mindset would go a long way to debunk Curtin's (1964) assertion that there "never was a civilized nation of any other complexion than white" (42). The African person is 'civilized' as he/she is conscious of his environment in the same light as Jomo Kenyatta knew that the English language was not making him authentic before his people and so "broke into Swahili to the applause of his auditors" (Skinner 2001, 31). Given the fact that Facebook opened the Afrikaans version on March 15, 2009, and since there is a possibility that in the near future Facebook will also be available in other African languages like Wolof, Hausa and Yoruba, one could say that the process of media decolonization in Africa has begun. Language is the vehicle of culture and culture is the mores of a people. Apart from language, African media content needs to be decolonized. African electronic media systems are the offshoots of ontological, and to a much larger extent, the axiological tenets of the west, thereby making African communication a pseudo-western system devoid of African culture. Examples abound: The west did not only colonize Africa to supplant political and economic control, they wanted assimilation in all spheres of African life. The newspaper, radio, television and now the Internet-mediated platforms on African soil are structured and programmed to fit and align with what pertains in the west. After all, there is no one transmission device for radio, television and Internet manufactured in Africa. So, African media organizations import finished products, including program materials from Europe, America and China, for wider dissemination on the continent in their original western languages. The same goes for news programs. According to Mazrui (2009) "Nigerian media (electronic or print) cannot afford to have their own correspondents in major African capitals, or war reporters in Darfur and the Democratic Republic of the Congo" (15). My own country, Cameroon, has never deployed its own reporters to major UDEAC, Francophonie or ECOWAS summits to cover the entire event beyond the short stay of its president and entourage. All other information from those events, including major conflicts in the region, is reported through the camera lens of western sources. With this type of mediascape in Africa, we can never decolonize. Ali Mazrui continues to state that: "Much of Africa has borrowed western tastes without western skills. It has borrowed consumption patterns without production techniques. It has promoted urbanization without industrialization and has learned capitalist greed without capitalist discipline" (21). These are the realities that Africa after more than 50 years of self-rule is witnessing after the colonial experience. To borrow western taste without mental re-evaluation is nightmarish. To continuously consume western digital communication gadgets in colonial languages without interrogating our minds and challenging western manufacturers to involve Africa and African languages in the process is to fall prey to Thomas Sankara's (Akomolafe 2014, 66) saying that "he who feeds you controls you". We have reputable African languages like Kiswahili, Yoruba, Hausa, Wolof, IsiXhosa, Zulu, Amharic etc even being taught in western universities, yet they are being paid lip services on digital media on the continent. Africa has been feeding fat on western production materials without looking back to where she belongs in the world gamut of world productions and consumption patterns.

Manufacturers of telephones, computers and most especially hardware and software destined to countries in Asia and Middle East integrate Arabic, Chinese, Korean and Indian languages etc in them, but when it comes to Africa, anything goes; so long as they are in English, French, Portuguese or Spanish, they will be consumed in Africa. I was impressed to see Arabic keyboards in Morocco, but unimpressed to find French and English keyboards in Internet café's in almost all of the tropical African countries (Nigeria, Cameroon, Ghana, Uganda and Kenya) that I have visited in the last six years. Some parents in Africa have cell phones but only a handful can actually send text messages in English or other European languages because of their incapacities to use western languages, let alone send emojis, yet no alarm bells are being sounded. Africans seem to be content with the status of being at the receiving end of imported western-mediated products. The continent of Africa is awash with imported mediated goods and services, none of which addresses Africa's indigenous communication needs. Just look at the modern media companies; none is designed to fit the communicative sociocultural contextual realities of the continent. From the studio construction to the broadcast green rooms, no research has been systematically carried out on African soil to integrate past communicative patterns like folktale night, moonlight storytellings, grandfather's fireside tales, mothers' lullabies, courtship wooing sounds, chieftaincy ritual dirges, divination songs, funeral drum sounds, war and mourning communicative techniques to align with western-imported stylistic studio designs in African media organizations. The continent is *forced* to only adapt (if possible) by working with letters and alphabets borrowed from Greeks and the Romans in order to survive in what Marshall McLuhan calls the "global village" (Antecol 1997, 455). But Africans are struggling to accommodate their unique village realities to that of the west that seems to embody what we now know as the world.

Electronic and digital media engineers from abroad never take pains to spend years and months in our countries to study our communicative cosmologies. When our own engineers are educated in the west they return and bring with them western ideologies on how our studios should be constructed. African countries continue to walk behind and not beside the west, and there is no end in sight. Our consumption patterns, as noted by Ali Mazrui, have been the sole driving force for our collective dependence on the west, and the effects of colonization on our minds, the brainwashing of our minds even after independence, has increasingly pushed us to the brink of creating pseudo-western states in Africa. Big media companies like Google, Apple, Verizon, Amazon and AT&T are leaving footprints all over the world, including Africa, especially with respect to online-mediated communications. Africa and Africans are only adapting and assimilating their erstwhile communicative patterns by westernizing African communications patterns and systems. Therefore, if we truly wish to decolonize mediated and communication systems in Africa, we need a paradigm shift made up of three approaches which I will be able to demonstrate using secondary data analysis i.e. (1) produce African-centered content in African languages like Kiswahili, Yoruba, Wolof, Zulu etc with subtitles in western languages; (2) fund, promote and deploy Afrocentric journalists in African countries for regional reporting; 3) internationalize the African News Agency (ANA); and (4) create more Uniform Resource Locators (URLs) whose server and content are operated and managed by Africans. The answers provided by these research questions should provide clues to the validity of Molefi Asante's theory of Afrocentricity. According to Asante (2007b, 16), "Afrocentricity is . . . a consciousness, quality of thought, mode of analysis, and an actionable perspective where Africans seek, from agency, to assert subject place within the context of African history". He goes further to state that ontological and epistemic priorities that involve and include Africa as agency should consciously attempt to make it Africa centered. The emphasis of the theory of Afrocentricity is on Africa and Africans conscious state of being.

Background/literature

"Africa is the only continent where the majority of children start school using a foreign language" (UNESCO 2010, 4). Reasons given by this organization include Africa's colonial past and the urgency of globalization. Because education is the foundation of human growth, foreign language education has been deeply seeded in the African academic soil and in almost all mediated facets of life. In order to stem the tidal wave of foreign languages in Africa, the 2015 United Nations Economic Commission for Africa meeting in Addis Ababa came out forcefully in support of the World Summit on Information Society (WSIS) resolution of encouraging the teaching of African languages in schools. This was done because the lack of online content in African languages for Africans in Africa is dismal. A plethora of media scholars (Asante 2013; Mazrui 2009; de Beer and Saliba 2000; Park and Curran 2000; Carey 1992) have decried the omnipresence and content of Western media on African soil that have stymied the growth and development of local Afrocentric media organizations. Their main criticism is similar in style with the lamentations of Lawino in Okot p'Bitek's poem "Song of Lawino". In that poem, Lawino mocks at her husband Ocol for rejecting her rich African food because he is in love with the food of a white woman called Clementine. In short, he is in love with the white man's way of life. Ocol speaks the local language with a white man's accent. All this is happening with the backdrop of Africa's knowledge economy and the quest to modernize the continent by following deeply ingrained western value systems. Africa can hardly disentangle herself from the cocoon of westernization if modernity is tied only to the Euro-American standard of evaluation. The continent continues to be the mullato or the imitator of everything western in terms of architecture, education, infrastructure, economic and political systems, culture, social status, class and value systems. In a study by Mbinjama (2013) carried out in a rural setting called King Williams Town in South Africa, participants preferred to be readily associated with western modernity than to associate themselves with that town. In fact, as the author states:

> It was also mentioned that being associated with King William's Town was like living in the "*Larlies*", a slang word often used by isiXhosa-speaking people to refer to the townships or squatter areas and signifying backwardness, lack of worldly wisdom and modernity. The adolescents want to belong to a modern society.
>
> *(Mbinjama 2013, 62)*

The colonial experiment on the continent of Africa created an epistemic inferiority in the cognitive abilities of her citizens. That surreptitious vicious experiment was to absolve them from knowing and respecting anything African. They were reduced to what Mazrui (1986) has referred to as passive participants in world affairs. African men and women, including their children, were brainwashed so as to feel ashamed of themselves vis-à-vis their colonizers. The only way for Africans, according to the imperialists and missionaries who invaded the continent, was to make them speak and act western before they could be recognized as human. According to the study by Mbinjama (2013), this is evident more than 60 years after Africa gained independence. Mbinjama (2013) also found that young South Africans also changed their identity while on social media because, according to them, "changing who they are online gratifies the need to appear richer, more westernized, and educated. In so doing, they create the illusion that they are of high status in the virtual community" (62). This is what has become ubiquitous in the geo-socio-psychological hemisphere of these natives. Language use online was equally a primordial consideration for users. Mbinjama's study also revealed "that adolescents would judge a contact's online writing, spoken dialect or accent to determine where they come from" (62). So, users prefer those proficient in English online but at the same time they would not like to interact with "whites" because it is symbolic to English and not isiXhosa. In fact, they preferred someone who can mix the two languages. It is this dichotomous ideological imbalance that African media users find themselves in today.

The colonial experiment imposed western language as the vehicle for educational quests in all schools. Birgit (2012), citing the World Bank report of 2011, discusses a rather disquieting phenomenon about language challenges for kids in Africa. Several studies illustrate the seriousness of the learning challenge. More than 30 percent of Malian youths aged 15 to 19 years who completed six years of schooling could not read a simple sentence; the same was true of more than 50 percent of Kenyan youths (World Bank Group 2011, 6–7). These kids grew up learning and speaking their mother tongues only to confront another new language in the western-style elementary schools. This classic display of cognitive dissonance as reflected is emblematic of the average African learning in schools and consuming western-driven media.

The tragedy is much more dire as more Africans seek to become information rich in an environment where the Internet comes in a foreign language. Halvorsen (2012) makes the case for Internet content to be in African languages:

> There is a call for more contributions from African scientists, scholars and creators of Internet content which is relevant, readily assimilated and in languages and contexts users can relate to and understand. The assertion is that a Western cultural and information imperialism, enabled through African countries' dependence on the more established and rich countries, still prevails.
>
> *(316)*

Halvorsen (2012) also remarks

> that it is imperative that the Tanzanian intellectual elite is active in creating Internet content which is relevant, readily assimilated, and in languages and contexts users can relate to and understand. To participate in information and knowledge societies people need to be able to create as well as utilize knowledge. As pointed out in the introduction it is essential for a participant not to regard Internet content as being predetermined and unchangeable, but to see the possibility of being an active participant rather than a passive consumer.
>
> *(319)*

Lor and Britz (2006, 18) suggest: "Ideally African countries should reduce their dependence on the information infrastructure of their former colonial rulers by improving national bibliographic control and developing regional resource-sharing schemes". This seems to be the panacea for closing the loopholes between the information-rich and information-poor countries with respect to media consumption. This is because Halvosen states "there is an ongoing cooperation between the Department of Kiswahili and the Faculty of Informatics and Virtual Education in creating Kiswahili software" (320). From the traditional media perspective, Kiwoya and Makokha (2009) make a strong case for creating a Kiswahili Broadcasting regional hub with member countries in East Africa which they called the East African Regional Broadcasting Service (EARBS) (28). We need to do this because, according to a speech by Bokova (2010), "We need to protect the over 201 African languages in danger of being extinct" (Kandybowicz and Torrence 2017). In an article on #RhodesMustFall published in *The Guardian*, Chaudhuri (2016) argues on the merits of the new epistemic dispensation post Cecil Rhodes, who is more often than not associated with racism in South Africa. The call for a new vista to dispense knowledge also includes language that is used in African universities to inculcate wisdom and values of the African world into the minds of African people. This of course should include the media that constantly bombards the people of Africa with images and sounds primarily emanating from the west. In support of this stance, two years later, Ndlovu-Gatsheni (2018) published "Epistemic freedom in Africa: deprovincialization and decolonization" and raised the issue of globalizing Africa's knowledge. The world should not deprive Africa's epistemic potency, and that should include African language perception across all new media platforms.

De-Europeanize mentality

Africans are still suffering from mental incarceration brought unto them by European conquest of the continent. For decolonization of the mind, according to Ngũgĩ wa Thiong'o, to materialize on bona fide Africans at home and in the diaspora a mental tsunami is needed to clean their mental hemispheres (Ngũgĩ 1988). The effect of European mental subjectivities and the internecine magnetic neocolonial machinations to subjugate Africans to secondary 'inferior' positions vis-à-vis global epistemologies has crippled us for decades. If W.E.B Dubois characterizes African Americans as suffering from double consciousness, the African in the continent and in the diaspora is suffering from triple consciousness, i.e using African, mulatto and Euro-American lenses to perceive the world. When Franz Fanon underscored the philosophical perceptions of the colonizer and the colonized in Africa, he was, in fact, seeking ways for mental liberation for the African. Presently, the African government-sponsored media reporter in the continent has three audiences to satisfy: the neocolonial master (to ensure continuous flow of foreign aid), the Black African on the continent (still suffering from the prestige of anything that is gold from Europe/America glitters) and the African in the diaspora (who worships and dines with the neocolonizer). When Water Rodney published his now famous "How Europe underdeveloped Africa", he was laying the ground rules for the decolonization of the mind of the African, but after his death, as well as after the deaths of his predecessors such as Chinua Achebe, Ali Mazrui, Bernard Nsokika Fonlon, Cheikh Anta Diop and Amilcar Cabral – all clamoring for decolonization – nothing has changed and 'things are still falling apart' on the continent. Presently, no amount of preaching and writing about mental awareness about total and unconditional dependency on the colonial master even after more than half a century of independence has helped to change the African mind. The average African on the continent still looks up to Europe and the United States as the model for development; after all, don't we still cling to the same European cultures and languages at our major summits, education, commerce, politics, culture and media on the continent, including the African Union? In fact, speaking English or French on the continent brings prestige, and one can lose a job/status for speaking African languages (see the example of Kings Williams town in South Africa) and also the Kamuzu Banda Academy in Malawi discussed in Nyamnjoh (2012), where kids are taught in schools to dress, think, write and act British. I propose a three-step process that can quickly bring an end to mental slavery in Africa.

1 Curriculum redesign

All elementary/primary schools on the continent should employ teachers of young children who can teach using what is popularly known as translanguages. This is the tendency to infuse local languages and realities in the pedagogy. By the time these students get into journalism schools, writing for the media, broadcasting in the electronic and digital media platforms will be well handled. They will be able to write and report using a mixture of local and international languages. At present, very few African languages have made it through the international vocabulary dictionary. Students should be able to have two or more dictionaries in schools, i.e. local languages, English or French. Courses in communications and journalism, such as public relations, ethical issues in journalism, introduction to African media and journalism, broadcast and print journalism, can be taught using translanguages. In rural parts of the continent, students find it hard to succeed in courses with colonial languages because these languages do not reflect their realities. Translanguages, or what Chinua Achebe calls "transliteration" (adapting what pertains in the west with local realities), can be very helpful in this regard. This is the only way to push forward local African languages like Kiswahili, Wolof, Amharic etc in print to force their way into the international vocabularies. After all, don't we have French-borrowed words in English and vice versa?

2 African Union and African languages

Kiswahili, Wolof, isiXhosa, Hausa, Yoruba and Amharic should become the official languages of the African Union. These languages are already enjoying wider appeal because they are being taught in schools. African slavery cannot end with our elected leaders still hanging onto the thread of English and French at the African Union Summit at Addis Ababa. They can employ a translation services, if need be, like China, North and South Korea, India and all Middle Eastern countries do when they have European/American visitors.

3 Recruit bilingual media gurus

All major media organizations on the continent of Africa, whether electronic or digital, should uphold Afrocentric standards of recruiting bilingual reporters, writers and broadcasters. For instance, in East Africa, such persons should have bilingual degrees in Kiswahili and English; in South Africa, IsiXhosa or Zulu or any other South African language and English. In West Africa, they should be bilingual in Hausa/Wolof and English or French, and in North Africa, in Arabic and English or French. In East Central Africa, they should be bilingual in Amharic/English, and for Lusophone countries, in local languages and Portuguese. These are the African media experts who will be deployed across the continent to cover events on behalf of their media organizations. These are the writers who should decolonize and recontextualize African events that are now covered by foreign news media like CNN, the BBC, Aljeezera, German DW, and Chinese STVs and CTVs. We cannot allow an entire continent to be covered by reporters educated in the west, living in the west and under the payroll of the west. Ministers of communication and culture, new media and information in all of Africa should hold regular summits to discuss plans to have their various governments fund reporters based in conflict-ridden parts of the continent. When major crises erupt on the continent, foreign media organizations rush to the scene to report with covert agenda.

Media and Afrocentricity

According to Asante (2007b, 16), "Afrocentricity is . . . a consciousness, quality of thought, mode of analysis, and an actionable perspective where Africans seek, from agency, to assert subject place within the context of African history". Therefore, consciousness of Africa's identity and centrality in anything that relates to the continent constitutes the overall aim of his Afrocentric theory. Mazama (2003) calls it a "paradigm" because it deconstructs and reconstructs the notion of African reality through a process of reconceptualization. It is a theory rooted in African culture and cosmology. Thus, traditional and new media activities on the continent ought to mirror Africa's socio-historical, anthropological and geo-political nature. Again, Asante (2007b) situates his theory as "a theory of agency, that is, the idea that African people must be viewed and view themselves as agents rather than spectators to historical revolution and change" (17). It is through this that proper identification and representations of African media by African media experts can be authenticated. The most efficient way to achieve such a goal is first and foremost for journalists and broadcasters to recognize the power of African languages and culture in print, radio, television and the online platforms. In the age of new media globalization, the use of African languages, as well as some European languages when needed, especially in the urban cities, is crucial. African languages such as Kiswahili, Yoruba, Wolof, Africaans, Zulu, Hausa and Amharic already have wider appeal and are taught in schools, so there is no need not to use these languages. If decolonization of African media needs to be a reality and not just a slogan, then pursuing this is the primary objective. The effect of Arab/European missionary activities and colonization of Africa left the continent eagerly yearning for authenticity, and that includes getting rid of impact and imbibe of colonial languages and culture. The indelible mark that it has created in the minds of Africans is palpable, but it is now time to cleanse, otherwise the continent will forever be dependent on outsiders.

Media content and adaptations (government policy)

The fact that in a continent of more than 54 nations only a tiny fraction has placed emphasis on developing their ethnic-driven languages for official use is regrettable. This is why development has forestalled. "There is a close relationship between language and development and meaningful development cannot take place where linguistic barriers exist" (Erastus 2013, 41). Vast populations of Africans in rural settings, suburban communities and cities have stuck to their indigenous languages. However, these populations are marginalized because priority is given to those proficient in the colonial languages. These communities do not read newspapers offline or online in either English, French or Portuguese. Countries in North Africa have Arabic languages that are used officially and in daily activities. While colonial languages have become the official languages of politics and commerce in mostly tropical African countries, Arabic has become the official languages of countries like Tunisia, Morocco, Egypt and Lybia. Only three countries in the tropical regions (Tanzania, Ethiopia and Somalia) do not have English, French or Portuguese as an official language. In a continent of more than 54 countries, this is an enormous tragedy with respect to development. For the African Union to still be using English and

French as its official language of operation, with no plans to Africanize its language policies, decolonization and development may still be a distant dream. Note that the majority of Africans live in the rural settings where indigenous languages are the only languages they can function with. If we wish to decolonize media in Africa, we need content, both online and offline, that is in African languages.

Conclusion

A new dawn needs to break in Africa for decolonization of the media to yield meaningful and long-lasting dividends. Years of subjugation of the African people to occupy the inferior position on the ladder of human progress has had a serious toll on them and the mental evolution of its subsequent generations. The curricula of most African countries still emphasize mastering western civilization in order to achieve any kind of developmental goals. The books written by westerners and teachers who have been educated abroad seem to have more credibility than those written by those trained at home, and this applies to professional schools, like journalism, and mass communication programs at universities. In 2015, I was a Fulbright Scholar at a mass communication department in a West African university, and 85 percent of the books used from first year to the final year were written and published by westerners. Even the pamphlets written by the instructors were heavily influenced by the so-called western mass media standards. These books are taught by those trained at home and abroad, but the emphasis was on what pertains abroad. These students when they graduate are the ones to influence media policies on the continent. They are the ones sitting in boardrooms and crafting legislation meant for the government. These students are the future journalists to be deployed to conflict regions and to accompany power wielders like ministers, governors and MPs to various national, regional and international summits and conferences. Africa does not need to rely on CNN and other foreign media entities to report events on the continent when we have tons of broadcast stations for electronic communications and blogs for digital communications. The same goes for creating URLs for digital communications that serve the needs of the African people. Africans studying journalism abroad have the duty to adapt their skills on Afrocentric requirements for the continent. The colonial conquest of the continent of Africa has been long gone since the 1960s. All African countries are now independent. If independence means subservience to the erstwhile colonial masters to achieve full sovereignty and restore dignity to Africans, then we are doomed. The pain of playing secondary roles as the means of achieving cherished dreams will be detrimental in the long run for generations to come. If globalization of media means that each continent plays an active role on the world stage in order to be recognized and valued by the international community, then Africa has a meaningful role to play. According to Afrocentricity theory by Molefi Kete Asante, the four research questions have provided sufficient responses that have adhered to the assumptions of the theory to put Africa and Africans in the epistemic and ontological sphere of influence through conscious awareness of the role Africa media should play in the world.

In my discussion of solutions to decolonize media content for African consumers, I have placed a lot of emphasis on language, dependency and culture. If we agree that language is the canopy under which all other elements of the cultural mores of a people are contained, then we only have to agree with Cheikh Anta Diop that for Africa to attempt at decolonizing, and in the same process create an atmosphere for mental reassessment and renewal for its people, language has to play a pivotal role. We cannot after 60 years of colonial rule still rely on foreign-imposed language for communication on the media and our educational institutions. One cannot avoid but hear the echo of the voices of Julius Kambarage Nyerere, Namdi Azikiwe, Osagefo Kwame

Nkrumah, Thomas Sankara, Jomo Kenyatta and Patrice Lumumba about nationalism and pan-Africanism in all spheres of our lives, including mediated communications. We seem to glorify the west, as evidenced in the majority of our clothing, food and shelter consumption on the continent, and that is affecting our dignity and reputation on the world stage. The languages that are used on mass media, whether on television, radio, newspaper or the Internet, are largely western and, as Anta Diop warned, we will not achieve development with that, because things will continue to fall apart, even after the deaths of Chinua Achebe, Ali Alamin Mazrui, Nelson Mandela and Walter Rodney, who is famous for having written the magnum opus "How Europe underdeveloped Africa". We pride ourselves with wearing western suits; writing and speaking impeccable English and French on our national televisions, seminars and classrooms; making these foreign languages official national languages in some of our countries, and worst of all at the African Union.

The second most important challenge facing Africa in the age of globalization, as discussed earlier, is dependency. One of the tenets of the theory of dependency is that what you have is considered inferior and what comes from somewhere is more valuable, and that is the fate of the media system in Africa. We produce films and television programs in Africa, yet we relish in importing Hollywood, European and Chinese films and programs because they are sold to us at a cheaper rate. This type of dependency makes Africa and Africans look to these foreign entities as the standard bearers, and what is produced at home is considered substandard and more expensive. For this mentality to change, a lot of effort is needed from power wielders on the continent to engage in a complete paradigm shift for us to be Afrocentric first and foremost before we can accommodate anything foreign. In this way, the decolonization of our minds and that of the media we use in Africa would see a new dawn.

References

Akomolafe, F. 2014. Burkina Faso: You cannot kill ideas. *New African Magazine*, December: 66–67.

Antecol, M. 1997. Understanding McLuhan: Television and the creation of the global village. *ETC: A Review of General Semantics*, 54(4): 454–473.

Asante, M.K. 2007a. *Cheikh Anta Diop: An Intellectual Portrait*. Los Angeles, CA: University of Sankore Press.

Asante, M.K. 2007b. *An Afrocentric Manifesto*. Cambridge: Polity Press.

Asante, M.K. 2013. The Western media and the falsification of Africa: Complications of value and evaluation. *China Media Research*, 9(2), 64–71.

BBC News. 2009. http://news.bbc.co.uk/2/hi/africa/8100295.stm.

Birgit, B. 2012. Language policy and science: Could some African countries learn from some Asian countries? *International Review of Education*, 58, 481–503. DOI:10.1007/s11159-012-9308-2.

Bokova, I. 2010. Speech, Norwegian National Commission to UNESCO, Oslo, 6 June. Referred to in Magasinet, Dagbladet, Oslo, 11 September 2010.

Carey, J.W. 1992. *Communication as Culture*. New York: Routledge.

Chaudhuri, A. 2016. The real meaning of Rhodes must fall. *The Guardian*, 16.

Curtin, P.D. 1964. *The Image of Africa: British Ideas and Action. 1780–1850*.Madison, WI: University of Wisconsin Press.

de Beer, A.S. and Saliba, H., 2000. Identifying and addressing racism in South African media –an introduction. *Equid Novi: African Journalism Studies*, 21(3), 153–156.

Erastus, K.F. 2013. Examining African languages as tools for national development: The case of Kiswahili. *Journal of Pan African Studies*, 6(6), 41–68.

Halvorsen, T.A. 2012. Participation in the ICT era: Implementation without humiliation, misconception and false consciousness. *International Review of Education*, 58, 313–334. DOI:10.1007/s11159-012-9291-7.

Kandybowicz, J. and Torrence, H. 2017. Africa's endangered languages: An overview. In Kandybowicz, J. and Torrence, H., eds. *Africa's Endangered Languages: Documentary and Theoretical Approaches*. Oxford: Oxford University Press, 1–9.

Kiwoya, V. and Makokha, J.S. 2009. The case for Kiswahili as a regional broadcasting language in Africa. *The Journal of Pan African Studies*, 2(8): 11–35.

Lor, P.J. and Britz, J.J. 2006. Knowledge production from an African perspective: International information flows and intellectual property. *International Information and Library Review*, 37(2): 61–76.

Mazama, A. 2003. *The Afrocentric Paradigm*. Trenton, NJ: Africa World Press.

Mazrui, A. 1986. *The Africans: A Triple Heritage*. Boston, MA: Little Brown Company.

Mazrui, A. 2009. Media messages: Sins of distortion and signs of wisdom. In Mbayo, R.T. et al., eds. *Communication in an Era of Global Conflicts*. Lanham, MD: University Press of America, 15–24.

Mbinjama, A. 2013. Language and cultural ideologies on the Internet: Social media use of adolescents in semi-rural South Africa. *Journal of Intercultural Disciplines*, 11, 58–70.

Ndlovu-Gatsheni, S.J. 2018. *Epistemic Freedom in Africa: Deprovincialization and Decolonization*. London: Routledge.

Ngũgĩ, W.T. 1988. *Decolonizing the Mind*. Goteborg: East African Educational Publishers.

Nyamnjoh, F. 2012. Potted plants in greenhouses: A critical reflection on the resilience of colonial education in Africa. *Journal of Asian and African Studies*, 47(2): 129–154.

Park, M.J. and Curran, J., eds. 2000. *De-Westernizing Media Studies*. London: Psychology Press.

Skinner, E.P. 2001. The restoration of African identity for a new millennium. In Okpewho, I.O., Davies, C.B. and Mazrui, A.A., eds. *The African Diaspora: African Origins and New World Identities*. Bloomington, IN: Indiana University Press, 28–45. www.uneca.org/sites/default/files/PublicationFiles/wsis10_and_beyond.pdf.

UNESCO. 2010. *Why and How Africa Should Invest in African Languages and Multilingual Education*. http://unesdoc.unesco.org/images/0018/001886/188642e.pdf.

World Bank Group. 2011. *Education Strategy 2020: Learning for All. Investing in People's Knowledge and Skills to Promote Development*. Washington, DC: World Bank.

7

Communicating the idea of South Africa in the age of decoloniality

Blessed Ngwenya

Introduction

The intensification of theoretical interest in the idea of decolonizing knowledge and ways of knowing is currently one of the most popular subjects in South Africa. This contested subject calls for the interrogation of the role of all sites of knowledge production and discourses that sustain the power structure of coloniality across all spheres in the country. My contribution to this volume is concerned with the incorporation of experiences and prevailing estrangement and subordination into the disconnected and 'vanguardist' epistemological method of approaching media theory in the global South media landscape, in general, and post-apartheid South Africa, in particular. I argue that the dominant discourse about South Africa in the media, with special emphasis on public service broadcast media, is not a South African idea but an externally generated idea. Public service media in South Africa is therefore an idea of South Africa and not a South African idea. It is one that is generated from outside instead of from within, through internally produced social and institutional constructions of a local experience. As a result, using a Cartesian examination, the media in South Africa is a mind that is detached from its own body that is not only on the side of power but also sustains its reinforcement and continuation. In this theoretical chapter, I investigate the complex set of inquiries that critical media theorists have pursued in the process of mounting intellectual and political entrenchment of the exclusionary predominant idea of South Africa in contemporary South African media. The chapter falls into three parts. In the first, I explore the Eurocentric foundations of coloniality of knowledge. In the second, I consider what might be the idea of contemporary South Africa and the historical nodes that frame its creation. In the third and final part, continuing in the historical method, I use some standard nodes in the development of media theory to trace the development of its thought and its theorizing as located in the global North. Marxism forms the key pillars of discussion in this section. The third part analyses how the epistemic (dis)'located-ness' of South African media in the global North serves to defend and preserve the vestiges of imperial South Africa. In this final section, drawing from theorists of liberation such as Boaventura Santos, Ngũgĩ wa Thiong'o, Ndlovu-Gatsheni, Walter Mignolo, Valentine Mudimbe and others does not only call for epistemic dis-obedience but for the imagining of a new locus of enunciation in articulating the media. This approach serves to unmask the institutionalized violence that compels African media to always seek validation from European media systems whereas understanding of the world far exceeds the Western understanding of the world (De Sousa Santos 2014, 134). In this chapter, I argue that the media in South Africa is not only complicit but also promotes the unquestioning modernity/coloniality slant of producing subjects and subjectivities that perpetually lend themselves to barometers and colonialist agendas imposed upon them. I suggest that there are strong lines of continuity between Westo-Eurocentric colonial strands of power, epistemology and public service broadcast media in South Africa.

Power, modernity/coloniality and the media

At the centre of this chapter is the question of power and epistemology. The media in South Africa is the product of a particular knowledge. This knowledge, I argue, is anchored on the Eurocentric foundations that esteem the idea of colonization as progress and development that needs to be emulated (Ndlovu-Gatsheni 2015; Ndlela 2009; Chukwudi 1997; Wiredu 1992). Consequently, the Eurocentric power of framing is directly relevant in not only understanding the South African media but African political structures as well. Owing to these foundations, the South African media therefore represents a particular form of practice, of reasoning, and of argumentation that is socially contrived and historically constructed and not wholly detached from coloniality. If the 'universal' imagination is colonial as implied, then analysis calls for attention to the need for political and epistemic de-linking as well as the detachment from knowledges that produce the *hubris of the zero point* which present knowledge as detached and neutral (Castro-Gomez 2007). In this pursuit, I ask questions addressed by eminent decolonial scholar Walter Mignolo (2009, 3): Who and when and why and where is knowledge is generated? In the process, I shift attention from the enunciated to the enunciation. To add to these questions: Who speaks, who listens and why? (hooks 1994). It is therefore important to consider how the logic of monoculture of scientific knowledge influence the locus of enunciation in the South African media (De Sousa Santos 2014, 188). To this effect, a number of questions suffice: What is the role of the media in general and public service broadcast media in particular in post-apartheid South Africa? What does this broadcast media mediate? How does this media interact with its social environment? What defines the South African public service broadcast media's locus of enunciation? Where does the South African public service broadcast media position itself in the global matrix of power? The range of these questions is, of course, immense, as are the epistemological positions that may be formulated in response to the questions. However, these questions anchor the central issues in this chapter, thus providing a framework that draws together the key arguments that run through the chapter.

In building a framework to address these questions, in this section I begin by giving a brief overview of the South African public service broadcast media. I then give a brief background on the vocabulary that anchors the decolonial epistemic lens, with the intention of laying a foundation to understand how the idea of the South African public service broadcast media took shape within the larger transformations of Westocentric cultural practices of public service broadcast media. I weave into the argument that decolonizing the media is a two-pronged process that seeks to re-constitute the epistemic foundations of the field as much as it is a project that aims to unmask the colonial, historical and hierarchical power structures that masquerade as emancipatory.

Louw and milton (2012) have demonstrated the importance of the South African Broadcasting Corporation in pioneering the post-apartheid transformation process. This claim on the importance of the media cannot be underestimated. For Marchall McLuhan (1964), communication institutions are the main force for change in human society. In consequence, the media plays a key role in post-apartheid South Africa in attempting to create transversal connections between people who had been deeply divided by the dehumanizing apartheid system. The media, particularly the public service broadcast media, has continued to take a central role in framing public discourse around socio-economic and political issues that deepen the South African democracy (Bosch 2017). In recognition of the importance of the media, a three-tier system based on section 192 of the Constitution of South Africa (Act No 108 of 1995) was established. The act established a three-tier system (community, commercial and public tiers) and an independent authority to regulate the entire broadcasting sector in the public interest.

The public service broadcaster is established as a public company with the state as the sole shareholder in terms of the Broadcasting Act, No 4 of 1999. The South African Broadcasting Corporation (SABC), which has 20 radio stations and 5 TV stations, has by far the largest footprint in South Africa with a weekly average listenership of 40 million and an adult weekly viewership of 20 million (SABC Report 2018). It follows then that with such a wide footprint the SABC has attracted public criticism on issues of being ANC controlled, self-censoring, lacking in objectivity, lacking in fairness and being subject to political and economic control by powerful individual and organizations. I note this in order to question the relevance of political economy in understanding South African public service media subjectivities. I want to move away from the constant continuity of mechanical sensibilities that continue to be trapped in the limited logic of capitalism or state power to explain the content and effects of the media. I move away from these mechanical ruses to expand conditions of possibilities that centre the impact of global power structures which shape global media and are not reducible to local political-economy paradigms. I deploy the decolonial epistemic paradigm to transcend the idiosyncratic limitations.

Decoloniality has meant different things to different people in different geo-political contexts. In this study, it is a theory and method of analysis that emerges from the underside, to counter and de-link from the Western imperial modernity which valorises the provincial foundations of Western concepts and accumulation of knowledges as universal (Ndlovu-Gatsheni 2018; Escobar 2012; Maldonado-Torres 2016). Walter Mignolo's claim that one of the accomplishments of imperial reason was to uphold itself as a superior identity by constructing inferior constructs, expelling them to the outside of the normative sphere of the real, chimes with the preceding observation and lays a concrete foundation for complementary discussion on decoloniality that centres on de-linking (Mignolo 2007, 2). Walter Mignolo (2007) emphasises that

> Decoloniality means thinking from the exteriority and in a sub-altern epistemic position vis-à-vis the epistemic hegemon that creates, builds, constructs an outside in order to assure its interiority.
>
> *(14)*

Drawing on this quote from Mignolo is a good way to begin a discussion of coloniality which is inseparably welded to the question of power. Moreover, to understand decoloniality and to de-centre European thinking in the analysis of the media one has to have a well-founded knowledge of coloniality. Coloniality is different from colonialism, the two exist on a labyrinth, and at times they are wrongly used interchangeably. Colonialism indicates a political and economic relationship in which a sovereignty of a nation or a people rests on the power of another nation, whereas coloniality refers to long-standing patterns of power that emerged as a result of colonialism (Maldonado-Torres 2007). As observed by Torres, coloniality survives colonialism. The long-standing patterns of power are largely maintained by three key pillars: coloniality of knowledge, coloniality of being and coloniality of power. There are other pillars, but these three are the key ones. Although the media constitutes an indispensable set of practises and discourses for the production and consolidation of existing societies, it should not be ignored how it is shaped by the same societies as anchored by the global matrices of power. These three pillars will contribute to an understanding of the formulation of the symbolic framework on which the role of the media in South Africa is built and sustained.

First, coloniality of knowledge is concerned with the control and monopolization of epistemological issues by the Western world. Contemporary epistemological projects find themselves caught up in this Western canon that continually reproduces coloniality in its domains of thought that privileges Western thinking and Western thinkers (Grosfoguel 2007, 212). This fundamentalist Eurocentric epistemological tradition highlighted by Grosfoguel which posits that there is only one sole epistemic tradition from which to achieve truth and universality tends to mask the power relations on the production of knowledge that hinge on who, whose, where and why is knowledge produced. Second, coloniality of being relates to how the Eurocentric ethics of domination giving meaning to being. This logic is well articulated by Nelson Maldonado-Torres (2007, 240–270) that

> the colonial dimensions of being, expressed partly in Western civilization by the West's philosophical discourse's monopoly on the meaning of Being, or to be more precise on its exclusive possession, control, and exercise of the philosophy on existence.

Coloniality of being is therefore strongly attached to the ontological hierarchization of being and the sense of being human. Torres further develops the idea of coloniality of being by introducing what he terms "imperial Manichean misanthropic scepticism". This scepticism is an attitude of being that positions itself at the apex of being and perpetually holds those it places at the base of humanity in permanent suspicion. The questioning of the humanity of others is not limited to individuals but also postures itself against the institutions they run. As I will illustrate in this chapter, this positioning also defines the media's gaze on the state and relationship with the state in the global South, a relationship of permanent suspicion that questions the humanity and capability of those who have been colonized in the past.

Third, coloniality of power is defined by Peruvian scholar Anibal Quijano (2000) as a historical process that views the present globalized world as a culmination of the consolidation of Western power via the colonization and the establishment of world capitalism in the 16th century by instituting racial categorization and imposing a division of labour structured by these categories. These global power structures continue to exist between the former colony and colonizer. The understanding of coloniality of power enables us to excavate how the current global political order which sustains the superiority of the global North was constructed and constituted into the asymmetrical modern power structure that Quijano terms the colonial matrix of power.

Quijano, in his seminal article, defines the colonial matrix of power as the four-pronged set of technologies of subjectivation that exist on a continuum of interrelated domains. First is the control of economy which includes but is not limited to land appropriation, exploitation of labour and control of natural resources. Second is control of authority (institution, army), control of gender and sexuality (family, education) and control of subjectivity and knowledge (epistemology, education and formation of subjectivity) (Quijano 2007, 168–187; Winter 2003; Ndlovu-Gatsheni 2013).

Discussions of the coloniality and the colonial matrix of power reveal the relation between epistemology, ontology and being and how it is foundational to understanding imperial projects and global designs that locate Europe as a model for the achievements of humanity. Eurocentric knowledges have postured Europe as a goal, and hence as modernity, reducing everything outside of European imagination as barbaric. Coloniality refutes this position and reveals itself as a darker side of modernity. In the words of Walter Mignolo, coloniality is a darker of side of modernity; it is constitutive of modernity, and there cannot be modernity without coloniality (2007, 155–162). Consequently, coloniality is explained as the enduring patterns of power. Modernity is therefore the name given for the historical process in which Europe begins its process towards world hegemony. It is the epistemological hegemony that seeks to present the media via one sole logic, a closed Eurocentric totality idea of the media. It is this hegemony that deforms and fragments the South African media's locus of enunciation. The colonization of the imagination of the dominated, also used as device of cultural and social control, is seductively presented such that the dominated can speak from the side of the oppressor, (Quijano 2007, 168–178). As result the locus of enunciation, which is epistemologically stuck in Eurocentric thought, is a strategy that has been crucial for Western global designs which hide the location of the subject of enunciation via a hierarchy of superior and inferior knowledge, influencing the oppressed to speak from the position of the oppressor. The subject has to aspire to Eurocentric knowledge considered as the only avenue to 'being' and therefore to be rewarded materially and symbolically through power. Since 'being' is a consequence of knowledge, to decolonize is therefore an epistemological reconstitution that fragments a singular modernity, therefore re-constituting power. In summary, the media is a reality born out of relations of power. The media's role in South Africa remains interpellated by its Eurocentric genealogy. The media has continued to be an appendix of and to the state that reinforces coloniality and the colonization of imagination of the colonized through key levers of ownership and ideology which dictate its role. In this chapter the public service broadcasting media's role is discussed through understandings of the birth of the state in South Africa and in the global South in general whose midwife was the language of progress, salvation and modernization.

Whose rainbow is it anyway? Configurations of the state and the history of the media in post-apartheid South Africa

Traces into the genealogy of the media reveal the 19th century as the era where globalization of communication was propelled by the media's transformation into large-scale commercial concerns as enhanced by key technological innovations (Thompson 1995, 79). It must however be noted that these communication technological innovations were intricately tied to political and commercial power. For example, Thompson observes that military interests played a vital role in the expansion of cable networks, where British, German and American governments played key roles in these technological developments (1995, 79). This historical framework of media development has always determined the role of the media in different contexts across the world. These foundations have also shaped the privileged position in Western society of viewing the media by means of Hallin and Mancini's (2004) four dimensions of media systems: structure of the market, political parallelism, professionalization of journalism and the role of the state. In this section, I am interested in the roles of the public service broadcast media in relation to the state in post-apartheid South Africa.

The role of the media in post-apartheid South Africa has largely been tied to ideas of nation-building that encapsulate reconciliation and democratic citizenship (Wasserman and de Beer 2012; Fourie 2002). This form of nation-building has largely been termed the 'rainbow nation', where a single nation of many cultures is constructed. The South African media was born into this framework which has largely remained the primary thread running through the fabric of media professionalism and independence. Despite this attractive and clearly defined role, the media not only remains divisive, but also fractured, fragmented and unconstitutive in its disposition. But we may need to arrive at the purpose of the media through understanding its origin, identity, meaning and significance. At the heart of the purpose is a misplaced conceptualization, that of the rainbow nation. The international and local framework in which the post-apartheid South African media was born into, especially the role of forging a nation and seeking to create some homogeneity, presents two emergent areas of concern.

The first concern is an epistemological one: Can we rely on the same knowledges that have been used in the past to divide people to forge unity? In South Africa, this epistemological challenge is solidified by the impossibility of reconciling people of whom there is no evidence of conciliation in any moment in history and who have never imagined themselves as a nation due to hierarchical historical racial configurations. The 'rainbowness' remains an illusion and a merchant of silences that somehow serves to 'restore' the very racial configurations it is committing to challenging by subjugation and subjectivation of those who have never had a voice to permanent silence. Consequently, the purpose of the media becomes that of mediating power. In this case, there is on the one hand debates on those who hold political power and their control of the public broadcaster as the focus of attention. For example, over the years, the ANC has largely been blamed by scholars, civil society and other groups for controlling the public broadcaster. These claims are not unfounded, because over the past 25 years the appointed CEOs have always been aligned with a ruling faction within the ANC. Wynand Harmse, who has served in the SABC for over 30 years, 7 of those as a CEO, has written a book that illustrates the apartheid seeds of political control that bedevil the ANC today (Harmse 2018). While it may not be disputed that the ANC does wield political control over the public service broadcaster, the differences with the apartheid broadcaster should not be air-brushed. The ANC is a false site of power. Real power lies with the economic power. The National Party (NP) had the advantage over the SABC because it controlled both economic and political power. And those with power are those who have benefitted from the previous state system of racial segregation. This stratification of power can be illustrated in the following example: In South Africa, uKhozi FM that broadcasts in iSiZulu is by far the most listened to radio station, with a listenership of 7 million people weekly. However, when it comes to advertising revenue, it is a distant seventh, trailing the English and Afrikaans broadcasting stations that have attractive audiences, namely, Highveld Stereo, Jacaranda, Metro FM, KFM, East Coast Radio and Talk Radio 702. The power is not only political but economic as there was no re-distribution of resources, and the inequalities remain largely racially stratified. The muzzling is also strongly attached to the class configurations which are racially hierarchized. This silencing of the previously oppressed is a characteristic of coloniality wherein heterogeneous societies there is a vertical structure of being. The modus operandi tends to privilege the voice of those at the apex of the colonial structure, silencing others at the base. This kind of stratification by default silences inquiry and distances the unequal historical configurations from contemporary events. In the very same country there are those who are citizens and consumers of the media while others are mere subjects (Mamdani 1996). An invisible line continues to exist between those at the apex and those at the base. Dos Santos points out that this line divides social reality in such a profound way that whatever lies on the other side of the line remains invisible and utterly irrelevant (2014, 70). Frantz Fanon calls this the zone of being and zone of none being (1952).

The second concern pertains to the post-apartheid media's urge to speak. Media roles and ideas are largely anchored on media liberties and freedom of speech. What is largely ignored is in whose interest the media does speak, and most importantly, what it wants to create. It is therefore important to state that another subliminal role of the media is to create. In his seminal work, *Pedagogy of the Oppressed* (1972), Freire speaks about the power of the word to create and transform. Freire's ideas on power of the word in creation is supported in theology where, in the beginning was the word and everything was created through it. The media in contemporary society is the word, and its function is to create. However, what the media can create can only be traced to on whose behalf it speaks. If historical foundations of framing epistemologies framing are Western, then the birth and the function of the media should be read within the frames of colonial matrices of power that may also determine not only ownership but ideological structures too. The media in South Africa finds itself as an appendix of coloniality as it aids the project of modernity in reproducing coloniality as a frame of reference. It is the same frames that position Western epistemology as not only frames of reference but a goal and a model. The barometer for the function and freedom of the media becomes wholly Western, and in a process of aspiration journalists and others are epistemically forced to perform media freedoms. This is recognized and chimed by Ndlovu who notes that the production of knowledge within formerly colonized states is generally underpinned by coloniality (Ndlovu 2013, 1–12). Consequently, we find the media narratives in the global South pre-occupied with silencing analysis in ways that limit what media thinkers and practitioners do within modernity. This fractured and aspiratory locus of enunciation buttresses the integration and appropriation of the media into modernity as a goal. The media is also used as a tool to usher the state into modernization.

Modernization, it must be noted, has connotations and involves coherence of state identity, a function of post-apartheid media, but what it really means is inserting and subjecting the state into the global matrices of power. The state is born into the crisis of modernity in the global South and has been implicated in a historical European process towards world hegemony, viewed on a progressive plane. If the state is born captured by these colonial matrices of power, which are contours that frame coloniality/modernity, how then do we discuss media roles or even freedoms? The response cannot be divorced to configurations of the state and interrogations of citizenship, especially when homogeneity is the official discourse but the praxis is exclusion.

To articulate the idea of South Africa is to understand how the project of modernity interpellates all aspects of life through the conduit of the media. On the one hand, the construction of the apartheid state had been a result of a failure to deal with difference/heterogeneity, yet on the other, the emergence of the post-apartheid state was a response to a dilemma of fighting for a common humanity that had been denied to the majority of the population. The hovering modernity posed a problem for the newly birthed South Africa. At the heart of this South African problem was a series of conceptual conflations. One example is the rhetoric and normativized idea of conflating the nation with the state. A South African state exists but not a South African nation, yet the media has been tasked with the role of promoting and creating a rainbow nation. This rainbow nation, I argue, is only about moving from hard apartheid to soft apartheid, a case of moving from the overt to the covert, where the media is not only an appendix, but is thrust within existing racial social formations and serves to sustain them. The media encourages the previously excluded to maintain the fake homogeneity in a 'carry your own cross' manner via the silences I point out in the preceding sections and those whose voice have always been heard continue to be heard. These media 'performativities' and self-congratulatory representations, it is clear, do not match the reality on the ground, where fissures are unmistakably visible.

The theatrical performance of nationhood or 'rainbowism' and racial 'invisibilizing' of the previously disadvantaged by the state can be traced to the configuration of the Westphalian, Eurocentric state. There is evidence in Africa that where the Eurocentric state does not correspond with the realities of diversity on the ground, it becomes characterized by the development of coercive tendencies where it has the power to claim the constitutional use of force within its defined territory. The post-apartheid project was that of 'civic nationalism', which promotes an inclusive form of a nation, a nation as a community of equal rights, with patriotic attachment to shared set of political practises and values regardless of race, colour or creed (Ignatieff 1994, 4). In such circumstances, the media, courts, church, education system and security sector seeks to unite the people subjected to this idea of the nation. In South Africa there is what one can call 'soft-coercion' by the 'independent' media. This is done by means of homogenization and banal nationalism where the pursuit of building a shared sense of belonging is performed to create a common culture. The spectacle includes symbols such as flags, values, truth and reconciliation commissions, use of sports, reviving traditions and formative myths of origin, and sometimes inventing and re-inventing them.

Ernest Renan (1947), the 19th-century French philosopher, even resurrects and adds to these antiquated divisive notions of the nation two key discordant concepts. These are namely 'forgetfulness' and 'extermination and terror'. These, according to Renan, are a means to an end. The end is unity and the nation. Renan claims that forgetfulness is a key component in nation creation. Drawing from the Eurocentric ethic of violence, Renan asserts that all nations are born out of violence, so the violent acts should be conveniently forgotten for a nation to be forged and unity to prevail. Renan believes that people unite in their memories of suffering because alleviating grief requires a "common effort" which serves as a foundation for unity. But Renan's idea of unity in itself is mottled. This contrived nationalism takes unity for uniformity, yet the two are different terms altogether. Unity is basically the harmony and togetherness of different populations or nations within a country, yet uniformity desires likeness, and any form of difference is not tolerated.

Consequently, if the media is not really at the coal face, but rather a mere appendice whose important work involves following, performing and mediating power, its essential purpose becomes that of promoting and sanctioning bias under pretences of objectivity, neutrality in its pursuit to create national identity and other homogeneity myths. The idea of South Africa which is promoted by the media in reality is two pronged. On the one hand, it reveals a triumphant nation that has against all odds washed away vestiges of apartheid; on the other hand, deeper analysis reveals an idea, one that is shunned by the media, that the nation symbolizes a fractured locus of enunciation, inequality, oppression and dispossession. If the latter is highlighted by the media, it is positioned using the barometer of 'rainbowism' which is itself flawed due to its emphasis on the government of the day whose abilities are questioned in an imperial Manichean scepticism trajectory. The subliminal message is about questioning the capability of the bodies that occupy state institutions. The black bodies whose humanity has always been questioned. Consequently, to challenge the idea of South Africa is to challenge the whole entire imagination of Europe of the idea of Africa and that of the state. Six eminent scholars have given various views that give inroads to different insights into the invention of Africa, as well as pointers and explanations as to why modernization imaginations continue in their diverse interpretations to be located within the one Eurocentric frame of knowledge – a frame of knowledge that stations itself as a goal and a model to other knowledges. These scholars are Valentine Mudimbe, Mahmood Mamdani, Eric Wolf, Ngũgĩ wa Thiong'o, Mabogo More and Bernard Magubane. The discussion of these six scholars overlaps into the next section that examines media theory.

First, Eric Wolf, in his seminal work, 'Europe and the people without history', highlights how the West has in the past positioned itself as a society and civilization independent of and in opposition to other societies and civilizations, (1982, 5). Wolf succinctly points out how the linearity in thinking by the West, of course not as a spatial space but idea, is imagined as a furtherance of virtue when he says:

> this West has a genealogy, according to which ancient Greece begat Rome, Rome begat the Christian Europe, Christian Europe begat the Renaissance, the Renaissance the Enlightenment, the Enlightenment political democracy and industrial revolution . . . industry, crossed with democracy, in turn yielded the United States, embodying the rights to liberty and pursuit of happiness.
>
> *(1982, 5)*

If this quote from Wolf is the anchoring position to Eurocentric imagination, it therefore comes as no surprise that developmental scholar Daniel Lerner, who emphasized the critical role of the media in the modernization process held the idea that the injection of Western values and systems would lead to the transformation of 'traditional' societies (1958). The neoliberalist rebuttals of Daniel Lerner that emphasized the development of different societies according to their contexts were also limited in that they fell into the trap of examining the phenomenon within the very same frames of Eurocentrism. Walter Mignolo, in his book *Coloniality, Subaltern Knowledges and Border Thinking* (2000), notes the need to break from these framed hegemonic forms of knowledge and critiques that are globally designed but create and masquerade as local histories (22).

In an attempt to trace designs that contribute to the larger whole that anchors the dominance of the modernity/colonial/Western imaginary, its reproduction and the role of epistemology in constructing and sustaining power, Valentine Mudimbe speaks of the invention of Africa. Mudimbe even traces the etymology of the word *colonialism*, which is derived from the Latin *colere*, meaning 'to cultivate or design'. According to Mudimbe, "colonists as well as colonialists have all tended to organise and transform non-European areas into fundamentally European constructs" (1988, 1). Robin Derricourt, buttresses this view by stating that, "The image of Africa was largely created in Europe to suit European needs – sometimes material needs, more often intellectual needs, (2011, 18). In his book *Race and the Construction of the Dispensable Other*, Bernard Magubane gives a closer analysis of the relationship between power and the production of knowledge when he demonstrates how exploitative and unjust systems require and perpetuate false and even absurd systems of thought to rationalize and sustain themselves (2007, 29). On this continuum, Mahmod Mamdani sheds light on the idea of South Africa and how unequal power relations that are exclusionary can be reinforced, in the process excluding from within and from the state epistemologically. These hierarchical configurations, founded on exclusions, imaginings that subliminally 'invisibilize' others pose a crisis of articulation for the media. But the media in South Africa is ensnared in a contradiction that besets modernity/coloniality institutions, that of pursuing autonomy but at the same time being entrapped in the domineering vagaries of modernity/coloniality. And these vagaries are informed by theory of the imperial paradigm which imposes and maintains the dominant view.

Of media theory and a fractured locus of enunciation

Theories have always been important in linking the domain of ideas and that of the empirical world to produce a knowable world. Theory can be defined as the total set of empirically testable, interconnected ideas formulated to explain a phenomenon (White and Klein 2002). However, there is what one may call dis-locatedness of theory where theories can be forklifted from different contexts, mainly dominant, to explain phenomena in geo-politically detached, mainly periphery, nations from where they are designed. This approach tends to create, a stretched case, of what scholar Achille Mbembe calls mutual zombification, where both the dominant and dominated rob each other of vitality and both are left impotent (2015, 104). Ngũgĩ wa Thiong'o presents an important insight with regards to theorizing from a lived experience and in the process addressing the zombification impasse. wa Thiong'o traces the etymology and meaning of word *theory*. He points out that,

> theoria, meaning a view and a contemplation. View assumes a viewer, a ground on which to stand, and what is viewed from that standpoint. A view is also a framework for organising what is seen and a thinking about the viewed.
>
> *(wa Thiong'o 2012, 15)*

Ngũgĩ's articulations could be used to pose questions for the South African media. What is the media's standpoint? How does it frame what it sees? What is its epistemic location? By and large, the role of the media has been discussed in relation to economic and political interests, with a large body of theory gravitating towards political economy theories. From this perspective, the media has been viewed largely as a sphere that mitigates against the encroachment of these false dichotomies of political and economic interests. The pursuit, therefore, has been autonomy. These debates have also raised a valid but limited point that the media enjoy autonomy only to the degree that it does not threaten dominant interests and hegemonic principles (Kupe, Fourie, Hall).

If these points are valid, they remain conspicuous for what they conceal. What the theories generally conceal, I argue, is what fuels a dislocated locus of enunciation. Locus of enunciation generally means to think and speak from where you are. At the centre of what the theories conceal is the racialized black subject. The black body does not have power, since media mediates power, so it does not have media, and to cap it all off, it is not a citizen or consumer, but rather a subject subjected to invisibility and devoid of voice. Mahmood Mamdani (2017) points this out when he states how direct rule denied rights to subjects on racial grounds and how indirect rule incorporated them into a 'customary' mode of rule. Frank Wilderson stretches Mamdani's position further when it comes to limitations of political economy discourses with regards to the black subject. Wilderson (2003, 225–240) establishes that a Marxist-derived lens interprets a state constructed at the intersection of both a capitalist and a white supremacist matrix a subaltern as structured by capital, not white supremacy. Race cannot be derivative of political economy he argues. This terrain punctuated with issues of race chimes well with the post-apartheid South African context. Philosopher Mabogo More extensively discusses the subjectivation of the black subject in post-apartheid South Africa:

> They tell us that the situation in South Africa is a class struggle than a racial one . . . black people are dependent upon the economic interest of white people. . . . the alienation suffered by the black worker is completely different from that suffered by the white workers.
>
> *(2017, 238)*

What can be drawn from More, Mamdani and Wilderson is that the black body has to reach the realm of the human first before it is parachuted into political economy theories as upheld by media thinkers. Issues of ownership, concentration and diversity in the media should not be the base of media discussions. The media should locate itself outside the coloniality/modernity frames of reference, as it is impossible to analyze a portrait whist being within the frame. What is therefore clear is how coloniality of power and knowledge capture any form of knowledge production by the media. It becomes even clearer how the media thinks, speaks and locates itself epistemically the dominant side. Another reason is the production of media personnel within the Area Studies domain.

Ndlovu-Gatsheni (2015) establishes how African scholars in the tradition of Area Studies tend to be native informants that valorize the production of fact and resist theory. This leads to debates of skilling and knowledge production. Journalists and media personnel are trained to reproduce coloniality instead of being critical thinkers, and if they are critical thinkers they are only cogs in wheels, serving to work efficiently in a well-oiled system. We can gain some insights into the whole process by considering in brief five key areas that the South African media has entrenched itself in to reproduce the Westo-centric modernity buttressed by coloniality of being, power and knowledge to maintain the racialized global matrices of power within South Africa. These are, mystification, economism, dis-embeddedness, projection and amplification.

First, *mystification*, in Marxian terms, refers to the impediment to critical consciousness. The media in this case presents itself as sacred and a conduit for truth. The media, courtesy of its epistemic foundations postures as non-situated, in the process hiding its location in the power structures. Mystification is closely linked with and enables projection. In psychology, *projection* refers to a defensive trait where one attributes perceived faults in themselves to others. The media as an appendice of coloniality/modernity, which always has coloniality as its darker side, tends to present Western media as a goal and model; all other ills and shortcomings are largely projected on the state in an imperial Manichean scepticism way. The framing of news can also be influenced by projection, for example, in the Marikana imbroglio striking miners were shot dead by the police, but the media highlighted the police brutality and not the capitalist hand and voice behind the massacre. Consequently, in South Africa, it has become the goal of research to examine the relationship between the state, which is read as the ruling ANC, and the media. This distortion of inquiry chimes with the proverbial dog barking at the wrong tree. Mystification and projection work together to cement the ideology of economism in the media. *Economism* "privileges the economic and political aspects of social processes at the expense of cultural and ideological determinations" (Grosfoguel 2008, 326). The power of projection and 'sacredness' brought about by mystification of the media, in its attempt to conceal the speaker, banks on the 'neutrality' of economics and uses it as a policing stick. For example, during the Jacob Zuma era, the falling rand and 'impending' economic crisis were used by the media to shape the citizens and subjects' view on the political arena. Political brinksmanship is played by the media which assumes the role of a 'guided dog' and not a watchdog. *Disembededdness* is another tool that the media uses to remove the subject that speaks from analysis. This is realized by removing media values and ideas from the concrete and local South African context by using an abstract de-contextualized barometer of Western states such as Australia. This kind of posturing presents a dilemma of the media being epistemically located far away from its social location. Ramon Grosfoguel explains this as the success of the modern/colonial world system where "subjects that are socially located in the oppressed side of colonial difference think epistemically like the ones on the dominant positions" (2007, 213). Finally, *amplification* refers, in this case, to the mischievousness of knotting every error to the government of the day. Instead of relegating issues that do not have a direct bearing to the livelihood of the people, these may be amplified. For example, one would question why Nkandla, former South African president Jacob Zuma's home, received coverage going over half a dozen years for irregularities in security details of about 20 million South African rands. This contributed to the president's demise, but Steinhoff, with fraud of over 100 billion rands, was largely ignored, not to mention bread companies which colluded on fixing bread prices.

It is necessary therefore to reexamine, within the framework of analysis I have proposed, to expand on the representation of the rainbow nation. First, granting that is a political project before a media one, the sequel to the events positioned both print and broadcast media as an appendage of the asymmetrical power relations that define the global power structure. In this instance, the media worldview, instead of being subversive, was made subservient to the dominance and importance of the 'nation-building' agenda. Undoubtedly, the media reinforced the idea that the fissure of inequality would fade off via a mere bandage of 'rainbowism'. The monological approach has not gone unnoticed by a number of scholars.

In his empirical study, Morgan Ndlovu reveals how the media, the state and the army stood in solidarity against the mineworkers (society) in its presentation of the Marikana massacre that happened in 2012 (2013, 49). The police fatally shot 34 mineworkers protesting against poor working conditions and low wages. In his piece, Ndlovu illustrates how the modern South African state, capital and media are part of the same 'colonial power matrix', and hence the three were bound to be on the same side against labour during the Marikana massacre and the events that followed (Ndlovu 2013, 46). In this monologic solidarity case we are forced to reconcile the idea of solidarity with that of erasure. The powerful, that is capital, the state and the media, converge, yet the larger society is erased from view. Schiller (1976, 9) asserts, "the sum of processes by which a society is brought into the modern system and how its dominating stratum is attracted, pressured, forced and sometimes bribed into shaping social institutions correspond to, or even to promote, the values and the structures of the dominant centre of the system"(cited in Willems 2014, 4). Wasserman and De Beer (2005) give evidence to this claim by locating it in the South African context. They point out that, although many debates around the media's role in post-apartheid society focused on the relation between the media and government's orientation toward economic power, relations often remained obscured.

Complementary to these claims is Shepherd Mpofu and Colin Chasi's (2017) work on Mandela, nation and symbolism. Mpofu and Chasi give an excellent discussion on how those who wield the legal monopoly of power try to invent traditions within which belonging to the nation is constructed through Mandela as a symbol of the nation. In their work, Mpofu and Chasi argue that the quixotic representation of the nation seals and hides those who encounter structured violence. The mythologizing of Mandela by the media chimes with the utopian representation of the rainbow nation by the media. Mpofu and Chasi conclude their work by making a strong claim that Mandela midwifed South Africa into a violent pluralism, which together with Mandela, is a creation of global American capital (18).

Mpofu and Chasi's stance provokes a number of critiques. Joseph Manzella (2008) in his 1999–2005 study of South African print newsrooms offers a thorough and insightful perspective on how the change and diversity in ownership structure impacts on organizational culture in print media in post-apartheid South Africa. Manzella (2008, 261) observes that, in this diversity, print media, such as the *Star*, have adjusted to the prevailing social order, and others, such as the *Mail & Guardian*, have attempted to reproduce the conditions of a previous sociopolitical order so that journalists may continue to define themselves in contradiction to the political system.

To others, the appellation 'diversity in South African media' is a contradiction in terms. A hasty surface analysis of the heterogeneity may lead to a conclusion that favourably depicts transformation within the South African media. Wendy Willems (2014) is quick to pick on this variance when she states that the process of diversity ownership or structure are subject to external forces ideologically. This argument of change in structure, newsroom or ownership conceals more than it reveals. The changes amount to de-racialization. De-racialization and decoloniality have contrasting pursuits. De-racialization assumes heterogeneity means a change in logic. This position in turn hides the pattern of coloniality and the enduring power relations using past tenses when discussing inequalities. In de-racialization, the logic of the media remains the same yet the players are different. This is a monologic practice by the media. The media performance takes a dialogic form that peddles ideas of solidarity, sameness and unified meanings in a single consciousness, albeit in a sharply unequal society.

A number of conflicts evidence the pursuit of monologic practice, despite diversity in ownership and structure in print media. For example, in 2003, the editor of *The Star*, Mathata Tsedu, was dismissed from his post, allegedly for the Africanization of the paper, to the dissatisfaction of the owners (Manzella 2008). This was three years after the South African Human Rights Commission (SAHRC) had held hearings to examine racism in the press which allegedly painted black leaders as corrupt (Jere-Malanda 2002, 146). The state of affairs has continued to this day. In another case, in 2017, Steve Motale, the former editor of the *Citizen Newspaper*, issued an apology to the then South African President Jacob Zuma. In a 27 January 2017 *News24* page, Motale was quoted as saying, "I have always maintained I was innocent and this was a glaring interference with editorial by management. They wanted to dictate which stories I could run". On 14 October 2018, in an editorial column, one of South Africa's leading newspapers, *Sunday Times*, admitted that it had run "tainted" scoops during the presidency of Jacob Zuma which turned out to be largely false but insisted it had been the victim of political manipulation. "We admit here today that something went wrong in the process of gathering the information and reporting" of several top stories, *Sunday Times* editor Bongani Siqoko wrote in a column.

Unless a nuanced explanation is provided, the preceding analysis implies insufficiency, and to a certain degree an inconsistency, with the monologic position. In effect the Mcquailian position of the media as a check on government appears to be met. In reality, and in the South African context, a tug-of-war between the media and the government does not mean the media stands for society; instead, it is a tug-of-war of ideologies – mainly neoliberalism versus a developmental state. The fight is only pitched at the elite level and therefore still qualifies as a monologue since both schools of thought are a product of the global power matrix. Jane Duncan captures this well when she says the developmental state is a variation of the neoliberal state and not an alternative to it. Privatization and centralization are the main pursuits, and both are crafted from the top and tend to be inherently authoritarian. In other words, they share a similar aesthetic (Duncan 2008). A decolonial perspective considers that there are other dimensions in the struggle between the media and the government. The media is not actually at loggerheads with the state, but it is against the party and bodies that holds state levers. For example, other levers of the state such as the judiciary are not at loggerheads with the media. Maldonado Torres calls this the imperial Manichean misanthropic scepticism where the very humanity and ability of colonized peoples is questioned as a deliberate strategy to justify all sorts of imperial and colonial interventions. Some of the interventions are done by the use of the media as a mouthpiece and watchdog.

Decoloniality therefore seeks to subvert the inverted relationship between power and society at large together with the scepticisms that are subliminally driven by the media. Instead of pegging the discussion and role of the media in South Africa at the elite level, decoloniality seeks to delink from the colonial matrix of power underlying Western modernity that hides behind political projects such as liberalism and the developmental state. In his outline of ten theses on coloniality and decoloniality, Torres is quick to point out that liberalism facilitates a transition from vulgar legal forms of discrimination by institutions to less vulgar but equally or more discriminatory practices and structures (Maldonado-Torres 2016, 5). Decoloniality is consequently both the analytic task of unveiling the logic of coloniality and the prospective task of contributing to build a world in which many worlds co-exist (Mignolo 2011, 54).

In closing, the understanding of the relationship between modernity and coloniality refers to an understanding of modern conceptualizations of freedom, progress, civilization, development, and democratic capitalism as themselves epistemic products of the subjugation and exploitation of colonized and enslaved peoples (Mignolo 2016). It is therefore important for the media in South Africa to move beyond categories created and imposed by Western epistemology; Mignolo calls this process pluri-topic hermeneutics. The pursuit to define a media role as an anchor and also appendice to nation-building should emerge from pluri-topic hermeneutics, because it is not the media that has control over its role, ownership or representations, but rather the epistemic configurations it locates itself in. Consequently, if our knowledges are always situated, as stated by feminist scholar Donna Haraway (1988), the media needs to free itself from the shackles of the hegemonic European paradigms that masquerade as universal, which by their disposition sustain and advance coloniality/modernity.

Conclusion

A central query I have addressed in this chapter has concerned the role of the media in post-apartheid South Africa. This has been discussed vis-à-vis the brand of state formation and 'civic nationalism' as representative of the interests of racial homogeneity armour-plated by the modernity/coloniality project. In the discussion, I have made the claim that the role of the media cannot be divorced from processes of state-making, construction of nation and citizenship. Consequently, the South African media is caught up in a world where it tries to manufacture homogeneity yet it is born out of a system of state formation that fails to manage difference. The inseparability of questions of the media, state, nation and citizenship led me to another fundamental concern of tracing and mapping out the contours of how the South African media is by and large an epistemic product of the conquest and exploitation of oppressed peoples of the world. The chapter has also examined how traditional approaches to the study of the media tend to conceal rather than reveal. Underpinning the analysis are issues of autonomy, class and power which obscure the fundamental issue of race. The media in South Africa remains an appendice of modernity/coloniality and continues to speak from the position of the powerful by epistemically locating itself on the dominant side of power.

References

Bosch, T. 2017. *Broadcasting Democracy: Radio and Identity in South Africa*. Pretoria: Human Sciences Research Council Press.

Castro-Gomez, S. 2007. The missing chapter of empire: Postmodern reorganization of coloniality and post-Fordist capitalism. *Cultural Studies*, 21(2): 428–448.

Chukwudi, E.M. 1997. The colour of reason: The idea of race in Kant's anthropology. In Chukwudi, E.M., ed. *Postcolonial African Philosophy*. London. Blackwell, 103–140.

Derricourt, R. 2011. *Inventing Africa: History, Archaeology and Ideas*. London. Pluto Press.

De Sousa Santos, B. 2014. *Epistemologies of the South: Justice Against Epistemicide*. London. Paradigm Publishers.

Duncan, J. 2008. Executive overstretch: South African broadcasting independence and accountability under Thabo Mbeki. *Communicatio South African Journal for Communication Theory and Research*, 34(1): 21–52.

Escobar, A. 2012. *Encountering Development: The Making and Unmaking of the Third World*. Princeton, NJ: Princeton University Press.

Fanon, F. 1952. *Black Skin White Masks*. New York: Grove Press.

Fourie, P.J. 2002. *Media Studies: Content, Audiences and Production*. Cape Town: Juta Limited.

Freire, P. 1972. *Pedagogy of the Oppressed*. Harmondsworth: Penguin.

Grosfoguel, R. 2007. The epistemic de-colonial turn. *Cultural Studies*, 21(2–3): 211–223.

Grosfoguel, R. 2008. *Transmodernity, border thinking, and global coloniality, Eurozone: Decolonizing Political Economy and Post Colonial Studies*. www.eurozine.com/articles/2008-07-04-grosfoguelpt.html (Accessed 12 June 2019).

Hall, S. 1980. Race, articulation and societies structured in dominance. In United Nations Education, Scientific and Cultural Organization, ed. *Sociological Theories: Race and Colonialism*. Paris: UNESCO, 305–345.

Hallin, D.C. and Mancini, P. 2004. *Comparing Media Systems: Three Models of Media and Politics*. Cambridge: Cambridge University Press.

Haraway, D. 1988. Situated knowledges: The science question in feminism and the privilege of partial perspective. *Feminist Studies*, 14(3): 575–599.

Harmse, W. 2018. *SABC 1936–1995: Still a Player- or an Endangered Species?* Johannesburg: Naledi Publishers.

hooks, b. 1994. *Teaching to Transgress: Education as the Practice of Freedom*. New York: Routledge, 167–175.

Ignatieff, M. 1994. *Blood and Belonging: Journeys into the New Nationalism*. London: Vintage.

Jere-Malanda, R. 2002. Press freedom and the crisis of ethical journalism in Southern Africa. In Atkins, J.B., ed. *The Mission: Journalism, Ethics and the World*. Ames, IA: Iowa State University Press, 143–152.

Lerner, D. 1958. *The Passing of Traditional Society: Modernising the Middle East*. New York: Free Press.

Louw, E.P. and milton, v.c. 2012. *New Voices Over the air: The Transformation of the South African Broadcasting Corporation in a Changing South Africa*. New York: Hampton Press.

Magubane, B.M. 2007. *Race and the Construction of the Dispensable Other*. Pretoria: University of South Africa Press.

Maldonado-Torres, N. 2007. On the coloniality of being: Contributions to the development of a concept. *Cultural Studies*, 21(2–3): 250–270.

Maldonado-Torres, N. 2016. Outline of ten theses on coloniality and decoloniality. *Fondation Frantz Fanon*. http://frantzfanonfoundation fondationfrantzfanon.com/article2360.html (Accessed 20 November 2019).

Mamdani, M. 1996. *Citizen and Subject: Contemporary Africa and the Legacy of Late Colonialism*. Princeton, NJ: Princeton University Press.

Mamdani, M. 2017. *When Victims Become Killers: Colonialism, Nativism, and the Genocide in Rwanda*. Kampala: Fountain Publishers.

Manzella, J. 2008. The star's first draft: A news organization revises the next narrative of race in post-apartheid South Africa. *Culture and Organisation*, 14(3): 261–277.

Mbembe, A. 2015. *On the Postcolony*. Johannesburg: Wits University Press.

McLuhan, M. 1964. *Understanding the Media: The Extensions of Man*. New York: New American Library.

Mignolo, W.D. 2007. Delinking. *Cultural Studies*, 21(2–3): 449–514.

Mignolo, W.D. 2009. Epistemic disobedience: Independent thought and de-colonial freedom. *Theory, Culture and Society*, 26(7–8): 159–181.

Mignolo, W.D. 2011. *The Darker Side of Western Modernity: Global Features, Decolonial Futures, Decolonial Options*. Durham, NC: Duke University Press.

Mignolo, W.D. 2016. Global coloniality and the world disorder. *World Public Forum* (blog), 29 January. http://wpfdc.org/blog/society/19627-global-coloniality-and-the-worlddisorder.

More, M.P. 2017. *Biko: Philosophy, Identity and Liberation*. Cape Town: HSRC Press.

Mpofu, S. and Chasi, C. 2017. Mandelaism in newspaper advertising that 'pays tribute' to Mandela after his death. *Journal of Literary Studies*, 33(4): 1–19.

Mudimbe, V.Y. 1988. *The Invention of Africa: Gnosis, Philosophy, and the Order of Knowledge*. Bloomington: Indiana University Press.

Ndlela, N. 2009. African media research in the era of globalisation. *Journal of African Media Studies*, 1(1): 55–68.

Ndlovu-Gatsheni, S.J. 2013. *Empire, Global Coloniality and African Subjectivity*. New York and Oxford: Berghahn Books.

Ndlovu-Gatsheni, S.J. 2015. Decoloniality as the future of Africa. *History Compass*, 13(10): 485–496.

Ndlovu-Gatsheni, S.J. 2018. *Epistemic Freedom in Africa: Deprovincialisation and Decolonisation*. London: Taylor and Francis.

Quijano, A. 2000. Coloniality of power, eurocentrism and latin America. *Nepantla*, 1(3): 533–580.

Quijano, A. 2007. Coloniality and modernity/rationality. *Cultural Studies*, 21(2–3): 168–178.

Renan, E. 1947. Qu'est-ce qu'une nation [1882]? In Psichari, H., ed. *Oeuvres complètes d'Ernest Renan*. Paris: Calmann-Lévy.

SABC Report. 2018. *Annual Report*. https://www.sabc.co.za/sabc/wp-content/uploads/2019/10/SABC_AR_2019_.pdf (Accessed 15 April 2019).

Schiller, H.I. 1976. *Communication and Cultural Domination*. New York: International Arts and Sciences Press.

Thompson, J.B. 1995. *The Media and Modernity: A Social Theory of the Media*. Cambridge: Polity Press.

Wasserman, H. and De Beer, A.S. 2012. A fragile affair: The relationship between mainstream media and government in post-apartheid South Africa. *Journal of Mass Ethics*, 20(2–3): 192–208. DOI:10.1080?0 8900523.2005.9679708.

wa Thiong'o, N. 2012. *Globalectics: Theory and the Politics of Knowing*. New York: Columbia University Press.

White, J.M. and Klein, D.M. 2002. *Family Theories*. Thousand Oaks, CA: Sage.

Wilderson, B. Frank. 2003. Gramsci's black Marx: Whither the slave in civil society. *Social Identities*, 9(2): 225, 240.

Willems, W. 2014. Beyond normative de Westernization: Examining media culture from the vantage point of the global South. *The Global South*, 8(1): 7–23. ISSN 1932-864.

Winter, S. 2003. Unsettling the coloniality of being/power/truth/freedom: Towards the human, after man, its overrepresentation – an argument. *The New Centennial Review*, 3(3): 257–337.

Wiredu, K. 1992. Moral foundations of an African culture. In Wiredu, K. and K. Gyekye, eds. *Person and Community: Ghanaian Philosophical Studies, 1*. Washington DC: The Council for Research in Values and Philosophy.

Wolf, R.E. 1982. *Europe and the People Without History*. Los Angeles: University of California Press.

8

Decolonising media and communication studies

An exploratory survey on global curricula transformation debates

Ylva Rodny-Gumede and Colin Chasi

Introduction

In 2015 and 2016, higher education institutions in South Africa were faced with widespread student protests calling for free access to higher education and broad-based transformation and decolonialisation of curricula. This triggered a nationwide debate around the lack of transformation and prevailing legacies of colonialism in higher education in the country. Such discussions are not necessarily unique, or isolated, to South Africa. Yet little is known about how these debates play themselves out within varying national, regional and international contexts, and importantly within different disciplinary fields.

It is generally accepted that the field and discipline of media and communication studies is becoming increasingly globalised and internationalised (Livingston 2007, 273). By media and communication studies we here refer to the broader discipline of communications, which we take to include subject fields such as media studies, journalism studies and strategic communication. At the very least there seems to have emerged a scholarly "consensus on the need to internationalize media studies . . . in an era characterized by an acceleration of globalization processes" (Ndlela 2007, 324). However, when scholars in the field speak of 'global' or 'international' scholarship, they rarely speak of theory of global or universal origins, diversity, inclusivity and significance. They instead tend to refer to theory from the global North (Willems 2014; Rodny-Gumede 2013; Freedman and Shafer 2010; Ndlela 2009; Curran and Park 2000; Sreberny 2000). The 'global' rarely means 'universal' (Sreberny 2000) and moves towards internationalising scholarship and the curriculum seemingly become exercises in extending the reach of a largely Westernised field of study rather than working towards a curriculum inclusive of a wide range of scholarship that goes beyond the Western cultural sphere of influence.

Instead of understanding the global South on its own terms and despite calls to "'dewesternize', 'decolonize', or 'internationalize'" the field of media and communication studies, the global South continues to be theorised from the vantage point of the global North (Willems 2014, 8). While scholarship in the global South as well as the global North in recent years has started to pay more attention to the polarisations of North and South, Chasi and Rodny-Gumede (2016) argue that such moves towards a recognition of a supposed changing global order and attempts at 'de-Westernising' (Curran and Park 2000) and even 'Southernising' (Rodny-Gumede 2015, 2013) of the discipline, have through Manichaean juxtaposing of North and South but reinforced the insularity of the discipline. Instead ideas of the global North continue to be the norm upon which the discipline is founded elsewhere.

This has the result that scholarship of the North as well as the South have "failed to acknowledge the agency of the global South in the production, consumption, and circulation of a much richer spectrum of media culture that is not a priori defined in opposition to or in conjunction with media from the Global North" (Willems 2014, 7).

This failure comes at the expense of recognising the fidelity for relevance of scholarly work, theory and experiences from the global South (Rodny-Gumede 2013; Comaroff and Comaroff 2011; Sreberny 2000, 114–115). Opportunities are thus tragically lost to see that the global South is not simply a victim of the North. The global South can, instead of being cast in victimhood terms, be seen "as a part of the world that has agency, a place from which we can start theorizing the human condition" (Willems 2014, 8). The renewed emphasis and calls for the decolonisation of all spheres of society, including higher education, have but emphasised the need for rethinking how scholarship not only maintains a Western domination of the field but also how it originates in, as well as perpetuates colonial legacies. As Moyo and Mutsvairo (2018, 29) say, the decolonisation of higher education and knowledge production is intimately linked to the false claims of universality of Western knowledge and the inherent Western geo- and body politics of knowledge production.

Through an exploratory reading of views on curricula from around the world, we ask whether the increasing calls for, as well as moves towards, the internationalisation of the media and communication disciplines also constitutes a move beyond the global North towards a truly global media and communication curricula that also recognises and encompasses the global South. And if so, we ask whether such curricula constitute a move towards a decolonisation of the curricula whether it is taught in the global North or global South. Thus, we seek to understand how decolonisation is understood and what constitutes the elements of decolonisation of the curriculum in differing contexts, as well as the challenges that confront efforts to decolonise the curriculum.

To do so, we engage local and international scholars from within our own discipline of media and communication studies, whose work variously safeguards and produces ideas of quality and relevance in higher education, around questions of, as well as meanings ascribed to, transformation and decolonisation of the curricula. We do this to contribute to disciplinary debates on transformation and decolonisation, and to contribute to the production of curricula that challenge the insularity of scholarship from the North, whether real or perceived. We seek to find ways in which to assert, as well as develop, media and communications curricula "symbolic of change, innovation, unity as well as diversity, rebirth and the development of adult learners to meet the challenges – locally and globally – of tomorrow" (du Plooy 2006, 190). In significant part we do this by drawing on the views of colleagues who kindly engaged with us through the survey, we provide an exploratory analysis that is firmly grounded in our own understanding of scholarly debates that foreground moral imperatives to produce a transformed and decolonised media and communication studies curricula.

In fairness to ourselves, we are not merely setting forth a select few views on the curricula. Instead, undergirding this chapter is the view that discourses on decolonisation do, and should, reaffirm "values and principles of integrity, social justice, fairness, and excellence" (du Plooy 2006, 189). We hope to hereby contribute to new processes that variously humanise ourselves and others involved in disciplines we research and teach in. In brief, our aim is threefold. First, we explore conceptualisations of decolonisation and what the elements of decolonisation of the curriculum are as well as the challenges posed to a decolonisation of the curriculum. Second, we hope the discussion will contribute towards the production of a decolonised curricula. Third, in doing so, we hope to contribute to a process in which we humanise ourselves as well as colleagues in the discipline.

Decolonisation debates

We are well aware that we write from a Southern African context lodged within centuries of colonialism and later apartheid and its aberrations. Here, as elsewhere where colonial relations have held sway, both colonisers and the colonised have left marks on each other (wa Thiong'o 2012, 51). One could fancy that the colonised appropriate the best of what their coloniser imposes, to produce an ideal new synthesis (ibid). But, then, one also has to contend with the view that the history of both colonies and of postcolonies involves repetitions and gross distortions of native cultures, customs and traditions, along with the entanglements, appropriations and deformations of the modernity that drove Western colonialism (Mbembe 2001, 25). The latter view is likely at stake in debates on transformation and decolonisation that continue to hold sway in Southern Africa today. For, throughout the region, amidst public concern about the stubborn persistence of colonial legacies, scholars as well as university leaderships continue to rethink their engagements with students and other stakeholders in ways that can be expected to change the structural and epistemic orientations of the higher education system. In this context, processes are underway to rethink the place of higher education in relation to political, economic, social and cultural developments and trajectories hereof.

Partially as a result of the influence of global movements that bring together new combinations of peoples, ideas, goods and services (wa Thiong'o 2012, 52), we also know that debates, on transformation and decolonisation, are of global relevance. In the West, when transformation issues are at stake within the discipline, diversity is couched as a question of dealing with new flows of people, goods, ideas and services that bring previously marginal international influences to bear (cf. wa Thiong'o 2012, 52). With regards to internationalisation, Livingston (2007) argues that it is not always clear what internationalisation means, and while it might mean the "exchanging knowledge and understanding across borders", equally it could mean a strive towards "achieving a shared consensus regarding theories, methods and approaches". If the latter, Livingston (ibid) argues that internationalisation stands the risk of

> becoming a Trojan horse, smuggling in the priorities or perspectives of some at the expense of others. Indeed, the more ambitious one becomes for the internationalising effort, the more sceptical voices come to the fore, concerned that the perspectives of the already-powerful dominate over that of others.

To paraphrase Grosfoguel (2008, 64), such projects instead become exercises in ensuring that we all think epistemically alike, i.e. aligned to Western dominant thought in whatever discipline or field we might be. In this regard, internationalisation projects fail to become projects of diversification and de-Westernisation (Curran and Park 2000, 3).

Global debates about the transformation of the media and communications curriculum are not new, and date back to the UNESCO International Commission for the Study of Communication Problems established in 1977 and the subsequent Many Voice One World, or the so-called MacBride report (UNESCO 1980), that called for democratisation of media and communication technologies. Importantly, the report warned against universally adaptable models, an argument also furthered in the 1982 Grünwald Declaration on Media Education (UNESCO 1982) which explicitly states that while "responsible" educators will not ignore international media developments and instead "work alongside their students in understanding them", they should not "underestimate the impact on cultural identity of the flow of information and ideas between cultures by the mass media". This statement reflects the need for a curriculum that reflects local realities as a basis for the analysis of global frameworks and developments rather than the other way around (cf. Rodny-Gumede 2013).

Neither are debates on transformation and decolonisation unique to South Africa or to postcolonial domains. Academics around the world need to continuously engage with questions of the relevance of curricula amidst changing global world orders. Across the world scholars face the need to rethink what is taught, including how scholarship and curricula can undo lingering colonial legacies and contribute to a humanising development. Arguably, the groundswell of pressure for change indicates it is time we recognise that experiences and scholarship of the global South are not only equal to those of the global North, but also necessary for the advancement of our discipline as a whole and more humanising bodies of scholarship. The theoretical point is that we need to find ways to rethink higher education and scholarship not only in South Africa and the greater postcolonial world, but also in the global North. In doing this we recognise that higher education programmes and research from the global North continue to be standard bearers, or markers of the norm for curricula and scholarship worldwide. At the same time, and to make the point, deliberately or otherwise, dominant Western scholarship reflects and treats Northern histories as though *the rest* either do not exist or only exist to the extent that they either aid or do not interfere with Northern doctrinal theorisations (cf. Chasi and Rodny-Gumede 2016; Willems 2014). To this end, and in the process, Western scholarship denies globally shared humanities, shared histories and shared futures (Chasi and Rodny-Gumede 2016).

There is little for us to gain here in tracing out all the similarities and differences between projects of internationalisation and de-Westernisation in the initial conceptualisation of the concept as set out by Curran and Park (2000). We do however note that Waisbord (2015) argues that the project of de-Westernisation entails much more than merely broadening the geographical scope of enquiries to also consider case studies from the global South, and that to think so narrowly of de-Westernisation might lead to a consolidation of our enquiries into balkanised forms of area studies. Instead Waisbord argues for a cosmopolitan approach to de-Westernisation and for an openness to studying a range of global problems and academic issues in such a capacious fashion that "rather than being restrained by geographical divisions, de-Westernisation should help to expand analytical perspectives and bring theoretical and comparative questions to the forefront of media studies" (ibid, 178).

And equally, while the projects of de-Westernisation and decolonisation of media and communications scholarship and the curricula are not comparable, there are overlapping concerns. An independently, projects of transformation within the discipline have neglected aspects of transformation lodge within the global South and many postcolonial societies in particular, where colonialism has left have left incommunicable scars on society and its citizens. The legacies of colonialism and the continuous inequities it has created has made sure that state formation, politics and socioeconomic development in the postcolony have remained premised on race. In the postcolony, "race continues to be a marker of social difference, hierarchy and pain" (Frassinelli 2018, 4). The formal end of colonialism or apartheid and its aberrations in southern Africa did not bring an end to the socioeconomic injustices, power hierarchies and suppression of indigenous and local knowledges that these systems created (ibid). This has also come with particular implications for women, and the particular bounds of black women, and the male dominance of the discipline is hard to ignore (Orgeret 2018, 352).

The call for the decolonisation of media and communication studies as Wasserman (2018, 50) argues inevitably is concerned with "the shared experience of a colonial subjection, struggles for independence and continued geopolitical and economic marginalisation in the era of globalisation suggest that a study of media on the continent should include a focus on the lived experiences of Africans in relation to such media, embedded as these are within unequal local and global power relations". Decolonisation efforts are thus efforts to break with Western modernity and to search for alternative modernities (Mignolo 2011). And beyond, in the words of Fanon (1963, 36), decolonisation is a programme of completely changing the world. Fanon talks about complete disruption, a disruption that within our discipline is yet to be felt, let alone realised.

Thus it is not the querying of colonial legacies and the challenging of them we are concerned with, however defining such efforts and the moments they have created have been through the work of African scholars such as Nyamnjoh (2011; 2005), wa Thiong'o (1986), Fanon (1963), instead what concerns us is the impact, or lack hereof, that the decolonisation project has had on the discipline. The transformational issues that are at stake when envisioning decolonisation, as du Plooy (2006, 189–190) sets out, have serious implications for everyone involved in higher education, and the media and communication discipline in particular. Most importantly, decolonisation presupposes transformations in intellectual discourses, in the formal and informal content of teaching/learning and in research endeavours and services to the community. It presupposes of such significance that the whole of the societies in question – including businesses and industries – come to address African needs in ways that are consistent with African values, worldviews and mindsets (Chasi 2018, 2015). And we add that decolonisation speaks to the emergence of new conceptions of the global–local nexus that more justly serve the needs and aspirations of people without subordinating some to centres that are not composed of their own needs. Ngũgĩ wa Thiong'o (1993) insightfully argued that decolonisation involves challenging the dominant and dehumanising Western centre. He contends that it does this by bringing to the fore complementary, supplementary, separate and related centres that take as their starting, or centering points, local experiences and perspectives of people from all over the world so that there emerge with multiple, complementary and competing centres (ibid). wa Thiong'o (2012) talks about a 'Globalectic' approach to the curricula founded on a mindfulness of reading texts from within their context, i.e. a curriculum fit for the purpose that it serves. Globalectics or the 'politics of knowing' entails the development of a new dialectic in which the curricula is "approached from whatever times and places to allow its contents and themes to form a free conversation with other texts of one's own time and place and to allow it to speak to our own cultural present and to read it with the eyes of the world and to see the world with the eyes of the text" (ibid, 38). A most important matter is that education should be centred on the needs and experiences of those it serves, the point of departure must always, as wa Thiong'o (2012, 57) says, be "from here to there". When this happens, education serves the ends of social justice. Social justice in education has often focussed on classroom pedagogies and educational practices to combat different forms of oppression such as racism and sexism. This needs to be taken further to recognise that as educators we have a role to play in dismantling all forms of oppression and the barriers and pain they create. Educators should be in the business of creating new and more just social orders both in and beyond classrooms and universities, and because justice truly knows no boarders. We should be involved in generating more socially just curricula, teaching environments, education systems and environments in the global South as well as in global North.

Thus, the fundamental aims of projects for the decolonisation of knowledge and of the curriculum must be linked to broader aims of ensuring relevance of curricula and teaching practices – challenging as well as changing normalised misanthropic orders. Decolonisation aims at overcoming legacies steeped in, as well as enforced through, the remnants of, and continuations, of our own (and global) histories of slavery, colonialism and apartheid with their aberrations that manifest throughout the world. Decolonial educators thus facilitate debates and research that etch out new notions and possibilities for more relevant universities that reflect and produce social justice.

Decolonial practices trigger debates around how we should better form, reform and adapt curricula in the different contexts in which these curricula are served. Most pertinently, the Western dominance has been taken as a colonial legacy, and as such calls have been heard for a decolonisation of the curriculum. In some instances, such calls have been expressed as a need for an Africanisation of the same (Motsaathebe 2011; Mano 2009; Nyamnjoh 2005). In other instances, decolonisation is equated with a more generalised idea of localisation of content to fit specific needs in the context that it serves. What remains constant is that such calls are for recognising that a broader transformation of the curriculum has to take place in order to challenge dominant and Northern epistemologies and ideas of truth within the media and communications discipline, and to thereby dare scholars to see the inherent insularity of the ways in which the discipline has continuously created and re-created an epistemology lodged in archaic, patriarchal and decidedly racialised ideas that principally emanate from, and favour, the West (Chasi and Rodny-Gumede 2016). As scholars of media and communication studies, we see that epistemologies and disciplinary foundations that guide teaching, research and resource allocations are increasingly being challenged. A feature of these fields is that our scholarship must confront how people live and express their modes of existence through communication in ways that are variously mediated. So, to think of humanising the world from the perspective of studies of media and communication is not just to question how people and scholarship are diminished and denied dignity and worth. It is also to call to question how scholars have thus far claimed to engage with humanity.

Our starting point, as set out earlier, is that perspectives emanating from the global South have for long been neglected in media and communication scholarship in both the global North and global South. No more evident is this than in media and communication studies curricula, where scholarship as well as theories of communication and media studies of the global North are taken as the norm for the development of the curricula in the global South (Chasi and Rodny-Gumede 2018; 2016; Rodny-Gumede 2015; Mano 2009). We know that the problem faced by scholars in differing disciplines, including media and communication scholars, particularly in the global South, is that curricula as well as literature from the global North are often copied/mimicked/repeated without change or without critical engagement. In the interest of advancing a decolonial perspective, with specific focus on media and communication studies, we will shortly go on to discuss views on current curricula from differing contexts, being particularly mindful of contending and complementary accents given to debates around transformation, diversification and decolonisation in various settings. Before this, let us briefly introduce the survey from which we draw the views to follow.

The survey

The findings are drawn from a survey sent out in the first quarter of 2016 to a broad scholarly community through 65 personal emails as well as through the email lists of the International Association for Media and Communications Research (IAMCR) and the South African Communications Association (SACOMM). In total, 31 responses were received and 30 were subsequently coded and recorded. The respondents represent 34 different universities (some respondents are associated with more than one university) from 14 countries (Australia, Brazil, China, Finland, France, India, Kenya, Nigeria, Norway, South Africa, Sweden, Switzerland, United Kingdom, United States and Zimbabwe).

Through the survey we sought answers to the following questions: What are the most pressing issues/debates with regards to questions of curricula and the relevance of curricula in different national/cultural contexts? Is Manichaean juxtapositions of global South and the global North a feature of debates around the curriculum, and if so, are such debates centred around a need to broaden the scope of scholarship, methodologies, course contents and teaching materials to encompass scholarship from the global South? To what extent are curricula centred on an epistemological approach that is inclusive of a diverse set of scholarship from a wide range of national and cultural contexts? What are some of the ways in which scholars from around the world understand and define the idea and call for a decolonialisation of curricula and knowledge production? And, what are the challenges of decolonising the curriculum? These questions correspond to the closed- and open-ended questions we posed to surveyed scholars. Respondents were informed that their identities would be held in confidence. As such, we have anonymised the identities of respondents in the text of this chapter, because we know these discussions are sensitive and, in some contexts, even shunned. We have ourselves seen the consequences of articulating the need for decolonisation in various forums and how divisionary these debates can be.

As noted earlier, we consider this study to be exploratory in nature. The findings, from the sample we use, cannot claim to be representative of what global or local bodies of media and communications scholars think about the issues we are discussing. Thus, we are cautious to use the data to make generalisations. Nevertheless, we hold that the information gathered and analysed does provide insights into, and in some instances even a rich understanding of, issues pertaining to the weight and meanings ascribed to the decolonisation of media and communications curricula. We hope that it can be used to start a discussion around varying takes on transformation, diversity and inclusivity of the media and communication curricula and contribute to further research.

We are also aware that discussions with samples and populations of academics can only constitute a start to what must become larger transformative conversations. After all a "university is not only a teaching/learning environment, it is also a life-world in which lecturers and learners meet in a context which is broader than the parochial didactic relationship" (du Plooy 2006, 206). Lecturers and researchers in higher education do not function in a political or social void, so our ability to conceive of and implement decolonising changes will have to entail "collaboration with diverse role-players, especially the adult learner" (ibid).

Our approach of engaging with our local and international survey participants is a significant but small nod to the serious need to heed Ngũgĩ wa Thiong'o (1993) and recognise, produce and respectfully represent multiple centres in our scholarship. We do this while trying to centre our own otherwise marginalised location in the world. However, we are very cautious of the need to not engage with the survey responses in a way that juxtaposes responses from the global South with those of the global North in a Manichaean zero-sum fashion. Instead, by being constantly self-reflexive about our positionalities as scholars of the South, we have attempted to ensure that our pursuit of a more just educational enterprise does not result in a reading that constantly, apologetically and even vengefully and unjustly pits scholarship from the North against scholarship from the South. We do not assume that all that is of the North is harmful and that all that is of the South is good and desirable. But admittedly we look to the data with the systematic objective of understanding how a decolonial agenda that is transformative towards inclusiveness and justice can be promoted and enabled through the curricula. To do otherwise, we contend, would be to deny the multitude of factors that play a role in scholarly engagements with, and developments around, curriculum development.

What follows is a discussion of the responses to our survey questions and some of the more salient themes that can be discerned.

Views on the decolonisation of media and communication curricula

In what follows various themes are identified as we seek to reveal, explore and interrelate views on curricula that arose from our reading of the responses to the survey. These themes are evidently not distinct and unrelated. Instead, as they speak to the same core concerns about decolonisation, they also variously speak across and into each other in ways that the reader is encouraged to enjoy and find additional insights from. We do however hope that our thematic organisation of what we found makes parsimonious sense of what we found while giving heuristic order to these findings.

A 'Western' bias in how curricula are established

The responses from all respondents emphasise that there is a clear 'Western' bias in how curricula are established, as exemplified by these responses: "In South Africa despite calls for transformation we still follow the same curricula as in the U.K. and the U.S. and we use the same teaching materials" (Respondent 13, South Africa) and "we are still beholden to a curriculum that is mainly European and 'Western' with little relevance to South Africa and the students we teach" (Respondent 23, South Africa). From African contexts other than South Africa, respondents equally emphasise that: "We follow a very Westernised curriculum in Kenya, local content is not valued" (Respondent 11, Kenya). Significantly, respondents from outside African equally lamented this state of affairs saying, for instance: "Journalism education in the US tends to be very US-centric" (Respondent 17, U.S.) or that "we almost only use US and British textbooks. . . . And experts from the global South really only come to us if they work elsewhere in the global North" (Respondent 5, U.S.). The point is not necessarily that there is a total absence of curricula materials that come from or that reference the South. Rather, it is that when the 'South' is factored in, it is done so in ways that are still mainly ad hoc and in separate courses or modules, and as "African examples as an exception and maybe even appeasement or to tick a box" (Respondent 30, Zimbabwe).

What is emphasised by the South African scholars is the imperative of striking a balance between influences, experiences, as well as a canon of scholarship from both the global South and the global North. This is also connected to an idea of not falling into or pandering to isolationist approaches that say reject all supposed Western ideas. This sentiment is well reflected in the following response:

> I am not saying we can or should completely discard the canon of literature that has informed much of the discipline, but it needs to be contextualised and new scholarly arguments and texts brought to the fore.
>
> *(Respondent 23, South Africa)*

Rather than accepting Manichaean juxtapositions or zero-sum curricula gamesmanship, what is asked for is a "more nuanced debate that does not assume that everything from the north needs abandoning and everything from the south is now relevant" (Respondent 16, South

Africa). The realisation here, which is echoed in the responses of many of the other southern African respondents, is that our scholarship is enhanced in its interactions with preceding bodies of scholarship. One function of a canon is that it elevates scholars by enabling them to learn from an organised and prearranged body of knowledge so that they conceptually stand on the shoulders of those who have preceded them. The nuanced thought is that scholarship from the South is part of human cultural evolutions of knowledge and is best developed when it plays, intermingles, interbreeds and freely cohabitates with other epistemic sources and forms.

While the balance between imperatives and scholarship is emphasised, this does not justify any minimisation of differences that are found between what scholars see. Differences in the historical positions that people occupy are significant; they yield valuable varieties of epistemic products. When different people, with their unique biographies, stand on the shoulders of scholars who preceded them, they will not see the same things in the same ways. Together with the call for a finer and fairer contextualisation of scholarship and literature, that recognises the legitimacy of different paths and places in which knowledge is sought and produced, a nuanced thought is that there are elevating prospects for all humanity wherever there is respectful meeting of knowledge practices that have different pedigrees, wherever people lift each other up so that each can see further than before. This value is lost wherever curricular remain colonial to the effect of blocking students from seeing from their own historical perspective, or from vantage points that value their own contextually encountered needs and concerns. Something of this is seen in responses from colleagues teaching in similar postcolonial contexts to that of South Africa who bemoan a lack of contextualisation by which local knowledge is neglected as universities fail to adequately train students to think critically about and from their own contexts. As this respondent says:

> there is a critical gap especially that of training students to be problem solvers within their unique contexts. Most 'western' theories have not been properly contextualized for the students to make sense of their relevance in their setting.
>
> *(Respondent 11, Kenya)*

And:

> I think one of the most pressing issues is about the curriculum reflecting the economic (industrial) political, social needs of the community in which it is tailored for. . . . It is about whether the current curricula connect the learner to his/her context of existence, or it is a perpetuation of the colonial system by 'softer' means?
>
> *(Respondent 3, Zimbabwe)*

We note such responses as an affirmation of how hermeneuticists and semioticians have long established the way in which texts are given different meanings in different historical contexts, by different people giving differing meanings to and conducting differing readings of texts. Realising this, and appreciating that canons can be made and unmade, arranged and rearranged, we note that what many scholars who are located in postcolonial contexts are calling for are *acts of appropriation of the media and communications canon that involve bringing old and new texts into conversations*. They are, in some respect affirming the fact that it is the readers, i.e. the scholars and students of today, whose interpretations are being facilitated and maybe also validated through this process. Part of the point is to recognise localities in the global South as points of reference alongside other histories. In one instance this entails recognising, for instance, that "Africa and

South Africa has a rich media and journalistic history that is all its own, and our teaching should draw on that extensively" (Respondent 27, South Africa).

There emerges a deep appreciation of what canons are and how they enable us to draw on archives of texts-of-practice that are developed by the intersecting paroles and histories of a South African and African "rich media and journalistic history that is all its own (sic)". Giving epistemic value to experiences, perspectives, practices and texts from the South is a vital political step that at base is about giving recognition to previously denied and marginalised peoples, their capabilities and their readings.

Nothing is left uncontested. How decolonisation is achieved, how imperatives are balanced, and how roles and weights are given to Manichaean juxtapositions between North/South, African/Western/European, global/local – these and more core issues are all contested. Beyond historical antagonisms between North and South, or the West and *the rest*, and beyond their "impact on the local identifications/definitions" (Respondent 1, South Africa), there is the overarching imperative to transformatively advance scholarship that is, as one South African respondent says, not "reactionary and mediocre", i.e. that valorises "local knowledge and its global relevance" while "critically examining, from a situated perspective, any important idea and theory, no matter where it comes from (Respondent 13, South Africa). It should "mean looking at the whole world from a critical perspective rooted in our own African context" (Respondent 13, South Africa).

What meanings then are ascribed to relevance and contexts in which curricula is developed?

The need to recognise context

The need for a revised curriculum whether articulated as 'decolonised', 'localised' or 'Africanised' is at the forefront of debates in South Africa and southern Africa. These debates are also tied up with wider debates around how "we problematize binaries of African/European/the West, in ways that does not reinforce, re-essentialise or also ignore intra-African/intra-Western differences and hierarchies" (Respondent 12, South Africa). This also applies to "binaries of constructions that homogenise racial groups, whether Black/White or African/Western" (Respondent 12, South Africa).

It is clear from the South African scholars surveyed that such debates are about the need for recognising the African and indigenous scholarship which is excluded from the curricula. This is in the interest of (1) addressing injustices of the past and (2) making curricula fit for the served contexts. What is clear from the responses from the South African scholars surveyed is that the imperative for localising and decolonising the curriculum has resurfaced as one of the most important aspect of transformation in higher education: "without a doubt the decolonisation debate is the most pressing one" (Respondent 19, South Africa) and "The decolonisation of the curriculum is a priority and we can no longer ignore our own context" (Respondent 23, South Africa). In addition, there is "urgency to support localised/Africanised content" (Respondent 1, South Africa).

With regards to debates around the curricula and the relevance of curricula in different national contexts, we know from the recent events that have rocked the South African higher education landscape that issues around transformation and a decolonisation of the curricula has been made a priority. Most South African universities have also formalised these discussions through university-wide structures such as their senate bodies and departmental teaching and learning committees. This also comes through in the responses from colleagues in the region and from scholars working in societies where the colonial experience has and continues to shape higher education and the curricula.

Defragmenting the hold of colonial epistemes

Independent of context or region, our surveyed scholars link the debates around the curricula to practical skills and employability of graduates. However there are variations in how this is interpreted from within local contexts. Our African respondents, in particular, argued that valuing employability and competitiveness does not entail accepting 'wholesale' or 'without change' ideas, epistemologies or schema from the North. They argued for "defragmenting the hold of colonial epistemes" (Respondent 16, South Africa) and for the emergence of "knowledge production that is sensitive to contexts and that thus addresses the history of South Africa" (Respondent 12, South Africa). They thus spoke for a curriculum:

> that undermines the power of canons, that integrates scholarship from around the world without assuming that source/location equates to value, that emphasises the importance of people speaking for and about themselves and their communities, that includes the voices of women, queer people, people with various genders and sexualities, people of colour, disabled people.
>
> *(Respondent 15, South Africa)*

And that:

> address issues that are relevant to students in the global South. Issues that have to do with governance in the African context for instance without just using the western concept of democracy, poverty, capitalism issues of ethnicity and identity should all form core of the curriculum to minimize 'confusion' and some sort of identity crisis of future generations.
>
> *(Respondent 11, Kenya)*

Most pertinently there seems to be a divide between the global South and the global North, with regards to the need for transformation and the reasons behind such transformation. Overall, scholars of the South emphasise breaking with Western hegemony and colonial legacies and the need for redress and social justice to higher extent than their global North counterparts who emphasise issues with regards to a changing media landscape as central to debates around a curriculum 'fit for purpose'.

Questions around employability of university graduates

And, while there is a stronger emphasis on the decolonisation of scholarship among scholars in the postcolony, the debate and considerations around the curricula outside of the postcolony are to a higher degree centred on issues around skills, employability in the context of a discipline as well as higher education landscape which are heavily influenced and challenged by rapid technological changes. Two colleagues, from Finland and the U.S. respectively, argued that "the most critical question is the employment of university graduates. . . . Job places of permanent employment is declining, the number of short contracts is growing" (Respondent 6, Finland) and "questions of curriculum have focused on what to teach students to prepare them for the changing journalism landscape . . . and how the curriculum can be adapted to include more technical components" (Respondent 17, U.S.).

This is not to say that these issues are not important or that they should not be considered in any context. Neither, is it to say that the decolonisation debate cannot be disassociated or delinked from debates concerning technological developments and the relevance of the curricula with regards to the employability of the students. However, as seen in the response from this respondent from India, the decolonisation debate demands that we contextually re-evaluate and rebalance the relative weight given to developing practical skills vis-à-vis focusing on theoretical knowledge – and even then while thinking carefully about what knowledge counts and why:

> We debate the relative value of developing practical skills versus more theoretical knowledge to a higher degree than a localized curriculum however.
> *(Respondent 7, India)*

And:

> Local content and context are important and so is the global. Media studies and the media is heavily influenced by global forces, however this does not mean that we do not use local examples. The Indian media sector is big and also counts many regional perspectives that have to be included in the curriculum.
> *(Respondent 7, India)*

This is all linked to globally shared concerns regarding the employability of graduates amidst a rapidly changing media industry. Scholars are constantly seized with the need to evaluate what this means for the training of media and communications students.

What could constitute decolonised curricula

This is expressed in questions around what could constitute decolonised curricula, as well as diversity in the curricula and to what extent the curricula is centred on an epistemological approach that is inclusive of a diverse set of scholarship from a wide range of national and cultural contexts. While the need for decolonising and revaluing African and Southern experiences is broadly shared by South African scholars, there are differences of interpretation and accentuations which are resultant from ancillary debates around the meaning of words such as 'local', 'de-Westernised', 'decolonised' and 'African'. These words remain unclear and are sometimes confusedly used interchangeably. How these expressions are applied and how meanings are ascribed to them remains a source of contention. One respondent explains this thus:

> That we need change I think is beyond dispute and as much as we might still find colleagues resisting change, the transformation of what we teach and how we teach is unavoidable and the demands of our students are clear. The 'what' and 'how' remains a question though, is a decolonised curricula a more localised curricula, or an African curricula? I see it as a curricula that takes account of varying influences and factors that have a bearing on the contemporary local as well as global political, social, financial, environmental landscape etc.
> *(Respondent 23, South Africa)*

Amidst fraught postcolonial histories and politics, contestations over readings of transformation is not so strange. Overall though, the scholars of the South that we surveyed mainly took decolonisation as meaning "social justices and redress" (Respondent 7, India), "enforcement of human rights" (Respondent 18, Brazil) and as referring to work that aims to "de-hegemonize higher education" (Respondent 10, Nigeria). In contrast, our respondents from the North rarely accentuate the colonial heritage and the need to decolonise as a means of undoing historical injustices and human rights abuses.

For our respondents from the global North, focus tended to still seemingly fall on the perceived 'global' and 'international' aspects of media and communications and technological developments. This is to say, "we are more inclined to speak of the 'internationalization' of media studies, by which we mean including non-European and non-Anglo-Saxon perspectives" (Respondent 2, Sweden). It is also to intimate that there is strong merit to "expanding the canon to go beyond Anglo-American scholars and include research and scholarship from other contexts especially the developing world" (Respondent 17, U.S.). So while "decolonisation is a good and accurate label for an important part of the gigantic tasks of defeating cultural (and political and economic) racism and imperialism in higher education, it would be a slightly less important sub-task" (Respondent 5, U.S.). This can be further explicated in terms of there being, among scholars from the North, "a tendency to concentrate on new technologies – gadget research [so that what emerges is] a very isolationist approach that defies an understanding of [other] historical contexts" and issues with their political and ideological considerations (Respondent 8, Norway).

To be sure, though, it is important to state carefully that our respondents from the North recognised that there is "need to mainstream equity, diversity and inclusion across all courses" (Respondent 4, U.K.). One spoke of the usefulness of courses that advance "cultural diversities" (Respondent 5, U.S.). Another said it is important to build decolonised curricula as a matter of "getting rid of stereotypes of thinking, which naturally inherent to those who know little or very little interested in other cultures or know only from books and movies" (Respondent 6, Finland). Yet another respondent from the North made the fundamental point that decolonisation can in these ways be thought of as a way "to redress the structural – often racially inflected – inequities that are the product of longer processes of colonialism within the institutional spaces of the university" (Respondent 4, U.K.). Seemingly, such discussions at British universities sometimes emanates from a need for being more inclusive of students from the former British Colonies with debates at British universities "framed in the context of globalization and the changing demographics of student populations at British universities" (Respondent 4, U.K.).

Yet other scholars challenge the idea of decolonisation, seeing it as "opportunistically led by people who feel discriminated because of their race, colour etc. [but have yet to] provide evidence that they can also perform at the highest level" (Respondent 24, UK) or even "[a]s a very isolationist approach that defies an understanding of historical contexts. Authoritarian and one that does not see the relationship between an historical political process and ideological concepts" (Respondent 8, Norway).

Such differing views also talk to the challenges faced by those who work to change the curricula and those who work towards a decolonised curriculum.

Challenges facing the decolonisation agenda

Part of the challenge facing the decolonisation agenda is that it is working to end something that has served some people well, even within the context of the generally marginalised South. Not everyone in the colonised world has been disadvantaged in the same way by the dominance of Western scholarship. Those who have been content to take up prominent roles in the 'global echo chamber of ideas' have been content to observe how they are cited and repeated – when they know that they themselves have merely echoed Western myths and misconceptions about Africans and about peoples of the South. To the extent that decolonisation is aimed at ending cycles of racism, exclusion and power imbalances, it threatens to unsettle established economies of priority and prestige. To this end, a decolonised higher education works against means and norms of "corruption, sexism, racism etc. in the workplace" (Respondent 12, South Africa). It is difficult to know "how to kill patriarchal sexist and racist colonial attitudes" (Respondent 16, South Africa), because this entails imagining and producing a whole new world that is beyond our ken.

For academics, administrators, managers and policy makers, decolonisation is challenging because it restacks and resets frames so that new stakeholder relationships arise as important where they were previously marginalised. Sometimes this means that decolonisation broaches new relational frontiers with the consequence that in certain instances curricula building and teaching are hamstrung by a severe shortage of both a scholarly canon and a substantial enough scholarly community to advance the requisite change. As this South African respondent says:

> I find it difficult to decide on new/other 'truths' when I myself have been schooled in the old truths. To recurriculise implies that whoever works with it, knows enough of the roots of our science, the inherent prejudices, traditional and current postcolonial and non-Western theory or paradigms and the relevance thereof in a 2016-and-beyond South Africa. There are precious few academics that have the competence to address that.
>
> *(Respondent 14, South Africa)*

This is emphasised not only by South African scholars but also by other scholars teaching and researching from with the context of the postcolony:

> In order to prepare relevant curricula for the global South in general and Africa in particular on journalism and media studies, I faced severe short of experts who can participate in this debate. I am writing this based on my experiences of teaching in Eritrea.
>
> *(Respondent 9, India)*

This is also emphasised by this U.K scholar who argues that much of the research done on African media and communications does not necessarily emanate from African scholars or localities:

> The decolonisation of curricula heavily depends on the availability of knowledge produced elsewhere. While in recent years, there has been quite a sharp growth in research on African media and communication (including a number of new journals), not all the research could be referred to as 'decolonised', and much work applies Western concepts to the African context rather uncritically.
>
> *(Respondent 4, U.K)*

In all respects, decolonisation brings with it the need:

> To bring in local examples and to recognize that we are not the US or Europe. We need to develop the curriculum to talk to our own nation and the problems we are facing. We need to start a national dialogue that raises questions of importance to us. And we need to have examples and learning material from around the world not only the US literature or European literature.
>
> *(Respondent 18, Brazil)*

In this conversation the previously marginal are radically made new centres of decision-making that must be engaged with respectfully. So, for example:

> We need to respect the value of the experiences of our students, as well as their expectations and perspectives on issues. And for those of us who bring privileges of gender, race, class etc. into teaching and into the debate about transformation, we need to be particularly aware of our own position.
>
> *(Respondent 27, South Africa)*

The latter also talks to how decolonisation debates brings to the fore the need for us as educators to become more self-reflexive. Without us necessarily having chosen this, we increasingly find ourselves positioned also as 'students' in the sense of having to learn new ways of relating to existing as well as discarded or forgotten scholarship and methodologies. No more so than in relation to our own students who show that we must go beyond our own miseducation, often shaped by 'Western' cognitive schema, perspectives and epistemologies, no matter how challenging and in addition from the perspective of one who is aware of the need to teach scholarship that is relevant to the deep and neglected needs of marginalised peoples of the South and other marginalised peoples, whose development needs do not need to be exaggerated to gain acceptance, there is something "offensive" about teaching from a curricula "fraught with Westernness or Europeanness . . . packed with stereotypes about third world countries and individuals and sings praises for the Western/European (so-called) modern societies" (Respondent 12, South Africa).

Thus, decolonisation implies saying 'no more' to historical legacies and social injustices that emanate from slavery, colonisation and apartheid which are then enforced and perpetuated through Westernised impositions and influences that disconnect the merit of education from needs and realities found in postcolonial contexts. Thus, the question is, as quoted earlier, whether "the current curricula connect the learner to his/her context of existence or is it a perpetuation of the colonial system by 'softer' means?" (Respondent 3, Zimbabwe).

The problem of how to decolonise is not just related to a real or perceived offensiveness of commentary and content, it is also one related to the productive and institutional consequences of the processes that, in the postcolony and wider global South, subordinate universities and their curricula to neocolonial positions and orders. Whereas universities may be ideally imagined to ceaselessly produce innovative research, and whereas scholars are expected to teach in ways that deliver and are informed by virtuous cycles of innovative insights, in many cases scholars find that, in their universities, they are instead made to adapt and to relay "models copied from the global North – that . . . renders the copiers inferior" (Respondent 10, Nigeria). This experience of undergoing cycles of repetition and duplication "stifles the creativities of the global South higher education system and perpetuates a hegemonic stance" (Respondent 10, Nigeria) in often viciously misanthropic cycles.

The decolonisation of the curriculum relates to a whole set of resource issues, pertinently summarised by this scholar:

> The issue of decolonisation is intricately linked to resources and cannot just be treated as an ideological issue. For it to be addressed, there is a need for a radical change in the structural inequalities between scholars and universities in different parts of the world. It would require more resources (i.e. time away from teaching and research funding without conditionality) to enable scholars in the global South to produce research, while at the same time, it would require scholars in the global North to engage more seriously with knowledge produced in/on the global South and to acknowledge that their own research on the global North is partial and contextual. . . . this is not unrelated to the conditionalities

attached to certain types of research funding and the rise of what Mandani has called 'consultancy culture'.

(Respondent 4, U.K.)

There are impediments to transformation that are caused by the increased commodification of higher education that "has eroded the very focus and role of higher education in developing societies" (Respondent 11, Kenya). A South African respondent says:

> the underlying question is whether the university can still be thought as a space for critical thinking and the pursuit of knowledge (or an approximation of it); or whether we should resign ourselves to the idea of the university as a managerial, top-down, commodified, branded, ranked, corporatized and securitised institution. If the latter, the question of decolonisation would be at best window dressing.
>
> *(Respondent 13, South Africa)*

Universities are not islands apart from other forces in the world. The possibility of decolonisation of curricula is tied to how other operations in the world determine what is feasible or not. Internally, within national boundaries, universities are subjected to economic and other pressures that drive the composition of curricula in various directions, even without these forces being fully deterministic. "With the current funding crisis in South Africa resources are going to be crucial. If not forthcoming we are unlikely to be able to bring about change" (Respondent 26, South Africa). Externally, Southern states and their universities are bound up in international, multilateral and global dynamics that carry and perpetuate colonial momentums. Just one tip of this is that "there are huge discrepancies in funding and the support received by scholars at African universities compared to their colleagues in the West" (Respondent 30, Zimbabwe). Largely, the global South continues to consume information the global North dumps. This is seen in how "course literature is imported from the north, for the simple reason that it is often cheaper than developing new scholarly material" (Respondent 18, Brazil). At the same time, generally, the global North does not cease to extract and process knowledge from the global South for its own ends. In consequence, "[t]he lack of necessary handbooks to support curricula based on a local/African epistemology will probably continue to hinder the Africanisation of curricula" (Respondent 1, South Africa).

Overall decolonisation remains a challenge, not only from perspectives of diversification and transformation of contents in the curriculum and the weight given to such a project, but also in terms of the question of how resources are to be found for purposes of actualising such projects. This is particularly pertinent if such projects are to be driven from comparatively under resourced universities in the global South.

Concluding remarks

Postcolonial universities have generally adopted Western communications and media scholarship, root and branch. This adoption is deep-rooted in the ways in which it is fed and grounded in national and international systems of governance and capital that determine much of what is visually observable at the surface. Those who fight for decolonisation of higher education must find ways to uproot systems which are currently in place and to replace these with new kinds that are democratic and answerable to previously denied and marginalised publics. It is then that we can begin to see the emergence of a university "whose identity is true to its contextualised existence. . . . [For] to decolonialize is to move towards one's own realistic, responsible essence"

(Respondent 14, South Africa). The resultant decolonised university is an ideal that humanises by making universities better reflective of both the differences, similarities, limitations and possibilities presented by peoples and their concerns.

Our exploratory survey shows a broad consensus around the need for transformation of the media and communications studies discipline, and the curricula in particular. However, how such transformations are defined and envisioned and how they relate and are interpreted from perspectives of a decolonisation agenda is contested. And where the African scholars surveyed as well as many other scholars from postcolonial societies emphasise the need, and actual calls for, curriculum transformation and a decolonisation of the curriculum, scholars from the global North seemingly emphasise slightly different issues influencing debates around the curriculum. Not unexpectedly, these differences come through in the relative weight given to debates around a decolonisation of the curricula premised on human rights, social justice, equity and redress versus an emphasis on broader inclusivity and diversity of scholarship from the South, that may or may not address deeper issues of colonial legacies and injustices, as well as debates centred on technological developments, quality assurance and employability of graduates.

The debate about decolonisation, to the extent that it entails questions of relevance, resourcing and the meeting needs, also has to be read as a confirmation of the relative weight given to debates around transformation of the curriculum, i.e. whether broader transformation debates are centred around the need for inclusivity, diversity and an undoing of a 'Western'-centric worldview shaped by, and enmeshed in, legacies of the colonial project. In this regard, the survey responses do reflect a disjuncture in the way that 'transformation' needs are interpreted as well as reflected in the curricula from within differing national, regional and international contexts. This is, as emphasised earlier, reflected through the way in which South African scholars, including many other scholars of the 'South', emphasise the need and moral imperatives for decolonising the media and communication discipline, including the curricula taught. However, such responses do not take away the additional needs for, and practical concerns around, transformation of curricula debates centred on a rapidly changing world order impacting on the higher education landscape, including the curricula, from perspectives of new technological developments and how such developments are read and emphasised, independent of geographical, political, or sociocultural location. We also note with concern the lack of discussions around gender and intersectionality in the responses and seemingly also in broader transformation debates.

Rethinking of curricula in communication and media studies ultimately converges with and requires the raising of a most pressing question: What is the university today, and what is its role in the context in which it operates? More precisely, the underlying question is whether the university can still be thought as a space for critical thinking and for the pursuit of knowledge (or an approximation of it); or whether we should resign ourselves to the idea of the university as a managerial, top-down, commodified, branded, ranked, corporatised and securitised institution. If the latter, the question of decolonisation would be at best a form of window dressing. This is confirmed wherever one sees the violent repression, by managerial and politically connected academic powers who are what are now claiming decolonisation as their own, of movements that put this demand on the agenda (Respondent 13, South Africa).

For those who look at the transformation of curricula, the South African lesson can be read to suggest that there is need to guard against losing the energy and focus that arise in moments of national strife and extended global interest in questions of transformation and decolonisation. To not produce more humanising curricula in such moments would be to affirm the worthlessness of the 'black pain' and of sacrifices of many for an education that meets their and our needs.

References

Chasi, C. 2015. How to speak of ending apartheid education: Transformation, renaissance, metamorphosis or resurrection. *Journal of Public Administration*, 50(2): 174–190.
Chasi, C. and Rodny-Gumede, Y. 2016. Smash and grab, truth and dare. . . . *Gazette Journal of International Communication*, 78(7): 694–700.
Chasi, C. and Rodny-Gumede, Y. 2018. Decolonising communication studies: A advancing the discipline through fermenting participation studies. In Mutsvairo, M., ed. *Palgrave Handbook on Media and Communication Research in Africa*. London: Palgrave Macmillan, 55–71.
Comaroff, J. and Comaroff, J L. 2011. *Theory from the South or How Euro-America Is Evolving Towards Africa*. London: Boulder.
Curran, J. and Park, M.J., eds. 2000. Beyond globalization theory. In *De-westernizing Media Studies*. London: Routledge, 3–18.
Du Plooy, G. 2006. Towards African communication science curricula: Challenges for higher education. *Communicatio*, 32(2): 189–209.
Fanon, F. 1963. *The Wretched of the Earth*. New York: Grove Press.
Frassinelli, P.P. 2018. Decolonisation: What it is and what research has to do with it. In Tomaselli, K.G., ed. *Making Sense of Research*. Pretoria: van Schaik Publishers, 3–9.
Freedman, E. and Shafer, R. 2010. Ambitious in theory but unlikely in practice: A critique of UNESCO's model curricula for journalism education for developing countries and emerging democracies. *Journal of Third World Studies*, 27(1): 135–153.
Grosfoguel, R. 2008. Transmodernity, border thinking and global coloniality: Decolonizing political economy and postcolonial studies. *Revista Crítica de Ciencias Sociais*, 80(1): 10–30.
Livingston, S. 2007. Internationalizing media and communication studies: Reflections on the international communication association. *Global Media and Communication*, 3(3): 273–288.
Mano, W. 2009. "Reconceptualising African Media Studies" in Daya K. Thussu ed. *Internationalising Media Studies*. London: Routledge, pp. 277–294.
Mbembe, A. 2001. *On the postcolony*. Berkeley: University of California.
Mignolo, W D. 2011. *The darker side of western modernity*. London: Duke University press.
Motsaathebe, G. 2011. Journalism education and practice in South Africa and the discourse of the African renaissance. *Communicatio: South African Journal for Communication Theory and Research*, 37(3): 381–397.
Moyo, L. and Mutsvairo, B. 2018. Can the subaltern think?: The decolonial turn in communication research in Africa. In Mutsvairo, B., ed. *Palgrave Handbook on Media and Communication Research in Africa*. London: Palgrave, 19–40.
Ndlela, N. 2007. Reflections on the global public sphere: Challenges to internationalizing media studies. *Global Media and Communication*, 3(3): 324–329.
Ndlela, N. 2009. African media research in the era of globalization. *Journal of African Media Studies*, 1(1): 55–68.
Nyamnjoh, F.B. 2011. De-Westernizing media theory to make room for African experience. In Wasserman, H., ed. *Popular Media, Democracy and Development in Africa*. New York: Routledge, 19–31.
Nyamnjoh, F.B. 2005. *Africa's Media: Democracy and the Politics of Belonging*. London: Zed Books.
Orgeret, K.S. 2018. Gender in African media studies. In Mutsvairo, B., ed. *The Palgrave Handbook of Media and Communication Research in Africa*. London: Palgrave Macmillan, 347–367.
Rodny-Gumede, Y. 2013. The local in the global: Challenges of teaching global journalism. *Ecquid Novi: African Journalism Studies*, 34(2): 128–141.
Rodny-Gumede, Y. 2015. Re-conceptualising the analysis of trajectories of media development in postcolonial societies. *Journal of Global Media and Communication*, 11(2): 131–146.
Sreberny, A. 2000. The global and the local in international communication. In Curran, J. and Gurevitch, M., ed. *Mass Media and Society*. London: Arnold, 93–119.
UNESCO. 1980. *Many Voices, One World* (International Commission for the Study of Communications Problems). Paris: UNESCO.
UNESCO. 1982. *Grünwald Declaration on Media Education*. Paris: UNESCO.

Waisbord, S. 2015. De-Westernization and cosmopolitan media studies. In Lee, C.C., ed. *Internationalizing "International communication"*. Michigan: University of Michigan Press, 178–200.
Wasserman, H. 2018. *Media, Geopolitics, and Power: A View from the Global South*. Cape Town: UCT Press.
wa Thiong'o, N. 1993. *Moving the Centre: The Struggle for Cultural Freedoms*. Nairobi, Kenya: EAEP.
wa Thiong'o, N. 2012. *Globalectics: Theory and the Politics of Knowing*. New York: Columbia University Press.
Willems, W. 2014. Beyond normative dewesternization: Examining media culture from the vantage point of the global South. *The Global South*, 8(1): 7–23.

9
Africa on demand
The production and distribution of African narratives through podcasting

Rachel Lara van der Merwe

Introduction

In Chimamanda Ngozi Adichie's TED Talk 'The Danger of a Single Story,' she notes that, 'Power is the ability not just to tell the story of another person, but to make it the definitive story of that person. . . . Stories matter. . . . Stories have been used to dispossess and to malign, but stories can also be used to empower and to humanise' (2009). Africa has long been subject to the West's single story about a dark continent, but for Adichie and many African writers before her, such as Ngũgĩ wa Thiong'o and Chinua Achebe, story can also be a tool of revolution. The introduction of new narratives shifts systems of power and fractures previously monolithic tales. Furthermore, Nick Couldry argues that, 'What we do . . . already comes embedded in narrative, our own and that of others. This is why to deny value to another's capacity for narrative – to deny her potential for voice – is to deny a basic dimension of human life' (2010, 7). Narrative is not simply a useful tool – possessing and sharing one's own narrative is key to human dignity.

The Internet, upon its emergence in the late twentieth century, was hailed as a utopian space for the distribution of everyone's narratives. A few decades later we have become accustomed to a less optimistic reality in which humans reproduce the inequitable social conditions of offline reality within the virtual, a practice that has been documented by scholars like Lisa Nakamura. Yet Nakamura also cautions against losing confidence in the Internet's capacity to be a socially transformative force (2002). In this chapter, I wish to suggest that perhaps one of these new forces for transformation might be the medium of podcasting. Podcasting has emerged at the intersection of narrative and new digital realities. Using the power, affordability, and intimacy of this medium to produce and distribute African stories, fiction or fact, is not only an opportunity to share our complex continent with the rest of the world, but it is also a way to build community and collaborations within Africa itself. Podcasting could be an antidote to the single story.

Within this chapter, I argue for the potential of the podcast in Africa. To do so, I address the distinction between podcasting and traditional radio, tracing podcasting's evolution from radio on the continent before identifying the unique benefits offered by this digital medium. Against this historical and theoretical backdrop, I briefly map out and consider the podcast scene in South Africa (SA) as an example of podcasting in Africa. Where has it been successful? What challenges does it face? I approach podcasting in this chapter not as a mere tool for the transmission of knowledge, but rather as a medium woven into the threads of society (Larkin 2008). I'm attentive to how people in Africa might take up this form of technology in creative ways unlike how it has been used elsewhere, and I am interested in podcasting as a site for cultural production and exchange.

Theorising media and cultural formation

Media and communication tend to be studied from two primary perspectives: the transmission view and the ritual view of communication (Carey 2008). While the transmission view focuses on media as a carrier for messages, the ritual view 'is directed not toward the extension of messages in space but toward the maintenance of society in time; not the act of imparting information but the representation of shared beliefs' (15). This perspective perceives media as participants in the formation of culture. In this chapter, as I consider the implications of podcasting for Africa, I approach the medium from the ritual view. How do podcasts allow for the circulation of ideas that maintain, renew, and transform cultural identity?

The recognition that media play a central role in facilitating identity is a core assumption in media and cultural studies. For example, Anderson (2006) highlights the role of print media in national formation, and Said (1994; 2003 [1979]), in his development of postcolonial theory, points out the role that art plays in developing European identity in opposition to its constructed perceptions of Middle Eastern culture. Hall provides robust theorisation about the role that popular media, like cinema, plays for communities in understanding and producing themselves (1993; 2000); furthermore, Larkin (2008) observes the role that infrastructural networks, which are produced by media, perform in shaping cultural flows. Media is something *lived*; it structures our lives, and we use it to give meaning to the surrounding world. How then could the podcast, weaving its way into the daily lives of South Africans, transform society?

Defining the podcast

The podcast is a digital iteration of radio, as reflected in its name, which combines references to the iPod, Apple's original MP3 player, and the act of broadcasting. The technical distinction between radio and podcasts can be found primarily in distribution – rather than hearing a story over the radio waves, a podcast is available for streaming or download over the Internet. However, it would be inaccurate to classify the podcast as just another form of distribution or as digital radio. While in some cases podcasts are radio shows repackaged for the Internet, generally the production of a podcast is approached differently from the production of radio. Even as it shares many characteristics with traditional radio, the podcast is its own medium. For example, unlike radio which is organised along a set schedule in accordance with available studio time and airtime to which listeners must conform their own schedules, podcasts are specifically designed with listener flexibility in mind. Mobile technology enables podcast listeners to choose not just when, but also where and how they listen to an episode. The expected asynchronous nature of podcasts translates to a lesser emphasis on live recordings for podcast producers, and as a result, podcast episodes can be more highly produced with more intentional editing, sound design, scripting, etc. Live recordings are still possible but are no longer an integral factor. Digital and mobile technologies make the medium of radio itself more accessible, but it is important to recognise the distinction between audio archives, material that is designed primarily for a synchronous radio distribution platform and later made available online, as opposed to podcasts that are designed for online, asynchronous listening but might also be slotted into a local radio station's schedule as a secondary distribution platform.

Though the technology to stream and download audio material is itself not new, podcasting as an identifiable medium is relatively novel, coming to initial popularity 'in 2006, when iTunes added podcasts to its menu, which lead to the influx of new podcasts and millions of new listeners' (Harding 2016). Since its initial advent, the medium has evolved, but it still generally can be recognised as a collection of connected episodes released at regular intervals, to which a listener can subscribe using a service such as iTunes. Some podcasts follow a seasonal cycle that resembles the television model in which there is a brief hiatus between sequenced sets of episodes, while others maintain year-round weekly or biweekly schedules. Still others do not follow any particular rigid schedule but are released as each episode is completed. Without a contract to make use of a radio station's airtime, podcast producers have reasonable flexibility to determine their schedule based on available resources.

The mobility and flexibility afforded by the podcast is the principle reason for its appeal. Berry (2016) notes that, while the podcast tends to draw in younger audiences than radio, it generally draws in a diverse audience because audiences are no longer constrained by the linear broadcast model and can download episodes (using Wi-Fi or data) and listen wherever. The podcast model also allows audiences to discover a podcast late, yet easily return to the beginning and 'catch up'. With the improvement and reduced cost of audio technology, more and more individuals are also joining the podcasting community as content producers, further expanding the appeal of podcasts by diversifying the content provided.

This chapter's focus on the podcast predicates a recognition that in the digital age, radio can no longer be understood as a 'unified and bounded medium'(Moyo 2013, 214). By discussing the podcast in Africa, I take into account the continent's long and rich history with radio while recognising that the evolution of the podcast signals a distinct new chapter of oral storytelling that must be addressed on its own terms. What significance do the unique characteristics and possibilities of the podcast hold for the construction and development of communal, national, and cultural identities?

Oral storytelling in Africa

The continent of Africa has a long history of oral tradition and culture (Miller 1980), but those dynamics have often been supplanted by the influx of US and European visual media, from the printed book to television, which have shifted African culture away from orality towards visuality. Yet there are still areas in which the oral remains significant for Africa, such as with radio. While the programming of visual media like television and film relies heavily on material produced in Euro-America, radio remains the domain of local programming since both its distribution and reception is cheaper, simpler, and more accessible than that of television (Mano 2010). Radio also has a long history of significance for the continent beginning during the age of colonisation and continuing throughout periods of resistance, decolonisation, democratisation, and digitisation.

During the colonial era, radio, upon its invention at the turn of the century, was quickly identified as a powerful medium by which to shape and influence colonised publics, especially those in less-accessible rural areas. However,

> designed primarily as a means of propaganda to serve the colonial empires, radio was always far more multifaceted and slippery than was intended by colonial powers. Language, and the ability of radio to work from within the thick medium of cultural knowledge, was

always a key element in its polysemic effectiveness and its ability to create new and sometimes unruly publics.

(Gunner et al. 2010, 6)

Writing in reference to French-occupied Algeria, Fanon (1994) makes a similar observation when he highlights the association of radio with colonial conceptions of civilisation but also outlines how the Algerians remade the medium for their own revolutionary purposes.

As resistance movements eventually became postcolonial state governments, radio continued to be a central tool for these organisations to foster solidarity and a sense of national community (Coplan 2010). Since national borders largely reflected borders drawn by the coloniser, an array of distinct people groups comprised each new nation, making national unity precarious at best. New governments had to develop compelling ideologies to justify participation in the state, despite the nonsensical geographies, and to promote a sense of brotherhood in the construction of these imagined communities. Around the same time as the height of the decolonisation process, between 1957 and 1967, the portable transistor radio became available on the continent. Its affordability resulted in the rapid expansion of radio listenership, which played a key role in the success and significance of these state broadcasting monopolies. Thus, radio in Africa has served as both a tool for the transmission of propaganda and for resistance and the development of counterpublics (Coplan 2010).

Commercial radio arose to challenge the one-way informative model of state-run broadcasting companies. Coplan notes that, by the twenty-first century, 'the number of nongovernment radio broadcasters in Africa had grown from three to three hundred' (2010, 139). Commercial radio, operated by independent corporations for profit, was accompanied by the emergence of community radio, 'which is run, owned and controlled by community organisations for their own communities, and funded from sources such as grants, sponsorships, donations and advertising' (Mtimde 2000, 177). Both commercial and community radio tend to be characterised by dialogic modes of communication in which the listener is directly addressed and is generally availed opportunities to respond in some form. Community radio, in particular, tends to be the most trusted (Coplan 2010, 144) due to its democratic and local commitments, but the popularity of both commercial and community radio serves as ongoing challenges to state-run media. Regardless, since the late twentieth century, deregulation of radio broadcasting across the continent and the development of institutions to protect private broadcasting, such as the Independent Broadcasting Authors (IBA) in SA, has allowed non-governmental radio stations to thrive and new media publics to form. Talk radio, in particular, is one subsection of African radio that has been particularly significant in creating spaces for citizens to engage and discuss important political topics (Odhiambo 2010; Bosch 2010).

Today some of the most widely listened-to radio stations in the world are in Africa, such as UKhozi FM, the SABC-run Zulu radio station in SA with over 7 million listeners, and African radio continues to evolve with the advent of the digital era. Radio can now be streamed over the Internet, and popular radio shows are often available for download in podcast format. Internet and mobile technology also provide new channels by which audiences can respond to the broadcaster. Listeners no longer have to use their precious cellular minutes to contact a station; their responses can take place through tools like SMS or Facebook, and many digital spaces allow for listeners to dialogue with each other (Chiumbu and Ligaga 2013; Willems 2013). However, despite these new channels for communication, it is important to remember that such spaces are not completely open; they are still moderated and censored by the broadcaster. The voices we see and hear are the voices that the broadcaster, whether public, private or community-sponsored, wants the listener to encounter.

Rachel Lara van der Merwe

The theoretical benefits of podcasting

Podcasting faces many similar challenges, but because it does not necessitate the fixed distribution node of the radio station, it has the capacity to support even more vibrant spaces of discourse, and it could nurture new transnational networks of communities and lived experiences.

The intimacy of the oral

If we first consider podcasting alongside its parent medium, radio, we can address the values of oral storytelling in general. Besides the fact that oral storytelling removes the requirement for literacy, perhaps its most prominent strength is the intimacy evoked through the aural. Cultural historian and philosopher Walter Ong explains (2002):

> Because in its physical constitution as sound, the spoken word proceeds from the human interior and manifests human beings to one another as conscious interiors, as persons, the spoken word forms human beings into close-knit groups. . . . Writing and print isolate. There is no collective noun or concept for readers corresponding to 'audience.'

The historical transition from an amplified spoken word in a public setting to the recorded setting of radio allowed for a new type of intimacy. Now that each listener had direct access to the speaker's voice, through the proximity of their radio, the speaker no longer needed to project his voice. John Brinkley, a charlatan of the early twentieth century, was one of the first individuals to recognise this affordance, using the medium to sell his wares by conspiratorially lowering his voice as if in personal conversation with his listeners (Reply All n.d.). Though Brinkley's use was unethical, we have since come to recognise the many possibilities for radio as 'intimate, personal, trustworthy, exploratory, live and immediate' (Edmond 2015). Podcasting extends these possibilities because the sound emissions can be directly centred around or in the ears: 'The latest manifestation of . . . what McLuhan called the "tactile embrace" of the oral-aural' (MacDougall 2011).

Beyond these auditory qualities, Couldry highlights the significance of voice 'as a process – giving an account of oneself and what affects one's life' (2010, vi) 'voice is the process of articulating the world from a distinctive embodied position' (8). As such, voice is an integral component of what it means to be human, and Couldry argues that 'effective voice (the effective opportunity to have one's voice heard and taken into account) is a human good' (2010, vi). Voice, as he understands it, is an expression of the individual but bounded by the resources made available by society. One is only able to express oneself as much as one has the tools by which to transfer one's interiority into exteriority through the use, for example, of language and technology, and as much as another is able to receive one's expression, materially and psychologically. One's symbolic and cultural capital also impacts voice. If a society does not recognise an individual with subject status, then that individual essentially has no voice. Voice 'values all human beings' ability to give an account of themselves; it values my and your status as "narratable" selves' (13), and it is about access to the act of self-narration. Thus, as we think about aural media technologies, it is important to ask who forms the narrative. Freedom to respond to a narrative through call-ins or Facebook is not the same as having the capacity to construct one's own narrative.

With both radio and podcasting, the act of listening extends beyond an act of acquiring information and becomes about 'being-with' – with the broadcaster, and with the others listening to the broadcast, wherever they might be. The ways in which radio and podcasting interweave media into the daily lives of listeners transform radio and podcast from performing simply as information to be consumed into media that function as daily ritual (Carey 2008). The prevalence of mobile technology in Africa and the rise of public Wi-Fi hotspots (Myburgh 2018; Wasserman 2011) makes digitised radio and podcasts more accessible to be taken with the listener wherever they might go. As a result, these forms of oral storytelling can become intimately woven into the fabric of listeners' daily lives as they carry voices into their homes, their cars, and their workspaces.

The affordability of the oral

The oral medium is also more affordable than its visual alternatives. On the level of production, high-quality audio recording and mixing equipment is much cheaper than high-quality video equipment. In addition, an audio project only requires the audio track – not a visual *and* audio track. This in turn affects the number of production crew required. Audio production and postproduction, in general, is easier to learn than video production and postproduction, and often audio recording, mixing, and editing can be performed by one individual or a very small crew. Audio files take up less space than video, and thus require less storage space. This is not to suggest that audio production is cheap; good high-quality audio is still a costly venture, but comparative to a full video production, it is much cheaper and much more versatile.

Furthermore, podcasting is cheaper than radio. Radio distribution requires a licence and/or a station willing to air your show on a particular FM or AM bandwidth, usually for a fee. The latter requirement also necessitates the social capital required to advance one's show past radio gatekeepers. A production must then be slotted into a specific timeslot, necessitating that one's audience show up at a particular time to a location with a radio. In contrast, podcasts only require an affordable digital space like Soundcloud to host one's productions, and it is free and relatively simple to distribute one's podcast through Apple's network. From those digital locations, audiences can download and listen at the time and place of their choosing. For production, anyone with access to a computer, a microphone or mobile phone, and Internet can download free or cheap software to record and edit their first story, though perhaps at a lower level of quality.

In addition, podcasts are oriented towards mobile technology, which aligns well with Africa's prevalent mobile technology usage. Already by 2017, 80 percent of the African population had access to a mobile phone (Oloyede 2017). Radio has thrived in Africa due to the affordability and accessibility of receivers; in the digital era, the mobile phone is widely prevalent in a similar manner, but it is also capable of doing much more than the transistor radio. For smartphones, access to the Internet characterises them as networked technology. Mobile devices provide new means by which both urban and rural audiences can engage podcast producers and fellow listeners, thus participating in the democratic process and circumventing the lack of fixed-line infrastructure in many areas of Africa. Such devices can also function as recording devices, making it easier for those who wish to narrate their own stories.

The community-building of the oral

Finally, podcasting, like community radio, tends to be a more audience-driven and crowd-sourced medium. Popular US podcasts, such as *Radiolab*, frequently make use of listener-contributed anecdotes and participation in activities like reading the credits. Edmond writes, 'Creating radio projects that are more social, immersive and engaging fosters a commercially valuable emotional attachment to a story, show, presenter, station and to a community of fellow listeners' (2015, 1578), which yet again speaks to the community that tends to emerge around oral media like radio and podcasting. For postcolonial nations, the significance of listener participation is particularly important as these nations are still in a pivotal formative era. State media tends to be at the forefront of shaping narratives about national identity, but the corporations behind private media play their own role in shaping a citizenry according to consumer logics. For truly democratic nations to succeed in Africa, the average citizen must have a voice in the formation of local and national identities. Radio has already opened up avenues within which educational endeavors have been made possible (Odine 2013) but as noted above, since media perform roles beyond information dissemination, Africans should also embrace radio and podcasting as spaces within which to share their stories and connect local communities.

Participation in the storytelling process takes on different forms. Talk radio has created space for listeners to engage broadcasters with their own perspectives, and mobile technology has provided new platforms to enable this. However, research shows that only a small portion of listeners actually use call-in opportunities and tend to use the space to build their own personal brands (Gagliardone 2016). For those callers who wish to express their opinion as a practice of democracy, they must abide by studio-set parameters and at any point might be censored or removed from air. The most successful callers must also learn to negotiate the communicative expectations and practices of on-air conversations. Simultaneously, as Willems notes, what externally may appear to be democratic engagement is often a strategy 'in which radio stations both aim to access personal data of their listeners as well as to attract revenue through premium-rated SMS messages and Facebook fanpage advertising' (2013, 230). To a certain extent, the market dictates everything within a capitalistic society, but podcasting allows for a new digital and oral space where more parameters of discourse can be set by the citizen.

The underlying logics of podcasting also transform the type of participation that might take place. The podcast no longer relies on a mass media model where the goal is distribution to the widest audience possible; instead the podcast is designed with a niche audience in mind. This is what Schutz calls 'directional intimacy' (Bratt 2017). Because of the affordances of digital technology, each podcast can cater their material for a particular audience. While the resulting audience may reflect a diverse geographic origin, unrestricted by access to a radio signal, the listeners tend to share similar interests, brought together by the niche content. Such specialised distribution produces small but strong, committed audiences that are deeply invested in both the show and the community.

Considering reality: the existing African podcast scene

While scholars have written extensively about radio in Africa, African podcasting is primarily the subject of online listicles and entrepreneur-driven business web articles. Academic research has focused on the role of the podcast for education or development, approaching the medium as a tool for transmission rather than as a site for cultural production. From journalistic coverage, however, it is evident that Africans across the continent are using this new medium to explore questions of individual and cultural identity with niche but geographically diverse audiences, both local and diasporic. Podcasts hail from all over the continent but the industry appears to be most prevalent in the countries of Nigeria, Kenya, and South Africa. Nigeria is home to podcasts such as *Not Your African Cliché*, hosted by four young Nigerian women seeking to challenge stereotypes about Africa, and *My Africa*, which Awachie describes as the *Fresh Air* of Africa (2016). Mnisi suggests that Kenyan podcasters 'are arguably the most astute in the long-term viability of the medium. This is largely evident in the conscious effort to target a young audience, between 18–34, with the realisation that Africa is a young continent whose conversations should centre around youth' (2017). Kenyan podcasts include *Afracanah*, about culture and current affairs; *The Spread*, about sex and relationships; *Otherwise?*, about politics, economy, and society; and *BenchwarmerzKE*, about sports (Mbugua 2017).

The South African context

If we take a closer look at podcasting within SA, it appears to have emerged during 2015 and early 2016. This follows a similar surge in podcasting in the US after the success of *Serial* at the end of 2014; however, the industry in SA is still unformed. Tracking down the 'most popular' SA podcasts proved difficult because listener data has not been aggregated, and much of what is labeled as podcasts are in fact repackaged radio content (Dias 2017). Even for podcast producers, comprehensive listener statistics are difficult to procure. In conversation with *Sound Africa* creator, Rasmus Bitsch (2017), he explained that neither Soundcloud nor iTunes provide data about listening habits such as how much, if any, of a podcast episode a listener actually engages after downloading. Since the time of the interview, Apple has agreed to release analytics that reveal users' stop/start/skip actions throughout an episode; however, this data only reflects the listening habits of users with devices upgraded to iOS 11. For SA, users with the requisite devices and software would reflect only a small wealthier subsection of the population. As such, any data gleaned wouldn't represent the podcast listening habits of the larger citizenry.

There are currently only two key sources of podcasting data within SA: PwC's annual *Entertainment and Media Outlook* (Myburgh 2018, 2019) and a recent study (Brown 2017) undertaken by SA podcast entrepreneur Matt Brown. Unfortunately, both of these data sources are produced by commercial entities in service of their own endeavors, so the statistics must be engaged with a recognition of how and why the data was initially procured. It's also helpful to note the entrance of Spotify to the SA market in March 2018. Spotify provides an affordable music streaming service to South Africans, in addition to being an easy channel by which to stream or download podcasts.

According to the 2018 PwC report, total data consumption by South Africans is forecast to reach almost 8 billion GB by 2022, and data traffic will surpass 7.9 billion GB by this time. Most data consumption in the country already takes place using smartphones, and PwC estimates the current penetration rate for Internet access is two-thirds of the entire SA population. The report argues that successful SA podcasts, such as *Alibi*, have given visibility to the medium and its market, resulting in greater interest from venture capitalists. It estimated 5.1 million monthly podcast listeners in 2017. Furthermore, the report identifies steady growth in podcast advertising revenue, estimating that by 2022, advertising revenue for podcasts will have increased by 50 percent. The 2019 report confirms that podcast advertising revenue almost tripled since 2017, from R38 million to R98 million, and in 2019, the report claimed that, "South African consumers find podcasts a fairly 'sticky' media format, with 80% of the audience listening to content through to the end. A majority also listen to a podcast within 24 hours of its initial download" (155). The report identified affluent citizens as the primary interest group for podcasts, but not the only audience.

According to Matt Brown Media, their study incorporated the responses of 15,682 respondents and comprises a representative sample of age, gender, location, and ethnicity. Without an IRB involved, it's impossible to evaluate the quality of their sampling and surveying methods but, according to their report, they estimate 6 million South Africans listen to podcasts on a weekly basis and 9 million South Africans on a monthly basis. Their study found that the key obstacle for the podcast market was *not* the cost of data, but rather knowledge of how to locate and download episodes. For those already listening to podcasts, the report notes that most listeners multitask while listening and view podcasts as an extension of the role that traditional radio plays in their life.

In order to obtain a better sense of the type of podcast material generated by South Africans, I compiled a list of popular SA podcasts using extensive Google searches and journalistic coverage to locate the podcasts that were most frequently discussed online and thus likely also the most popular. At the time of this investigation, from late 2017 through mid-2018, I identified and included all 13 podcasts (see Appendix 9.1) that received some form of national recognition and promotion. This list is not conclusive, but it reflects what an average South African would likely discover if they went in search of a SA-produced podcast. The sample is small but reflects the current size of the industry. In order to obtain a general sense of each podcast, I sampled the entirety of a recent episode and excerpts or full episodes from earlier in the archive. As an exploratory endeavour, my goal in sampling these episodes was to obtain a general sense of each podcast. This was not a form of detailed textual analysis but rather an act of cartography – a mapping of the terrain.

Of these identified podcasts, very few release a steady stream of episodes at a predictable pace. Among those I would describe as ongoing, only four had released an episode within the previous month. All the episodes that I sampled were high-quality productions but not at the level of technological sophistication that one would expect from a US-produced podcast, i.e. in terms of audio clarity and complexity. In terms of genre, the podcasts range from general audio documentaries appealing to a broader audience, such as *Sound Africa*, *Alibi*, and *First Person*, to productions catered for a more niche audience that are usually more interview-centric, such as *African Tech Round-Up* (about technology in Africa), *Amabookabooka* (about SA authors), and *The Sobering* (about SA hip-hop). Very few of the reviewed podcasts included commercials. These observations reflect an industry in its formative stages: the creativity and content are there, but the infrastructure still needs to be developed to support such endeavours.

Several of the podcasts are intentional efforts to develop cultural identity. For example, *Sound Africa* shares fascinating, lesser-known histories about the continent, in the style of a show like *This American Life*. By fleshing out or challenging officially taught narratives, this show has the potential to reshape continental and national collective memories. Another example is *First Person*, which introduces the listener to extraordinary, yet regular, individuals from all over SA. Each episode transcends mere interview and invites the listener into the person's local community to see inside their fridge or watch them at a local football game. These stories transport a listener out of their own narrow understanding of what it means to be South African into other iterations of lived identity and experience.

The existing challenges to developing infrastructure

Despite the popularity of mobile technology in Africa, several obstacles exist that have slowed the progress of podcasts across the continent: data costs and the digital divide, language, and the limitations on profitability.

While many Africans may have access to a mobile phone or even smartphone, data and cellular costs on the continent are high, discouraging the downloading or streaming of media such as podcasts (Wasserman 2011, 149). In addition, limited access to data shapes the way mobile technology is used and, subsequently, the population's familiarity with the full potential of their devices. While one study discovered that university students had ubiquitous access to mobile devices regardless of socioeconomic status and most used them to access the Internet (Brown and Czerniewicz 2010), another study revealed that students are not using those same devices to perform digital tasks such as listening to podcasts (Gachago et al. 2016). At a structural level, this suggests that until Wi-Fi is more readily accessible to the majority of the population or until data costs drop, the necessary digital lifestyle to support a developing podcast audience won't exist. However, there are some, like Elna Schutz from Wits Radio Academy (Bratt 2017), who disagree with this assessment and point out the proliferation of public Wi-Fi hotspots, such as those created by the Western Cape Government's Broadband Game Changer. If people wish to access a podcast, the resources, though not ideal, exist to accomplish such a task.

Public Wi-Fi is an insufficient infrastructure, however, in order for podcasts to facilitate voices and distribute new narratives. The potential for podcasts to serve as a means of expression for previously disenfranchised African communities will require attentiveness to how the digital divide implicates production processes. Even if more than half of South Africans have mobile Internet access (Myburgh 2018) and the ability to record on their phones, very few have access to editing software, along with the skillsets with which to produce a marketable audio story. This technological disparity maintains the economically privileged minority in control of both digital *and* radio airwaves.

Another challenge is language: with 11 official languages in SA, it is difficult to create broadcasts that cater to the home language of all citizens. Language plays a significant cultural and communicative role in a society (Thing'o 1986), and studies show that listeners respond better to broadcasts in their own language (Chibita 2010; Tsarwe 2014, 98). SABC has turned its focus to programming in all official languages, but they must determine multilingual programming choices based on available resources. A mass media broadcaster may have greater resources, but its size also limits its agility. The niche nature of podcasting allows for a space where it might be possible to offer more diversity in language options. No limit in stations and lower production costs affords existing shows to be translated and new shows to be produced by native speakers. Partnerships between community radio stations and podcast producers might be one effective way to address this challenge and serve local communities, while also providing a platform for those stories to be shared at a national level to other local communities.

Finally, a key obstacle to address is profitability. In the US, most podcasts are funded through advertisements, grants, subscriptions, or listener donations. Bitsch (2017) explained that, at the time, most SA podcasts don't contain advertisements because advertisers do not yet see the value. With new Apple Podcast and Spotify analytics, SA podcasters are better able to prove the significance of their audiences, and thus increase this revenue stream. The success of SA shows like *Alibi* is also helping producers obtain advertising (Myburgh 2018). The other revenue models, while familiar and accepted in the US and even parts of Europe, are unlikely to be successful in SA (Dias 2017) where citizens already spend less on entertainment media. In addition, while costs for producing podcasts may be low, the process is time-consuming, and the average working individual is unlikely to have time to produce and edit a podcast (Tulley 2011, 260–261) – further contributing to the podcasting digital divide. Thus, a serious challenge facing the podcast is how to identify productive revenue streams, while simultaneously addressing the question of time costs.

Concluding thoughts

In conclusion, podcasting holds true potential within Africa to serve as a medium that transcends mere information dispersal. Podcasts could be a powerful means for strengthening local communities and drawing them into the larger process of shaping national identity and sharing their many-storied identities with the world. This evokes the rich cultural exchange that Arjun Appadurai defines as the translocal (Appadurai 1996), which might allow listeners to 'imagine themselves as both global and local citizens' (Gunner et al. 2010, 10). As Couldry (2010) reminds us, voice is important, and African voices should play a significant role in the trajectory of our planet, along with the trajectories of their local and national communities. Podcasting is a powerful, flexible, and increasingly popular tool that could empower the facilitation and circulation of these voices both globally and locally.

This vision, however, remains idealistic until the necessary technologies and production instruction become available to the larger public. One possible key to unlock that potential is for existing African podcasters to demonstrate to their peers the value that this medium offers their lives and the community, so that infrastructural concerns can be addressed. Those in the technology community and public sector need to consider how to make data and production tools more affordable to the average African, and those in media communities must consider how to support partnerships between community radio and potential podcast producers across the country. For those of us in academia, there is substantial research that has yet to be done on both podcasting in general and across the continent. We need to gather more data on how the average citizen uses cellular data; the differences in how listeners engage with radio as opposed to podcast; and on the popularity of US and foreign podcasts within SA. It would also be valuable to do closer studies on the content, production, distribution, and success of existing SA podcasts. Providing this type of intentional foundation and context for the medium of podcasting could be an incredible catalyst within SA and the greater continent to shift more power into the hands of the people, to be an antidote to the single story.

Appendix 9.1
South African Podcasts Reviewed

Data updated as of October 8, 2020

Title	Began	Ended or Latest	Host	On iTunes?	Produced By	Based In
African Tech Round-Up	5/15/15	Ended – latest 05/14/2020	Andile Masuku & Osarumen Osamuyi	Yes	Independent	Johannesburg
Alibi	3/5/17	Ongoing-Season 2 released Spring 2020	Freddy Mabitsela & Paul McNally	Yes	For SAFM w/ Wits Radio Academy, Wits Justice Project & as part of Citizen Justice Network.	Johannesburg
Amabookabooka	9/1/15	Ongoing-latest 05/21/2020	Jonathan Ancer & Dan Dewes	Yes	Sound Media Productions	Cape Town
Creative Underground	7/3/16	Ended – latest 04/03/2017	Katlego Makhudu & Jonas Radunz	No	Independent	Johannesburg
First Person – Ordinary People . . . Extraordinary Lives	6/6/16	Ended - latest 12/10/16	Marianne Tham	Yes	A Kagiso Media initiative	N/A

(Continued)

(Continued)

Title	Began	Ended or Latest	Host	On iTunes?	Produced By	Based In
The Gareth Cliff Show	2014	Ongoing & daily	Gareth Cliff	Yes	CliffCentral	Johannesburg
Kiss & Tell with Lady Skollie	9/21/15	Ended – latest 03/09/16	Laura Windvogel	No	Independent	Cape Town
Lesser Known Somebodies	2/22/16	Ongoing- 09/07/2020	Simmi Areff	Yes	Independent	Johannesburg
The Sobering	10/5/15	Ongoing- 09/09/2020	Javas Skolo & Kitso Moremi	Yes	Indie Creative Network	N/A
Sound Africa	11/4/15	Ongoing- 10/05/2020	Assorted	Yes	Independent	Cape Town
Talking Heads	3/10/14	Ended – latest 10/5/16	N/A	No	Africa Centre Production	Cape Town
Quit Safari	N/A	N/A	Assorted	No	Quit Safari Label	Cape Town
Tune Me What	5/17/13	Ongoing- 08/14/2020	Leon Lazarus & Brett Lock	Yes	Independent	N/A

References

Anderson, Benedict. 2006. *Imagined Communities: Reflections on the Origin and Spread of Nationalism*. New York: Verso.

Appadurai, Arjun. 1996. *Modernity at Large: Cultural Dimensions of Globalization*. Minneapolis: University of Minnesota Press, 1st ed.

Awachie, Ifeanyi. 2016. 6 hot African podcasts you should be listening to. *OkayAfrica*, 29 February. www.okayafrica.com/culture-2/african-podcasts-you-should-be-listening-to/.

Berry, Richard. 2016. Part of the establishment: Reflecting on 10 years of podcasting as an audio medium. *Convergence*, 22(6): 661–671. https://doi.org/10.1177/1354856516632105.

Bitsch, Rasmus. 2017. Sound Africa and podcasting in South Africa. *Skype*.

Bosch, Tanja. 2010. Talk radio, democracy and the public sphere: 567MW in Cape Town. In Gunner, L. and Ligaga, D., eds. *Radio in Africa: Publics, Cultures, Communities*. Johannesburg: Wits University Press, 197–207. http://ebookcentral.proquest.com/lib/ucb/detail.action?docID=3545144.

Bratt, Michael. 2017. Podcasting in South Africa: Not profitable yet, but a powerful medium. *The Media Online* (blog), 29 November. http://themediaonline.co.za/2017/11/podcasting-in-south-africa-not-profitable-yet-but-a-powerful-medium/.

Brown, C. and Czerniewicz, L. 2010. Debunking the 'digital native': Beyond digital apartheid, towards digital democracy. *Journal of Computer Assisted Learning*, 26(5): 357–369. https://doi.org/10.1111/j.1365-2729.2010.00369.x.

Brown, Matt. 2017. The impact of South African storytelling and the power of podcasting. *Bizcommunity.com*, 17 July. http://search.proquest.com/docview/1919999573/citation/42EAE655ADE64866PQ/1.

Carey, James W. 2008. A cultural approach to communication. In *Communication as Culture, Revised Edition: Essays on Media and Society*. New York: Routledge, 2 ed., 11–28.

Chibita, Monica B. 2010. Multiple publics, multiple languages: Radio and the contestations of broadcasting language policy in Uganda. In Gunner, L. and Ligaga, D., eds. *Radio in Africa: Publics, Cultures,*

Communities. Johannesburg: Wits University Press, 270–285. http://ebookcentral.proquest.com/lib/ucb/detail.action?docID=3545144.

Chiumbu, Sarah Helen and Ligaga, Dina. 2013. 'Communities of strangerhoods?' Internet, mobile phones and the changing nature of radio cultures in South Africa. *Telematics and Informatics, the Digital Turn in Radio: Understanding Convergence in Radio News Cultures*, 30(3): 242–251. https://doi.org/10.1016/j.tele.2012.02.004.

Coplan, David B. 2010. South African radio in a Saucepan. In Gunner, L., Ligaga, D. and Moyo, D., eds. *Radio in Africa: Publics, Cultures, Communities*. Johannesburg: Wits University Press, 134–148. http://ebookcentral.proquest.com/lib/ucb/detail.action?docID=3545144.

Couldry, Nick. 2010. *Why Voice Matters: Culture and Politics After Neoliberalism*. London: Sage. DOI:10.4135/9781446269114.

The Danger of a Single Story. 2009. *TEDGlobal 2009: TED*. www.ted.com/talks/chimamanda_adichie_the_danger_of_a_single_story.

Dias, Paulo. 2017. Dear radio: The podcast conundrum in South Africa. *Marklives.com*, 12 September. www.marklives.com/2017/09/dear-radio-the-podcast-conundrum-in-south-africa/.

Edmond, Maura. 2015. All platforms considered: Contemporary radio and transmedia engagement. *New Media & Society*, 17(9): 1566–1582. https://doi.org/10.1177/1461444814530245.

Fanon, Frantz. 1994. *A Dying Colonialism*, trans. Chevalier, H. New York: Grove Press.

Gachago, Daniela, Livingston, Candice and Ivala, Eunice. 2016. Podcasts: A technology for all? *British Journal of Educational Technology*, 47(5): 859–872. https://doi.org/10.1111/bjet.12483.

Gagliardone, Iginio. 2016. 'Can you hear me?' Mobile – radio interactions and governance in Africa. *New Media & Society*, 18(9): 2080–2095. https://doi.org/10.1177/1461444815581148.

Gunner, Liz, Ligaga, Dina and Moyo, Dumisani, eds. 2010. Introduction: The soundscapes of radio in Africa. In *Radio in Africa: Publics, Cultures, Communities*. Johannesburg: Wits University Press. http://ebookcentral.proquest.com/lib/ucb/detail.action?docID=3545144.

Hall, Stuart. 1993. What is this 'Black' in Black popular culture? *Social Justice*, 20(1/2 (51–52)): 104–114.

Hall, Stuart. 2000. Cultural identity and cinematic representation. In Miller, Toby and Stam, Robert, eds. *Film and Theory: An Anthology*. Malden, MA: Blackwell Publishers, 704–714.

Harding, Warren. 2016. The 2016 podcast push in South Africa | BizTrends 2016. *Biz Community*, 25 January. www.bizcommunity.com/Article/196/687/139413.html.

Larkin, Brian. 2008. *Signal and Noise: Media, Infrastructure, and Urban Culture in Nigeria*. Durham: Duke University Press Books, unknown ed.

MacDougall, Robert C. 2011. Podcasting and political life. *American Behavioral Scientist*, 55(6): 714–732. https://doi.org/10.1177/0002764211406083.

Mano, Winston. 2010. Why radio is Africa's medium of choice in the global age. In Gunner, L. and Ligaga, D., eds. *Radio in Africa: Publics, Cultures, Communities*. Johannesburg: Wits University Press. http://ebookcentral.proquest.com/lib/ucb/detail.action?docID=3545144.

Mbugua, Melissa. 2017. The dawn of podcasting in Kenya. *IAfrikan*, 9 March. www.iafrikan.com/2017/03/09/the-dawn-of-podcasting-in-kenya/.

Miller, Joseph Calder. 1980. *African Past Speaks: Essays on Oral Tradition and History*. Folkestone and Hamden, CT: Archon.

Mnisi, Kagiso. 2017. Is podcasting the way to open up African media? *The Media Online*, 18 September. http://themediaonline.co.za/2017/09/is-podcasting-the-way-to-open-up-african-media/.

Moyo, Last. 2013. The digital turn in radio: A critique of institutional and organizational modeling of new radio practices and cultures. *Telematics and Informatics, the Digital Turn in Radio: Understanding Convergence in Radio News Cultures*, 30(3): 214–222. https://doi.org/10.1016/j.tele.2012.10.003.

Mtimde, Lumko. 2000. Radio broadcasting in South Africa: An overview. *International Journal of Cultural Studies*, 3(2): 173–179. https://doi.org/10.1177/136787790000300205.

Myburgh, Vicki. 2018. *Entertainment and Media Outlook: 2018–2022 (An African Perspective)*, 9. South Africa: PricewaterhouseCoopers.

Myburgh, Vicki. 2019. *Entertainment and Media Outlook: 2019–2023 – Africa*, 10. South Africa: PricewaterhouseCoopers.

Nakamura, Lisa. 2002. *Cybertypes: Race, Ethnicity, and Identity on the Internet*. New York and London: Routledge.

Odhiambo, Christopher Joseph. 2010. From Diffusion to Dialogic Space: FM Radio Stations in Kenya. In Gunner, L. and Ligaga, D., eds. *Radio in Africa: Publics, Cultures, Communities*. Johannesburg: Wits University Press, 36–48. http://ebookcentral.proquest.com/lib/ucb/detail.action?docID=3545144.

Odine, Maurice. 2013. Use of radio to promote culture in South Africa. *Journal of Radio & Audio Media*, 20(1): 181–196. DOI:10.1080/19376529.2013.777341.

Oloyede, Olaoluwa. 2017. Jumia unveils its third white paper on Nigerian mobile trends 2017. *Jumia Lounge*, 19 April. https://blog.jumia.com.ng/jumia-unveils-third-white-paper-nigerian-mobile-trends-2017/.

Ong, Walter J. 2002. *Orality and Literacy : The Technologizing of the Word*. New Accents. London: Routledge. http://search.ebscohost.com/login.aspx?direct=true&db=nlebk&AN=102902&site=ehost-live&scope=site.

Reply All. n.d. *Man of the People*. Podcast. https://gimletmedia.com/episode/86-man-of-the-people/ (Accessed 5 July 2017).

Said, Edward W. 2003 [1979]. *Orientalism*. New York: Vintage Books, 25th anniversary ed.

Said, Edward W. 1994. *Culture and Imperialism*. New York: Vintage Books.

Tsarwe, Stanley. 2014. Voice, alienation and the struggle to be heard: A case study of community radio programming in South Africa. *Critical Arts*, 28(2): 287–310. https://doi.org/10.1080/02560046.2014.906345.

Tulley, Christine. 2011. Itext reconfigured: The rise of the podcast. *Journal of Business and Technical Communication*, 25(3): 256–275. https://doi.org/10.1177/1050651911400702.

Wasserman, Herman. 2011. Mobile phones, popular media, and everyday African democracy: Transmissions and transgressions. *Popular Communication*, 9(2): 146–158. https://doi.org/10.1080/15405702.2011.562097.

wa Thiong'o, N. 1986. *Decolonising the Mind: The Politics of Language in African Literature*. Oxford: James Currey Ltd, Heinemann.

Willems, Wendy. 2013. Participation – in what? Radio, convergence and the corporate logic of audience input through new media in Zambia. *Telematics and Informatics, the Digital Turn in Radio: Understanding Convergence in Radio News Cultures*, 30(3): 223–231. https://doi.org/10.1016/j.tele.2012.02.006.

10

The African novel and its global communicative potential

Africa's soft power

Mary-Jean Nleya

Introduction

Media and communication gives life to the "right to narrate" (Bhabha 1994, xx). However, ways of narrating information and messages are often subject to the contest of complex economic, political and social processes in the contemporary global order (Bhabha 1994, 245). It is submitted that at the core of media and communication are the politics of representation that are informed by historical, ideological and cultural perspectives (Bhabha 1994, 245–246). The purpose of this chapter is to include cultural production – in the form of literature – as a medium with communicative potential. The chapter is situated within the oppositional forces of representation that are directly and indirectly linked to economic and political authority within the contemporary global landscape and the "discourses of 'minorities' within the geopolitical divisions of North and South" (Bhabha 1994, 245). The chapter will advance the argument on the role of literature, in communications, in the following four ways: firstly, the role of language as a medium through which literary expression takes its form. Secondly, an analysis on the feasibility of a pan-African notion of African literature. Thirdly, a discussion on three novelists who are the subjects of the discussion and their respective literary works. And fourthly, the role of literature (a communicative medium signifying cultural agency) as a form of Africa's soft power.

The next section will provide an overview of the historical underpinnings that undergird Africa's communication landscape in the modern world.

A historical overview of the continent

In 1963 when the Organisation of African Unity was formed, Emperor Haile Selassie of Ethiopia said:

> Thousands of years ago, civilisations flourished in Africa. . . . Their social patterns were their own and their cultures truly indigenous. . . . During those long years, Africans were born, lived and died. Men on other parts of this earth occupied themselves with their own concerns and, in their conceit, proclaimed that the world began and ended at their

horizons. All unknown to them, Africa developed in its own pattern, growing in its own life and in the Nineteenth Century re-emerged into the world's consciousness.[1]

Africa's reality, its diverse cultures existed long before many in distant shores knew of her actuality. Africa's existence was on her own terms. However, as a result of slavery and colonialism, Africa was to be interpreted and perceived through a lens unknown to her. Foreign journalists and novelists often used a frame of reference that dated back to that of European explorers to imagine Africa and its challenges (Rothmyer 2011, 6–7). Such narratives were used to justify the slave trade across the Atlantic and the subsequent colonial conquest by defining a people (Africans) who had had *their own* civilisation and identity, just defined in different ways. Today, Africa lacking its own international media house is still battling with the colonisation of its people's stories by another (Achebe 2000, 43). By taking back the ability to tell one's own stories, that is a form of "taking back the narrative" (Achebe 2000, 44).

For Africa to adequately communicate herself to the rest of the world, Africa will have to define her intellectual capabilities and sensibilities to develop this "frame of reference".[2] Modern African literature opens a window to the authentic stories of a people and thus becomes a communicative vehicle through which societies express themselves (Diamond 1989, 435). Political sociologist Larry Diamond succinctly captured the role of fiction in his book review of Chinua Achebe's *Anthills of the Savannah* saying: "[L]iterature may provide a precious and indispensable window into a society, a people and an era" (Diamond 1989, 435). Modern African literatures rose into the global literary scene and proliferated the consciousness of a local and international audience through wide dissemination because of the widespread use of the English language that bypassed the need for translation to reach English readers (Orthofer 2016, 2). The availability of fiction in English, particularly fiction from the African subcontinent enables the exposure of "readers to new stories, voices and places" (Orthofer 2016, 3).

In this modern 21st-century era, the ability to communicate has, arguably, been somewhat eased with the emergence and almost universal use of the English language as the "undisputed *lingua franca*" of the age especially in English-speaking African countries because large publishers and English-speaking readers are drawn to works that are not in translation (Orthofer 2016, 2). Modern African literature has traces in the works of the likes of Amos Tutuola's *The Palm-Wine Drinkard* and many others, including Achebe's *Things Fall Apart*. However, as far back as the 1930s African writers began writing literary works. Sol T. Plaatjie became the first black South African author of an English novel, titled *Mhudi* (Orthofer 2016, 194; wa Ngũgĩ 2018, 4).

Narratives in the fiction genre became (and are) a force for decolonising social constructs in a continent whose discourses were formerly hijacked in the years of colonial conquest. It is argued that just as the scholarly episteme currently grapples with decolonising knowledge production, modern African literature plays the role of "epistemological decolonisation" in its own right because fiction has a legitimate "place in social science scholarship" (Nyamnjoh 2012, 67; Mamdani 2016, 79).

Language choice in modern African literature

The emergence of the postcolonial novel exists at the intersection of a centralised linguistic system with colonial origins and the consequent quest for linguistic agency, autonomy and identity (Bolland 1996, 4). The use of the English language in the postcolonial African novel is indicative of using the tools bestowed upon the African people to communicate their identity and personhood to the rest of the world. The normative language choice has origins from the African Writers of English Expression Conference of 1962 that was held at Makerere University (wa Ngũgĩ 2018, 2). The conference was attended by young African writers who included Chinua Achebe (32 years), Christopher Okigbo (32 years), Wole Soyinka (28 years), Bloke Modisane (39 years) and others, with the aim of conceptualising "an African literary aesthetic" conveyed in English – as the title of the conference suggested (wa Ngũgĩ 2018, 2, 4). There are African writers who view the very use of the English language (or other European languages), as a means through which African writers express themselves, as a kind of Western imperialism to which Africans subject themselves and are accomplices, today (wa Thiong'o 1986, 8). One such an individual is the notable Kenyan writer Ngũgĩ wa Thiong'o in his book *Decolonising the Mind* (1986). In 1978 wa Thiong'o stopped using English as a medium for writing his fiction (wa Thiong'o 1986, 1–2; 2012, 9–10); while the now late Nigerian writer Chinua Achebe, one of the foremost respected African novelists, however, pointed to a more historical complexity with regards to the use of English (or other European languages) that serve as a *lingua franca* for African literature. Achebe said it is neither an either/or question, but rather a matter of using both English and indigenous African languages for this purpose – a hybridised linguistic strategy that reflects contemporary Nigeria (Bolland 1996, 5, 19). Because, as Achebe writes, "the only reason these alien languages are still knocking about is that they serve an actual need" particularly because of the "linguistic pluralism" distinct to Africa (Achebe 2009, 105).

In addition to the linguistic plurality on the continent, there are the practical concerns which include the following: the existing models of large publishers and the competitive nature of marketing budgets, and dissemination to as wide an audience as possible (Orthofer 2016, 2–3). Notwithstanding the validity of wa Thiong'o's arguments, Achebe's more pragmatic stance is often reflected in the fact that those countries whose "literary language is English are at an obvious advantage" because translations are a major challenge for publishers; and publishers often turn to books in English when "seeking foreign titles because it is the most widely understood language" (Orthofer 2016, 5, 11).

It is argued that not all languages are equal, for example "many European languages, including French and only recently Arabic and Chinese are relatively well represented in translation" (Orthofer 2016, 5) while others are not as represented. Therefore, the "practical" decisions associated with writing in English as opposed to other African indigenous languages is also reflective of colonial education that has strong remnants today, which takes the form of the linguistic hegemonic structures within which communication – in the form of fiction – takes place (Orthofer 2016, 11). Since the emergence of modern African novelists, they have been susceptible to the linguistic hegemonic structures because of restricted domestic production due to the uneven development of "literary and publishing infrastructure" at the local level (Orthofer 2016, 7). It was the British publisher Heinemann's African Writers Series that normalised English writing in Western and African markets (wa Ngũgĩ 2018, 17). As a result, the trend has been such that often some African novelists seek to have wide distributions of their works disseminated abroad and are bolstered because of their access to established metropolitan publishing houses. And often English-speaking African novelists are connected to Anglo-American publishing houses, Anglophone academia and therefore Anglophone book distribution networks (Orthofer 2016, 10). However, there is a caveat in that African novelists in various countries have different experiences. For example, in South Africa, there is a considerable body of work in Afrikaans, this however, is closely related to South Africa's history, which is beyond the scope of this chapter.

Nonetheless, the potency of English is a strong current which is mirrored in the fact that even writers who write in other African languages often ultimately translate their works into English. wa Thiong'o, an advocate for writing in indigenous languages, is a prime example as he is said to also "translate many of his works into English himself" (Orthofer 2016, 11).

Mary-Jean Nleya

A Pan-African notion of African literature

This chapter recognises the multiplicity of African stories, and does not seek to canvas the "African novel" as a monolith. The different regions of the continent are in themselves varied and diverse, and an attempt at painting the entire continent with one brush would be a disservice to the plurality of voices and complexities that do exist that all in their own way offer a communicative aspect for the continent. Southern Africa's literary scene cannot be compared to West Africa's, just as South Africa's cannot be compared to Nigeria's – the novels are each contextualised to the domestic social and historical processes innate to the specific country. As a point of departure, missionary printing presses, for example, Lovedale, became significant in growing early South African writing in the early 1900s (wa Ngũgĩ 2018, 4–5). South African writers of the early 1900s (prior to the wave of decolonisation) wrote in South African indigenous languages: Xhosa, Zulu, Sesotho and others (with translations in English). These writers included Thomas Mafolo's 1907 novel *Moeti oa Bochabela* (translated into English in 1934 into *Traveller to the East*) and *Chaka* written in 1925 but published in 1931. However, the trajectory of writing changed with the emergence of the "Makerere writers" during the wave of decolonisation, signaling an age of writing the African novel in English (wa Ngũgĩ 2018, 7). In African literary recollection there is a preoccupation with (and a celebration of) modern African literature in English (the Makerere writers) to the exclusion of early African writing – namely, as noted earlier, in South Africa in the early 1900s which featured indigenous African languages in creative writing (wa Ngũgĩ 2018, 7–8); however, an in-depth discussion on this is beyond the scope of this chapter.

It should also be noted that economic factors and structures play a significant role in the uneven development of domestic literary scenes in each African country. This is important in understanding book distribution networks, publishing houses, budgets for marketing new novels for the purposes of understanding the barriers to entry into publishing and maintaining a local literary culture (Orthofer 2016, 9).

The chapter focuses, for pragmatic reasons, exclusively on three Nigerian authors who have gained international literary significance and have been marketed as both Nigerian and African novelists; this does not ignore the literary vibrancy in the other African regions. The discussion here is also only limited on one (out of several) of the respective authors' literary works.

The argument this chapter seeks to advance is to highlight the importance of fiction as a form of "socioeconomic political thought" (Diamond 1989, 435) by using the selected works of inquiry and authors as a gateway into exploring the communicative potential of fiction, particularly employing a Pan-African notion of African literature. The next section of the chapter is to delve deeper into the literary works of the selected authors and their role as channels of communication, starting first with Chinua Achebe, followed by Chimamanda Ngozi Adichie and finally Wole Soyinka.

Chinua Achebe and Things Fall Apart's contribution to World literature

At the heart of human existence is the instinct to communicate, as Achebe puts it, humans are "story-making animals" and do not miss the opportunity to relate with others on "matching stories" (Achebe 2000, 59). The study of communication as a historical, linguistic, political and socioeconomic discourse through the lens of postcolonial literature permits a reimagining of social realities. The use of literary fiction as a "source of insights and understanding" is neglected in mainstream media and communications studies (Nash 1997, 13). Culture, societal norms, historical accounts and personal narratives are often encapsulated and captured in postcolonial African literatures and to this end literary narratives are a useful tool in media and communication studies. Those who view the world from different vantage points never quite view the world on the same terms; therefore, literature has the capacity to act as a bridge to make disparate people's cultures, languages, stories, histories connect in their shared humanity (Nyamnjoh 2012, 67 & 89–90). Chinua Achebe's *Things Fall Apart* (1994), originally published in 1958, a work of art and literary fiction, explores thematic issues of modernity – the elements wherefrom discourses on development were birthed. The novel and its characters provide an African perspective on the "reorganisation of their world, the alteration to their consciousness and redefinition of their values and developmental processes" resulting from colonialism (Agwuele 2012, 2) through the complex character of Okonkwo. The novel also presents an alternative epistemology to the social, political and cultural effects of the origins of development practice and European colonialism.

This novel is relevant because for centuries Africans, African institutions, African behaviours were presented in literature as homogenous and as "the negation of all human decencies" (Hammond and Jablow 1992, 20–23). African literature's contribution to World literature is an alternative form of African communication to the rest of the world, to convey voices that for many centuries had been subaltern to others. Literary fiction is more than merely the unknowing, passively consolidated fictitious stories, Achebe notes that such stories could be true or false, not in the way of news items, but rather as to their "genuineness and sincerity" (Achebe 2000, 33–34). Literary fiction is not only about the ability of a writer to weave words together in lyrical prose, bursting with tangible imagery; it is about the authenticity with which such stories are told. According to Achebe, "The stories we [Africans] have to tell could not be told for us by anyone else no matter how gifted or well-intentioned" (Achebe 1988, 25).

Achebe's *Things Fall Apart* recognised the importance of reclaiming the African story (Achebe 2000, 79). Achebe portrays a complex character, Okonkwo, whose complexity challenges Western historicity of European colonialism. The novel is set in Nigeria and follows the life of Okonkwo, who ascends to be a respected Igbo warrior, and is determined to live a life different from that of his father who died indebted and in disrepute. However, the trajectory of Okonkwo's own life is disrupted by European colonialism as he, a traditionalist, is unable to adapt to the changes brought by colonial rule. Achebe uses the tale of an African tragic hero (Okonkwo) and his experiences and response to colonial rule and his inability to modernise and hybridise his cultural ways. This tale also reflects the disruption of traditional African society.

Achebe known as the "father of modern African literature" was a postcolonial writer who told distinctly African, namely Nigerian stories, and who portrayed nuanced Nigerian characters against the backdrop of colonialism and its effect on human existence as well as the paradoxes in postcolonial Nigeria of power and revolution in his novels. Achebe opined that it was clear that an "African literary renaissance" was overdue and it was his goal and a major objective to "challenge stereotypes and the image of ourselves and our continent, and to recast them through stories, prose, essays" (Achebe 2012, 29). Achebe's earliest 1958 novel emerged as a contribution to the so-called modern African literature, providing the inclusion of the African voice and perspective to literary text that often neglected to give the other side of the African story. Achebe made use of literature as a "process of re-storying peoples who had been knocked silent by all kinds of dispossession" (Achebe 2000, 89). It was through the continual process of "re-storying" that would eventually result in a balance of stories in the global arena.

In one of Achebe's interviews he spoke of how he received letters from students in South Korea who had read his book, *Things Fall Apart*, and could identify with the main character,

Okonkwo. He spoke of how he realised that any dispossessed people could have easily identified with the novel, and how he would not have not thought of that at the time of writing the book.

In his reflections titled "Africa Is People", Chinua Achebe recalled a meeting with economists he was invited to attend in France in 1989 held by the OECD (Organisation for Economic Co-operation and Development). As a writer, he wondered how he, "an African novelist among predominantly Western bankers and economists", would participate in a meeting of this kind. He later made his own remarks prompted by the tangent the discussion on the 1980s structural adjustment policies (SAPs) in Africa had taken. He reflected in his essay that he "signalled his desire to speak and was given the floor", when he informed the meeting's attendees: "Here you are, spinning your fine theories, to be tried out in your imaginary laboratories. . . . I have news for you. Africa is *people*, real people. Have you thought, *really* thought, of Africa as *people*?" (Achebe 2009, 157).

Achebe, a novelist, was pleading for the economists at the OECD meeting in Paris that day to remember that behind the statistics and figures in matters of economics are actually real human faces, African faces. During the same conference, Achebe went further to personalise the implications of the SAPs by giving his native Nigeria as an illustration (Achebe 2009, 157–158). This speaks to the importance of Africa's inclusion in framing issues and thinking about creative avenues to imagine Africa's development and vis-à-vis ways to communicate such to the rest of the world.

The three-centuries-long Atlantic slave trade saw disparaging stories, and accompanying images, of Africa that attempted to justify the existence and continuance of the Atlantic slave trade, and later similar tropes were also used to defend imperialism and colonialism (Achebe 2009, 79). Contemporary forms of communicating stories that reflect Africa and her stories to a global audience grapple against the centuries-old legacy of stereotypes (Achebe 2009, 78–79). Achebe noted that it is impossible to simply "turn off" such a practice in one day, or in one lifetime.[3]

Africa, its complexity, nuance and the constituent countries, are yet to be discovered and truly understood and not simplified to the traditional news media binaries of good or bad, poor or rich, corrupt or not corrupt. The binary stories arise from having journalistic material that need to fit into media narratives. The gatekeepers of the news hold power in making editorial decisions on the kinds and perspectives of information their audience, from the rest of the world, wants to consume in published or broadcast news.

During the postcolonial period, Achebe used both fiction, nonfiction and personal essays to disgorge colonial stereotypes and colonialism as a whole in his writings. The perspective that Achebe brought into his stories attracted a wider audience to an alternative perspective that was not previously afforded to them, and the wide dissemination of his works was also bolstered by the mastery of the language choice he employed, English.

The African perspective told by Achebe empowered and emboldened other African writers to write their own literary texts, including authors such as Chimamanda Ngozi Adichie.

African woman and international pop-culture influencer, Chimamanda Ngozi Adichie: realist fiction, Half of a Yellow Sun

Adichie, an African woman and international pop-culture influencer, has used the power of words to rise to international prominence: among other things, being quoted in lyrics of pop-icons and having her words printed on the clothing of an affluent fashion house. Adichie's TED Talk, "The Danger of a Single Story", also had its own trajectory. In the TED Talk, she highlights the perils of blanketing one experience as representative of the whole. The multiplicity of stories, given a platform to be told, have the ability to connect cultural barriers and therefore shift people's perceptions of the world around them.

Adichie says, "When we reject the single story, when we realise that there is never a single story about any place, we regain a kind of paradise" (Adichie 2009 TED Talk). Adichie's notion of rejecting a single story can be used as a prism through which to analyse communicative methods that relate to representing Africa to the rest of the world in various forms: media, literature and culture. Prior to the emergence of modern African literature in the 1950s and 1960s, Africa was the subject of numerous stereotypes in the fictitious stories told: "The problem with stereotypes is not that they are untrue, but that they are incomplete", Adichie says. "They make one story, the *only* story" (Adichie 2009 TED Talk).

Adichie's 2006 realist fiction, *Half of a Yellow Sun*, is set in postcolonial Nigeria in the 1960s, before and during the Biafran Civil War. Adichie gives a tale of ordinary people, families and couples caught in between a catastrophic battle driven by more than just a binary of ethnic or religious strife. She portrays varied types of characters: from your learned professors in a university town, to the village boy, to the wealthy businesspeople; poor families to affluent ones simply trying to survive the ordeal of war. She delicately weaves in history, the complexity of ordinary people, issues of colonialism and its effects on nation-states and its constituent ethnicities. She also uses the conversations of a formerly colonised group of learned professors in a university town of Nsukka to challenge colonialism, the meddling of internal domestic affairs by foreign powers for their own neocolonial interests and also the imperial boundaries of the Berlin Conference that originally formed Nigeria.

The underlying forces that resulted in the Biafran Civil War and it lasting for as long as it did were mostly overshadowed by the visceral reports on hunger, famine and kwashiorkor-ridden children in international news media. Afua Hirsch's 2018 BBC radio documentary on the Biafran Civil War referenced how this kind of reporting set the precedent for the reportage that relates to Africa and other Third World countries today.[4] Adichie's novel, however, uses realist narrative prose to engage with the social and political narrative that surrounded the time-period in Nigeria. Adichie's *Half of a Yellow Sun*, like other well-written and researched realist fiction novels, solidify what Achebe said during an interview that "the truth of fiction is sometimes stronger than the truth of the newspapers".[5] This speaks to the importance of literature in communicating a truth that is deeper than that which the news media can communicate, particularly in creating empathy and building bridges across disparate peoples (Nyamnjoh 2012, 67 & 89).

Adichie's *Half of a Yellow Sun* uses three separate narrative points of view: that of Ugwu, a houseboy from a rural background – who views things from his vantage point and interprets things from his own lived experiences; Olanna, an educated woman from a wealthy family; and Richard, a British expatriate, the Other, who is also the observer. These perspectives Adichie uses to tell the story are relevant in guarding against telling a single story. The themes that run along the novel are modernity and tradition, history and politics, love and betrayal, poverty and wealth and many others.

Adichie's imagination, informed by history, enables the reader to familiarise oneself with the time-period in a humanising way. Similarly, Adichie's 2009 short story, *A Private Experience*, chronicles the meeting of two Nigerian women from different socioeconomic backgrounds who are both fleeing a violent outburst in the marketplace. The two main characters are Chika, an Igbo Christian from an affluent background who is also a student; while the other character is an unnamed woman, simply referred to as The Woman. The Woman is a Hausa Muslim, who is not from an affluent background, but is market trader in Kano. Adichie uses Chika's perspective, in the third person, to tell the story and bridges the often-divisive rhetoric of religious, social and ethnic difference to connect readers to the ways in which two people from opposing backgrounds can be each other's help-mates and be united by loss, violence, need and shared humanity.

Adichie's stories, both her novels and short stories, attempt to tell various perspectives to a social or political occurrence. Of course, her stories are fictitious, but borrow from a realist occurrence. She expands her imagination to the point of offering various perspectives of a single story, thereby proffering deeper levels of the human experience and, in so doing, enabling the reader to empathise with her characters. This speaks to the effect of literature and the underlying power of literature to expand the world's definition of a certain peoples it has often viewed as "Other" (Nyamnjoh 2012, 89).

The first African Nobel laureate in literature, Wole Yoyinka and his play Death of a King's Horseman

In 2012, Wole Soyinka opined:

> The African continent is an intimate part of the histories of others, both cause and consequence, a complex organism formed of its own internal pulsation and external interventions, one that continues to be part of, yet is often denied, the triumphs and advances of the rest of the world.
>
> *(2012, 1)*

African writers have been using their creativity, as intellectuals and social critics, to question and mirror Africa's place in a global context (Adebanwi 2014, 411–412), aware of the political and sociocultural contexts in which they operate and often using their realist writings as dialogic to anticolonial and postindependence movements (wa Ngũgĩ 2018, 6). Soyinka (like many of his contemporaries) "did not separate their literary aesthetics from the material work of politics" and he specifically faced detention in 1966 and was later exiled (wa Ngũgĩ 2018, 3).

One of Soyinka's plays, *Death and the King's Horseman* (2002) written in 1975 (derived from the occurrence of an actual historical event of 1946 in Oyo, an ancient city of Nigeria), illuminates the conflicts that arise as a result of the colonial effects of ideological projections that cause binary oppositions whereby positive representations are the norms of the West. However, Soyinka's play is not a condemnation of the West, but rather illuminates a tragedy that is precipitated by the intervention of an outsider in the affairs of the protagonist. Soyinka achieves this by making use of an alternative form of communication – a cultural production, a play.

The play depicts a British district officer (who is deployed to the British colony of Nigeria) interjecting to prevent the ritual-suicide of the dead king's horseman, a traditional practice. According to custom, the horseman was required to perform the ritual-suicide in order to accompany his dead king to the "other world". Soyinka uses poetic rhythmic sentences in the play to offer a complex play that not only shows the British district officer's intervention to suit his interests of impressing the British prince who is in Nigeria, but also the lack of understanding of culture, custom and sacred practices of the people whom he is there to preside over. The play makes use of a thematic portrayal to convey a complex meaning to the play. Soyinka does not simplify the play, squarely placing the blame on the British colonialists in preventing ritual, sacred Yoruba practice; however, he illustrates the role of the Yoruba horseman's delay in undergoing the ritual as one of the reasons that leads to his own demise. Yet, Soyinka nonetheless reveals that the lack of understanding by the British district officer (who occupies the geographic space of the Yorubas and who merely dismisses the cultural and religious practices of the "Other" as barbaric) precipitates the tragedy.

Soyinka's play introduces an unfamiliar reader to Yoruba culture and the time-period in which Nigeria was subject to colonial rule. This play also reveals the customs and conflicts that arise from the transformations that arose from the co-existence of two distinct cultures within one geographic space. Soyinka also depicts the African (Yoruba) worldview in a manner that is neither belittling nor elevating of their cultural practice – leaving it to the reader to read deeper into the self-actualisation and agency of the characters.

The first African to be awarded the Nobel Prize in Literature in 1986, Soyinka revealed the tensions that arise from societies that coalesce – Yoruba cultural and religious practice with European culture and domination. In the preface of the play, Soyinka admonishes readers from interpreting the play simply, singularly and as merely a depiction of "culture clash". However, when reading the play, it is apparent that the play offers a complex glimpse into the lives of ordinary Yorubas of the time. The contribution of this piece of creative work to World literature, familiarises unfamiliar peoples with a culture different to their own and which could easily be "othered" and dismissed. The play was specifically referenced as one of Soyinka's seminal works when he was awarded the Nobel Prize in 1986, and this piece of literature, the *Death and the King's Horseman*, illuminates the notion that alternative forms of communication (of African identity and culture) can be communicated without binary representations. And engages with traditional dance and music to enhance its themes.

To this end, Soyinka, Achebe and Adichie (as have other early and modern African novelists not included herein) have become tellers of diverse powerful – and in many cases relatable – African stories that have gone on to tell truths that are "sometimes stronger than the truth of the newspapers".[6] This kind of genre, fiction, has a legitimate place in social science as a discipline, as it is an "alternative space" for the marginalised voice to be presented in "its complexities and nuances" (Nyamnjoh 2012, 67). The next section of the chapter will underscore the importance of Africa's cultural production in solidifying its soft power in the global political economy.

Modern African literature as Africa's soft power: a look at Joseph Nye's concept of soft power

The pattern of Africa's history (slavery, followed by colonialism and apartheid) reveals the continent's historical deprivation in its ability to use its cultures to influence both local and global discourses because African cultures were portrayed as the antithesis of modernity and progress (Nyamnjoh 1999, 30). This has conversely resulted in Africa's current engagement with the rest of the world to be on unequal terms and has deprived the continent with equal opportunities to "prove itself on the world's marketplace of cultures" (Nyamnjoh 1999, 34). In essence the global system and its attention glorified that which was pointed away from Third World (African) countries' culture and cultural production (Bhabha 1994, xi). However, it is argued in this chapter that the marketplace of cultures is poorer without encountering Africa's myriad of cultures (Nyamnjoh 2015, 1).

As a point of departure, it should be noted that it is paradoxical the way in which the execution of African countries' cultural production (in English) as a form of soft power is reliant on the "soft power" of English as an important element of international communication. The use of English, as the abovementioned subsection on the language choice discussed, can be used as a communicative strategy to assert Africans' agency and outward self-actualisation, particularly because of the international communicative potential of English. The use of English establishes modes of agency and recognition in the current "cultural world order" of literary production (Bhabha 1994, xviii). It is in the context of cultural production that the following discussion on "soft power" is situated, namely cultural production as the locus of Africa's soft power, and the soft power of English as an external communicative strategy.

Joseph Nye, American political scientist, coined the term "soft power" in the late 1980s and states that "it arises from the attractiveness of a country's culture, political ideals and policies" (Nye 2004, 7–10). The term soft power emanates from the following sources: firstly, culture; secondly, political values and thirdly, foreign policies (Nye 2004, 11). For purposes of this chapter and specifically this section, culture will be the main focus point.

What does culture mean? Culture refers to the consolidation of shared knowledge, beliefs, principles and ideals that are significant and practiced in a society or a group of people within a certain society (Nyamnjoh 1999, 19; Nye 2004, 41). Literature, art and education are referred to as "high culture", whilst mass entertainment, such as music and films, are referred to as "popular culture" (Nye 2004, 41). The primary currencies that soft power engages with are values, culture, policies and institutions, and the main aim of soft power is to induce and attract others into its way of life and by virtue of this phenomenon sets the agenda. In essence, the politics of soft power is the "contest for attractiveness, legitimacy and credibility". The only way in which one can be attracted to something is if they are exposed to the particular culture in ways that do not undermine it, and the only way to familiarise others with varying cultures (in the soft power contest for legitimacy and attractiveness in the eyes of other societies) is the propensity to distribute information, which in turn becomes a source of soft power (Nye 2004, 31, 41–42, 54). However, it is fundamental to note that Euro/American soft-power dimensions emerge as dominant because of a particular kind of Western modernity that was historically seen as "worthy of recognition" that was driven by colonial conquest and the civilising mission (Nyamnjoh 2015, 1).

Nye posits: "Winning both the hearts and minds [of people] has always been important" (Nye 2004, 8, 30). In an interview,[7] Nye noted that the attraction and appeal of the US can emanate from varying features, ranging from Harvard to Hollywood, Starbucks to McDonalds, Microsoft to Michael Jordan etc. Nye, however, also cautions against merely thinking about soft power as likened to the influence of "Coca-Cola, blue jeans" and the like. Nye's earliest conception of soft power and his analysis of the same relates to the soft power of the US in the realm of international politics, in the eyes of global and domestic audiences. And to this end, he recognises that "America has long had a great deal of soft power" (Nye 2004, 11). However, in this chapter the relevance of this concept is centred on the role of cultural production in asserting agency and recognition to peoples once knocked silent in the global communication realm.

African countries can harness the communicative effect of modern African literature (and its contribution to World literature) to portray African culture in a way that familiarises international readers with African culture and identity. Indeed, in the "traditional balance-of-power politics", Africa neither has military nor economic power (hard power) comparable to high-income countries to afford the continent to "get what it wants" in the global political economy, whether through policies or regulations. And at the same time, Africa faces dilemmas in terms of global inclusion, as a site controlled economically at the global structural level (whether through governance structures within international financial institutions or its subjection to lopsided international trade rules). As a result, cultural production emerges as a way that "minorities" in the geopolitical world order antagonise and challenge the normative parameters set by such global (as well as local) power structures (Bhabha 1994, xvii–xviii). Therefore, harnessing the literary role in order to mould the dignity of African culture and identity in global discourses is imperative (quite apart from those to be pitied, aided or modernised).

The respective cultures and ideologies of powerful countries such as the US and Britain are viewed as attractive and, as a result, other countries are more willing to adopt and follow them

(Nye 2004, 33–35). The emergence of such cultural powers are the remnants of the "civilising mission" of the 18th century's Enlightenment period, which today subjects African cultures to "unfair competition" which emanated from "Westerners' glorifying of themselves and their cultures" while at the same time "devaluing the African and his creative initiative" (Nyamnjoh 1999, 34).

Nye submits that, in the near future, countries that will be seen to be more attractive and vis-à-vis to gain soft power in the global information age are those "with multiple channels of communication that help to frame issues" and who have a dominant culture that are linked to universal norms (liberalism, pluralism and autonomy) and who are also seen internationally as credible as a result of their domestic institutions, policies and values. As technology continues to make information flows easier and as a result makes the world increasingly smaller, soft power is set to become an important and dominant factor in the information revolution (Nye 2004, 41).

These conditions suggest that the US is most likely to bear the fruits of soft-power domination, and much of Nye's analysis is with respect to the US (Nye 2004, 33). However, the US does not dominate in all factors of attraction, as attraction is tailored to specific audiences. Additionally, the US has seen a rapid decline in terms of desirability and credibility in the eyes of the international community as a result of the country's recent divisive social and political climate ahead of the 2020 presidential elections. In terms of quality of life, in 2018, Norway was ranked as the best country to live in, while the US was ranked 23rd.[8]

Despite the least attractive aspects of America, it should be borne in mind that economic prowess significantly contributes to wealth, but more so to reputation and attractiveness. With regards to economic indicators, the US is the largest economy and over half of the world's brands are American;[9] whereas social indicators show that the US is the world's major exporter of television programmes, movies and music, the US publishes the most books in comparison to other countries, and also has the second largest number of Nobel laureates in literature (closely after France).[10] Europe is close competition to American soft power resources. As former colonisers of African states, Europe has familiar links to the continent, and therefore European art, music, literature, fashion and food are strong cultural attractions (Nye 2004, 75–77). France is the lead in Nobel Prizes for Literature, while Britain is third.[11] Britain is also third in music sales. France attracts more tourists than the US. Soccer, a European sport, enjoys more global popularity than typical US sports (American football or baseball) (Nye 2004, 75).

In television news, there has been a diversification in the framing of issues quite apart from an Anglo-American reference point or perspective with the emergence of Al Jazeera – this has resulted in the pluralism of global communication and information flows (Nye 2004, 54).

As a result of America's lead in many of the conditions that attribute to soft-power dominance, the modernisation process has been subject to external standards of America (Nye 2004, 41–42). During colonialism, Africa was narrated and interpreted in terms of the Eurocentric prism that was dominated by the colonisers, whereas in the contemporary age, American imported culture pervades many aspects of African life and it is "a medium through which people around the world constantly reorganise their individual and collective identities" (Nye 2004, 41 citing Notoji 2000, 225). The importance regarding the dynamics of cultural production proffers a profundity to mirror and express critiques to the status quo and thereby directs the conversation towards a path "not entirely dominated by [Western] forces of economic and social control" (Bhabha 1994, 29).

Therefore, what is required is an African experience to be given voice and legitimacy in today's global discourses because the world's marketplace of cultures and ideas is poorer with an absent, disengaged Africa (Nyamnjoh 2015, 1 & Nyamnjoh 1999, 34). Euro/American domination in the global communications sphere have created a hunger for something different. This was evidenced by the global success and wide reception of *Black Panther* – the Marvel film that was set in a fictional African country (Wakanda) with a predominantly black cast, partly spoken in Xhosa (an African indigenous language) and signifying parts of African culture. Despite the film's critiques, as essentialising and romanticising the continent, which go beyond this chapter, the reception of the film worldwide speaks to a place for Africa and its cultures in the global imagination and the marketplace of cultures.

Conclusion

The standards and tools which African novelists use to communicate Africa to the rest of the world today in modern African literature are those that originated from the historical and contemporary hegemonic structure, either from former colonisers or the Americanisation of global information networks. However, needless to say, African writers such as the earlier-cited Soyinka have enriched the English language with narrative prose (Aidoo 2014, 9).

The view of Africa as inferior exists even up to today. However, modern African literature is about reclaiming the narrative that was for so long told by others, other than Africans themselves. By virtue of this, African literature is a decolonising force in modern communication structures that are historically known to be dominated along Euro/American dimensions. Literature as a form of communication – communication bursting with imagery and colour, narrative prose and history – has the potential to eliminate a paradigmatic perception of Africa's "alienness" in global discourses. Larry Diamond said this in his book review of Achebe's *Anthills of the Savannah*: "The fiction of a certain country, culture or period may reveal more of its values, customs, conflicts, stresses, changes and transformations than does all the formal scholarship of historians and social scientists" (Diamond 1989, 435).

Communicating Africa's culture and identity, particularly through the media camera lens has often been to contrast African norms that have been "fuelled by assumptions that Africa has little to offer" (Nyamnjoh 2015, 1), and never quite through the lens of conversation, understanding and respect. The modern way of communicating Africa to the rest of the world has progressed over the years and surely the media's portrayal, and indeed media audiences, are not overtly narrow-minded. The transformation of news headlines being from: "The Hopeless Continent" to "Africa Rising" or "Aspiring Africa" have attempted to assuage the gloom. Such recognition has conditioned a kind of "convergence and mimicry imposed on Africa by the prescriptive gaze of those claiming civilizational superiority" (Nyamnjoh 2015, 2). However, there is still a lack of adequate understanding of the diversity and distinctiveness of African culture, identity and history, and the nuance of these. And African fiction, particularly in a widely spoken language such as English, has the global communicative potential to assert both externally and internally – to a global audience as well as among Africans – Africa's social agency through the diverse cultural representations.

Africa may not have an international news outlet with which to contribute to the world's consciousness Africa's framing of issues. However, Africa has established and emerging novelists and writers who constitute part of Africa's intelligentsia who have the propensity to be a conduit of communicating Africa both to herself and to the rest of the world,[12] thereby launching modern African literature's contribution to World literature as Africa's very own soft power to decolonise global discourses.

Notes

1 As seen in T. Mbeki. 2014. Africa's renaissance and new partnership for development. In Agyeman-Duah, I. and Ogochukwu, P., eds. *Essays in Honour of Wole Soyinka at 80*. Oxford: Ayebia Clarke Publishing.

2 Ibid.
3 Bacon, K. 2000. An African voice. *The Atlantic*, August. www.theatlantic.com/magazine/archive/2000/08/an-african-voice/306020/ (Accessed 23 June 2018).
4 BBC Radio 4. 2018. *Afua Hirsch, Archive on 4*. Britain and Biafra 50 Years on, 28 April. www.bbc.co.uk/programmes/b0b0lxm3 (Accessed 2 May 2018).
5 *The Harvard Crimson*. 2008. Chinua Achebe Explores Legacy After 50 Years, 21 November. www.thecrimson.com/article/2008/11/21/chinua-achebe-explores-legacy-after-50/ (Accessed 9 October 2020).
6 Ibid.
7 Joseph Nye. Interview by *Philadelphia Inquirer* foreign policy columnist Trudy Rubin, 12 February 2009. https://www.youtube.com/watch?v=F8udhM8QKxg (Accessed 10 June 2018).
8 World Economic Forum. 2018. *The Inclusive Development Index 2018: Results and Key Findings*. http://reports.weforum.org/the-inclusive-development-index-2018/results-and-key-findings/.
9 Daneshkhu, S. and Campbell, C. 2017. *Top 100 Global Brands, 2017*, August. https://ig.ft.com/top-100-global-brands/, as seen in Nye, J. 2004. *Soft Power: The Means to Success in World Politics*. New York: Public Affairs.
10 The Nobel Prize. *All Nobel Prizes in Literature*. https://www.nobelprize.org/prizes/lists/all-nobel-prizes-in-literature/ (Accessed 5 October 2020).
11 Ibid.
12 As seen in Mbeki (2014).

References

Achebe, C. 1988. *Hopes and Impediments: Selected Essays*. New York: Anchor Books.
Achebe, C. 1994. *Things Fall Apart*. New York: Anchor.
Achebe, C. 2000. *Home and Exile*. Oxford: Oxford University Press.
Achebe, C. 2009. *The Education of a British-Protected Child*. New York: Penguin Books.
Achebe, C. 2012. *There Was a Country: A Personal History of Biafra*. London: Penguin Press.
Adebanwi, W. 2014. The writer as social thinker. *Journal of Contemporary African Studies*, 32(4): 405–420.
Adichie, C.N. 2006. *Half of a Yellow Sun*. New York: Alfred A Knopf.
Adichie, C.N. 2009. A private experience. In C.N. Adichie, *The Thing Around Your Neck*. New York: Alfred A. Knopf.
Agwuele, A. 2012. *Development, Modernism and Modernity in Africa*. New York: Taylor & Francis, Routledge.
Aidoo, A.A. 2014. Death and the King's Horseman: Ten of one in ten. In Agyeman-Duah, I. and Ogochukwu, P., eds. *Essays in Honour of Wole Soyinka at 80*. Banbury: Ayebia Clarke Publishing.
Bhabha, H.K. 1994. *The Location of Culture*. New York: Routledge.
Bolland, J. 1996. *Language and the Quest for Political and Social Identity in the African Novel*. New York: Woeli Publishing Services.
Diamond, L. 1989. Fiction as political thought. *African Affairs*, 88(352): 435–445.
Hammond, D. and Jablow, A. 1992. *The Africa That Never Was*. Prospect Heights, IL: Waveland Press.
Mamdani, M. 2016. Between the public intellectual and the scholar: Decolonization and some post-independence initiatives in African higher education. *Inter-Asia Cultural Studies*, 17(1): 68–83.
Nash, H. 1997. *A Novel Approach to Education and Development: Insights from African Women Writers*. https://mro.massey.ac.nz/bitstream/handle/10179/2186/02_whole.pdf?sequence=1&isAllowed=y (Accessed 23 December 2018).
Notoji, M. 2000. Cultural transformation of John Philip Sousa and Disneyland in Japan. In Wagnleitner, R. and May, E.T., eds. *Here, There, and Everywhere: The Foreign Politics of American Popular Culture*. Hanover: University Press of New England.
Nyamnjoh, F. 1999. African cultural studies, cultural studies in Africa: How to make a useful difference. *Critical Arts*, 13(1): 15–39.
Nyamnjoh, F. 2012. Intimate strangers: Connecting fiction and ethnography. *Alternation*, 19(1): 65–92.
Nyamnjoh, F. 2015. Incompleteness: Frontier Africa and the currency of conviviality. *Journal of Asian and African Studies*, 1–18.
Nye, J. 2004. *Soft Power: The Means to Success in World Politics*. New York: Public Affairs.

Orthofer, M.A. 2016. *The Complete Review Guide to Contemporary World Fiction*. New York: Columbia University Press.

Rothmyer, K. 2011. *They Wanted Journalists to Say 'Wow': How NGOs Affect U.S. Media Coverage of Africa*. Joan Shorestein Center Discussion Paper Series, D-61. https://shorensteincenter.org/they-wanted-journalists-to-say-wow-how-ngos-affect-u-s-media-coverage-of-africa/.

Soyinka, W. 2002. *Death and the King's Horseman*. New York: W. W. Norton & Company.

Soyinka, W. 2012. *Of Africa*. New Haven: Yale University Press.

wa Ngũgĩ, M. 2018. *The Rise of the African Novel: Politics of Language, Identity, and Ownership*. University of Michigan Press: Ann Arbor.

wa Thiong'o, N. 1986. *Decolonising the Mind: The Politics of Language in African Literature*. London: Heinemann.

wa Thiong'o, N. 2012. *Globaletics: Theory and the Politics of Knowing*. New York: Columbia University Press.

11

Citizen journalism and conflict transformation

Exploring netizens' digitized shaping of political crises in Kenya

Toyin Ajao

Introduction

In 2018, the global number of Internet users rose significantly to over 4 billion, in comparison to the 750 million Internet users in view in 2001 (Internet Live Stats 2018). About 453 million of these worldwide Internet users reside in Africa (Internet World Stats 2018). They account for only 35 per cent of the continent's entire population. Nonetheless, the impacts of the African Internet users' sociopolitical engagement, especially through citizen journalism, are telling. The concept of citizen journalism, which is based upon 'ordinary' citizens "playing an active role in the process of collecting, reporting, analysing, and disseminating news and information" (Bowman and Willis 2003), according to Watson and Wadhwa (2014) has moved from its infancy to a matured platform where citizen journalists' multiple roles include conflict management. These amateurs, who sometimes include professional journalists who prefer a less constricting echo chamber in which to air their views, have revolutionized the way in which news is produced and consumed. They have also shown there is inherent democratic power in the user-generated content that has demonopolized traditional media, challenged dictatorial regime, and provided organic realities from peoples' lived-experiences (Banda 2010; Moyo 2011; Mutsvairo and Columbus 2012; Allan 2013).

For instance, the Kenyan new media platforms have continued to stand as one of the most vibrant and palpable online communities in Africa with 85 per cent of the population utilizing the Internet (Internet World Stats 2018). Thus, in the age of the new media, where chaos sometimes reigns on the Internet, members of the general public have devised a nonviolent techno-response to and engagement with violence (Bock 2012). Back in 2008, when the new media were still nascent in Kenya, four Kenyan bloggers engaged in a timely citizen journalism activity by creating the Ushahidi Platform to fill the information void created through the banning of the live broadcasts by the Minister of Internal Security, John Michuki, during the post-election violence (PEV). While both the burgeoning online community and the mass media were criticized for fuelling the embers of violence through ethnicized hate speech, these netizens decided to utilize the ubiquitous new media to provide alternative actions for conciliation and justice

(Jeffery 2011). According to Banda (2010) and Junne (2013), the Ushahidi's open-source software contributes to the significance of citizen journalism platforms for nonviolent technological interventions.

Also, Ushahidi crisis mapping and other relevant information gathered about the hotspot of violence in the Rift Valley were used for Red Cross humanitarian deployment and police intervention. Beyond the mapping, Ushahidi undertook other projects, such as the Uwiano early warning multiagent consortium and the Uchaguzi constitutional referendum and election monitoring mechanism. Furthermore, in a bid to mitigate partisan ethno-nationalism, and demand transformative governance beyond 2008, other nonviolent technological initiatives sprang up among Kenyan netizens. Among which are the Mzalendo platform that keeps a watchful eye on the parliamentarians, Afroes that invests in online games for community peace education, Sisi Ni Amani Kenya (SNA-K) that synergized local peace actors for distribution of peace messages in the 2013 general elections, the Map Kibera that presents verified figures of its inhabitants for political inclusion and the Twitter Chief who governs his community via Twitter.

This chapter is based on interpretivist qualitative research using nonprobability snowball sampling technique. In-depth interviews of 28 research participants, including the Ushahidi platform founders, partnered organizations, and intermediary institutions were carried out in Nairobi from August to November 2016. Data were amassed through semi-structured and unstructured interviews of four members of the Ushahidi platform, six other bloggers/citizen journalists outside the Ushahidi platform, seven civil society organization leaders/workers, three governmental workers, five writers/journalists, two activists and one politician. Two more members of the civil society were interviewed via email exchanges in April 2017 to supplement new questions that emerged during data analysis. The particular interest in Kenya and Ushahidi was as a result of the growing scholarly interest in broadening the new terrain of people-centred approaches to peacemaking in the twenty-first century context.

Data were analyzed with thematic techniques. The data thus revealed a conflict transformation paradigm in the cumulative efforts of Kenyan interventionist netizens who are committed to nonviolent digitized intervention in shaping political crises. In the context of this chapter, how several initiatives of the netizens under discourse are addressing political crises through nonviolent approach is highlighted. Finally, this chapter provides the empirical accounts of Ushahidi, Sisi ni Amani, Mzalendo, Map Kiberia, Afroes and the Twitter Chief's post-conflict nonviolent technological interventions and their conflict transformation influences.

The dynamic of the media in the context of Ushahidi in Kenya's 2008 PEV

Owing to election irregularities resulting in the deaths of over 1,000 people and the displacement of another 500,000 (Mwiandi 2008), Kenya witnessed its cruelest bloodbath since independence. According to Mwiandi (2008), the 2008 PEV brought to the fore deep ethnic divisions among the public rooted in socioeconomic and political problems. Other scholars pin the cataclysmic events on generational conflicts around land disputes, unfair distribution of resources, tribalism, human rights abuses, corruption, despotism, oligarchy, and colonial legacy.

The presidential elections that were conducted on the December 27, 2007, with Mwai Kibaki and Raila Odinga as its main contenders, had plunged the country into an unprecedented political, security, and humanitarian crisis. In the accounts of several scholars and human rights reports, the initial violence was spontaneous as a reaction to the perceived rigging of the elections by the government (Kagwanja 2009). Subsequently, while more facts emerged about the election and Kibaki hurried oath taking, more violence erupted in the Nairobi slum and the Rift Valley province. Odinga's supporters likewise declared him a winner, leading to Kenya contending with two presidents in one political seat. After the double-declarations, the spontaneous pandemonium became retaliatory and later morphed into more organized and state-driven strife.

The mass media houses were alleged to have accelerated the violence by spreading "alarmist information", which further sent the nation into bedlam (Makinen and Kuira 2008). While the divisive nascent online community began to engage in ethnicized tirades, four citizen journalists teamed up to create the Ushahidi (a Kiswahili word for "testimony" or "witness") crowdsourcing platform to document the extent of the violence. This platform emerged as a result of citizens' desire 'to do something' when information became truncated due to the ban of Kenyan's broadcasting houses by the Ministry of Internal Security (Makinen and Kuira 2008). The four bloggers, namely, Ory Okolloh, Juilana Rotich, David Kobia, and Erik Hersman, went to work swiftly via the Ushahidi platform to report, document, and provide information to the wider populace and the international community on the extent of the upheavals. This documentation resulted in a 'mashup' of information leading to a graphic representation of the crisis on Google Maps for the purposes of documentation, justice, and conciliation (Jeffery 2011).

On the ground, the Kenyan populace felt betrayed by the national and the international media during the 2008 onslaught (Mackay, Interview by author. Skype Call. Nairobi, October 5, 2016). Several research participants state that the mass media engaged in divisive and biased practices during the 2007 elections. Kenya's mass media, which include the print media, radio, and television, were a triad of complicit professional journalists who fuelled the 2008 PEV with what they reported and how they reported. Their broadcasts and materials were skewed towards agitating one ethnic group against another. For instance, one of the local-language radio stations, Kass FM, was accused of spreading ethnicized messages that fuelled the 2008 PEV. During the International Criminal Court (ICC) investigations and proceedings, Joshua Arap Sang, the head of operations at Kass FM, was arraigned to answer for his instigative role in intensifying the 2008 PEV via ethnicized broadcasts favouring the Kalenjins.

Mochama (Interview by author. Tape recording. Nairobi, September 22, 2016), a Kenyan journalist, puts the situation in this perspective:

> Of course, more vernacular radio stations took on even more, should I say violent messaging? We saw that with people like Joshua Arap Sang accused in the ICC. And three days after conflagration began to happen in Kenya, there was a general headline, you know of "We Want Peace" across all the major newspapers in Kenya and that was in 2008; January 3rd actually. Three days after you know, what people now acronym as the PEV, the post-election violence had begun. Which is the media's attempt to overcorrect the situation.

Mochama (Interview by author. Tape recording. Nairobi, September 22, 2016) believes the mass media could do better in scrutinizing what these politicians' intentions are for leading the country by not effectively questioning politicians' agendas and manifestos. Thus, the government gets away with cosmetic truth that contributes to the polarization and convulsion of the country, which is one of the reasons why most interviewers see citizen journalism as a positive platform that brings out hidden truths, exposes injustices, and provides organic realities on different matters. Not that Kenyan society has entirely turned to citizen journalism platform as the main source of information, but the growing consumption of information and netizens' actions are more visible in the Kenyan cyberspace – from the blogosphere of Bikozulu to the Twitter-yard of #KOT. Smart (Interview by author. Tape recording. Nairobi, November 16,

2016), reflects on "Citizen journalism as a platform that has become effective in watching the watchdog, which is the mass media". Ngito (Interview by author. Tape recording. Nairobi, September 7, 2016), founder of Map Kibera, proclaims that "Citizen journalism works because it is a people-focussed platform". He explains further that the platform could cut like a knife when taking the government or the mass media to task, even in the face of political oppression and repression. He concludes that it is also a platform burgeoning with divergent representations of the sociopolitical and economic needs of all sectors of society – from the upper elites to the lower working class.

Smart (Interview by author. Tape recording. Nairobi, November 16, 2016) relates to citizen journalists as a community mouthpiece and harbingers of needed information for intervention. To him, it is easier for citizen journalists to bring out the truth as they see it as opposed to the profit-oriented mass media burdened with heavy equipment and different agendas. Mwangi (Interview by author. Tape recording. Nairobi, October 17, 2016) also worries about the tenacity of the mass media to maximize profit, which has changed the way they were the truth-bringers in the Moi political dispensation.

Conversely, the director of the Kenya Human Rights Commission (KHRC), Kegoro (Interview by author. Tape recording. Nairobi, September 29, 2016) underscores the stark division permeating the Kenyan sociopolitical sphere and how the new media helped promote division and hatred in Kenya's 2007 elections. He blames the mass media for their lack of adherence to the ethics and standards of journalism in the way they had regularly succumbed to government pressure and manipulation, especially in 2008.

By and large, both the online platform and mass media promoted ethnicized biases in the Kenya's 2008 PEV, which, according to Kobia (Interview by author. Skype Call. Nairobi, October 3, 2016), made the fresh avenue that Ushahidi provided for documentation unique in shifting the people's attention to do something more positive. Thus, when Ushahidi emerged out of the concern of a few Kenyan bloggers to do something about the violence ravaging Kenya in 2008, it stood out among the polarizing voices on the Internet. Wanyeki (Interview by author. Tape recording. Nairobi, September 15, 2016) illustrates the positive efforts of Ushahidi, as she highlights the two trends of Kenyan netizens during the 2008 PEV. She calls the first, the panicky diaspora, with distorted interpretations of occurrences, and citizens who leaned towards a particular political orientation with a disruptive agenda. The second trend consisted of the progressive voices helping fellow Kenyans through the humanitarian response and offering reflective thoughts on why the violent conflict was raging. Therefore, a citizen journalism platform became an active reporting avenue by the Ushahidi team, in collaboration with other citizen journalists, to crowdsource information on the extent and magnitude of the violence among the Kenyan populace (Goldstein and Rotich 2008; Jewitt 2009; Banda 2010).

Not only did Ushahidi map the 2008 PEV, the platform also went ahead to become a hybrid of citizen journalism and technological platform offering open-source software for crisis and disaster mapping in various countries such as Chile, South Africa, USA, Haiti, India, the Philippines, and Pakistan (Banda 2010, 57). Kobia explains why he thinks the Ushahidi platform is a relevant netizen undertaking:

> Initially, I didn't think Ushahidi would have that big an impact. I was happy we made something and we could record this information but it was quite shocking to see how much impact it had. Almost immediately we were contacted by guys in South Africa, saying the needed a way to record xenophobic violence that was breaking out. So, what did

we achieve? I felt like we went far, above and beyond what we had hoped to do. We actually created a platform that we shared with other people that allow them to create similar communities. We made it easy for people to do what we did. They multiplied that effort. And on 2008 PEV, the immediate impact was having these data informing the Kenyan media and the world what was really going on and how bad the situation was at the time. Again Ushahidi had set out to have this information recorded for posterity, so there was a reference point. So obviously, after the dust had settled, people have a mechanism, a way of looking back to timeline event: a way to perform a post-mortem. Not just policy makers but the average person had finally had a way of looking into how things had played out and why they happened.

Ushahidi did not stop at mapping crises or providing the global community access to its open-source software; it upscaled its efforts by providing the software for the multiagent early warning mechanism platform called Uwiano in Kenya. Formed in 2009, Uwiano (www.nscpeace.go.ke/108/), a multistakeholder consortium, responds to imminent conflict through an early warning mechanism operating on the open-source software of Ushahidi to crowdscource information. Funded by the United Nations Development Programme (UNDP), the platform includes the Ushahidi platform, the National Cohesion and Integration Committee (NCIC), the National Steering Committee (NSE) on conflict management and peacebuilding, the Independent Electoral and Boundaries Committee (IEBC), and PeaceNet.

Shalakha, the progamme manager of PeaceNet (Interview by author. Tape recording. Nairobi, November 21, 2016), elaborates that through the locals the Uwiano platform is able to facilitate information gathering before there is an uncontrollable outbreak of conflict in Kenya's 47 counties. At the grassroots level, the Uwiano platform collaborates with local organizations, as well as individuals, whose roles are dubbed "peace actors". The peace actors consist of the community members (i.e. the district committee members, the police, local NGOs, and inter-religion councils) of each county where the consortium operates. Data collection as well as real-time reportage of brewing disputes or violent conflict are part of the peace actors' mandates. PeaceNet, in which the Ushahidi open-source software is used, mitigates unrest when it is reported to the online alert system through the organization's peace actors. This method assists in notifying the police and dispatches a swift response. With the Uwiano mechanism, the communities are coordinating themselves to reduce violence.

Also, in the 2013 general elections, Ushahidi's Uchaguzi electoral monitoring mechanism was used to monitor the election for transparency, fairness, and tranquility. The members of the public used the platform to report on voting and any suspicious activities. This was in response to the 2007 elections and the violence that occurred. Therefore, no chances were taken, especially where accurate and timely information could save the day. As reported on the Uchaguzi platform, of the 4,964 reports published on the Ushahidi website during deployment 2,699 were swiftly verified (Ushahidi n.d.). He describes this exercise as Ushahidi's way of contributing further to Kenya's political and conflict transformation.

While Ushahidi continues to build technology to elevate human conditions within a local context, several other netizen platforms are matching some of the platform's efforts on the people-centred paradigm. As Map Kibera, Sisi Ni Amani Kenya, Afroes, and the Twitter Chief discussed in the next section show, the nonviolent technological uptakes by Kenyan netizens, be it through citizen journalism or interactive websites, are a force of change that is influencing political crises towards conflict transformation.

Toyin Ajao

The Map Kibera project

Kibera is known as one of the most notorious slums in Nairobi, especially for its allegedly unprecedented crimes rate, unemployment, and extreme poverty. It has been said that Kibera, a slum in the midst the cosmopolitan essence of Nairobi, houses over a million Kenyans. However, Kepha Ngito, who grew up in Kibera, started a mapping project called Map Kibera to ascertain the real number of Kibera residents. He came up with 600,000. The information that Kibera was overpopulated had led to the government underfocusing on infrastructural development and job opportunities for the people of Kibera. Ngito states:

> A lot of stories have been told by others not from within, people are not telling their own story; people are spoken about, people are decided for, project are designed by other people for people in Kibera and other slums but not with them in the planning, they don't listen to their side of the story. Of course, when projects are designed like that, they do not work successfully. So, my first question is, could it be because the story of these people have not been heard that things are not working and could it also be that there is a conspiracy to keep them silent or to ignore when they speak or to push down their ambitions and desires?

With Map Kibera, Kepha Ngito showed the real population figure that could assist in facilitating the necessary amenities and employment opportunities for the Kibera populace. Map Kibera is a creative digital tool that presents the voices of the marginalized community of Kibera. This initiative that began in 2007 and launched in 2009 has extended to other slums such as Mathare and Mukuru in Kenya for creative mapping for better representation of these communities to the government. The Ushahidi platform open-source software was used in extending the work of Ngito and his team.

According to Ngito (Interview by author. Tape recording. Nairobi, September 7, 2016), Kibera, a scar in the conscience of Kenyan leaders with its glaring inequality, is no longer a negligible place as a result of the participation of the youth through the new media to speak to their reality. So, the advent of the new media has amplified the voices of the youth through different platforms, including social media and the Kibera News Network and Voice of Kibera, where the youth of the community are documenting and reporting sociopolitical concerns. This way, the government is alerted for immediate actions and the community is participating in its own affairs. Since the 2008 PEV and the Map Kibera project on the government's tail, a few developments have occurred in terms of the provision of amenities such as water and electricity in Kibera.

Mzalendo: interactivity between the people and the parliamentarians

Mzalendo exists to reach out to Kenyan parliamentarians so that they can hear peoples' concerns and act. According to the platform's website, the purpose of Mzalendo is to "keep an eye on the Kenyan parliament" and "promote greater public voice and enhance public participation in politics by providing relevant information about the National Assembly and Senate's activities". Mzalendo (meaning 'Patriot' in Swahili) is a nonpartisan project that began in 2005 and was revamped in 2012. Kenyan activist, blogger, and lawyer, Ory Okolloh, who was also instrumental to the formation of the Ushahidi platform in 2008, started Mzalendo alongside Conrad Akunga, an experienced software architect, engineer, and tech-entrepreneur. Mzalendo became a more effective parliament-monitoring platform after it was relaunched in 2012.

When the political environment was different in 2005 with the Official Secrets Act, information was only leaked to Mzalendo about the deeds and misdeeds of the parliament. But with the 2010 referendum and a new constitution in place, public participation is emphasized and access to information guaranteed. This allows for free flow of information between the citizens and the parliament. On the Mzalendo site, all the parliamentarians' information, including biographic information, contact details, and the committees on which they sit, is made public. This way, the people are able to reach out to their leaders directly. Where a parliamentarian is unreachable, Mzalendo is alerted, and if an issue is controversial, Mzalendo takes up the matter and tries to reach out to the concerned parliamentarian. This is to ensure that the job in which a parliamentarian is voted in to do is prioritized. Soft copies of parliament proceedings are also made available on the Mzalendo site. As an online site that serves as a bridge between the people and the parliament, Mzalendo considers the new media a catalyst for inclusive governance through an avenue that fosters cohesive information and feedback. Mzalendo has been replicated in a few African countries, namely Nigeria, Morocco, Tunisia, Ghana, Zimbabwe, and South Africa.

Mindset education: Afroes Haki 2 online peace game

In the age of Internet games, some violent, some educative, a group of people led by Kenyan-South African Anne Githuku-Shongwe decided to start to unlock the potential of young Africans. Transforming their entrenched belief system and mental model through play, games, and digital interactive media has become Afroes' focus. In 2013, Afroes (short for African Heroes and Heroines), an NGO that runs different transformational programmes both in South Africa and Kenya, decided to develop an online peace game (Afroes 2013). According to the Kenya Programme Manager of Afroes, Mwai Gathoni, local research was conducted, especially in the hotbed of the 2008 PEV, the Kenyan Rift Valley region, to understand where the community needs help in facilitating and nurturing a unified society. The research outcome led to the development of a mobile game called Haki Chaguo Ni Lako (aka Haki 2), designed to educate the players about peace and tolerance (Afroes 2015).

Although it is has not been an easy task to measure the impact of the game, several youths in the targeted communities have acquired information and awareness about the importance of the game as well as its overarching effect in promoting peace during and beyond election times (Gathoni. Interview by author. Note taking. Nairobi, April 19, 2017). Among the games that Afroes has developed for online civic education are Jobhunt (a game that educates players about online jobs), Moraba (used in South Africa to educate the youth audience on sexual health and prevention of gender-based violence), Haki to educate on the danger of depletion of ecosystem (in honour of Kenyan environmental activist and Nobel laureate Wangari Maathai), and Chamchase to educate the audience on child abuse, safety, protection, and rights.

Peace in Our Pockets: the work of Sisi Ni Amani

While Ushahidi's crisis mapping focussed on hotspots of violence to make a difference, Sisi Ni Amani Kenya (SNA-K), a local NGO in Kenya, decided to take it a step further by mapping peace. This is to make several peace initiatives by Kenyans more coordinative and collaborative. Sisi Ni Amani, meaning "We are peace' in Kiswahili, was conceived by undergraduate students at Tufts University, Rachel Brown and Cody Valdes (Parker 2011). The SNA-K programme started out in 2010 standing at a vantage point of consolidating the lessons learnt from the 2008 PEV to make a difference while working with local peace leaders and activists in the 2013 general elections. Using text messaging, SNA-K educates members of several Kenyan communities where its work is located, including Baba Dogo, Mathare, Dandora in Nairobi, and the Rift Valley. Through a USSD code, *762#, a Safaricom subscription donated to the SNA-K project, the SMS-based programming for peace-mapping and civil education for violence prevention is operated (Sisi Ni Amani unknown).

Using similar crowdsourcing technology as Ushahidi, SNA-K provides a leverage-networking platform for Kenyan peace leaders who are members of different communities to better collaborate. Face-to-face peace workshops are organized for sharing experiences, creating synergy, and building skills. One critical way that SNA-K text messaging had worked was in stopping the land dispute in Mulot, Narok County in 2012, where the violent actors received text messages urging them to consider peace. Heeding this advice, the warring factions met with a local religious leader to mediate (PopTech 2012). To this effect, inspired by the SNA-K, SMS-based peace mapping and civic education projects, Groove Productions made a documentary titled *Peace in Our Pockets* in 2012.

The documentary showcases the power of the effective use of mobile devices by Kenyan citizens and peace activists to broker peace (Peace in Our Pockets 2012). Through subscriptions to USSD code *762#, community members can access SNA-K's database and send information out to others. The messages are sent out in numerous languages, including English, Kiswahili, and Sheng. With a donation of over 50 million free text messages received from Safaricom to promote SNA-K activities, peace actors were able to send messages such as "let us desist from violence and always embrace peace", "we are brothers and sisters let's stay in peace", "let's build our nation by voting peacefully" to members of their communities. By 2013, over 30,000 members of the targeted communities had subscribed to SNA-K text-messaging services and several influential leaders and peace actors had converged to promote peace. Having 30,000 subscribers to SNA-K text-messaging services is considered an indicator of a community willing to try another alternative to violence. However, research is needed to ascertain to what extent this anecdotal evidence can be applied to broader outcomes.

The Twitter Chief Magic

Chief Francis Kariuki, popularly known in the Rift Valley, Nakuru County, specifically Lanet sub-county, as the "Twitter Chief", is a government administrator handling education, health, and security. Chief Kariuki utilizes Twitter effectively among and within his county. He currently has over 63,000 Twitter followers. When asked why he uses Twitter and the effectiveness of this digital platform in his work, Chief Kariuki states:

> Twitter, I think is the best communication tool among the communities. They have two platforms, one is through the Internet and the other one is through the SMS without having to activate their Internet bundles to be able to communicate. Every service provider works by assigning short and long codes that help convert Twitter messages to SMS messages and vice versa without being charged to receive the text messages. This becomes an effective mode of communication especially since not everybody has a smart phone. That's what I have been using in the community to communicate. So, whenever anything happens say may be an outbreak of a disease like polio, I use the platform to mobilise for immunisation.

Through efficient communication with his county, he sees less violence and more cohesion. The use of SMS and Twitter, according to the Chief, has been very resourceful in sharing information and coordinating for action. Training on the use of social media, most especially on the use of Twitter and Facebook for coordination, sensitization, and sharing of the information, is part of Chief Kariuki's regular engagement across Kenya.

Kenyan netizens' contribution to conflict transformation

Conflict transformation is a concept that "envisions and responds to the ebb and flow of social conflict as 'life-giving opportunities' to create constructive change processes that reduce violence, increase justice in direct interaction and social structures, and respond to real-life problems in human relationships" (Lederach 2003, 14). Lederach (2003) argues that conflict transformation addresses some of the elements missing in other approaches to peace, including the lack of a bottom-up, durable construction of long-term advocacy and strategic planning, especially in relation to conflict management and conflict resolution.

According to Lederach (2003, 12), conflict transformation is a peacemaking mechanism that is focussed on creating a more holistic framework of addressing the content, context, and structure of a given conflict. Looking at the utilization of new media by the people, it has not only allowed the amplification of peoples' voices to discuss the content, context, and structure of a given conflict, but it has also allowed for conflict-addressing innovations. For instance, through the Uwiano platform, a consortium is organized to see to the prevention of future violent conflict, and through the Sisi Ni Amani project, it is facilitating a solution-orientated process whereby relational coexistence is preached via text messaging. In addition, Mzalendo and the Kibera projects are not only intensifying the voices of the marginalized, but they are also providing evidence on the perennial sociopolitical and economic inequalities and injustices yet to be addressed.

Lederach (2003, 14) envisions conflict as "life-giving opportunities" to create "constructive change processes that reduce violence, increase justice in direct interaction and social structures, and respond to real-life problems in human relationships". In this case, Lederach (2003, 27) offers four levels of constructive change processes that must be engaged in to rebuild relationships and failed institutions, including personal, relational, structural, and cultural. The personal as minimizing the destructive effects of social conflict and maximizing the potential for the person's holistic growth and well-being; the relational hinges on minimizing poorly functioning communication and maximizing understanding; the structural as uprooting causes and conditions creating violent conflicts to promote nonviolent mechanisms for long-term peace and foster the necessary development structures to meet basic human needs; and lastly the cultural identifies and understands the contributing patterns in the rise of violence, which in itself assists in building mechanisms for constructive responses to conflict.

Since 2008, from Ushahidi to SNA-K, some Kenyan netizens have continued to converge as nonviolent digital interventionists. Several of the initiatives of these platforms have become proactive in creating a bidirectional if not multidirectional flow of information. Although, further research is needed to measure how increased access to information gathering and sharing have continued to amplify the concerns of marginalized communities for tangible political inclusion, nonetheless these platforms have shown that change can happen through nonviolent technological uptakes that focus on structural, cultural, relational, and personal issues that obstruct human development and coexistence. From the Uwiano early warning system, to keeping a watchful eye on the parliamentarians, to mapping Kibera for sociopolitical inclusion and the synergy of peace actors to utilize the new media for peace, Kenyan netizens are investing in ground-up conflict transformation.

Conclusion

People-centred digital platforms such as SNA-K, Mzalendo, the Ushahidi citizen journalism platform and netizens' nonviolent endeavours such as Map Kiberia are highlighting important sociopolitical issues and empowering the public to take charge of their own peace and invest in a model of governance that serves them. The nonviolent technological interventionists platforms of several Kenyan netizens presented in this chapter illuminate a ground-up conflict transformation endeavour. These netizens are using the new media to lead crucial conversations, share significant information, and develop innovations to prevent violent conflicts in direct response to real-life problems, which is important in addressing structural, cultural, and relational injustices that affect human development and peace. Conflict transformation, as Lederach (2003) posits, is a long-term venture, which enables continual voicing of concerns and innovations of the public. Therefore, the nonviolent digitized efforts of several of these platforms, including the Ushahidi, SNAK-K, the Twitter Chief and Afroes, have continued to engage and challenge the media, the government, and the public to not only invest in sociopolitical transformation and better governance but also to collectively participate in conflict transformation.

References

Afroes. 2013. *Haki 2 – Behind The Scenes*. YouTube. www.youtube.com/watch?v=0VXl6y3FV9c (Accessed 20 April 2017).
Afroes. 2015. *Mobile Games That Change Culture: Anne Githuku-Shongwe at TEDxSoweto 2012*. http://afroes.com/%E2%80%AAmobile-games-that-change-culture-anne-githuku-shongwe-at-tedxsoweto-2012/ (Accessed 19 April 2017).
Allan, S. 2013. *Citizen Witnessing: Revisioning Journalism in Times of Crisis. Key Concepts in Journalism*. Cambridge: Polity Press.
Banda, F. 2010. *Citizen Journalism and Democracy in Africa: An Exploratory Study*. Grahamstown: Highway Africa.
Bock, J.G. 2012. *The Technology of Nonviolence: Social Media and Violence Prevention*. London: MIT Press.
Bowman, S. and Willis, C. 2003. *We Media: How Audiences Are Shaping the Future of News and Information*, ed. Lasica, J.D. Reston: The Media Center at the American Press Institute.
Goldstein, J. and Rotich, J. 2008. Digitally networked technology in Kenya's 2007–2008 post-election crisis. *Internet & Democracy Case Study Series*, 1–10.
Internet Live Stats. 2018. *Internet Users in the World*. www.internetlivestats.com (Accessed 9 October 2018).
Internet World Stats. 2018. *Usage and Population Statistics*. www.internetworldstats.com/stats1.htm (Accessed 9 October 2018).
Jeffery, S. 2011. *Ushahidi: Crowdmapping Collective that Exposed Kenyan Election Killings*. www.theguardian.com/news/blog/2011/apr/07/ushahidi-crowdmap-kenya-violence-hague (Accessed 20 October 2014).
Jewitt, R. 2009. The trouble with twittering: Integrating social media into mainstream news. *International Journal of Media and Cultural Politics*, 5(3): 233–240.
Junne, G., 2013. *The Role of Media in Conflict Transformation*. www.irenees.net/bdf_fiche-analyse-1002_en.html (Accessed 21 October 2014).
Kagwanja, P. 2009. Courting genocide: Populism, ethno-nationalism and the informalisation of violence in Kenya's 2008 post-election crisis. *Journal of Contemporary African Studies*, 27(3): 365–387.
Kepha Ngito, 2013. Interview by author. Tape recording. Nairobi, September 7.
Lederach, J.P. 2003. *The Little Book of Conflict Transformation*. Intercourse: Good Books.
Makinen, M. and Kuira, M.W. 2008. Social media and post-election crisis in Kenya. *Information and Communication Technology- Africa*, 1–15.
Moyo, L. 2011. Blogging down a dictatorship: Human rights, citizen journalists and the right to communicate in Zimbabwe. *Sage*, 12(6): 745–760.

Mutsvairo, B. and Columbus, S. 2012. Emerging patterns and trends in citizen journalism in Africa: The case of Zimbabwe. *Central European Journal of Communication*, 5(1): 121–136.

Mwiandi, S. 2008. *Moving Beyond Relief: The Challenges of Settling Kenya's Internally Displaced*. USIPeace Briefing. New York: USIP United States Institute of Peace.

Parker, P. 2011. *Sisi Ni Amani, 'peacemapping' in Kenya: Insight on Conflict*. www.insightonconflict.org/blog/2011/09/kenya-peacemapping/ (Accessed 24 April 2017).

Peace in Our Pockets. 2012. http://peaceinourpockets.com/background/ (Accessed 4 April 2017).

PopTech, 2012. Rachel Brown: Communicate peace. *Vimeo*. https://vimeo.com/52166705 (Accessed 14 April 2017).

Sisi Ni Amani, Unknown. *Safaricom Donates 50 Million Texts*. www.sisiniamani.org/safaricom-donates-50-million-texts-to-sisi-ni-amanis-election-activities/ (Accessed 2 April 2017).

Tony Mochama, 2016. Interview by Ajao, T. Tape recording. Nairobi, September 22.

Ushahidi (n.d). "Uchaguzi: During the Kenyan General Election in 2013, Ushahidi customized and deployed its software to map the vote and ensure a peaceful, fair election process". Available at: https://www.ushahidi.com/case-studies/uchaguzi (accessed 6 September 2020).

Watson, H. and Wadhwa, K. 2014. The evolution of citizen journalism in crises: From reporting to crisis management. In Thorsen, E. and Allan, S., eds. *Citizen Journalism Global Perspectives*. New York: Peter Lang, vol. 2, 321–332.

12

Ghetto 'wall-standing'
Counterhegemonic graffiti in Zimbabwe

Hugh Mangeya

Introduction

Previous research on [traditional] African communication systems and modes have mainly focused on the use of fire, drums, music, dance, and tribal markings, among others (Wilson 1987; M'bayo and Nwanko 1989; Orewere 1991; Bussotti 2015). In Zimbabwe, graffiti has been mainly regarded as a rural phenomenon with Chitauro-Mawema (2006) dismissing its presence in the urban space. This chapter takes graffiti as a form of mediated civic agency which enables grounded communication in various African communicative settings. Willems (2015) characterises mediated civic agency as the wide spectrum of actions through which citizens can engage power via a wide range of media forms. Zimbabwe's urban political graffiti is distinct from its much-studied Western hip-hop–based counterpart which is mainly based on 'bombing' and 'jamming' (Powers 1999, Hookstra 2009; Morgan and Louis 2009; Ouzman 2010; Mrsevic 2012; Blomkamp et al. 2014). Inherent mobility constraints of the medium dictate that it be consumed only *in situ* and makes it a potent barometer of the sociolinguistic distribution of specific political attitudes. Graffiti messages therefore act as informal truncated local bulletins akin to the in-built checks and balances of African traditional political structures encapsulated by the proverb 'a king/chief is defined by his subjects' which ensured that power dynamics between the ruling elite and their subjects were seldom biased towards the rulers.

African media and communication have generally been conceptualised in the paradigm of 'rural' forms of communication. As such, an idealised/traditional African rural–urban dichotomy has predominantly been used in defining and characterisation of the cultural bases/drive of the two 'distinct' societies. The urban society has been, by and large, perceived as a 'cultureless' society where mainly mass and new media are the predominant communication modes. Whilst the rural is seen as that place where the 'center' still holds and traditional media are still prominently used. The chapter argues that traditional modes still underpin communication philosophy in urban societies. This is interrogated through the analysis of political graffiti in Zimbabwe's urban areas. Mangeya (2014) shows how graffiti produced by high school students in Zimbabwean urban areas is not just a result of random petulance by a cultureless youths. Rather, it is a text that is greatly informed by a sense of moral and cultural correctness.

The urban society is not a homogenous body. There are demographically and socio-politically distinct groups which can be categorised on a variety of factors. The chapter uses the ghetto ('location' in Zimbabwe) and suburb distinction to show that graffiti production is socio-politically driven. Although this distinction is not by any means entirely definitive, it is employed from a sociological perspective, to distinguish different levels of cultural dominance and prominence accorded and/or practiced by the two groups in question.

Defining African media and communication

Lang and Lang (2009) observe that it is not uncommon to associate the media with modern institutions as these have access to modern technology enabling them to disseminate information to dispersed multitude. Studies on African media and communication systems, however, have largely used the traditional paradigm as the conceptual basis; that is, exploring 'indigenous' communication forms whose way and manner of communication is predicated on the institutions and ethos of their host culture (Ansu-Kyeremeh 1998). As such, 'traditional', which has also been interchangeably with 'oral/folk' (Desai 1977; Sharma and Singh 2015; Wilson 1987) and 'rural'/'village' (Abebe 2013; Ansu-Kyeremeh 1998; Jinadasa 2011; Orewere 1991), has been used to refer to cultural institutions, ceremonies, events, and arts of African ancestors observed, practiced, and perpetuated by successors from generation to generation. Importantly, these are creations of human interactions, consensus, and conflicts (Orewere 1991).

A salient concern in media studies is 'the power' of mass media, and in particular their roles as vehicles of culture and grassroots mobilisation. For example, there are approaches which explore the mass media as forces that provide audiences with ways that ultimately shape their very existence and participation within a given society. That is, they may be used to reveal ideologies and the nature of discourses in any given social milieu.

African notions of governance

Each and every society has its own peculiar model of governance, distinguished by various degree of formalisation and codification of rules, principles, and laws conditioning governance (constitutionalism). Unlike in western countries where the periodic election is the yardstick of democracy that determines political legitimacy (Abebe 2013; Anyanwu 2005), African societies have always had forms of democratic governance peculiar to them. These forms operated in accordance with their traditions and belief systems. Majoritarian democracy entailed a unilateral/dominant form of governance where the need for a controlled, formal, governmental authority, as seen in western societies, is expressed. Social contracts, predicated on consensual democracy, provided the basis for indigenous African ideas of governance (Wiredu 1997).

Kanu (2015) argues that governance and its associated democratic principle is a cherished African value which existed in precolonial Africa as a pattern of African administration, despite arguments to the contrary. The foundation of governance in precolonial Africa was based on the African conception that 'the King [or Queen] ruled but at the pleasure of the people, for a King without subjects is no King [or Queen]'. A leader could not rule if the people did not sanction his leadership. This is one of a number of checks and balances that were critical in regulating the power relations between leaders and their subjects. In traditional philosophy this phenomenon is encapsulated in the proverbs 'a king/chief is defined by his subjects' and 'leadership alternates'. The two proverbs underscore how traditional philosophy engendered a sense of democracy as the leader could only govern at the behest of his subjects.

In spite of its predominant hereditary nature, African leadership systems were supported by built-in formal checks and balances and political accountability which ensured that power relations between the leaders and their subjects were not too lopsided. Not only were important decisions arrived at through healthy negotiation between the leader and the people, the people also had the ability to voice their concerns via other leaders who were considered to be the voice of the politically oppressed and marginalised, to shift their allegiance to another leader, and, in extreme situations, to overthrow or depose the leader (Wiredu 1997; Crook 2005; Karim 2012; Abebe 2013; Kanu 2015). Significantly, specific genres of poetry enabled subjects to correct their leaders without fear of political victimisation. Chiwome (1992) explains how such poetry is an important institution which allows aggrieved subjects to vent their political frustration and disillusionment, and thereby ensure healthy power relations. The people could therefore meaningfully participate in a political climate defined by trust, confidence, and support. They regarded themselves as the mandate-givers of the chief/king which is a crucial precondition for democratic governance (Anyanwu 2005). The leader's political authenticity and legitimacy therefore derived from the people, who constituted a 'jural community' (Skinner 1998) which mitigated against autocratic tendencies in African governance.

The African postcolonial state however brought with it an inevitable clash of civilisations between the emergence of modern conceptions of democracy and principles of human rights, on the one hand, and the entrenched cultural governance traits in Africa, on the other hand (Abebe 2013. Western institutions of governance, such as electoral polls and other democratic structures, for example, are often at odds with traditional African cultural values and the region's contemporary socio-economic realities. The in-built checks and balances seemed to work very well during the precolonial times, and in fact continue to work "in rural communities where the visibility of modern institutions is largely absent" (Abebe 2013, 430). This has left the continent at crossroads in relation to the alternative forms of governance available to move Africa forward. Migration laws as well as a battery of laws that curtail freedoms of expression and assembly, for instance, have seriously limited the operation and utility of the traditional checks and balances. Resultantly, citizens are then faced with the task of searching for alternative spaces on which to register their discontent. Graffiti is explored as a form of mediated civic agency that politically disenfranchised groups appropriate to negotiate unequal power relations within the urban setup.

Political graffiti as a cultural medium

Wilson (1987) argues that the use of the qualifier 'traditional', associated with African media is, potentially, semantically and conceptually misleading. It is generally used to invoke elements of outdatedness and primitiveness, especially in Third World countries. Resultantly, traditional communication is considered mutually exclusive and alien from what is considered more modern and technological communication systems. Thus, African media is inevitably seen as impediments to both change and modernisation. Graffiti is by no means an inherently cultureless artefact. Its origin in any given social milieu is inextricably linked to its cultural heritage. The more-studied western version has hip-hop as its cultural basis. The tagging of walls becomes much more than a simple petulant act of vandalism, but a culturally driven socio-political statement that can only be appreciated in its social context. This highlights the constructed nature of graffiti and the definitive role which cultural convention plays in that construction.

In this light, Zimbabwe's urban political graffiti is conceptualised as a communication form intrinsically connected to a country's political heritage. It is a medium shaped by traditional conceptions about the nature of relations between a leader and their subjects as well as the discursive ways in which they are negotiated. Thus, the proverbs defining the nature of the African governance and the associated institution of 'correcting a chief/king' are central to the understanding of the nature of political discourse subsisting on this medium.

Graffiti is defined as an alternative media form that is used to challenge the status quo, particularly in the absence of state-controlled mainstream media (Copland 1985; Nixon 1994; Rosenberg 2002). Although graffiti is predominantly defined as the visual manifestation of the American hip-hop movement that started in the mid-1970s, Bodunrin (2014) and Pare (2009) state that it has been a means of communication for many centuries. Bodunrin (2014) notes two distinct traditions of South African graffiti. The first relates to apartheid graffiti linked to the 1960 Sharperville Massacre and the 1976 Soweto Uprising. Whilst this type of graffiti was mainly subversive in nature, the second type of graffiti, occurring in post-apartheid South Africa, has undergone a paradigm shift. The opening up of democratic spaces has transformed it into a more aesthetic form that captures South Africa's sociopolitical diversity. For Gaynor (2017), this is encapsulated in the 'Diverse people united' graffiti. It has now been commodified, being bankrolled by big organisations, government, and NGOs. Barnett (2018) explores the legalities of copyrighting this form of graffiti. It emerges that present-day South African graffiti is viewed more as a commercialised aesthetic street art form than as a subversive discourse.

Pare (2009) explores graffiti practices in Zimbabwe, as well as in the Middle East. Of particular interest is how Zimbabwean graffiti has been appropriated by a solidarity group called Woza (Women and Men of Zimbabwe Arise). This group paints graffiti on road signs to express anti-disestablishment sentiments. Significantly, the group has vowed to continue writing graffiti until their establishment takes heed of their dissatisfaction. Jena (2013) notes how increasingly more people are resorting to graffiti to register their discontent. It is little wonder Bodunrin (2014) argues that African graffiti has a different agenda to that of its spray-canned western counterpart. Alonso (1998), Brighenti and Reghellin (2007) and Brighenti (2010) explore western graffiti from a territorology paradigm. They argue that signature graffiti is crucial in boundary-making practices. This body of work explores how graffiti crews/communities define themselves, and how they trace their own boundaries in relation to other communities and different practices. Tagging has not yet caught up, especially, in the Zimbabwean sociolinguistic context. Much of the graffiti is textual, rather than visual, aimed at expressing dissatisfaction towards a variety of authoritarian figures and institutions.

Public space and political discourses

The notion of space is inextricably linked with the notion of media. It defines both the parameters within which participants can take part in events and processes that condition their daily lives. Discursive space is generally controlled by clearly defined boundaries that distinguish between the public and the private (Brown 2006). Political economy determines the extent of individuals' participation in or on these spaces. Space is crucial in the construction of discourses as it is the specific site(s) on which specific discourses are constructed. It determines the access and nature of participation, in terms of linguistic resources at the participants' disposal. As such, urban spaces enable varying degrees of civic and political engagement, and the nature of that participation.

The enactment of media censorship laws, mostly curtailing the freedom of expression, has resulted in the shrinkage and/or closure of spaces on which meaningful political engagement can occur as there would be limited spaces within which citizens can freely express anti-establishment sentiments, anger and frustration without fear of victimisation. Significantly, graffiti offers a situation in which the discourse is brazenly displayed out 'in the open' for everyone to see.

In this context, 'openness' refers to three important aspects of the graffiti. First, it refers to how there is no attempt to hide the inscriptions. Secondly, the discourse used allows for a high degree of bluntness that may not be found in more conventionalised media. It is not affected by ethical/moral conventions that constrain more informal media forms. Thirdly, it is easily accessible for both production and consumption of the discourse. Anyone literate is a potential writer and reader of graffiti. Thus, graffiti becomes a significant discursive platform on which anti-establishment sentiments can be expressed.

Discussion

Each and every nation has its own brand of political engagement. Whilst constitutionalism may be the operative model of political participation the world over, there are national peculiarities in terms of how democracy, in its various guises, is practised. There is therefore a need to take into account local political realities when approaching the African political terrain. These realities inform the nature of political negotiation subsisting in any given country.

In Zimbabwe, ZANU (PF), like most revolutionary parties in Africa, has systematically created conditions and institutions which ensure it stays in power for a long time. Machaya (2016) opines that:

> It is the fear of a total ejection from the political arena, and becoming politically obsolete, with very marginal chances of staging a comeback that motivates many hegemonic political parties in Africa and elsewhere, to employ exclusionary political tactics that guarantee them perpetual control of the government.

Such tactics include the setting up of repressive media laws and institutions that do not encourage freedoms of expression and assembly. These include laws such as the Access to Information and Protection of Privacy Act and the Public Order (AIPPA 2002), the Security Act (POSA 2002), and The Broadcasting Services Regulation Act (2007). The setting up of the Media and Information Commission, which was initially created through section 68(1) of AIPPA, complemented the laws in creating a legal smokescreen for undermining both freedom of expression and opposition politics in Zimbabwe (Mukasa 2003).

The closure of democratic spaces make graffiti a viable and attractive medium in environments which do not allow for the engagement of the individual's right to freedom of expression (Bolazzi 2012, 2). Peteet (1996) not only characterises graffiti as a cultural artefact but also as interventions in power relations. She shows how graffiti writers in the intifada have taken a stand on walls in a 'last-ditch effort to speak and be heard' (142). Approached from this perspective, political graffiti can be viewed as a renegotiation of the right to freedom of expression seriously lacking on more official and conventional platforms. In this way, it truly becomes an intervention in skewed power relations (Peteet 1996). Just as the stone wall was a revolutionary device in the intifada, the durawall can also assume the same crucial political function in the Zimbabwean context. It is within this political climate that political inscriptions written on durawalls in Zimbabwean urban areas are analysed.

Expression of political identity

Political identity, taken in the wider context of identity politics, is an integral aspect of a person's total identity. It is crucial when taken in the context of collective affiliation and mobilisation.

Jenkins (2000) considers collective identity/affiliation, which are central to party politics, as playing a powerful and defining role in contemporary societies. It can actually be placed more or less on the same level as religious identities which are capable of creating fanaticism, among other effects. Political identities have the potential to condition voting behaviours and other political forms of action, such as demonstrations and petitioning the government, among others.

The collective identity one derives from supporting a political party can function as a crucial rallying point. Its suppression can potentially present a variety of socio-political challenges to the affected individual. It is not a coincidence that AIPPA and POSA came into operation immediately after the formation of the Movement for Democratic Change (MDC) which came as an immediate danger to the ruling party's hegemonic ambitions. It presented the most realistic chances of unseating the ruling party.

Machaya (2016) notes how the ZANU (PF)-led government has employed exclusionary political tactics which have ultimately led to the "refusal to recognise in principle the existence of alternative centres of power" (a fact which is also going to figure significantly in so far as the party's succession discourses). The result is a farcical multiparty democracy, but one that has failed to create a level playing field that allows for opposition competitiveness. This has basically led to the degeneration into a de facto one-party state where no other political party can rule the country. As a result, the mere expression of one's support for the opposition is, for all intents and purposes, an act of treason. It became next to impossible to openly support the opposition, more specifically the MDC. This brought in an interesting discursive trend in political graffiti which mainly appeared in two main discursive forms, as shown in in Figures 12.1 and 12.2.

Figure 12.1 MDC

Figure 12.2 MDC Ndizvo (MDC is great/good/the answer?)

Denying opposition supporters the right to publicly express their collective political affiliation is akin to Lord Voldemort's 'He who must not be named' in that it is an attempt to erase the existence of a formidable political entity by simply refusing to identify it by name. This represents something close to the linguistic nullification/decimation of the opposition party by making it difficult for the people to both identify each other and publicly fraternise. Following on Jenkin's (2000) argument that "identity has become a legitimate political good *sui generis*" the linguistic blackout of the name MDC is a calculated strategy to decimate their collective political identity. The inscriptions in Figures 12.1 and 12.2 are therefore read as much more than the expression of the opposition party's presence in Zimbabwe's political arena. In an environment where its only ZANU (PF) supporters who can openly declare their allegiances without fearing any adverse ramifications, the durawall offers the chance of levelling that part of the field to the writers. The wall thus presents the opportunity to exercise one's political identity. Its effect from a solidarity perspective cannot be overemphasised. The inscription in Figure 12.2, in particular, can also be read in the context of state discourses relating to the MDC and its western sponsorship and leadership by the urban lumpen and how it is therefore culturally unsuitable to govern the country. Thus, it is an act of both linguistic and political defiance whereby the inscription is denying the unsuitability of the party and, at the same time, reasserting it as even better compared to what is considered to be the default political choice, ZANU (PF).

Call for Mugabe to step down

The proverb *'ushe madzoro hunoravanwa'* (Shona for 'leadership [is a race, it] alternates') is a philosophy that engendered the need to freshen up institutional leadership, be it political or otherwise. It is a philosophy similar to the characterisation of leadership as a relay race where the baton is supposed to be exchanged at predetermined intervals. Former President Mugabe ruled Zimbabwe for up to 37 years. In spite of the long term in office, Mugabe continuously refused to pass the leadership baton and step down. In fact, political discourses unsurprisingly carried undercurrents of how people were fed up by his continued reign. The inscriptions shown in Figures 12.3 and 12.4 typify the discursive negotiation of this position in graffiti:

The two inscriptions are imperatives. They presuppose a certain level of power that presupposes the ability to carry out the drastic suggestion in Figure 12.4; that is, 'pushing' Mugabe out of office. They also presume a situation where the citizens had been monitoring the situation in the country. The assumption is now that things have deteriorated to a position whereby the only way forward is for Mugabe to vacate his political office. It is also important to appreciate the inscriptions in light of growing dissent and anti-government protests that rocked the country from the latter half of 2016. Notable are the #ThisFlag and *Tajamuka/Sesijikile* (Shona for 'we protest') movements which brought in an Arab Spring-type of social media-motivated political movements. When the 'dots' are connected, it does not come as a surprise that the movements came to be. On the one hand, the 'enough' graffiti offers clear suggestions of people who are ready to 'alienate' a despotic and autocratic leader and shift their allegiance to someone else. On the other hand, the social media-instigated movements, and the subsequent march by the citizens of Zimbabwe, is then read as the fulfilment of a prophecy already foretold through political graffiti inscribed on the durawalls. Ironically, this type of civil action is one of the four viable scenario that could result in Mugabe's stepping down from office. This underlines the notion that a leader derives his power and mandate from his subjects. Thus, a leader gets his legitimacy from the support of the people. It is not

Figure 12.3 Zvakwana (enough [is enough])

Figure 12.4 Zvakwana Bob out (enough Bob out)

a matter of election results, fraudulent, rigged, or otherwise, but the fact that subjects are behind you and have trust, confidence, and support of the political regime. In this way, the subjects become the jural community.

Whilst the common/popular assumption is anti-Mugabe sentiments are produced by opposition supporters/members, it is also noteworthy that they could also be equally as a result of ZANU (PF) supporters as well. This is in light of Magure's (2014) allusion to the *bhora musango* (Shona for 'kick the ball [out of the goal] into the bushes') campaign by ZANU (PF) legislators who actually encouraged their own party supporters not to vote for Mugabe in the 2008 harmonised elections. This was apparently done in a bid to punish him for not relinquishing power to a younger presidential candidate. The fact that Mugabe could not garner the required majority vote for an outright win and was forced to enter into a run-off with Tsvangirai underscores the potential vulnerability of leadership to changes in political allegiances and underlines the critical role the electorate plays in modern-day democratic governance. In fact, the threat of 'dissident voting' has not completely passed with the ousting of Mugabe and rise to power of Mnangagwa. There is still genuine fear within the party structures of a repeat of the 2008 *bhora musanga*-type of voting (Kwaramba 2018; Staff Reporter 2018). This intraparty antihegemonic, or anti-Mugabe, graffiti highlights the succession and factional war that have threatened to tear the ruling party apart.

The question of age was a nagging constitutional issue for the elder statesman. It therefore comes as no great surprise that there were inscriptions which explicitly make reference to the age issue. These are presented in Figures 12.5 through 12.7.

The inscriptions in Figures 12.5 through 12.7 reveal that the people know what they want in so far as the person running for the presidency is concerned. The inscriptions do not make

Ghetto 'wall-standing'

Figure 12.5   Elected presindend + 5 year term + age limit 65 years (*sic*)

Figure 12.6   Presidence age 40–65 yrs (*sic*)

Figure 12.7 *Bvuma kuchembera* Mugabe (concede that you are [too] old [to rule])

reference to any other political office which suggests that the production is not as random as it might appear. Figures 12.5 and 12.6 both make explicit reference to 65 years as the age limit for standing for the highest political office. They are an overt bid to eliminate Mugabe, who stood for his seventh term as the head of government in 2013. The inscription in Figure 12.7 mentions the aspect of old age in so many words. It defines or characterises Mugabe as an old man (and probably therefore a spent force) who should not be allowed to run for office. The inscription in Figure 12.6 also underlines the importance of age whereby the age limit is also set regarding presidential candidature. It emerges that the candidate must be mature enough (at least above 40 years) but also not too old to be incapacitated to discharge the expected duties. Issues of senility might be a significant factor in the setting of the maximum age limit. It is also important to note questions on Mugabe's old age are part of a political narrative that gained currency just after the formation of MDC. Insinuations about Mugabe's age were believed to have been made in Oliver Mtukudzi's (2002) song 'Wasakara' (You are worn out) – popularly known as 'Bvuma' (concede [that you are too old]).

Anti-Mugabe hate speech

Hate speech is broadly defined as the conscious, deliberate, and intentional use of language (which can be in the forms and videos, among other linguistic resources) that is aimed at demeaning, insulting, denigrating, or threatening another party (Magure 2014; Crisis Coalition 2012). Such speech may foster a climate of prejudice and intolerance and may actually be used to fuel political discrimination, hostility, and violence (Community Empowerment for Progress Organisation n.d.). In Zimbabwe, hate speech is considered to have

> become an endemic and poisonous epidemic that has fractured and polarised society by extreme levels of political and social intolerance and hostility towards any group or individual that disagrees with ZANU PF's perspective of reality.
>
> *(Crisis in Zimbabwe Coalition, 2012)*

Tsvangirai was a victim of hate speech in the state's popular discourse. He was variously labelled a teaboy, a coward who ran away from the liberation war while real heroes fought against white colonialists, too ugly, and uneducated, among others.

Graffiti provided members of the community who might not have access to the media fight back such hate speech with their own. Most of it was directed to Mugabe whilst some was directed at the state of the ruling party as a political institution. These are presented in Figure 12.8.

The inscription plays into a trend that is dominant in most sub-Saharan subordinate and dissident discourses. Mbembe (2001) observes a pathological obsession of dissenting populations with orifices. This is by no means a phenomenon that is only restricted to the political arena. Telling someone '*mhata yako*' (your anus/vagina) is a very common insult that is uttered on a regular basis. (It has to be appreciated that the word *mhata*, as noted by Tagwirei and Mangeya (2013), is a social corrective label that enjoys free semantic variation. It can be taken

Figure 12.8 Mugabe imhata (Mugabe is an asshole)

to either refer to the vagina or the anus. Its meaning depends on the social context in which it is deployed.) It however becomes significant when the same insult becomes banal in political arena. More so, when it is directed at the country's ruling party in an environment where negative statements against the person or office of the president are outlawed.

Mbembe (2001) observes that in Togo and Cameroon obscenities were sometimes disguised in ceremonies that were superficially meant to exalt the ruling parties. Indeed these ceremonies were even held under the noses of the officials to whom the insults and discontent were targeted. The fact that these insults were hidden in such linguistic devices as tone and intonation might mean that the politicians would miss this important voicing of discontent. Graffiti, on the other hand, allows disgruntled parties to voice their discontent in an explicit manner, albeit anonymously. The disgruntlement is not disguised by any element of language. The disgruntlement is made explicit for anyone to decode.

Allport, cited in Texeira et al. (2003), distinguishes types of violent and prejudicial actions based on the extent of their energy. These actions range from antilocution, avoidance, discrimination, and physical attack to extermination. The levelling of insults against an individual, as is the case in Figure 12.8, is no more than the verbalisation of prejudice. In such an instance, the insult is regarded as one of several ways through which opposing parties engage in political violence. It is a case of the people refusing to take political hate speech lying down and therefore choosing to fight fire with fire. The walls become a site where the political jousting takes place.

Conclusion

Graffiti is much more than the result of juvenile delinquency or random acts of petulance by maligned segments of the society. Above all, it does not randomly appear on the urban landscape. It is, historically, a product of the linguistic expression of disenfranchised groups. Its actual form depends on the local traditions conditioning the existence. Whichever it may be, it is still a truncated form of cultural production. Zimbabwe's political graffiti is appreciated within the general context characterised by the institutionalised closure of discursive spaces for political engagement. As such, it's an alternative site of political engagement. Informed by traditional Shona notions of governance and democracy, political graffiti urgently calls upon the establishment to open up spaces for open dialogue with the people. The recent initiative by President Mnangagwa to engage with people on his Facebook page is a step in the right direction in re-establishing healthy dialogue between the state and its citizens.

References

Abebe, S.G. 2013. The relevance of African culture in building modern institutions and the quest for legal pluralism. *Saint Louis University Law Journal*, 47: 429–446.

Alonso, A. 1998. *Urban Graffiti on the City Landscape*. Western Geography Graduate Conference, San Diego University, February.

Ansu-Kyeremeh, K. 1998. Indigenous communication systems: A conceptual framework. In Ansu-Kyeremeh, K., ed. *Perspectives on Indigenous Communication in Africa: Theory and Application*. Legon: School of Communication Studies Printing Press, vol. 2.

Anyanwu, C.S. 2005. *Is the African Traditional Institution (Chieftainship) Compatible with Contemporary Democracy? A Case Study of Bochum in Limpopo Province South Africa*. Masters in Social Science, School of Development Studies, University of KwaZulu Natal.

Barnett, J. 2018. Where does graffiti stand when it comes to copyright? *Bizcommuninity*. www.bizcommunity.com/Article/196/825/181034.html.

Blomkamp, E., Hager-Forde, S. and Flemming, T. 2014. *Graffiti Vandalism Prevention Programme Design: Insights and Case Studies Prepared for Community Developed and Safety Unit, Auckland Council.* www.innovatechange.co.nz (Accessed 25 July 2016).

Bodunrin, I. 2014. Rap, graffiti and social media in South Africa today. *Media Development*, 61(4): 10.

Bolazzi, D. 2012. *Painting the Revolution: An Analysis of the Graffiti Movement in Post-Revolutionary Egypt.* BRISMES Annual Conference. Revolution and Revolt: Understanding the forms and causes of change, 26–28 March. https://brismes2012.files.wordpress.com/.../daniele-bolazzi-painting-the-revolution.pdf (Accessed 23 May 2018).

Brighenti, A.M. 2010. At the wall: Graffiti writers, urban territoriality, and the public domain. *Space and Culture*, 13(3): 315–332.

Brighenti, A.M. and Reghellin, M. 2007. Writing, etnografia di una pratica interstiziale. *Polis*, XXI: 369–398.

Brown, A. 2006. Urban public space in the developing world – a resource for the poor. In Brown, A., ed. *Contested Space: Street Trading, Public Space, and Livelihoods in Developing Cities.* Cardiff, Wales: ITDG Publishing, 17–35.

Bussotti, L. 2015. Short reflections on the history of African communication. *Historia y Communicacion Social*, 20(1): 205–222.

Chitauro-Mawema, M.B. 2006. *Gender Sensitivity in Shona Language Use: A Lexicographic and Corpus-Based Study in Words in Context.* Oslo: University of Oslo.

Chiwome, E.M. 1992. Traditional Shona poetry and mental health. *Zambezia*, XIX(i): 1–17.

Community Empowerment for Progress Organisation (CEPO). n.d. *Introduction to Hate Speech on Social Media.* https://defyhatenow.net/wp-content/.../defyhatenow_whatishatespeech_JUL27.pdf (Accessed 23 May 2018).

Copland, D. B. 1985 *Township Tonight! South Africa's Black City Music and Theatre.* London: Longman

Crisis in Zimbabwe Coalition. 2012. *State Media Continues to Endorse Hate Speech.* www.swradioafrica.com/Documents/Crisis%20Report%2004-07-2012.pdf (Accessed 23 May 2018).

Crook, R. 2005. *The Role of Traditional Institutions in Political Change and Development.* Briefing Paper. www.odi.org/publications/1325-role-traditional-institutions-political-change-and-development (Accessed 23 May 2018).

Desai, M.V. 1977. Dynamics of folk media. *Folk Media and Mass Media in Population Communication*, 5–8.

Gaynor, T.S. 2017. Street art as protest discourse. *PatTimes.* https://patimes.org/street-art-political-discourse/.

Hookstra, C.L. 2009. *Adolescent Graffiti Vandalism: Exploring the Root Causes.* Masters of Science in Leadership and Management Project, University of La Verne.

Jena, N. 2013. Graffiti: A powerful form of expression. *The Standard*, 29 September. www.thestandard.co.zw/2013/09/29/graffiti-powerful-form-expression/.

Jenkins, R. 2000. The limits of identity: Ethnicity, conflict and politics. *Sheffield Online Papers on Social Research*, 2.

Jinadasa, M.P.K. 2011. Community development programmes and folk media: A communication model for Sri Lankan rural society. *Global Media Journal – Indian Edition*, 2(2).

Kanu, I.A. 2015. *African Traditional Democracy.* https://igwebuikejournals.com/pdf%20created/1.1.1.pdf (Accessed 23 May 2018).

Karim, A.A. 2012. *Trust in Modern and Traditional Political Institutions in Africa: Determinants, Winners and Losers.* Master of Science in Globalisation: Global Politics and Culture. Department of Sociology and Political Science, Nowergian University of Science and Technology.

Kwaramba, F. 2018. Witch-hunt in Zanu PF . . . as party preempts bhora musango. *Daily News Live.* www.dailynews.co.zw/articles/2018/06/02/witch-hunt-in-zanu-pf-as-party-pre-empts-bhora-musango (Accessed 24 June 2018).

Lang, K. and Lang, G.E. 2009. Mass society, mass culture and mass communication: The meaning of mass. *International Journal of Communication*, 3: 998–1024.

Machaya, C. 2016. Beyond violence and intimidation: Explaining possible ZANU (PF) victory in 2018. The role of third parties. *African Politics and Policy*, 2(4).

Magure, B. 2014. Land, indigenization and empowerment: Narratives that made a difference in Zimbabwe 2013 elections. *Journal of African Elections,* 13(2): 17–47.

Mangeya, H. 2014. *A Sociolinguistics of Graffiti Written in Shona and English Found in Selected Urban Areas in Zimbabwe.* PhD Thesis submitted to the African Languages Department, University of South Africa.

M'Bayo, R. and Nwanko, R.N. 1989. The political culture of mass communication research and the role of African scholars. *Mass Media Review,* 3(2): 1–15.

Mbembe, A. 2001. *On the Postcolony.* London: University of California Press.

Morgan, A. and Louis, E. 2009. *Key Issues in Graffiti.* Research in Practice No. 6. Canberra: Australian Institute of Criminology. https://aic.gov.au/publications/rip/rip06 (Accessed 23 July 2013).

Mrsevic, Z. 2012. *Street Graffiti: Between Amnesty of Our Children and Moral Panicking.* www.zoricamrsevic.in.rs (Accessed 12 June 2013).

Mtukudzi, O. 2002. *Wasakara: Bvuma-Tolerance.* Sheer Sound. https://www.letssingit.com/it/oliver-mtukudzi-album-testo-bvuma-tolerance-638w9x.

Mukasa, S.D. 2003. Press and politics in Zimbabwe. *African Studies Quarterly,* 7(2): 172–183.

Nixon, R. 1994. *Homelands, Harlem and Hollywood: South African Culture and the World Beyond.* New York: Routledge.

Orewere, B. 1991. Possible implications of modern mass communication media for traditional communication in a Nigerian rural setting. *African Media Review,* 5(3): 53–65.

Ouzman, S. 2010. *Graffiti as Art(e) Fact: A Contemporary Archaeology.* www.uj.ac.za/EN/.../departments/.../Ouzman%202010%20Graffiti.pdf (Accessed 23 July 2013).

Pare, A. 2009. *Graffiti as Social Protest.* www.comminit.com/democracy-governance/content/graffiti-social-protest.

Peteet, J. 1996. The writing on the wall: The graffiti of the intifada. *Cultural Anthropology,* 11(2): 139–159.

Powers, L.A. 1999. Whatever happened to the graffiti art movement? *Journal of Popular Culture.* 29(4): 137–142.

Rosenberg, S. 2002. Youths popular culture and identity: American influences on South Africa and Lesotho. *The Journal of South African and American Comparative Studies,* 9.

Sharma, A. and Singh, N. 2015. Role of folk media in rural development. *International Journal of Education and Science Research Review,* 2(2): 59–63.

Skinner, E.P. 1998. African political cultures and the problems of government. *African Studies Quarterly,* 2(3): 17–25.

Staff Reporter. 2018. Mnangagwa in 'bhora musango' dilemma. *Bulawayo 24 News,* 12 April. https://bulawayo24.com/index-id-news-sc-national-byo-132919.html.

Tagwirei, C. and Mangeya, H. 2013. 'Juvenile' toilet door posting: An expression of gendered views on sex and sexuality. In Wanjiku Khamasi, J., Longman, C. and van Haegendoren, M., eds. *Gender, Sexuality, and the Media: A Question of Accountability.* Eldoret: Moi University Press, 27–42.

Texeira, R.P., Otta, E., and Siqueira, J. 2003. *Between the Public and the Private: Sex Differences in Restroom Graffiti from Latin and Anglo-Saxon Countries.* Working Paper No03/007. Retrieved from University De S.o Paulo. http://www.ead.fea.usp.br/WPapers/2003/03-007.pdf.

Willems, W. 2015. Alternative, mediation, power and civic agency in Africa. In Alton, C., ed. *The Routledge Companion to Alternative Community Media.* London: Routledge, 88-99.

Wilson, D. 1987. Traditional systems of communication in modern African development: An analytical viewpoint. *Africa Media Review,* 1(2): 87–104. www.eldis.org/document/A37138.

Wiredu, K. 1997. Democracy by consensus in African traditional politics: A plea for a non-party polity. In Eze, E.C., ed. *Postcolonial African Philosophy: A Critical Reader.* Cambridge: Blackwell Publishers Inc, 303–312.

13

"Arab Spring" or Arab Winter

Social media and the 21st-century slave trade in Libya

Ashley Lewis, Shamilla Amulega, and Kehbuma Langmia

Introduction/background

The world reacted with shock to the news of West African migrants to Libya having been captured and sold into slavery. American news network Cable News Network (CNN) is being touted as responsible for bringing national attention to the travesty in a November 2017 newsbreak entitled "People for Sale: Where lives are auctioned off for $400" (Elbagir et al. 2017). In this report, CNN sought to further investigate a grainy video image that had been circulated, which featured a young adult Black male being auctioned off for farm work in Libya. After traveling to Tripoli to validate the legitimacy of the video, undercover journalists witnessed first-hand about a dozen men being sold off for work. Refugees from conflict-laden countries in West Africa, migrants to Libya are leaving turbulent lives behind in search of better opportunities in Europe but instead are being captured at the Libyan border and thrust into an age-old institution of forced labor accompanied by human degradation, humiliation, and abuse. Scholarly inquiry into the practice of slavery has resurfaced amid recent reports of human trafficking in Libya.

Increasingly, social media access and use now permit everyday citizens to dialogue about social and political issues like the practice of slavery in Libya, independent of the institutions that typically monopolize these discussions. This work employs the use of critical discourse analysis in exploring rhetoric around the capture and unlawful detainment of West and East Africans in route to Europe for the purpose of selling them into slavery. In order to achieve this objective, three research questions have been posed: (1) What is the discourse around slavery in Libya as discussed by anti-slavery Facebook groups? (2) How is Facebook being used as an alternative public sphere for the advocacy of human trafficking victims in Libya? (3) How do Facebook users' discourse concerning the slave trade in Libya compare to that of early abolitionists in North America? As the Pew Research Center reports that Facebook is one of the most widely used social media platforms (Pew Research Center 2018), we will rely on this medium for data collection and analysis. To provide answers to these three questions, our data was elicited from Facebook groups that were created by everyday citizens spreading awareness about this issue, also advocating on behalf of the enslaved. This research contributes to re-emerging inquiries about modern-day slavery and civic abolitionism by first historicizing the institution of slavery, and by examining the role of Facebook as an alternative sphere in which everyday citizens commune.

Modern slavery as the new global trade

The silence of advanced nations is complicit with the hegemonic structures that create the conditions for unlawful slavery. Class and race dominance, paternalist thought, religion, and capitalism have historically served as systematic and ideological mechanisms used to restrict populations in the West. Simultaneously, these ideologies and structures benefit others by exalting them and placing them in positions of power. For instance, Wilson (1976) notes that while capitalism made the idea of free labor appealing to White southerners during slavery in the United States, Christianity reinforced the paternalistic values of White slaveholders. Religion was used to solidify in the minds of slaves that as they were being protected and cared for by their masters, they were then obligated under Christian morals and values to obey their enslavers as the Christian bible requires dutiful children to do and provide free labor to their slaveholders as part of a reciprocal relationship (Wilson 1976). In modern-day practices, religion and paternalism continue to be used as devices to ensure obedience and complacency among slaves.

It is difficult to comprehend the value of humans being measured per their physical capabilities, yet this is how slaves were sold in tropical Sahel markets. During the 15th through the 18th centuries slaves were obtained by trading with indigenous kingdoms of the Savannahs and captives captured in local wars were taken to markets where they were bought by Muslim merchants from the north (Alexander 2001, 49). Norris (1982) found that much of the work done at salt extraction sites in the Sahara was done by slaves, providing salt for the extensive trade through the tropical Savannah populations in the 19th century.

Currently, more people are being trafficked across borders now than at any point in the past (Kapstein 2006). It is therefore crucial to bring awareness of the modern slave trade to spark a recognition of the flaws in our contemporary economic and political environment. Irrefutably, modern slavery is comparable to the acrimonious facts of the Atlantic slave trade that led to a reexamination of U.S. history – largely celebratory until the 1960s (Kapstein 2006, 103). Additionally, the United Nations estimate that human traffickers earn around $10 billion per year and that the average sale price for a slave is around $12,500. Subsequently, operating costs are approximately $3,000 for each slave and traffickers can earn over $10,000 per victim (Kapstein 2006). This system is analogous to ancient slavery practices and profitable structures such as providing cheap domestic labor to European countries.

Slave trade in Libya

Historical analysis of the slave trade in Libya helps illustrate its evolution and illuminates its significance to contemporary human trafficking operations. Picarelli (2008) found that "contemporary trafficking is but the latest form of a trade in human beings practiced for millennia, where comparisons are often drawn between contemporary sex trafficking and the White slave trade of the early 1900s" (Picarelli 2008, 1). The historical significance of the slave trade in Tripoli is pertinent to understanding Libya's past with slavery as it relates to the current issue of human trafficking.

In his analysis, Picarelli (2008), identified four factors that frame the evolution of the trade in human beings: economic foundations, ideological positions, state responses, and organizational dynamics of the trade in human beings. These four factors mirror the current issues that impact contemporary slave trade operations in Libya and in other African countries. Altaleb (2016) offers insight into the social and economic relationships of slaves in Libya by evaluating Ali Abdullatif Ahmida's research on Libya, from the early 19th century to the early 20th century. Ahmida (1994) highlights the role of tribal peasant groups in the social and political transformation of Tripoli, Fezzan and Cyrenaica, arguing that "due to the extension of control over the countryside by the central administration, at first that of the Ottoman, and later that of the colonial powers" (Ahmida 1994, 5). The local response to stop slavery was strongly constrained by the agrarian regions that relied on slaves to work on the farms.

Nineteenth-century agrarian practices took precedence as one of the leading contributors to the Libyan economy due to the decline of the caravan trade. Ahmida (2010) noted that the Fezzan population was established by three main groups: landowners, small peasantry, and sharecroppers. Therefore, the aristocratic tribal clans (represented by a class beneath the landowning class), owned most of the small farms and employed freed slaves under sharecropping contracts, as slaves were needed to cultivate their farms. Furthermore, Ahmida (2010), noted that the population was divided into two groups: the notables, merchants who owned the land – the Ghadamsiya class versus the peasant class, which consisted mainly of freed slaves or their descendants who worked the land under the control of the Ghadamsiya. Additionally, De Agostini (1974) described Libya's ex-slaves, commonly referred to as shwashna, as being individuals with low immigration status from tribal backgrounds who were secured for farming by a percentage of the farmland produced.

Methodology

Critical discourse analysis (CDA) has been selected as this research's method of analysis given its appropriateness for investigating the prevailing discourses in a society and how these discourses reinforce power and privilege within that society (Wodak and Meyer 2009). Unveiling these dynamics is thought to be necessary because discourse allows certain populations to maintain power through the use of discourse, while all others live in a constant state of subjugation. What's more is that those who are oppressed by discourse or "language in action" might not be privy to their oppression because the discourse has been normalized and is therefore uneasily uncovered.

Through CDA, the marginalized are given the necessary information about their oppression to become empowered to act on dominant forces within a society. Theoretically, discourse analysis seeks to excavate the existence and maintenance of power by institutions and the elite through language and practice. Moreover, CDA is used to reveal the active injustice and oppression that language and practice allows to function in society. Activists are then charged with the task of striving to make concrete change where a specific injustice is concerned, taking all required measures to ensure this.

Critical discourse analysis was used to examine public and private anti-slavery Facebook groups, identified through a Facebook search using the phrases "slavery in Lybia" and "slave trade in Lybia", with variations of each phrase containing the same words also included in the search. Among those groups that the search yielded, five groups containing 350 members or more were included in our study's sample. Each Facebook group's description, wall posts, and any comments on a post were coded using a method similar to that which appears in Shortell's (2004) work around abolitionist rhetoric found in anti-slavery newspapers published between 1827 and 1861 (Shortell 2004, 84–88). In his work, Shortell (2004) uses a unique computer application, *SemioCode*, to construct a diagram of semantic relations to reveal a socio-cognitive map that shed light on abolitionist discourse, the ultimate goal of revealing a shared discourse and worldview among actors within the abolitionist movement (Shortell 2004, 85). Shortell

(2004), a social psychologist and spatial semiotician, created *SemioCode*, a statistical application designed to quantitatively study relationships among textual elements. The application uses algorithms to create frequencies and co-occurrences to find probabilistic relations; it uses coding algorithms to operationalize themes in a text as sets of keywords, illuminating semantic links. Shortell (2004) used this software to find common themes and keywords present in abolitionist newspapers published in New York between 1827 and 1860. Shortell's computerized content coding yielded 16 themes. As this study is critical, it is important to note that the idea of an alternative public sphere, a modification of Habermas' theory of the public sphere, which was relative to uncovering abolitionist undertones in citizens' discussions about the Libyan slave trade crisis. Jurgen Habermas' initial conceptualization of a "public sphere", first proposed in 1962, referenced interactions between free citizens in a democratic society, from the bourgeois class, in open arenas where civic engagement is promoted. What should be highlighted about these spaces is the element of critical discourse that takes place within them. In these arenas, the material and ideological contingency of the public sphere is said to vary from society to society and is heavily influenced by the spatiotemporal specificity of a given social reality within a society (Susen 2011).

The global popularity of social media and their propensity to blur the lines between public and private life has changed the material and ideological contingency of Habermas' original conception of a "public sphere" (where public and private were once separate). It is now necessary to consider that both spaces exist simultaneously. Additionally, whereas in Habermas' early conception of the public sphere both public and private spaces were dominated by the White male perspective, the Pew Research Center reports that today's social media users are predominately Black, Hispanic, and female (Pew Research Center 2018), groups that have traditionally been excluded from earlier conceptions of the public sphere.

Shortell (2004) contends that social movement discourse cannot be isolated from hierarchical social relations and the process of domination because though arguments contest particular arrangements, they can simultaneously consent to others (Shortell 2004, 77). This research acknowledges that though users with access to social media platform like Facebook are using it to engage in dialogue about the evils of modern-day slavery in Tripoli, the platform itself is still under the ownership of a larger media entity and is therefore subject to some rules of censorship as set forth by the platform itself.

Data analysis

Sixteen themes were generated through computerized content coding of the abolitionist newspaper *The Working Man's Advocate* (1830–1844) included in the study's sample: JUSTICE, LIBERTY, RIGHTS, UPLIFT, AMERICA, SLAVERY, GOD, BROTHERHOOD, COLORED, PROPERTY, LABOR, CHARACTER, SUFFERING, NATURE, POLITICS, and LAW (Shortell 2004, 86). Overall, *SemioCode* was used to illuminate the construction of abolitionists' arguments, which Shortell contends are designed to describe the social world, explain it, or evaluate it (Shortell 2004, 87). Each unit was coded for the aforementioned themes, a rhetorical mode that was assertive, evaluative, or explanatory; a rhetorical tone that reflected anger, joy, sadness, or irony; and a rhetorical basis of either similarity or difference. Whereas paragraphs were used as coding units in Shortell's (2004) work, each Facebook group description, each Facebook post, and each Facebook comment was coded as a unit of analysis. To better suit the purpose of this research, Shortell's original 16 themes have been adjusted in order to more accurately examine this special case of slavery in Tripoli.

Table 13.1 Anti-slavery Facebook groups

Group	#of Members	Group Type	Languages
Stop Slavery in Libya! Action Now	350	Support, Open	English, Spanish, Portugese, French, Dutch
Slavery in Libya and around the World	676	N/A, Closed	N/A
Stop Slavery in Libya #slaveryinlibya	392	Custom, Open	English, Spanish, Portugese, French, Dutch
A Call to Action: Community Movement Against Slavery and Injustice in Libya	1094	Support, Open	English, Spanish, Portugese, French, Dutch
SAY NO to slavery in Libya	1594	Support, Open	English, Spanish, Portugese, French, Dutch

Themes AMERICA, RIGHTS, COLORED, LIBERTY, COLORED, UPLIFT and BROTHERHOOD, were replaced with themes AFRICA, AFRICAN, LIBYA, TRIPOLI, HUMAN RIGHTS, HUMAN, ATROCITY, and FREEDOM. Advertisements, images, videos, and organized demonstrations notices were not examined, but are noted in our analysis.

Though a total of five Facebook groups were examined for their content, one of the five groups was closed and did not permit non-members to access its content (see Table 13.1). Nevertheless, the group's description was available to non-members for examination and therefore has been included in our analysis.

Findings

Of the five groups examined, three were led by women. One of the three groups, which was closed, was an entirely female group. Each group had an international membership and was primarily composed of non-White members. As each group was multicultural, some postings were not written in English, the language that is primarily used by the researchers who conducted this analysis. Members in four of the five groups appeared to vary in age (this information was not accessible in the closed group). Every group in the sample had a prepared description of the group in its "about" section, and in each description, expressed a goal of either educating others about the slave trade crisis in Libya or contributing to the end of the slave trade in some way. All groups contained textual posts including posters, images, and videos that in some way connected to the issues of slavery (some covered incidents of slavery in other places besides Libya).

There were also the very assertive modes of expression present in each group's description post. All five groups examined use the description to state the group's purpose and their mission. While the tone of group descriptions tended to be assertive, the description of a group entitled STOP SLAVERY IN LIBYA! ACTION NOW seemed explanatory as it discussed the lack of government intervention for slavery, citing this as one of the main reasons why the group had been developed. The other group titled A Call to Action: Community Movement Against Slavery and Injustice in Libya, galvanized around mobilizing people to go out and fight slavery.

The group also provided insight on the possibilities of eradicating slavery by shedding light to the people and countries supporting it. For example, "The countries who fund these detention centers need to be held accountable". The posts and wall comments that depicted the JOY rhetorical tone basically was in reference to victory over slavery, such as the Nigerian slaves in

Libya being taken back to their country, a container full of clothes and amenities landing in Libya to assist the slaves, and a collection of money that was raised to help the Libyan slaves being released from a European organization, that had earlier branded the Facebook group as a "terrorist funding group" and had seized the total contributions.

Most of the anti-slavery discourse was found in group wall posts, many of which either urged group members to become active in helping to end the suffering of African migrants by ending the slave trade or sought to persuade group members of the evils of slavery. The majority of these posts were created by one of the group's administrators or moderators. The purpose of many of the posts was to inform others in the group about the dire situation in Libya, as well as assert the importance of concerned citizens intervening on behalf of the captured. While anger and sadness were the tones of many of these posts, most of them expressed unbridled anger at this situation that had previously been hidden, and anger at government failure to put an end to the fiasco. For example, one wall post contained a map that showed that Libya currently has no anti-slavery organizations, reiterating the importance of the involvement of everyday citizens in helping to bring trafficking in Libya to cessation.

The bulk of the comments that were examined not only issued blame to the European Union, intergovernmental organizations, NATO, and the United Nations for the dire state of affairs in Libya that would permit such atrocities to take place, but members also used their comments to indict the U.S. government. These comments accused the U.S. of not only being passive, but also for creating the circumstances in Libya that allowed for such deplorable activities to take place. One member's comment read:

> Libya had the highest human development index in the Islamic world/Middle East as according to a UN report before US-NATO sought destruction and regime change.

Another member with similar sentiments posted the following:

> Look what those devil Obama and Killary [Hilary] and that liser [loser] French Sarkoz . . . did to the beautiful progressive Libya.

This user was referring to the former president of the United States, Barack Obama, and the former U.S. First Lady and secretary of state, Hilary Clinton. Both worked closely with Nicolas Sarkozy, former president of France, to drive out the presently deceased Colonel Muammar Gaddafi, former leader of Libya, who had been criticized internationally for running a seemingly ruthless regime and committing various crimes against humanity. He was killed in 2011, an incident that some have referred to as a catalyst for the destabilization of the Libyan government. Yet, other comments made statements that accused the U.S. and the U.K. of supporting the war on Libya, therefore making them responsible for what one commenter called an "inhumane scenario".

Though most comments issued blame to the Western world, one commenter, who did not appear to be a member of the group (this was determined from a lengthy discussion that the commenter had with the one of the group's administrators), asserted that there is, in fact, no slavery happening in Libya, only human smuggling, which the commenter alleged is taking place all over Africa. This commenter is referring to the human smuggling that many young men living around the Horn of Africa (Djibouti, Eritrea, Somalia, and Ethiopia) find themselves involved in due to the low availability of job opportunities in their home countries. In another thread of comments, two people went back and forth about whether Arabs were African or European. In one of the most controversial comments examined, a user discussed America's

"Arab Spring" or Arab Winter

recent "border situation", alleging that the coverage that receives serves to distract the wider populace's attention away from slavery in Libya. This user is of course referring to immigrant Mexican families who are being detained and separated at the U.S.–Mexico border.

Other common themes that emerged dealt with the atrocities of slavery and the grave injustices and abuse against African migrants. One such comment discussed Britain turning a blind eye on the torture, rape, and abuse that refugees are subject to, and also accusing Britain of supporting the Libyan coast guard. The tone of this post and those like it was either sad or angry. One lone post did contain a more joyous tone, and this post dealt with news of the Republic of Chad's involvement in helping to liberate enslaved Africans in Libya. The *Washington Post* reports that in November 2017 the Republic of Chad was involved in a multicountry initiative to liberate slave camps in Libya (Bearak 2017).

In order to establish bonds between themselves and those affected by the slave trade, many group members used a basis of similarity to show solidarity between themselves and others. In both wall posts and comments, many group members referred to the enslaved in Lybia as their "brothers" and their "people". One particular user referred to the enslaved as his/her "fellow Africans".

Call to action

A few of the groups examined did issue a call to action or urge the wider populace to not only take active stances against slavery in Libya, but to also take substantive action in helping to eradicate the system. One group challenged others to "keep raising our voice to save our people from the hands of animals called 'Lybia'". Another group provided practical measures for people to follow in an effort to help prevent slavery. These measures are discussed thoroughly in Research Question 2.

Discussion and conclusion

Research Question 1: *What is the discourse around slavery in Libya as discussed by anti-slavery Facebook groups?*

Most anti-slavery discourse found in group wall posts either urged group members to become active in helping to end the suffering of African migrants by ending the slave trade or sought to persuade group members of the evils of slavery. Many posts like these were created by one of the group's administrators or moderators. The purpose of many of the posts was to inform others in the group about the dire situation in Libya, as well as to assert the importance of concerned citizens intervening on behalf of the captured. While a tone of sadness pervaded many of these posts, most of them expressed unbridled anger at this situation that had previously been hidden, and anger at the failure of various governments to put an end to it. For example, one wall post contained a map revealing that Libya currently has no anti-slavery organizations, reiterating the importance of everyday citizen involvement in helping to bring trafficking in Libya to an end.

Other comments that were examined not only issued blame to the European Union, intergovernmental organizations, NATO, and the United Nations for the dire state of affairs in Libya that would permit such atrocities to take place, but members also used their comments to indict the U.S. government. These comments accused the U.S. of passivity and for creating the circumstances in Libya that allowed for such deplorable activities to take place. One member's comment read:

> Libya had the highest human development index in the Islamic world/Middle East as according to a UN report before US-NATO sought destruction and regime change.

Another member with similar sentiments posted the following:

> Look what those devil Obama and Killary [Hilary] and that liser [loser] French Sarkoz . . . did to the beautiful progressive Libya.

This user was referring to former U.S. president Barack Obama and former First Lady and secretary of state Hillary Clinton, both of whom had worked closely with Nicolas Sarkozy, former president of France, to drive out the presently deceased Colonel Muammar Gaddafi, former leader of Libya, who had been criticized internationally for running a seemingly ruthless regime and committing various crimes against humanity. He was killed in 2011, an incident that some have referred to as a catalyst for the destabilization of the Libyan government. Yet, other comments made statements that accused the U.S. and the U.K. of supporting the war on Libya, therefore making them responsible for what one commenter called an "inhumane scenario".

Research Question 2: *How is Facebook being used as an alternative public sphere for the advocacy of human trafficking victims in Libya?*

A few of the groups examined did issue a call to action or urge the wider populace to take active stances against slavery in Libya and take substantive action in helping to eradicate the system. One group challenged others to "keep raising our voice to save our people from the hands of animals called "Libya". Another group provided practical measure for people to follow in an effort to help prevent slavery. This included:

> one, "Support your fellow human beings in a peaceful protest. Stop UAE funding of armed groups in Libya which imprison, torture and kill African migrants in addition to selling them as slaves. Two, stand up against human rights abuses, Mobilize, Organize, Speak-up, Speak out. Three, "UN action against Africa (Gaddafi) must stop".
>
> Four, "Stay informed and keep others informed, raise awareness in your community about the issue, write a letter to your Member of Parliament and demand action". Five, "Government should protect the working class and fight against poverty that lead to slavery". "The countries who fund these detention centers need to be held accountable".

These examples demonstrate the contentious discourse powering Facebook activism. Discourse can also be a mediator and a source of power (Steinberg 1999, 14). Steinberg asserts that discourse mediates power by facilitating the social action of control and exploitation. Further, discourse shapes consciousness and empowers possibilities for action and change that are culturally constituted.

Research Question 3: *How do Facebook users' discourse concerning the slave trade in Libya compare to that of early abolitionists in North America?*

Very similar to early abolitionist discourse, common themes that emerged in the examined Facebook groups dealt with the atrocities of slavery and the grave injustices and abuse against African migrants. One such comment discussed Britain turning a blind eye to the torture, rape, and abuse that refugees are subject to, and also accusing Britain of supporting the Libya coast guard. The tone of this post and those like it was either sad or angry. One lone post did contain a more joyous tone, and this post dealt with news that the Republic of Chad had become involved in helping to liberate enslaved Africans in Libya. The *Washington Post* reports that in November 2017 the Republic of Chad was involved in a multicountry initiative to liberate slave camps in Libya (Bearak 2017).

In order to establish bonds between themselves and those affected by the slave trade, many group members used a basis of similarity to show solidarity between themselves and others. In both wall posts and comments, many group members referred to the enslaved in Libya as their "brothers" and their "people". One user referred to the enslaved as his/her "fellow Africans"

A critical discourse analysis revealed that Facebook groups were not only used to encourage global citizens to take a stand against the inhumane practice of slavery in Libya, but posts were also used to criticize larger institutions, like the United Nations, to which Libya claims membership, who seemed to be compliant with this formidable practice. Facebook users, either consciously or unconsciously, used the language of 19th-century American abolitionists to indict the Libyan government and other key political figures for engaging in and permitting these atrocities, in alignment with critical discourse, which takes a stand against the powerful and elites, namely those who abuse their power. The majority of posts showed anger for the situation in Libya, with commenters being assertive about putting it to an end. Though they did not possess the power or influence of the institutions that they criticized to put a stop to it, many felt empowered by their abilities to be active in what they perceived to be effective ways to address this travesty; through attending a rally, or creating and sharing anti-slavery wall posts to spreading awareness to others. Some users gave donations to anti-slavery organizations that vowed to send clothing and food to African refugees in Libya. Other groups took their activism a step further by searching for anti-slavery organizations in Libya to contact, reiterating the importance of their own advocacy after finding none. Others were empowered by sharing news of Africans who had been rescued from Libya and returned to their homes, although it is not clear if commenters understood that these men were leaving one undesirable condition, only to return to another.

Most of the moderators and administrators for the examined Facebook groups were women. This is significant in relationship to Habermas' theory of the "public sphere", which historically excluded women and people of color. The theory of the alternative public sphere fittingly describes how social media has extended communal spaces to those who would have traditionally been denied access. The analysis also revealed that many Facebook users who expressed discontent with Africans being enslaved are citizens of the Western countries that encourage illegal means of immigration by not allowing Africans to come migrate over legally, or making legal immigration impossible because of restrictive policies, tedious processes, and high costs. While everyday citizens may not have the hard power of governments and organizations to put an end to human trafficking in Libya, social media use has made it possible for them to exercise soft power, by urging capable parties to act on behalf of the oppressed.

Though the evils of American slavery are now widely known, during its operation, there were no devices or tools comparable to today's social media that allowed for dispersed populations and networks to convene together in one space at a given time to share their ideas, displeasure for the practice of slavery, and advocate on a mass scale on behalf of the oppressed. Further, social media and the Internet now allow practices that were once easy to conceal to not only be uncovered, but to be broadcast widely for all to see, critique, and hold accountable parties responsible for their unlawful actions and injustice.

A few comments were particularly significant as they revealed a deeper concern with the relationship between Libyans and other Africans. One comment read, "Why aren't other Libyans stopping the cruelty", and another:

> From one side you want the polices, from the other side the slavery, which I assure you that there is no slavery in Libya, there is only human traffic [smuggling], which our brothers from Africa are doing it and they fully understood that Libya is a failed state and war zone.

Finally, one last comment implored others to "keep raising our voice to save our people from the hands of the Animals called Libya". It is also necessary to highlight the back-and-forth conversation between two male users asking each other whether Arabs are African or European. These ironic remarks illuminate the alleged fragile relationship between Libyans and the rest of Africa. For example, Mazrui (1974) posits that Arabs have played two major roles in Africa: first as accomplices in African enslavement, and then in the 20th century as allies in African liberation (as exemplified by Gaddafi, the Libyan revolutionary who dreamed of Africa as a centralized power against the West). However, Wai (1984) believes that President of Malawi Kamuza Banda's criticism of Arab involvement in the slave trade in Africa excludes them from being considered Africa's genuine friends. Hence, President Banda emphasizes that present cases of slavery in Southern Sudan, where Africans have been oppressed, repressed, and subjected to varied human indignities by Arabs, is a case in point. This is analogous to the fate of African men in Libya, where they are treated as sub-human and sold into slavery. This is suggestive of possible Arab superiority to darker-skinned Africans, a dynamic that is worthy of further exploration.

The institution of slavery is an age-old practice that has affected millions. These effects are especially known by African populations. Systems of complacency and compliance allow this diabolic practice to thrive, creating monetary profit for nations looking to benefit from free labor. The abuse, humiliation, and degradation that its victims are subject to has sparked international outrage, with many vocalizing their opposition to slavery. These early protests were spearheaded by abolitionists of the late 19th century. Today's widespread use of social media platforms have not only revolutionized advocacy and means of resistance but has also granted expanded access in terms of those who are able to become politically involved. Going forward, emancipation of modern slavery needs not just to be examined, but to bring to light the underlying causes that permeate its existence and derive practical solutions, such as enacting policies that can address the problem. Slavery emancipation means little to poor people, and immigrants who are continually trapped in systems that essentially benefit from their disadvantage, which essentially leads to modern slavery. There is a need for developed nations, such as Britain, France, and the U.S. to re-evaluate their restricted labor laws and immigration policies. Increased regulations in broken systems also serve to stipulate illegal migration and thereby increase the level of exploitation of many workers who do not have legal protection in labor markets. Conclusively, social media will continue to remain an open forum for those with oppositional viewpoints who look to challenge the dominant narrative.

References

Ahmida, Ali Abdullatif. 1994. *The Making of Modern Libya: State Formation, Colonization, and Resistance, 1830–1932*. Albany: SUNY Press.

Ahmida, Ali Abdullatif. 2010. A problematic view on Libyan history: The emergence of Libya: Selected historical essays. *Journal of African History*, 51: 420-422)

Alexander, John. 2001. Islam, archaeology and slavery in Africa. *World Archaeology*, 33(1): 44–60.
Altaleb, Amal Mehemed. 2016. *The Social and Economic History of Slavery in Libya (1800–1950)*. PhD diss., University of Manchester.
Bearak, Max. 2017. African and European Leaders Want to Evacuate Thousands Mired in Libyan Slave Trade. *The Washington Post*, 30 November. www.washingtonpost.com/news/worldviews/wp/2017/11/30/african-and-europea-leaders-want-to-evacuate-thousands-mired-in-libyan-slave-trade/?utm_term=.f71261b976de (Accessed 16 July 2018).
De Agostini, Enrico. 1974. *Sukan Libya*, trans. al-Tillisi, Khalifa. Tripoli: al-Dar al'Arabiya lil-Kitab, vol. 1.
Elbagir, N., Razek, R., Platt, A. and Jones, B. 2017. *People for Sale: Where Lives Are Auctioned for $400*. www.cnn.com/2017/11/14/africa/libya-migrant-auctions/index.htm (Accessed 13 December 2017).
Kapstein, Ethan B. 2006. The new global slave trade. *Foreign Affairs*, 85: 103.
Mazrui, Ali A. 1974. Black Africa and the Arabs. *Foreign Affairs*, 53: 725.
Norris, H.T. 1982. Bulletin of the School of Oriental and African Studies. *University of London*, 45(1): 174–176. http://www.jstor.org/stable/615218 (Accessed 3 October 2020).
Picarelli, J.T. 2008. *The "Modern Day" Trade in Human Beings: How Historical Experience Influences the Contemporary Trafficking in Persons*. Dissertation, American University.
Shortell, Timothy. 2004. The rhetoric of Black abolitionism: An exploratory analysis of antislavery newspapers in New York state. *Social Science History*, 28(1): 75–109.
Pew Research Center. 2018. *Social Media Fact Sheet: Internet, Science & Tech*, 5 February. www.pewinternet.org/fact-sheet/social-media/ (Accessed 16 July 2018).
Steinberg, M.W. 1999. The talk and back talk of collective action: A dialogic analysis of repertoires of discourse among nineteenth-century English cotton spinners. *American Journal of Sociology*, 105(3): 736–780. DOI:10.1086/210359.
Susen, Simon. 2011. Critical notes on Habermas's theory of the public sphere. *Sociological Analysis*, 5(1).
Wai, Dunstan M. 1984. African-Arab relations from slavery to Petro-Jihad. *Issue: A Journal of Opinion*, 13: 9–13.
William, J. Wilson. Slavery, paternalism, and White hegemony. *American Journal of Sociology*, 81(5): 1190–1198. www.jstor.org/stable/2777568.
Wilson, William J. 1976. Review: Slavery, paternalism, and white hegemony. *American Journal of Sociology*, 81(5): 1190–1198.
Wodak, Ruth and Meyer, Michael, eds. 2009. *Methods for critical discourse analysis*. Thousand Oaks: Sage.
Wright, J. 2008. *The Emergence of Libya: Selected Historical Essays*. London: Silphium Press, 121–151.

14

On community radio and African interest broadcasting

The case of Vukani Community Radio (VCR)

Siyasanga M. Tyali

Introduction

A large body of research and theoretical outputs has been generated from the community radio sector of South Africa (Berger 1996; Teer-Tomaselli 2001; Bosch 2003; Tyali and Tomaselli 2015). Such outputs have focused on multiple themes, including the health communication role of the industry, its history and development as well as the democratic role of such a broadcasting sector within the country. Using a case study approach, the focus of this chapter is on theorising the decolonisation role of the community radio sector by understanding its cultural "liberatory" role in relation to the history and memory of a particularised African community. Fanon (1961, 51) in his attempts to make sense of the continuing legacy of colonialism on "postcolonial" societies suggests that "because of the various means whereby decolonisation has been carried out have appeared in many different aspects, reason hesitates and refuses to say which is a true decolonization, and which is a false". Though this is acknowledged, scholars such as Tuck and Yang (2012, 13) have however argued that "decolonisation specifically requires the repatriation of indigenous land and life". In dealing with the existence of coloniality or none thereof in "postcolonial" societies, Castro-Go´mez (2007, 428) ponders "do we live in a world where the old epistemological hierarchies made rigid by modern colonialism have disappeared, or on the contrary, are we witnessing a postmodern reorganization of coloniality?" Should it be that coloniality is acknowledged in such societies, thus decolonisation and repatriation of indigenous life is an antidote to such coloniality. Repatriation of such life requires communities to not only decolonise the current moment, but to mainly understand how the current moment is connected to history and memory. Thus, the dominant question that underpins the chapter is: how does a community radio such as Vukani Community Radio (VCR) (as a case study) adapt its broadcasting content to suit the everyday need of the African community it serves? Through this central question, I further aim to understand the manifestation of African memory on the airwaves of a media institution and how this speaks to the question of the making and the re-making of "previously" colonised "spaces" into African interest-driven spaces.

The objective of this chapter is therefore connected to the larger idea of understanding how media institutions play an identifiable decolonisation role by reflecting the subliminal and overt means of resistance by an African community against the philosophies of colonialism, coloniality and Western imperialism. Figuoera (2015, 50) argued that "though colonization and slavery ended, their structures remain deeply embedded in the spaces they once occupied and in the psyche of the people they dominated". Wigston (2008, 4) also notes that "our understanding of the nature and structure of the present media environment is largely influenced by what happened in the past". These perspectives therefore affirm the quest of the chapter in exploring the decolonising role of a community radio platform that is operating in the contemporary era of "postcolonial" South Africa.

As a result of their identity and cultural impact on societies of reception, media institutions continue to be covertly and overtly underpinned by deep ideological foundations that may impact such societies of reception. Thus, whether liberalist, communist or authoritarian, media platforms are naturally ideological in their production of content. According to van Dijk (2000), ideology seems to constitute certain forms of systematic ideas that are most prevalent in social, cultural, political and religious settings of a society. These are related to the lived thinking of social groups or movements within such societies. Some scholarship has emphasised that "ideologies are belief of a group and its members" (ibid, 7). As an ideological platform embodying philosophies of African culture, how it is lived, expressed and shapes a community in South Africa's "postcolonial" era, understanding a community broadcaster that is underpropped and centred on African belief systems is in this context essential to the idea of decolonising the airwaves through the project of making and re-making itself as an African media institution. Thus, decolonisation in the context of this chapter needs to be understood within the bigger project of repatriating African indigenous life from the jaws and impact of colonialism. Central to this investigation of a community radio platform is the historical understanding of colonialism as a cultural bomb which aims to destroy and denigrate all forms of African identities that emerge from colonialism (cf. wa Thiong'o 1986).

Brief background: the case study of a community radio station

In 1996, the broadcasting licence dispensation gave broadcasting rights (initially on a temporary basis) to a community broadcasting sector that had been officially recognised during the postapartheid negotiations of South Africa. Among such licence-granted broadcasters was a university student–aligned broadcasting institution named VCR. This community broadcaster was and still is situated in a small IsiXhosa-speaking semi-rural town known as Cala in the Eastern Cape province of South Africa. It was established by a group of students who were then known as Cala University Students Association (CALUSA). The community radio station started broadcasting on April 9, 1996, and since then it grew and established itself as a stable community broadcaster. From its initial development and association with a group of university students, the history of VCR is similar to that of a number of community radio stations in South Africa. In their initial development phase, these radio stations were incubated at university campuses. In some cases, and at the height of the antiapartheid movement (Bosch 2003), some of these stations were established by students who acquired broadcasting skills from university campuses and then later used their skills to build broadcasting facilities in their respective communities. Whilst in its initial years of establishment, VCR started broadcasting through a temporary licence, but in 2000, the radio station was granted a renewable medium-term licence that allowed it to broadcast for a four-year period. It is this same broadcasting licence condition that still allows VCR to broadcast until today. Broadcasting on the 90.6–98.4 frequency, VCR together with Bush Radio (Bosch 2003) are some of South Africa's oldest community radio broadcasters.

VCR and the rest of the community radio sector of South Africa emerged from a long and evolving conceptual contestation on the meaning of community radio and community broadcasting in general. With regards to this evolving discourse, some scholarship has concluded that there is still a lack of consensus on how the community radio sector should be defined (Banda 2006; MISA 2000). Largely this is because the term "community radio", according to Guy Berger (1996, 3), has become less rigidly defined over the decades, especially in terms of ownership and control. Historical and socio-political contexts of community stations offer different approaches with regard to ownership and community participation. On a general level, community radio signifies a two-way process that entails the exchange of views from various sources and the adaptation of media for use by communities (AMARC 1998). MISA (2000) states that community radio is a station built by the community, used by the community and serving the interests of the community. Emphasis is on community ownership, autonomy, participation and representation. Programmes are produced by the community, while in the case of a public broadcaster programmes are largely imposed to the community by the broadcaster (cf. Mhlanga 2006). In critiquing the various notions and objectives of community radio, Teer-Tomaselli (2001) notes that, taken together, the aspirations of community radio stations are onerous, and few stations anywhere have been able to achieve them in their entirety. This therefore means that the understanding of the term "community radio" or even its objectives should be adapted on a case-by-case basis. Hence, Fackson Banda (2006) concludes that at a conceptual level, community radio has undergone some paradigm shifts, and these need to be contextualised at a local level. It is the conclusion of this chapter that such conceptual contestations will redefine the role of community radio stations as well as their roles in "postcolonial" Africa.

Continuities and discontinuities: on the media and the colonial project

Whilst VCR has been operating in the "postcolonial" moment of South Africa, its origin as a modern-day media institution that is operating in Africa can be directly traced to the colonial project, which led to the cultural destruction of some African communities within the continent. In this section, the aim is to understand the colonial role of the media with an idea of making sense of the community radio broadcaster as an offshoot of the media genealogy in Africa. Thus it is vital to trace the history of the media in Africa and how it relates to the colonial project. This task seeks to understand the contemporary project of decolonising the role and practice of community radio stations in modern-day South Africa. Nyamnjoh (2005, 172) argues that "just as it is dangerous to blame everything on the past, it is equally dangerous to deny the power of the past in shaping the present". Thus, an analysis of the historical roles of the media potentially illustrates the continuities and discontinuities of these institutions initial colonial mandates. Taking into context the question of coloniality, studies of postcolonial Africa suggests that colonial legacies are still prevalent (Mbembe 2001; Tuck and Yang 2012; Fanon 1961) in the contemporary moment of postcolonies. In reference to the media industry, some research literature suggests that the radio medium as well as other media platforms existing today, including the press, were designed to support colonial ideologies and their related policies (Mano 2011; Rønning and Kupe 2000; Rosenthal 1974; Switzer and Switzer 1979; Mhlambi 2015). For instance, it was Fanon (1965, 69) who argued that in the then French occupied

Algeria, Radio-Alger, a then French broadcasting station which had been established in that country for decades, was a re-edition or an echo of the French National Broadcasting System which was then operating from Paris. On the relationship of the colonisers and modern media industry he further stated that (1965, 71–72):

> among European farmers, the radio was broadly regarded as a link with the civilized world, as an effective instrument of resistance to the corrosive influence of an inert native society, of a society without a future, backward and devoid of values.

Therefore, in this sense, the modern media industry was proven to be directly connected to the many colonial and cultural institutions that were used to support Western imperialism and colonial cultures. Some scholarship has also demonstrated that such roles continue to affect contemporary private and public spheres in Africa (Ziegler and Asante 1992). Though their history and development are nuanced in South Africa, as part of the broader media industry, community radio platforms have a direct link to the colonial situation of the African continent (Rønning and Kupe 2000), and hence their role in the current era of "coloniality" of the global South needs to be analysed. Whilst community radio stations were officially introduced in South Africa's during the country's "postcolonial" moment, their genealogy as offshoots of the broader media industry and the continuing question of coloniality in "postcolonial" societies compels us to re-visit the theory of the colonially untainted community radio sector. After all, the legacies of colonialism continue to live on in the "postcolonial" moment (Figuoera 2015). It is for these reasons that the focus of this chapter is on the intersection of a community radio station with memory and how such creates a possibility of the making and the re-making of a decolonised African media institution.

Media and memory: when the African subject re-members itself

Though still somewhat anchored to its historical mission, in contemporary discussions the often unacknowledged role of some media institutions is how they can serve as re-membering tools. This role is based on their feature of continuously re-living the past through certain means of broadcasting and contributing to various forms of memory and thus leading to communities of remembering. Fokasz and Kopper (2010, 1) argue that "parallel to its topicality, the media creates the communities of remembering in modern societies". Largely it acts as a notional spaces of recollection through "shared reference points for the community to recognise itself and to remember the past" (ibid). The act of re-membering needs to be taken into consideration when we theorise how media in Africa can make and re-make themselves as African media institutions. In a way, the airwaves as a space for memory have a potential to anchor and connect current generations to their history and memory. Thus, this role needs to be analysed and theorised with reference to the decolonising and cultural roles of media institutions and particularly the community radio sector in Africa. wa Thiong'o (1986) argued that colonialism was meant to subject African identities to a "cultural bomb" where subsequent African generations would not be able to see anything positive in their African cultures. He further noted that (1986, 4):

> The effect of a cultural bomb is to annihilate a people's belief in their names, in their languages, in their environment, in their heritage of struggle, in their unity, in their capacities and ultimately in themselves. It makes them see their past as one wasteland of non-achievement and it makes them want to distance themselves from that wasteland.

However, whilst this colonial act was unleashed on Africans, the research data underpinning this chapter illustrates that a "postcolonial" broadcasting institution such as VCR can be used to recognise the value of cultural memory. This act also needs to be seen within the wider scopes of contemporary decolonisation movements that aim to instil social/African community cohesion through history and culture at a time when these were meant to be obliterated by colonialism and the continuing project of coloniality (cf. Quijano 2007; Said 1989) in the global South. Regarding the social value of memory in decolonisation, Dudai and Edelson (2016, 275) note that "we are to a large extent the product of our memory. Besides the fleeting instant captured in the present, we continuously re-enact the past and imagine the future by relying on our recollections". The idea of memory is important in how African societies conceive, imagine, make and re-make themselves by relying on memory as means of re-membering (wa Thiong'o 2009) their societies. Fokasz and Kopper (2010, 2) further argue:

> It is memory that creates the link between the past, the present and the future and enables members of the community to identify who they are, because it is common reference points in the past that brings them together, and allows them to recognize themselves as a community.

Some societies have their own forms of remembering. With regards to making use of such forms of remembering, Gqola (2004, 6) postulates that "collective memory prompts engagements with some form of historical consciousness, and requires a higher, more fraught level of activity in relation to the past than simply identifying and recording it". She further suggests that "memory activity is crucial for the symbols through which each community invents itself because it resists erasure" (2004, 6). Another question that is at the core of this chapter, is how does a media institution re-member (wa Thiong'o 2009) societies and communities through memory? Furthermore, how does this act of re-membering re-define media institutions in Africa?

Decolonial theories contextualised: memory against the epistimicide of culture and being

As has been noted, media institutions have historically participated in the oppression of the colonised beings, and more specifically on the oppression of the African beings and their associated cultures and identities. These institutions achieved this through their affiliation to the colonial projects (cf. Fanon 1961). In this section, the focus is on the decolonial theory that was used to read and understand the lasting legacy of colonialism: "coloniality of being" and how today's presence of African memory in media content challenges the on-going "coloniality of being" of the African subject in the particular location of the study underpinning this chapter. Generally, the impact of the "coloniality of knowledge" and the "coloniality of power" are often experienced at the level of "being" (individual or collectively). The "coloniality of power", "coloniality of knowledge" and "coloniality of being" combine to form a matrix of control-advancing coloniality. Torres-Maldonado (2007) indicates that "coloniality of being" is a theoretical framework that emerged from academic work focussing on coloniality and decolonisation. It arose as a way of theorising and understanding the "coloniality of power" and its related implications on individuals and communities under a "colonial situation".

The theoretical framework (coloniality of being) deals with the results of colonialism in the psychological and cultural standing of people who emerge from administrative/settler colonialism and later being subjected to ongoing legacies of colonialism (Quijano 2007; Torres Maldonado 2007). Additionally, "coloniality of being" also closely contends with the lived experience of colonisation and coloniality with a special reference to language as well as identity and culture. Torres-Maldonado (2007) also argues that languages are not only sites of identity affirmation, but they are also the sites of knowledge storage and memory (cf. wa Thiong'o 1986). It is in this similar school of thought where Fanon (1952, 9) argues that in "every colonized people – in other words, every people in whose soul an inferiority complex has been created by the death and burial of its local cultural originality – finds itself face to face with the language of the civilizing nation; that is, with the culture of the mother country". Thus at the level of "being", identity informing concepts such as language and historical narratives have immense psychological implications in how colonised subjects perceive themselves in relation to their cultures.

In this chapter, the theory detailing the "coloniality of being" is used to understand how the airwaves of a media institution such as VCR potentially delink from legacies and the historical project of media institutions that were established by settler/administrative colonial societies in Africa. For instance, an understanding of the cultural impact of language concludes by stating that a people deprived of their languages among other variables of affirming one's humanity are people who were deprived of their memory and communal ontologies. Such an argument also applies in the context of a colonised people who have been systematically and historically deprived of their memory. Therefore, in the current context of coloniality, these are people whose "being" continues to being in question as a result of existence which has been systematically denied by identity and cultural informing institutions, including broadcast media. Du Bois (1903) argues that for the African, the site of existence in the modern world is a constant psychological battle against one's oppression based on the traditions of questioning and inferiorrising the African "being" and their African identity. According to Du Bois (1903, 9), the modern world is:

> a world which yields him [the African] no true self-consciousness, but only lets him see himself through the revelation of the other world. It is a peculiar sensation, this double-consciousness, this sense of always looking at one's self through the eyes of others, of measuring one's soul by the tape of a world that looks on in amused contempt pity.

Most importantly, at the level of media representation by a media institution championing the voice of African ontologies, how does this form of double consciousness manifest itself? Du Bois (1903) maintains that at the level of "being", the subject emerging from colonialism and subjected to coloniality is split into two: (1) the European aspirational self and (2) the reality of being "trapped" into an African body. This twoness is as a result of the "coloniality of being" and the continuing legacy of colonialism in Africa. Quijano (2007) concluded that through modernisation, Europeanism was transformed into a project of inspiration for the rest of the world. The "being" that is not emerging from Europe and settler North America is therefore subjected to this aspiration which leads to a constant questioning of itself. Thus in the context of this chapter, the theory has been crucial in understanding how the question and presence of African memory in a media institution delinks from its colonising mission and thereby ultimately illustrates a trajectory towards the decolonisation of African memory and the making of some media institutions as African media institutions, proper.

A note on the research method

In research, decolonisation is often concerned "with [unsettling] how settler perspectives and worldviews get to count as knowledge and research and how these perspectives – repackaged as data and findings – are activated in order to rationalize and maintain unfair social structures" (Tuck and Yang 2012, 2). When considering the African worldviews and local rationalities, there is a need to change the complete structure of colonial or neocolonial research system. For instance, discourse on the need to decolonise "research methods" has gained momentum over the years (cf. Smith 1999; Tomaselli and Dyll-Myklebust 2015, Tuck and Yang 2012; Sithole 2014). Smith (1999, 1) in her seminal work on "decolonising methodologies" argued that as a practice, research as a scientific tool has traditionally been associated with the worst excesses of colonialism and continues to be remembered with execration by those who have been subjected to the darker side of modernity. This means that, "just knowing that someone measured our 'faculties' by filling the skulls of our ancestors with millet seeds and compared the amount of millet seed to the capacity for mental thought offends our sense of who and what we are" (Smith 1999, 1). Therefore, the study underpinning this chapter was conducted using a critical "qualitative case study" approach. The aim was to suspend the rationalities of the colonial method (Smith 1999) by experimenting with the idea of decolonising the research method. The study enunciated the cultural and identity functions of VCR in reference to the African communities that are targeted by the broadcasts of this media institution. It relied on an autocritiqued and decolonised critical interpretive paradigm format of the "case study research design" so as to make sense of the community radio station as a living cultural tool that champions the epistemologies and ontologies of an African community (cf. Yin 2014). Therefore, in its entirety, this study employed such a case study approach – the case of VCR – in its assessment of the presence of African memory as a decolonising project for a community media platform. While the focus was on the entire functioning of the community radio station, I also chose to give special attention to some selected radio programmes at the radio station with a focus of targeted analysis. Yin (2014) informs us that the manner in which a case study was understood over the years continues to evolve. The use of a case study as a research design tool therefore allows global South researchers to use it with a purpose of contextualising research as well as understanding the nuances of the multi-world approach – the upholding of the plural world and ideas.

In the context of this chapter, I therefore present findings from an analysis of an African cultural based programme [Amasiko NeZithethe] that broadcasts on VCR. The study was conducted from 2014 to 2017 with an intention of understanding Africanisation and decolonisation of the media institution. In this chapter I present sampled content that was undertaken with a purpose of analysing the airwaves as a source of memory. The details of such content are captured in Table 14.1.

Table 14.1 A complete biographical summary of the selected media programme

Name	Genre	Slot Time	Number of Episodes Analysed
Amasiko ne Zithethe (culture and traditions) (presented by Mnyamezeli Mpumela)	Africa cultural lifestyle radio programme that is geared towards the revival and appreciation of African culture and traditions	18:00–20:59	30 episodes

The table provides some descriptive information of the content that was used to understand the decolonisation of African memory as read from the airwaves that constitute VCR. In addition to such programme content, I also used unstructured interviews and processes of content analysis to solicit data from respondents that design, structure and present the content of this community radio programme. For the study underpinning this chapter, the units of analysis included the following: (1) the use (and relevance) of African languages by the community radio station as a means of promoting local identity, revisiting cultural memory and cultural pride; (2) the assessment of content and its relevance to the immediate needs of the local African community surrounding the community radio station; (3) a focus and presence of content relating to local cultural and traditional practices; (4) and perspectives, contradictions and other local views on what is considered to be the role of the community radio station in contributing towards an African identity for the broadcasting platform.

In this chapter, I therefore present key themes that emerged in relation to the idea of content relevance to the African community where VCR broadcasts. The key thematic areas that underpin this chapter include: (1) airwaves as a centre of cultural memory and (2) media content as the site of nostalgia and belonging.

The airwaves as a centre of cultural memory

As argued earlier, the role that the media should play in South Africa still informs an important part of evolving discourses on decolonising and indigenising the country's media in a manner that reflects the media industry's geographical and cultural particularity (Fourie 2008; Sesanti 2010; Berger 2002). While this is the case, research data emanating from the unstructured interviews of the study underpinning this chapter illustrates that in some instances, rural and semi-urban African-based communities in South Africa continue to rely on oral traditions as a means of passing information from one generation to the next. For instance, data in the study underpinning this chapter illustrates that cultural-related family practices in the area of broadcasting by VCR are often passed from one generation to the next through the tradition of oral cultural practice. Regarding the strengthening of such practices, the idea of VCR as a customary tool as well as traditional and cultural memory depository tool illustrates that African traditions and cultural norms can still be accommodated by the modern contexts of an African society. In the context of VCR, it was indicated that on a number of occasions, the station sometimes serves the role of being a centre of memory for cultural practices and customs. It is especially valuable medium for practices and norms that are often not clearly remembered by the local people and those who wish to observe and perform certain African traditional and cultural rituals within the contemporary era of South Africa. For instance, it was indicated by one interviewee:

> As an example one listener would write down a topic and send it through as a result of not having answers to whatever it is that is bothering them. So you find that as the topic has been written, yourself as a broadcaster/journalist of the show, there are areas that you need further explanation on, and so you arrange to meet the person who wrote the topic so that they can clarify the topic as to what is happening, what is it that they would want clarity on. And then after that, you go to people who have more knowledge on this issue, like elders, the red people [abantu ekuthiwa ba bomvu] those people that are often said to be uneducated, the people that are said to be traditional people [emaXhoseni]. The people who undertake such practices, people who do these African traditional and cultural rituals. Then you ask from them and they would explain to you how they wish to explain.
> *(Mnyamezeli Mpumela, VCR Producer and On-Air personality, March 30, 2016)*

In this instance, the media platform performs the role of being an African cultural memory tool by facilitating discussions in matters relating to the de-archiving of cultural knowledge. Such a role benefits current African generations who may have lost such knowledge as a result of colonialism and modernity (wa Thiong'o 1986) as well as through the partial fading of oral traditions that are practiced in the geographic areas in which VCR broadcasts. The community radio station therefore acts as a wise "grandfather/mother" who is able to provide cultural counselling for current African generations who don't necessarily have access to particular forms of cultural memory. The community that VCR broadcast to is still predominantly that of a society which observes and cherishes African customs and traditions. These traditions thus seem to be kept relevant by this station in an increasingly imperialised and neocolonised global South society. "Because when I look at it, the people in this area that we are in, predominantly still observe customs, cultures and traditions" explained a producer and broadcaster of VCR. Unfortunately, the passing of knowledge – from one generation to the next – around African knowledge systems pertaining to these customs can at times elude the current generation of communities that observe such cultural practices. Thus, most of the members of the communities who need knowledge and advice on their cultural practices often rely on the community radio station to elucidate on the correct practices and manner they should be following in observing African ontologies.

Data from the study underpinning the chapter also illustrates that in most instances the advice offered on such community "traditions" often validates discussions that are debated over various African cultural-related issues of VCR. In some instances, this cultural memory role of VCR even extends to the idea of tracing one's lineage through clan names that are a reference point for the family genealogy of an individual. Neethling (2004, 5) demonstrates the value of clan/lineage names by arguing that "Xhosa speakers, through their clan names (*iziduko*), are linked to a common ancestor. Should Xhosa speakers meet for the first time, they will usually ask about clan affiliation: *Ngubani isiduko sakho*? (What is your clan name?)". Regarding clan/lineage names and the discourse around them on VCR, I established from interviews that:

> On Friday I change the order and do lineages and clan names. When I talk about lineages and clan names. . . . This one is on Friday at 8. And even little kids with no knowledge of topics that we discuss during the week, here they are able to ask their parents as to "who am I?" "You are Bhele, Qunta, Mafu, Dlambu. . . [African family genealogy]" and they will memorise this and on Friday will call and say "Hi presenter and I am this". I am trying to make sure that this culture does not end [of tracing your lineage]. That is the main reason of this show.
>
> (Mnyamezeli Mpumela, *VCR Producer and On-Air personality*, March 30, 2016)

The findings therefore suggest that VCR is instrumental in availing knowledge of historical practices. Such includes the value of clan names to a generation of Africans who may not be familiar with the cultural symbolism of tracing one's ancestry. On the importance of the past and its relevance to the future, Quijano (1993, 150) argues that:

> among ourselves [the colonized], the past is, or can be, a personal experience of the present, not its nostalgic recovery. Our past is not lost innocence but integrated wisdom, the unity of the tree of knowledge with the tree of life, which the past defends in us as the basis for an alternative rationality against the instrumental rationalism that dominates our present.

To some extent, this community radio station performs the role of being a "virtual museum" where people tune in to make sense of their African lineage, identities and cultural practices that may not often be available to the current crop of Africans residing in the area of broadcasting.

Nostalgia and belonging

The analysed content of the study underpinning this chapter also illustrated that African memory also survives through the process of re-member(ing) dispersed "family" (clans) of the African community. For instance, in this specific area of the cultural role of VCR, the media content that was analysed revolved around the AmaGcina clan, which forms part of the greater "traditionally" ruling AbaThembu clan that used to oversee most of the area of broadcasting by VCR. On-air content of VCR revealed that major discussions on the airwaves included ongoing meetings within various members of this clan groups. They also involved means of trying to unite the different members of the group so that they may be familiar with one another as clan family members – an explanation that was repeatedly emphasised to contextualise the on-air discussions within the programme. As a way of providing background information to the context of discussions for this particularly form of re-member(ing) the various members of this clan group, the analysed content revealed an on-air personality of the community radio programme who often recalled different community meetings that took place to familiarise the clan members (AmaGcina) with each other. Furthermore, the announcer would for instance give dates of upcoming meetings that were to be held in areas such as Molteno, Ezibeleni and Hofmeyer in the Eastern Cape Province, South Africa. Furthermore, in the analysed content, the show announcer would introduce an on-air guest who was invited to unpack the meaning behind these clan meetings. These discussions and the overall analysis of the programme content also illustrate that clans or the existence of clans and ethnicity still informs the cultural mantra of the VCR programmes. However, unlike the negative connotations characterising postcolonial Africa and the negative discourse of ethnic groups within the continent (Mamdani 1996), the discussions at VCR in general, and more specifically in the African cultural programming of this station, illustrate that ethnicity and Africanity in general can be rescued from colonial cultural engineering. Thus, the conclusion reached from the data of the study underpinning this chapter was that the programme is playing a vital role in decolonising ethnicity as well as memory associated with ethnic and clan politics of some African communities. This conclusion was reached as a result of the positive contributions of the discussion and how even clan members who are not affiliated to the AmaGcina clan positively contributed in the discussions surrounding this topic.

The data of the content sampled from the particular programme (Amasiko Nezithethe) illustrated that the programme itself is specifically designed to underscore the re-member(ing) of the African family as well as discussions on African cultures, customs, "traditions" and current cultural affairs within the area of VCR broadcasting. Findings from the study underpinning the chapter illustrated that the VCR programme content is specifically focused on an African community that does not use this media platform to listen to and discuss mainstream and often Western popular culture on its airwaves. The data indicated that context and particularity of the community of broadcast is important in planning topics of discussions. Therefore, from the perspective of the analysed content, the on-air broadcasting of this particular programme seems to resemble intricate matters that appear to be held dearly by the African community of broadcast. This particular focus of VCR therefore again attests to the manner in which a media institution can privilege local concerns, local identities and the preoccupations of a people that reside within a specific locality in South Africa. Through its content, the station therefore re-centres the history, memory, identity and cultures of a particular African community (cf. Asante 2003) in its broadcasting location. Considering the location of the community radio station and the broadcasting mandate of community radio stations in South Africa, the programme indicates the particularity of Africanity and the visibility of an African community as a form of re-member(ing) themselves within the airwaves of a media institution.

Making sense of it all: on VCR and the decolonisation project

The continuing call for decolonising media institutions and their associated role of eliminating the legacy of colonialism (cf. Said 1989; wa Thiong'o 1986) needs to be understood within the wider context of challenging the epistimicide (Grosfoguel 2007) of African subjects and their cultural realities. As illustrated by some scholarly literature, media institutions have played a significant role in the subjection of the colonised subjects (Fanon 1965; Ziegler and Asante 1992). Thus, in grappling with the role of a media platform which aims to turn the tide against this "historical" colonial role of media institutions, a case exists for the re-reading of the contemporary role of media institutions. At a community media level, some broadcasting institutions are meant to serve the immediate interest of the "historically" oppressed communities of reception. It is within this context that the chapter focused on the role of VCR in re-membering displaced African communities. The chapter also grappled with the manifestation of African memory within the airwaves of VCR. These two thematic areas in this chapter were used to "meditate" on the meaning and role of such broadcasting activities within the continuing discourse of decolonising media institutions. As described previously, the colonial legacy of media institutions is being challenged by the growing quest of using such media institutions to mirror African lived experiences that were meant to be shattered by the colonial "cultural bomb" (wa Thiong'o 1986, 4). Whilst the chapter attempted to illustrate this role, Tuck and Yang (2012, 1) warn that:

> Because settler colonialism is built upon an entangled triad structure of settler-native-slave, the decolonial desires of white, nonwhite, immigrant, postcolonial, and oppressed people, can similarly be entangled in resettlement, reoccupation, and reinhabitation that actually further settler colonialism.

It is for these reasons that this chapter looks up to the agency of Africans in a particularised location, their media platforms and how such can be used to re-read the everyday role of such a media institution in advancing the struggle of decolonisation. The chapter illustrates that the struggle for the emancipation of the colonised can also be waged through platforms that had historically aimed to oppress them. It was wa Thiongo (1986) who initially looked up to theatre and stage plays as ways of emancipating the oppressed and the colonised from the shackles and legacies of settler colonialism. This chapter therefore advances this historical theorisation of decolonisation by understanding the role of media institutions in refashioning themselves as African interest–driven platforms. By re-reading the role of African memory on the airwaves, the chapter grappled with how media institutions *in* African can become African media institutions.

Conclusion

Within present-day coloniality of South Africa, various scholarly research endeavours continue to tackle diverse and converging means of resisting colonisation and imperialism of media spaces within the postcolonial moment of the country. In this chapter, the intention was therefore to understand the decolonisation of memory as undertaken through the airwaves of a media institution. Furthermore, the objective was to understand how the process of broadcasting history, memory and nostalgia illustrates the everyday stance of African communities in the process of resisting media imperialism and the coloniality of the airwaves. The chapter thus argues and illustrates that media content has a vital role of connecting contemporary African communities to their ancient past. In this sense, the celebration, visibility and input of African voices on their past illustrate important steps in decolonising memory.

References

AMARC. 1998. *What Is Community Radio? A Resource Guide' in a Report by AMARC Africa & Panos Southern Africa*. www.amarc.org/documents/manuals/What_is_CR_english.pdf (Accessed 12 May 2014).

Asante, M.K. 2003. *Afrocentricity: The Theory of Social Change*. Chicago: African American Images.

Banda, F. 2006. *Alternative Media: A Viable Option for Southern Africa?* A Report published by the Open Society Initiative for Southern Africa (OSISA). https://core.ac.uk/download/pdf/145046852.pdf (Accessed 18 March 2018).

Berger, G. 1996. *What Is the Community Media?* Paper presented at the Community Voices Conference, Malawi, 6–11 October. www.journ.ru.ac.za/research (Accessed 13 February 2014).

Berger, G. 2002. Seeing past race: The politics of the HRC's inquiry into racial representation. *Ecquid Novi*, 23(1): 254–277.

Bosch, T. 2003. *Radio, Community and Identity in South Africa: A Rhizomatic Study of Bush Radio in Cape Town*. Unpublished PhD thesis, Ohio University.

Castro-Go´mez, S. 2007. The missing chapter of empire: Postmodern reorganization of coloniality and post-fordist capitalism. *Cultural Studies*, 21(2): 428–448.

Du Bois, W.E.B. 1903. *The Souls of Black Folk*. New York: Barnes & Noble Classics.

Dudai, Y. and Edelson, M.G. 2016. Personal memory: Is it personal, is it memory? *Memory Studies*, 9(3).

Fanon, F. 1952. *Black Skin, White Mask*. London: Plato Press.

Fanon, F. 1961. *The Wretched of the Earth*. London: Penguin Books.

Fanon, F. 1965. *A Dying Colonialism*. New York: Grove Press.

Figuoera, Y. 2015. Reparation as transformation: Radical literary (re)imaginings of futurities through decolonial love. *Decolonization: Indigeneity, Education & Society*, 4(1): 41–58.

Fokasz, F and Kopper, A. 2010. *The Media and the Collective Memory: Places and Milieus of Remembering*. www.lse.ac.uk/media@lse/events/MeCCSA/pdf/papers/FOKASZ%20and%20KOPPER%20-%20MEDIA%20AND%20COLLECTIVE%20MEMORY%20-%20MECCSA%202010%20-%20LSE.pdf (Accessed 10 December 2016).

Fourie, P.J. 2008. Ubuntism as a framework for South African media practice and performance: Can it work? *Communicatio*, 34(1).

Gqola, P. 2004. Where have all the rainbows gone? *Rhodes Journalism Review*, 24.

Grosfoguel, R. 2007. The epistemic decolonial turn. *Cultural Studies*, 21(2–3).

Mamdani, M. 1996. *Citizen and Subject: Contemporary Africa and the Legacy of Late Colonialism*. Princeton: Princeton University Press.

Mano, W. 2011. Why radio is Africa's medium of choice in the global age. In Gunner, L., Ligaga, D. and Moyo, D., eds. *Radio in Africa: Publics, Cultures, Communities*. Johannesburg: Wits University Press.

Mbembe, A. 2001. *On the Postcolony*. Johannesburg: Wits University Press.

Mhlanga, B. 2006. *Community Radio as Dialogical and Participatory: A Critical Analysis of Governance, Control and Community Participation, a Case Study of X-K FM Radio*. Unpublished MA Thesis, University of KwaZulu-Natal, Durban.

Mhlambi, T. 2015. *Early Broadcasting History in South Africa: Culture, Modernity and Technology*. Unpublished PhD Thesis, University of Cape Town, Cape Town.

MISA (Media Institute of Southern Africa). 2000. *Community Level Baseline Research into Community Media Attitudes and Needs in Zambia and Namibia*. Windhoek: MISA.

Neethling, B. 2004. Name choices among the Xhosa of South Africa. *Verbatim*, XXIX(4).
Nyamnjoh, F. 2005. African journalism: Modernity, Africanity. *African Journalism Studies*, 25.
Quijano, A. 1993. Modernity, identity and Utopia in Latin America. *Boundary 2*, 20(3).
Quijano, A. 2007. Coloniality and modernity? Rationality. *Cultural Studies*, 21(2–3).
Rønning, H. and Kupe, T. 2000. The dual legacy of democracy and authoritarianism: The media and the state in Zimbabwe. In Curran, J. and Park, M., eds. *De- Westernizing Media Studies*. London: Routledge, 157–177.
Rosenthal, E. 1974. *You Have Been Listening . . . The Early History of Radio in South Africa*. Cape Town: Purnell.
Said, E.W. 1989. Representing the colonized: Anthropology's interlocutors. *Critical Inquiry*, 15(2).
Sesanti, S. 2010. The concept of 'respect' in African culture in the context of journalism practice: An Afrocentric intervention. *Communicatio*, 36(3): 343–358.
Sithole, T. 2014. *Achille Mbembe: Subject, Subjection and Subjectivity*. Unpublished PhD thesis, University of South Africa.
Smith, L.T. 1999. *Decolonising Methodologies*. Donadon: University of Otago Press.
Switzer, L. and Switzer, D. 1979. *The Black Press in South Africa and Lesotho*. Boston: GK Hall & Co.
Teer-Tomaselli, R. 2001. Who is the community in community radio? A case study of community radio stations in Durban, KwaZulu-Natal. In Tomaselli, K. and Dunn, H., eds. *Critical Studies on African Media and Culture: Media, Democracy and Renewal in Southern Africa*. Boulder: Colorado Press.
Tomaselli, K. and Dyll-Myklebust, L. 2015. Public self-expression: Decolonizing researcher-researched relationships. *Communitio*, 4(3).
Torres-Maldonado, N. 2007. On the coloniality of being: Contributions to the development of the concept. *Cultural Studies*, 21(2–3).
Tuck, E. and Yang, K.W. 2012. Decolonization is not a metaphor. *Decolonization: Indigeneity, Education & Society*, 1(1): 1–40.
Tyali, S. and Tomaselli, K.G. 2015. Assessing 'beneficiary' communities' participation in HIV/AIDS communication through community radio: X-K FM as a case study. *Communicare*, 34(2).
van Dijk, T.A. 2000. *Ideology and Discourse: A Multidisciplinary Introduction*. Barcelona: Pompeu Fabra University.
wa Thiong'o, N. 1986. *Decolonising the Mind*. London: Heinemann.
wa Thiong'o, N. 2009. *Something Torn and New: An African Renaissance*. New York: BasicCivitas Books.
Wigston, D. 2008. History of the South African media. In Fourie, P.J., ed. *In Media Studies: Media History, Media and Society*. Claremont and Cape Town: Juta Publishers.
Yin, R.K. 2014. *Case Study Research Design: Methods*. Los Angeles: Sage.
Ziegler, D. and Asante, M.K. 1992. *Thunder and Silence: The Mass Media in Africa*. Trenton, NJ: Africa World Press.

15

Not just a benevolent bystander

The corrosive role of private sector media on the sustainability of the South African Broadcasting Corporation

Kate Skinner

Introduction

Post-apartheid, South Africa's public service broadcaster, the South African Broadcasting Corporation (SABC), has been one of the only examples of public service (as opposed to state) broadcasting on the African continent (Bussiek 2013). Once one of Africa's most notorious state broadcasters, the SABC was transformed post 1994 into a public-service broadcaster through a number of policy and legislative processes. This, however, has been a difficult, stop-start process. The corporation has experienced challenges at the level of governance, management, finances and editorial independence. These problems intensified from 2007 onwards, with the SABC experiencing near constant board and management instability and also financial instability (Lloyd et al 2010; Ad hoc Committee 2017).

Throughout these challenges the dominant explanations and narratives in the media – but also in academic debates – have centred around the SABC's 'incorrigible incompetence and corruption'. The story told is one of a technology luddite, a lumbering, wasteful public institution under constant government encroachment, an institution that should ultimately be privatised (see De Vos 2018). But there is another important set of explanations that is more rarely explored – the constraining role of private sector broadcasters on the SABC and on the broadcasting environment as a whole in South Africa.

The dominant narrative, especially in the media, has been that subscription broadcaster MultiChoice – a company that operates across Africa – has exhibited 'breath-taking technological innovation', financial astuteness, efficiency and effectiveness (Harber 2012). And it is true that MultiChoice has been at the forefront of implementing new technologies (ibid). It is also true that it has become a hugely successful and profitable international business, with its parent company Naspers dominating the Johannesburg Stock Exchange. However, alongside, and core to these successes have been 'cut-throat' business practices including the strong lobbying (manipulation) of a number of broadcasting players, including the Independent Communications Authority of South Africa (ICASA), its predecessor the Independent Broadcasting Authority (IBA), the SABC and government itself.

This chapter explores this private sector impact on public service broadcasting, using the South African case study of the SABC and subscription broadcaster, MultiChoice. The focus is specifically on television. Broadcasting policy debates in South Africa – over the last decade – have been focussed particularly on television transformation and the digital migration from analogue to digital terrestrial television (DTT).

A critical political economy approach

The chapter adopts a primarily critical political economy of the media analytical frame. At the centre of critical political economy critiques are analyses of power and inequality (McChesney 2013; Wasko et al. 2011). Critical political economists examine the socio-economic aspects of media systems. They acknowledge that in the new evolving digital media environment there has been an explosion of content, channels and programming – and with the proliferation of "on demand content" and social media – greater interactivity and audience participation. They agree that this is an important starting point for the production and distribution of a diversity of content and citizen engagement with this content, all essential to the deepening of democracy (McChesney 2013; Wasko et al. 2011; Durdag 2016).

However, simultaneously, critical political economists also make important observations about the *nature* of content and audiences' *access* to content. Here they distil some important challenges to media and democracy developments in the digital environment which is pertinent to this study.

Critical political economists focus on the important issue of diversity – an issue that lies at the heart of media and democracy debates. The theorist Napoli, for instance, looks at issues of 'source', 'content' and 'exposure' diversity. Napoli (2001) refers to 'source' diversity as the diversity of ownership of media outlets, ownership of content/programming, and diversity of the workforce within individual media outlets. He considers 'content' diversity as including format-programming diversity, demographic diversity reflected in programming and the diversity of ideas in programming. Finally, he refers to 'exposure' diversity as the diversity of content received by audiences (Napoli 2001). Napoli argues that there may be a cornucopia of content produced but what is critical is that this media is in fact consumed, engaged and interacted with – and by all citizens.

Taking all these aspects of diversity into account, critical political economists point to the fact that diversity principles are in fact (strongly) compromised by market conditions and in market-led economies – and at all three levels.

Critical political economists point to global, regional and national concentrations of ownership of the media – and the impact on content – which is a significant problem in South Africa, across the broadcasting landscape (see Bagdikian 2004; Rumney 2014; Dugmore 2018).

In terms of 'content diversity' they point to the strong growth in the commercialisation of content, over time, including the dissolving of the Chinese walls between editorial and advertising, and with this the growth in native advertising and product placements. They point to the explosion in light entertainment and with this the marginalisation of more democracy-enriching content including news, current affairs, foreign and local news, especially for poorer, lower living standards measure audiences (Lowe and Berg 2013; BBC 2015).

Finally, critical political economists highlight issues of access and the growing cost to the ordinary media user of accessing content. Critical political economists point to the costs of data, the cost of upgrades to devices and the growth of pay-walls and subscriptions to access "quality" content (see Reid 2016).

It is in this unequal context of media ownership concentration and unequal access to quality programming and content, especially for poorer audiences that this study is located. The chapter can be read in terms of the broader efforts at post-colonial transformation and indigenisation of public media institutions.

Qualitative research methods

In line with a critical political economy frame the chapter has adopted a primarily qualitative methodological approach. The chapter presents the information gathered from a series of in-depth interviews with policy makers (including government representatives, representatives from the regulator, ICASA and members of parliament) and other key stakeholders (including broadcasters, independent producers and civil society organisations) "pushing" to shape and influence policy and policy-making processes. Further, it presents the analysis of a number of policy documents, particularly DTT policy documents.

Twists and turns: developments in South Africa's broadcasting policy

Broadly, there has been one major restructuring process in broadcasting in post-apartheid South Africa – and two failed attempts. The first was the restructuring process initiated after the passing of the Independent Broadcasting Authority Act of 1993 – this established South Africa's three-tier broadcasting system (including public, commercial and community broadcasting). The second and third processes include South Africa's failed Integrated Information Communication Technology (ICT) policy process and the digital terrestrial television (DTT) migration process. The focus of this chapter will be on the first restructuring process and the failed DTT migration – these processes were most directly impacted by MultiChoice.

First phase of broadcast restructuring: SABC transformation but fiscal austerity and MultiChoice constraints

During apartheid, the SABC dominated the broadcasting landscape as a state broadcaster. However, even before the end of apartheid, significant policy changes were implemented. The appointment of the first democratic board of the SABC in 1993 was seen as critical to transforming the SABC into a public broadcaster, a move that was seen as essential for the holding of free and fair elections. The board selection process was broadly open and democratic and stood in sharp contrast to apartheid days when the president, in line with the Broadcasting Act of 1976, appointed the board and selected its chair (see Duncan 2001; Horwitz 2001).

Simultaneously with the appointment of the new democratic board the Independent Broadcasting Authority Act of 1993 was passed, also before the end of apartheid. One of the central purposes of the act was to create a new diverse broadcasting landscape. The law established an independent regulator for broadcasting, the Independent Broadcasting Authority (IBA), to regulate public broadcasting in the public interest, open up the airwaves and promote the provision of:

> A diverse range of sound and television broadcast services on national, regional and local levels which when viewed collectively, cater for all language and cultural groups and provide entertainment, education and information.
>
> *(RSA 1993, IBA, Section 2)*

The IBA Act required that the regulator conduct an inquiry into three key issues (public broadcasting, cross-media control and South African content) before fully commencing re-regulation of the broadcasting sector. The Triple Enquiry Report, drafted as a result of this inquiry, adopted a rich and multifaceted view of diversity focusing on access, equality, independence and unity. Further to this, the report put forward a set of recommendations to implement a new, diverse post-apartheid broadcasting landscape. The report included a detailed financial modelling exercise. It linked this model to concrete ways in which the SABC and the broadcasting landscape as a whole could be restructured (Duncan 2001; Horwitz 2001).

In terms of the broadcasting landscape, the recommendations included a call for the SABC to sell eight regional stations and one of its three television channels and to re-licence this channel as a free to air commercial channel with significant public service obligations. The understanding was that the funds generated through these sales would return to the SABC (see Lloyd et al. 2010).

In terms of the SABC, the report called for a mix of advertising and sponsorship, licence fees and government grants. Advertising was to be reduced to approximately 50 percent of the SABC's total revenue. The report called for significant local content, educational and African language programming targets and for provincial programming (IBA 1995, 47).

This carefully balanced set of proposals, however, was overturned in Parliament. The SABC was allowed to retain its third television channel and to sell off six rather than eight radio stations. Further, the money made on these sales was handed over to the national fiscus and not to the SABC as promised. The SABC thus had a huge public mandate, many channels and limited funding. This created an immediate financial crisis for the corporation – in 1997 it recorded a deficit of R64m with predictions of much higher sums in future years (see Horwitz 2001).

In an environment of strong fiscal austerity in South Africa, international consultants, McKinsey, were then contracted. McKinsey's key objective was to make the SABC sustainable without accessing public funds. The diversity targets initially implemented were then reversed. Certain public programming (including local content) was removed from primetime in favour of more commercially viable programming. Further, the SABC decided to outsource all production except news and current affairs (Lloyd et al. 2010).

The Broadcasting White Paper, 1998 and Broadcasting Act, 1999 consolidated these recommendations by proposing and implementing a cross-subsidisation, commercial funding model. The SABC's television and radio channels were divided into public and public–commercial channels and stations, with proposals for the public–commercial channels to aggressively pursue advertising and for these channels to then cross-subsidise the public channels. The ultimate outcome of these proposals was a cumbersome, bureaucracy-heavy model that was never fully implemented. Ironically the public channels made more money than the commercial channels, entirely undermining the model (see Lloyd et al. 2010). Further, it was a model that – because it did not place caps on advertising – encouraged the aggressive pursuit of advertising across all channels and stations. The implications of this was that the SABC found itself significantly constrained in terms of fulfilling its diversity targets, specifically its African-language targets (see Tleane and Duncan 2003).

While government was taking decisions that directly constrained the SABC and its long-term possibilities for stability and its ability to deliver on its content diversity mandate for all citizens, it was simultaneously taking decisions that directly benefited and bolstered the subscription broadcasting sector – and in particular MultiChoice – targeted at more elite audiences.

Background to Naspers, M-Net and DSTV

The original print media company, Nasionale Pers (later Naspers), was established in 1915. The company played a specific role in bolstering apartheid (see Horwitz 2001; Matisonn 2015; Van Vuuren 2017).

In the 1980s, South Africa's print media companies started to lose advertising revenue due to the advent of television in 1976. A plan was then made to launch a subscription channel owned by the print media companies. Although all four major newspaper groups originally owned shares, Naspers ultimately became the sole owner. M-Net was launched in 1986 (see Harber 2012).

A number of decisions were taken in the apartheid and post-apartheid periods that specifically bolstered the power of M-Net – and eroded the power of the SABC. Firstly, it is critical to note that the IBA Act included a grandfather clause protecting the M-Net Licence "under existing conditions" for 13 years (Matisonn 2015). As part of this arrangement, M-Net was allocated valuable, scarce terrestrial frequencies – a highly unusual allocation for a subscription broadcaster (Horwitz 2001; Matisonn 2015).

Then, in addition to occupying valuable spectrum, M-Net was allowed to continue with its lucrative initially one-hour and then two-hour daily "open time" window. This "open time" slot allowed M-Net to broadcast its signal unencrypted during primetime television viewing, giving M-Net access to significant advertising revenue and opportunities to lure wealthier audiences over to pay-TV. The "open time" window was to be closed as soon as M-Net broke even, namely, as soon as it signed up 150,000 subscribers. M-Net achieved this in 2 years, but the window was allowed to continue for 21 years (see Harber 2012). The SABC fought this arrangement. The Corporation argued that the window's closure was essential to freeing up advertising revenue for itself and also for South Africa's new proposed free-to-air commercial broadcaster, launched later as eTV. This plea fell on deaf ears (see Horwitz 2001).

Not only was M-Net given specific privileges, so was Naspers' satellite service, DSTV. As Teer-Tomaselli (2011) points out, the IBA Act failed to provide specifically for satellite broadcasting:

> The IBA was responsible for the regulation of terrestrial broadcasting. While aspirant entrants to the satellite sector waited in vain throughout the 1990s, the terrestrial subscription broadcaster, M-Net used the opportunity and the gap in policy prescription to declare itself exempt from the need to apply for a licence for satellite activity and established a direct-to-home digital satellite television service, DSTV.

DSTV was launched in 1995 and the service grew without a licence and without competition until 2007, when it was finally licenced and when ICASA (the IBA's successor) moved to introduce new subscription broadcasters into the market. At this point however DSTV was already so dominant that it was difficult to introduce new players. Four subscription services were awarded licences after a competitive bidding process. However, only one service – On Digital Media – launched. Within a year, however, it went into business rescue (see Lloyd et al 2010).

In 2012, ICASA introduced another subscription licencing process. Again, ICASA licenced a number of new stations. This time the process was entirely unsuccessful – no new stations launched (SOS and MMA 2017; ICASA 2017)

By 2017 MultiChoice owned 98.2 percent of the subscription market. It was beamed into more the 50 percent of all households. It consumed almost 100 percent of all subscription revenue and a substantial proportion of all advertising revenue (more than 50 percent). The overall largest percentage of revenue in the television sector is subscription revenue, i.e. 76 percent (SOS and MMA 2017; ICASA 2017). In a nutshell, MultiChoice, a subscription broadcaster, was now the dominant player in the post-apartheid South African broadcasting landscape, dwarfing all other broadcasters, certainly on the revenue front.

The second phase of broadcast restructuring: MultiChoice plays an active limiting role

As stated previously, there have been one major broadcasting restructuring process and two failed attempts. The two failed processes have included the DTT and the integrated ICT policy processes. As discussed, this chapter focuses on the DTT process.

To understand the DTT restructuring process – and its failures – it is critical to understand the original promises of DTT. Over the decades a number of television technologies have developed internationally, including terrestrial, cable and satellite technologies. Over time these technologies have shifted from less efficient analogue technologies to digital versions (Galperin 2004; Marsden and Arino 2000; Madikiza 2011).

DTT specifically affects terrestrial television technologies i.e. technologies that use Earth-based (terrestrial) broadcasting transmitters. Terrestrial technologies have dominated the South African television environment.

DTT technologies most importantly free up valuable spectrum important for mobile broadband services. Further, on the television front, they allow for a significant number of channels to be broadcast in the place of a single analogue channel. As the technologies have gained efficiency it has become possible for up to 20 channels to replace a single analogue television channel, allowing for the possibility of significant quantities of programming to be delivered cheaply and efficiently.

A number of policy processes have influenced the overall outcome of the DTT project. As stated previously, these have included government's digital migration policy (including various amendments) and various sets of DTT regulations, issued by the Regulator, ICASA.

My focus in this chapter is on the digital migration policy.

South Africa's digital migration policy: MultiChoice moves to protect its interests

South Africa's Department of Communication's original Digital Migration Policy of 2008 detailed the following, among a number of objectives for the migration: creating an environment for the uptake of DTT by all households including the poor; ensuring a future for existing services and introducing new services; filling information gaps in the present analogue environment in terms of government, provincial and parliamentary information; ensuring better coverage of all languages; ensuring more programming for people with disabilities; and developing South Africa's creative industries (RSA 2008; Waghorn 2011; Reid 2012).

There were three further sets of important issues covered by the policy. These included mechanisms to ensure universal access (including subsidies for poor households); mechanisms to ensure support for local content (including proposals for the establishment of digital content generation hubs) and a series of technical specifications for set-top boxes/decoders. This was to ensure interoperability (ensuring a number of services could be accessed from a number of service providers on the same box) and a "return path" capability (facilitating audiences' access to the Internet).

In summary, the original vision for the digital migration process was the creation of a 'smart box'/decoder with subsidies to facilitate citizens' acquisition/purchase of the decoder and subsidies to ensure that quality content could be accessed via the decoder. The original digital migration policy of 2008, however, was subject to major contestation. There were multiple amendments and multiple new start dates. The constant delays eventually threatened to render the entire DTT policy and its benefits obsolete as new technologies developed and started to overtake DTT.

The first set of amendments was tabled on 19 August 2011. The policy adopted a new digital standard – DVB-T2 in place of the DVB-T standard originally adopted – this allowed for up to 16 standard definition digital television channels for every 1 analogue channel (RSA 2011). This created the technical possibility for a significant plurality of content. However, the haggling that proceeded this decision led to loss of money, time and momentum on the project (see Armstrong and Collins 2011).

The second set of policy amendments was tabled in February 2012. Again, there were shifts to the 'digital switch-on' deadlines. Further, amendments were made to introduce new players during the 'dual illumination' period. (The dual illumination period is the period where both digital and analogue signals run simultaneously before the analogue signal is switched off.) This amendment potentially increased the diversity of broadcasters and content. However, no particular support measures were proposed as to ensure the sustainability of these new players (see RSA 2012).

The third set of policy amendments was then tabled in December 2013. Again, this set a new digital switch-on date as 1 April 2014, just over a year before the International Telecommunication Union's (ITU) June 2015 deadline for analogue switch-off (RSA 2013). At this point, battles that had quietly simmered around the issue of 'set-top box control'/encryption 'exploded' into the policy arena. Contestations brought the migration process to a shuddering halt. It is during these policy debates that MultiChoice chose to flex its muscles and became a major campaigner against encryption (Gedye 2015a, 2015b).

The arguments for and against encryption

'Conditional access' is an encryption or signal-scrambling system. Encryption is usually used in the pay-TV environment. However, more recently, a number of countries have started to adopt encryption systems in the free-to-air environment e.g. Germany. In the pay-TV environment, encryption allows only those who pay for the service to watch the service.

In the free-to-air environment, encryption is used for other purposes such as preventing the copying of television content or restricting the geographic area in which the set-top box/decoder can be used. Finally, importantly, it allows for the launch of new services including subscription services. ('Set-top box control' is the South African term for conditional access (Lewis, 2014)).

MultiChoice put forward a number of arguments against encryption. They argued that one of the most important issues in the DTT process was to ensure that the costs of set-top boxes were kept as low as possible to ensure maximum uptake. They argued that conditional access/encryption would necessarily make the migration more expensive, as both the boxes and the call centres (needed to support the boxes if encryption was used) would be expensive. Most importantly, however, they argued that it was unfair for the government to support encryption because it could give an 'unfair advantage' to new pay operators – encryption would allow these operators to launch their services with government effectively subsidising their encryption systems. MultiChoice argued strongly that free to air broadcaster, eTV was intent on launching a new pay service.

On the other side: eTV argued that an encryption system was in fact critical for issues of diversity, the long-term survival of free-to-air television and diversity of content across the broadcasting landscape.

eTV argued that to allow free-to-air broadcasters to effectively compete with pay operators – in particular, MultiChoice – some form of encryption was essential. They stated that encryption would help stem the tide of grey boxes coming into the country as had happened in places like Mauritius during their migration process (see Berger 2010). eTV argued that without encryption, any box would be able to pick up the signal, allowing for the distribution of cheap and often ineffective boxes undermining the DTT experience and pushing people with money to pay options. Encryption, however, would create uniformity to the viewing experience as regards the electronic programming guide. It would assist installers and call centre staff to more effectively assist viewers with installation and reception issues. Further, it would allow free-to-air broadcasters to access high-definition 'premium content' more easily – international content sellers are worried about piracy and prefer high-definition content to be encrypted. They argued that encryption would ensure a strong, diverse, quality offering to begin to compete with pay-television (see Gedye 2015a). Finally, eTV flatly denied that they intended to launch a subscription service.

The different broadcasting roleplayers lined up to take up the different positions. eTV had a number of supporters, including the SOS: Support Public Broadcasting Coalition, Media Monitoring Africa, a section of the National Association for Manufacturers in Electronic Components (Namec), the South African Communications Forum (SACF) and the community broadcaster, Cape TV.

MultiChoice's fierce lobbying created splits in two organisations. For example, Namec split to create two Namecs – one supporting encryption, the other opposing it. Also, splits developed within the community broadcasting body – the Association of Community Television, South Africa (ACT-SA). Both groupings were susceptible to this lobbying – community broadcasters were dependent on MultiChoice to broadcast their channels on DSTV to gain national coverage and to grow audiences and advertisers. Also, the faction of Namec that supported MultiChoice's 'no encryption' stance was offered a major joint contract with MultiChoice and a Chinese manufacturer, Skyworth Digital, to manufacture set-top boxes (Gedye 2015a). There were no clear benefits to either Namec or ACT-SA for supporting MultiChoice's position. Namec stood to gain more from the manufacture of encrypted boxes and community broadcasters had more to gain from supporting a robust free-to-air market.

MultiChoice also strongly lobbied the SABC. The SABC had originally been one of the key innovators and drivers behind encryption.

The SABC's decision to abandon encryption was linked to a confidential contract signed between the two players. The contract had a history. For a number of years, the SABC was under pressure to launch a 24-hour news channel. There were several international 24-hour news channels on MultiChoice's subscription platform, DSTV. Then, in 2008, eTV launched eNCA, the first South African 24-hour news channel. By 2013, however, there was still no free-to-air or public service South African 24-hour news channel available to all.

The reasons for this were numerous, but chief amongst these was National Treasury's strong fiscal austerity stance and thus resistance to funding public broadcasting. They continued to push for the SABC to be sustainable through mainly commercial funding streams making it difficult, if not impossible, to launch new channels (Underhill 2013).

It was at this point that MultiChoice stepped into the breach and agreed to pay the SABC R553m over five years to launch the channel (Underhill 2013). Further, MultiChoice pushed for the launch of an SABC entertainment channel – *Encore* – using SABC archival material. Both channels were to be hosted on MultiChoice's DSTV platform with an understanding that the 24-hour news channel would be launched on the DTT free-to-air platform once this was (finally) launched (Underhill 2013). *Encore* however was to remain restricted to the DSTV pay platform.

The SABC was not in a strong negotiating position. MultiChoice had superior finances and given government's resistance to fund new channels the SABC had few places to turn. In their secret contract, which was later leaked to the media, MultiChoice stipulated that the deal could only go ahead if the SABC agreed to drop its demands for encryption (Ad hoc Committee 2017).

The MultiChoice/SABC deal was a turning point – it pushed government to change its position on encryption. However, Communications Minister Carrim staved off this decision – but only for a while (My Broadband 2017).

A compromise is crafted, then scuppered

Minister Eunice Carrim, appointed by President Zuma in 2013, moved into the fray to find a compromise over encryption. He proposed a number of amendments that confirmed the inclusion of an encryption system in government-subsidised set-top boxes – but its use was not mandatory. Also, if it was to be used at some later point the subscription operator would have to pay. He thus created the possibility for the benefits of encryption to be realized, including the possibilities for new subscription services to be launched.

MultiChoice's opposition to these amendments was strong and immediate. The pay operator took out expensive full-page adverts in a number of Sunday newspapers in 2014 accusing the Minister of siding and materially supporting eTV. Carrim was then removed from his post after the 2014 elections. Speculation was rife that his removal was linked directly to his compromise position around conditional access (Gopal 2015).

A fourth set of policy amendments was then tabled in March 2015 by Carrim's successor, Minister Faith Muthambi. These policies moved to reverse Carrim's proposals. A number of paragraphs were inserted into the policy that stated that set-top boxes should 'not have capabilities to encrypt broadcast signals' (RSA 2015). Further, the policy stated: 'Depending on the kind of broadcasting services broadcasters may want to provide to their customers, individual broadcasters may at their own cost make decisions regarding encryption of content' (RSA 2015). It was eTV's turn to state their strong opposition, and they immediately took the Minister to court. eTV lost this court case, took it on appeal and won. The Minister, SABC and MultiChoice then took the matter to the Constitutional Court. The case was heard in February 2017 and judgement was handed down in June 2017. The matter was finally resolved in favour of the Minister, the SABC and MultiChoice (see TechCentral 2017; Karim 2017).

The Constitutional Court however was not ruling on the substantive issues. The legal arguments revolved around the rationality of Minister Muthambi's policy-making process and her reversal of Carrim's policy amendments. The final Constitutional Court majority judgement was that policy making was 'fundamentally a power assigned to the executive' (TechCentral 2017). A dissenting judgement however stated that the Minister's policy amendment should not be 'immunised from scrutiny as her disregard for her constitutional and statutory obligations was patent' (TechCentral 2017). Consequently, the court was 'not only entitled but obliged to intervene' (TechCentral 2017). This, however, was the dissenting judgement.

Ultimately, MultiChoice emerged victorious. Their subscription broadcasting monopoly remained intact. The prospects of launching a new subscription channel became more remote. In the context of the broadcasting landscape as a whole they remained the only substantive player that could offer a host of channels and host of quality content. They remained the only player that could easily access premium content.

South Africa missed the international analogue 'switch-off' deadline of June 2015 set by the United Nations' International Telecommunications Union. Some months later, on 1 February 2016, the government quietly, with little fanfare, 'switched-on' the digital signal thus launching the 'dual-illumination' period and the start of the migration. However, as no set-top boxes were yet commercially available this launch in effect gave terrestrial pay-TV broadcaster, Naspers-owned M-Net, a 'boost' as it was ready with its 'GoTV' offering and their specially designed boxes. The free-to-air broadcasters, SABC and eTV, made no announcements (see McLeod 2016).

Conclusion – the overall undermining of free-to-air television and the SABC

The original promises for DTT for the country and specifically for the SABC were substantial. The major promise for South Africa was the release of very valuable spectrum for new telecommunication and mobile applications – and in terms of television more content and programming for all South Africans in all South Africa's official languages.

In terms of content, the SABC was originally to have eight free-to-air digital DTT channels. Then, as the efficiency of the technology improved further, the promise was for the SABC to broadcast close to 20 channels. However, to date, the SABC has only been able to produce two new channels and only one for free-to-air TV.

When digital 'switch-on' was finally launched in February 2016, the SABC launched its original three channels (SABC 1, SABC 2 and SABC 3) and their 24-hour news channel. The *Encore* channel was restricted to DSTV.

This launch was a shadow of the original promise and what made matters more challenging was that the SABC had, through abandoning its rights to encryption, relegated itself (and all free to air broadcasters) to a cheap 'dumb box' for the future.

In summary, the near collapse of the DTT programme has left the free-to-air environment bereft of development and innovation. The SABC has been reduced to a four TV channel, technology laggard. Also, in the process, the very concept of public service broadcasting and its possibilities to innovate, re-create and re-imagine itself, in the digital environment, has been undermined. And sadly, the SABC has colluded in its own demise. Its secret deal with MultiChoice did not strengthen the public broadcaster but only further strengthened MultiChoice.

References

Ad Hoc Committee of Parliament on the SABC Board Inquiry. 2017. *Final Report of the Ad Hoc Committee on the SABC Board Inquiry into the Fitness of the SABC Board*, 24 February. http://www.governmentpublications.lib.uct.ac.za/news/final-report-ad-hoc-committee-sabc-board-inquiry-fitness-sabc-board.

Armstrong, C. and Collins, R. 2011. Digital turmoil for South African television. *International Journal of Digital Television*, 2(1): 7–29.

Bagdikian, B. 2004. *The New Media Monopoly*. Boston, MA: Beacon.

Berger, G. 2010. *Challenges and Perspectives of Digital Migration for African Media*. Dakar, Senegal: The Panos Institute, West Africa.

British Broadcasting Corporation. 2015. *Future of News: News Versus Noise*. BBC Research Report. London: BBC, 28 January. http://newsimg.bbc.co.uk/1/shared/bsp/hi/pdfs/28_0115futureofnews.pdf (Accessed 6 February 2015).

Bussiek, H. 2013. *Public Broadcasting in Africa Series: An Overiew*. Johannesburg: Open Society Foundations.

De Vos, D. 2018. The SABC is largely the same creature inherited from the apartheid years. *Daily Maverick*, 21 August. www.dailymaverick.co.za/opinionista/2018-08-21-the-sabc-is-largely-the-same-creature-inherited-from-the-apartheid-years/ (Accessed 16 June 2019).

Dugmore, H. 2018. *Paying the Piper: The Sustainability of the News Industry and Journalism in South Africa in a Time of Digital Transformation and Political Uncertainty*. Grahamstown: Digital Journalism Research Project, Rhodes University. https://themediaonline.co.za/wp-content/uploads/2018/05/PAYING-THE-PIPER-The-sustainability-of-the-news-industry-and-journalism-in-South-Africa-in-a-time-of-digital-transformation-and-political-uncertainty.pdf (Accessed 17 June 2019).

Duncan, J. 2001. *Broadcasting and the National Question: South African Broadcast Media in an Age of Neo-Liberalism*. Johannesburg: Freedom of Expression Institute and the Netherlands Institute for Southern Africa.

Durdag, B. 2016. Creating the myth of the better future: Technological determinism and reproducing social inequalities. In Servaes, J. and Oyedemi, T., eds. *Social Inequalities, Media and Communications: Theory and Roots*. London: Lexington Books.

Galperin, H. 2004. *New Television, Old Politics: The Transition to Digital TV in the United States and Britain*. New York: Cambridge University Press.

Gedye, L. 2015a. Multichoice accused of hijacking digital TV. *AmaBhungane*, 29 May. http://amabhungane.co.za/article/2015-05-28-multichoice-accused-of-hijacking-digital-tv (Accessed 28 March 2017).

Gedye, L. 2015b. *Theme 3: Making Monopolies*. An Unpublished Working Paper Written for the SOS: Support Public Broadcasting Coalition on Critical DTT Policy Issues, August.

Gopal, S. 2015. Koos Bekker knew Minister would be axed: Claim. *TechCentral*, 29 May. www.techcentral.co.za/koos-bekker-knew-minister-would-be-axed-claim/57046/ (Accessed 25 August 2016).

Harber, A. 2012. *Gorilla in the Room: Koos Bekker and the Rise and Rise of Naspers*. Johannesburg: Parktown Publishers (trading as Mampoer Shorts).

Horwitz, R.B. 2001. *Communication and Democratic Reform in South Africa*. Cambridge: Cambridge University Press.

Independent Broadcasting Authority. 1995. *Triple Inquiry Report*. Rosebank and Johannesburg: IBA, August.

Independent Communications Authority of South Africa (ICASA). 2017. *Government Gazette No. 41070*. Discussion Document: Inquiry into Subscription Television Broadcasting Services, 25 August.

Karim, S.A. 2017. Constitutional court decision could change the television landscape. *Daily Maverick*, 16 March. www.dailymaverick.co.za/article/2017-03-16-groundup-constitutional-court-decision-could-change-tv-landscape/#.WUJruJCGNPY (Accessed 15 June 2017).

Lewis, C. 2014. *DTT, Conditional Access and You*. Presentation to the SOS: Support Public Broadcasting and Link Centre Seminar – DTT, Conditional Access and You, Johannesburg, 21 May.

Lloyd, L., Duncan, J., Minnie, J. andBussiek, H. 2010. *Public Broadcasting in Africa Series: South Africa*. Johannesburg: An Open Society Initiative for Southern Africa.

Lowe, G.F. and Berg, C.E. 2013. The funding of public service media: A matter of value and values. *International Journal on Media Management*, 15(2): 77–79. DOI:10.1080/14241277.2012.748663.

Madikiza, L. 2011. Broadcast digital migration policy in South Africa. In Adoni, E. E., ed. *Handbook of Research on Information Communication Technology Policy: Trends, Issues and Advancements*. Hersley: Information Science Reference, vol. 1.

Marsden, C. and Arino, M. 2000. Digitisation and convergence of interactive platforms. In Brown, A. and Picard, R.G., eds. *Digital Terrestrial Television in Europe*. Mahwah, NJ: Lawrence Erlbaum and Associates.

Matisonn, J. 2015. *God, Lies and Spies: Finding South Africa's Future Through its Past*. Vlaeberg, Cape Town: Missing Ink.

McChesney, R.W. 2013. *Digital Disconnect: How Capitalism Is Turning the Internet Against Democracy*. New York: The New Press.

McLeod, D. 2016. Finally, digital TV era arrives in South Africa. *TechCentral*, 3 February. www.techcentral.co.za/finally-digital-tv-era-arrives-in-sa/62948/ (Accessed 30 November 2016).

My Broadband. 2017. Communication minister will make sure set top boxes are encrypted. *My Broadband*, 13 June. https://mybroadband.co.za/news/broadcasting/215166-communications-minister-will-make-sure-set-top-boxes-are-encrypted.html (Accessed 15 June 2017).

Napoli, P.M. 2001. *Foundations of Communication Policy: Principles and Progress of Electronic Media*. Cresskill, NJ: Hampton.

Reid, J. 2012. The digital disaster that we know nothing about. *Daily Maverick*, 3 December. www.dailymaverick.co.za/opinionista/2012-12-03-the-digital-disaster-that-we-know-nothing-about/#.WHP5uxt95PY (Accessed 1 December 2016).

Reid, J. 2016. Media content diversity in SA: Why is government still asking all the wrong questions? *Daily Maverick*, 29 August. www.dailymaverick.co.za/opinionista/2016-08-29-media-content-diversity-in-sa-why-is-government-still-asking-all-the-wrong-questions/#.V9KKXih96hc (Accessed 9 September 2016).

Republic of South Africa. 1993. Independent Broadcasting Authority Act, Act No. 153 of 1993.

Republic of South Africa. 2008. Government gazette no. 31408. *Broadcasting Digital Migration Policy*, 8 September.

Republic of South Africa. 2011. Government gazette no. 34538. *Amendment of Broadcasting Digital Migration Policy*, 19 August.

Republic of South Africa. 2012. Government gazette no. 35014. *Amendment of Broadcasting Digital Migration Policy*, 7 February.

Republic of South Africa. 2013. Government gazette no. 37120. *Amendment of Broadcasting Digital Migration Policy*, 6 December.

Republic of South Africa. 2015. Government gazette no. 38583. *Amendment of Broadcasting Digital Migration Policy*, 18 March.

Rumney, R. 2014. *Twenty Years of SA Media Ownership (1994–2014). Media Landscape 2014: Celebrating 20 Years of South Africa's Media*. Pretoria: Department of Communications.

SOS and MMA. 2017. Joint Submission by the SOS Coalition and Media Monitoring Africa on the Discussion Document on the Inquiry into Subscription Television Broadcasting Services, 4 December.

TechCentral. 2017. TV encryption: Muthambi wins concourt battle. *TechCentral*, 8 June. https://techcentral.co.za/encryption-muthambi-wins-concourt-battle/74777/ (Accessed 13 June 2017).

Teer-Tomaselli, R.E. 2011. Transforming State-Owned Enterprises in the Global Age: Lessons from b; Roadcasting and Telecommunications in South Africa. In Olorunnisola, A. and Tomaselli, K.G., eds. *Political Economy of Media Transformation in South Africa*. Cresskill: Hampton Press.

Tleane, C. and Duncan, J. 2003. *Public Broadcasting in the Era of Cost Recovery: A Critique of the South African Broadcasting Corporation's Crisis of Accountability*. Johannesburg: Freedom of Expression Institute.

Underhill, G. 2013. SABC launches 24-hour news channel on DSTV. *Mail & Guardian*, 1 August. http://mg.co.za/article/2013-08-01-sabc-launches-24-hour-news-channel-on-dstv (Accessed 4 February 2017).

Van Vuuren, H. 2017. *Apartheid Guns and Money: A Tale of Profit*. Sunnyside, Johannesburg: Jacana Media.

Waghorn, R. 2011. *Delivering a Successful Migration to Digital TV*. Unpublished Paper Delivered to an SOS: Support Public Broadcasting/Sparks Seminar held on 6 October 2011 at the Institute for Advancement of Journalism, Parktown, Johannesburg.

Wasko, J., Murdock, G. and Sousa, H. 2011. The Political economy of communications: Core concerns and issues. In Wasko, J., Murdock, G. and Sousa, H., eds. *The Handbook of Political Economy of Communications*. Oxford: Blackwell.

16
Health communication in Africa

Elizabeth Lubinga and Karabo Sitto

Introduction

Health communication is an emerging field within the broader study of communication. Health communication occurs in various contexts; intrapersonal, interpersonal, small group, organisational, mass and public. This chapter focuses on and operationalises communication for health as interpersonal when occurring between healthcare provider and patient; small group among teams of healthcare professionals; within organisational settings such as hospitals, clinics or health promotion and education organisations and at mass or public level often involves the media. This chapter mostly addresses the interpersonal, organisational and mass contexts, because communication in these core appears to affect most of Africa's population in relation to existing health needs.

Nonetheless, the chapter briefly addresses other contexts of communication. The two main contexts, both pillars of health communication – mass and interpersonal – rarely interface. Interpersonal interaction between health practitioner, whether nurse, doctor or traditional healer in the African context, and their patient(s), offers a personalised approach and appears to run parallel to mass communication. On the other hand, messages communicated to the public by governments through health departments, by health promotion organisations and other interested international and national parties, are often homogenous, yet in Africa, target broad heterogeneous audiences. It is factors such as inequitable rates of literacy, mostly rural populations; lack of access to health care and related facilities; as well as cultural barriers among others, that influence the heterogeneous nature of target audiences. Languaging in health messages presents an ever-present barrier in Africa, given the framing of the messages in *lingua francas* such as English, French, Portuguese, Swahili and Lingala for example and subsequent translation into multiple African indigenous languages. In addition, the indirect communication of sensitive health-related content in an attempt by healthcare providers, health promotion organisations and governments to accommodate cultural taboos and stigma, often results into a loss of message meaning.

The chapter commences with a contextualisation of health communication, with a focus on mass communication at international, African regional and national levels. A critique of some major commonly cited existing Western health communication theories, as often applied to African contexts, is conducted. The critique raises questions about the need for African scholars to conceptualise newer fit-for-purpose health models in order to augment the existing culturally relevant PEN-3 Cultural Model developed by Airhihenbuwa in 1989. Notions of culture and activism and their influence on health communication are scrutinised as well as the introduction of artificial intelligence and robotics' growing use and effects of information and communication technologies (ICTs).

Contextualising health communication in Africa

Various players operate in the field of health in Africa. At a global level, organisations whose funding for health-related and other needs is solicited from multiple governments and non-governmental sources and is distributed among many different countries are classified as multilateral, as is the case of the World Health Organisation (WHO). Global health organisations typically map out areas of policy development and research, which countries are often required to adhere to; offer technical support to governments or non-governmental organisations (NGOs); and engage in advocacy. The dynamics between WHO and various countries were emphasised in 2020, when the organisation pronounced COVID-19 as a pandemic on 11 March (WHO 2020a). The pronouncement of pandemic attested to the global spread but also required individual countries to put measures into place to mitigate the risk of spread. Global organisations hardly formulate messages targeting national audiences, but often require accountability from various countries regarding the implementation of health-related programmes.

Bilateral agencies such as the United States Agency for International Development (USAID) are government agencies or non-profit organisations (NPOs) based in a single country and provide funding to developing countries. For example, in South Africa, for HIV/AIDS, the USAID has partnered with the South African government at various levels, faith-based organisations (FBOs) and NGOs to provide training and support for personnel working with people living with HIV/AIDS. Specifically, the USAID has sponsored provision of antiretroviral treatments to over 1.4 million people and supported other organisations such as President's Emergency Plan for AIDS Relief (PEPFAR) in providing care and support services to more than 2 million HIV-infected people (USAID 2018).

At the regional level in Africa, bodies such as the Economic Community of West African States (ECOWAS) and Southern African Development Community (SADC) have formulated health-related policies to cater for the health needs of their citizens. For instance, SADC has a Health Policy Framework, which proposes policies, strategies, and priorities in areas such as health research and surveillance; health information systems; health promotion and education; HIV and AIDS and sexually transmitted diseases as well as communicable and non-communicable disease control, among others (SADC 2012).

In individual African countries, NGOs play a pivotal role in providing support for health care. NGOs are non-profit, voluntary citizens' groups organised at the local, national or international level, such as Doctors Without Borders/Médecins Sans Frontières. The NGOs are often task-oriented and usually organise based on particular issues such as health, among others. In South Africa alone, there are more than 100,000 registered non-profit organisations, while in Kenya the number of NGOs grew by over 400 percent between 1997 and 2006 (The Conversation 2017). Because they operate at national levels, NGOs typically construct and disseminate homogenous messages to their target audiences. Such messages are often ineffective because audiences may not understand them, or such NGOs conceptualise the messages internationally and transfer the same ideas to national contexts. Such was the case of health promotion organisation loveLife, which ran provocative HIV/AIDS campaigns between 2000 and 2009 in South Africa with concepts that were too complex for targeted audiences to comprehend or were too culturally explicit for certain segments of those audiences. The motivations put forward by loveLife for the use of such messages, taken from numerous media interviews and coverage, was their desire to shock the public into speaking about the "incommunicable" issues surrounding HIV and AIDS. As Refilwe Africa, then editor of loveLife's *Uncut Magazine* stated,

> We want people to think about our posters. Either they understand it from first-hand or they get angry and say: I do not know what you are trying to say. At some point in our campaign, we will get people to wonder. This creates conversation between parents and children, dialogue between peers.
>
> *(Hollemans 2005)*

At no point were their communication tactics strategies linked to or substantiated by them through any communication theories that may have informed their communication execution. In a literature review conducted on their programmes, there was a recognition that their subsequent messaging needed to change significantly from their entry into South Africa, informed by research outcomes in their target communities (loveLife 2010).

Contemporary health theories: fit for African contexts

The dominant health communication theoretical approaches that are central to the understanding and prediction of media campaigns are behavioural theories. Behavioural theories are distinct from other bodies of theory. They focus on the individual's behaviour change, describe relationships between constructs and inherently offer guidance for implementation of health campaigns by organisations and other players that use them in applied, practical settings. Dominant behavioural theories like the Health Belief Model (HBM) (Janz and Becker 1984; Rosenstock 1974), the Theory of Reasoned Action (Fishbein 1980; Fishbein and Ajzen 1975) and the Extended Parallel Process Model (EPPM) (Witte 1992; Witte and Allen 2000) acknowledge that behavioural intentions are important to determining ultimate behaviour. The HBM and EPPM place communication at the centrecore of the promotion and education of health to targeted audiences with predictable results. As they interrogate behaviour, they also attempt to predict the individual's reaction to health campaign messages. Both theories have been criticised for focusing on the individual and on predicting how each individual is likely to react to messages. They do not take a collectivist stance, thus making them an ill-fit for application to collectivist cultures as are prevalent in African contexts (Dutta-Bergman 2005).

In addition, behaviour change is not always an individual's decision because there are many other influencing factors such as peers, society, culture and many others.

Airhihenbuwa's (1989) PEN-3 Cultural Model was developed as a framework for health promotion and disease prevention in African countries, and has over the years, bridged the gap between health communication and culture. The model has three primary domains: Cultural Identity, Relationships and Expectations, and Cultural Empowerment. Each of the domains consists of three elements with an acronym of PEN, which are different for each. For example, the Cultural Identity domain entails human influences including People, Extended Family and Neighbourhoods. The relationships and expectations domain which is about perceptions and attitudes towards health problems includes: Perceptions, Enablers and Nurturers, while the Cultural Empowerment domain identifies and examines the role of Positive, Existential and Negative cultural beliefs and practices in affecting a person's health behaviour (Iwelunmor et al. 2014). It has successfully enabled health research that is culturally responsive because of its particular focus on cultural identity and cultural empowerment, but with consideration of relationships and expectations (Whembolua et al. 2015). The theory promotes culture as an enabler in the process of empowerment. This culture-centred body of knowledge highlights work by Airhihenbuwa (1995) and Dutta-Bergman (2005), among others. It upholds narratives by marginalised communities and highlights the interaction between agency, culture and structures. It integrates different levels in terms of how structures such as community medical services, transportation and media at micro-levels, as well as policies, civil society organisations and media platforms at meso-level and at macro level how national and international bodies interact and drive policy formulation (Dutta 2008).

In terms of the way forward concerning developing other culturally responsive theories relevant to the African context, for consideration is positioning the important, yet oft unrecognised role of traditional doctors and traditional (herbal) medicine. It is common knowledge that common practice among many Africans when faced with disease is that patients may use both traditional and Western medicine concurrently or interchangeably. A bidirectional relationship thus exists in praxis among patients, between traditional and Western medicine. For consideration too is the idea of whether a hybrid between dominant Western behavioural theories and cultural approaches would be relevant to the research of health communication in African contexts. After all, health research in Africa has always relied on both paradigms, albeit independently, to answer pertinent questions. Researchers could better consider the role of spirituality and/or beliefs in communicating health and how these influence health behaviour within the African context.

Case Study: the case of Ebola in West Africa

This chapter focuses on Ebola that has intermittently broken out in West, Central and East Africa unlike the more recent global COVID-19. Nonetheless, lessons from the fight against Ebola have been instrumental in the fight against COVID-19 with countries such as the Democratic Republic of Congo, Uganda Nigeria, Gambia and Liberia among others redirecting resources for tracing Ebola cases to COVID-19 (NBC News 2020).

The Ebola breakout in West Africa was announced by the WHO in 2014, reporting cases of Ebola Virus Disease (EVD) in Guinea, marking the beginning of the largest historical epidemic to date which swept across West Africa (CDC 2017a). The epidemic took the world by storm, as patients from across the globe became infected with the deadly virus.

The start of the epidemic in Guinea West Africa was reported under the suspicion that the patient had been infected via an animal, as it is a zoonotic disease. Only after five fatalities was an outbreak official health alert declared, at which point the virus was already spreading across borders in the region to other parts of West Africa. Death rates increased significantly, and it took three months and 29 deaths for the outbreak to be declared by the WHO.

The delay in global alerts being issued about the disease appeared to have accrued from slow interventions in the countries that were initially affected by the earlier cases. Blood testing (the only method of confirming cases of Ebola) received cultural resistance with respect to people's blood being drawn (Dionne 2014). Those that had come into contact with unsuspecting sick people and had become infected moved across borders and there was little monitoring of their movements, nor was there communication of the outbreak. The rallying call of the WHO for the globe to help the worst-affected countries and put monitoring mechanisms in place brought into place the needed interventions.

Standardised messages were developed to inform the world about Ebola and how to possibly identify the disease. Through continuous communication on global news networks, updates on local broadcast channels and health ministries of countries investing in information campaigns were employed to help allay fears of infection and further spreading of the virus. Organisations at risk, from all over the continent, for example in South Africa, South African Airlines, one of the largest airline carriers in Africa, developed information campaigns for travellers, to reduce panic and respond to customer concerns about various destination countries (Vuso 2014).

Communication about the outbreak became a multidirectional coordinated effort, bringing traditional figures and other cultural influences, multiple countries' politicians, international and local organisations and the modern medical fraternity together in a concerted effort to spread accurate information to people and reduce the global level of panic. With great messaging efforts conducted at all levels of communication, local and global as well as across power spectrums from community members right up to politicians/policy makers, information fell into relevant hands. The powerful key that began to break the chain of information asymmetry about the virus was the involvement of local/traditional leaders and influencers in crafting of the communication messages (CDC 2017a).

In West African countries affected by the outbreak, integrated digital media were used to support on-the-ground efforts to disseminate information, whilst enabling people to participate in mapping where cases were growing (Dionne 2014). Such integrated campaigns included SMS/text messaging campaigns, social media campaigns, word-of-mouth through local traditional leaders and door-to-door digital capturing of suspected cases.

The combined challenges of on-the-ground cultural resistance to the most effective method of diagnosis, as well as delays resulting from politicians' culture of communication often characterised by face-saving, resulted in a delay in combating the Ebola virus. The outbreak was only successfully contained when the communication process involved stakeholders at all levels, was in a language that local people could connect with and involved strict monitoring. Most important was that all the communication was coordinated across multiple media in multiple local languages, in a multidirectional manner.

While the virus is not completely eradicated and a cure or commercially licensed vaccine is yet to be confirmed for the disease, the 2014 outbreak helped put in place communication mechanisms that have made it quicker and easier to contain outbreaks of disease. Screenings at ports of entry, buy-in from critical stakeholders as well as simplified communication to inform communities about the disease have contributed to better surveillance mechanisms across the globe. Establishing communication mechanisms is important because of the intermittent outbreaks of Ebola on the African continent. A study about the latest outbreak in the Democratic Republic of Congo in 2019 shows that a quarter of the participants believe that Ebola is not real (Al Jazeera 2019). For such a highly contagious disease, health workers said that public mistrust, including people concealing symptoms, refusing treatment and vaccines were the biggest obstacles to stopping an epidemic that has reportedly killed more than 630 people from August 2018 to March 2019.

Regulatory environment

Health care is highly regulated, beginning with the various oaths e.g. the Hippocratic Oath that upcoming practitioners are expected to take in order to practice in their chosen medical fields. In addition, various professional bodies monitor and enforce proper practice. This is because human life is at the centre of health care, and the protection of it is central to society. Politicians in Africa hold significant power and influence over communication in general, including health communication. They are able to make and amend laws regulating media content, messaging and placement, including social media. In 2020, politicians in Africa and globally had to evoke disaster laws in individual countries to manage the COVID-19 pandemic with advice from WHO (WHO 2020c). In places such as Uganda and Benin, people on the ground have felt the full might of political power over media as both countries have recently implemented heavy social media taxes as a disincentive, especially for young people, not to criticise their governments. While Benin has since reversed its decision in response to the different types of protests by the Beninese to the social media tax since its announcement, other countries remain unyielding (Tobor 2018).

Politicians are also in control of budgets allocated towards health communication and decide to invest it in line with policies and political patronage; this includes power over the message communicated, what is expressly said and what is deliberately not mentioned. Political will, particularly in Africa, plays a critical role in health communication and its effectiveness in helping those intended to receive the message.

Many politicians on the African continent are much older than their constituencies, with presidents typically being well over 60 years of age (Kiwuwa 2015), while the median African population age is 19.7 years of age (WorldOMeters 2020). The stark age differences between populations and regulation/policy makers pose challenges particularly in health communication because of a generational divide. Health communication norms in Africa tend to be steeped in a language of age, and communication tactics are perceived to be dated or modernist in approach by recipients of the communication. In such modernist health communication approaches, communication is evaluated in terms of its effectiveness only, and questions of ethics and values are taken for granted (Pal and Dutta 2008), with tools such as scare tactics, fear-mongering, punitive measures, shaming and authoritarianism used to drive intended messages. Uganda's President Yoweri Museveni, who is one of the oldest presidents in Africa, in April 2018 made a public announcement vilifying oral sex, emphatically stating (allAfrica 2018):

> Let me take this opportunity to warn our people publicly about the wrong practices indulged in and promoted by some of the outsiders. One of them is oral sex. The mouth is for eating. *Okulya* [to eat in *Luganda*] . . . chum (onomatopoeia). The mouth is for eating; not for sex.

Such communication from an aging calibre of African politicians does not allow for effective influence in their engagement with mostly young constituencies about contemporary health issues such as oral sex and alternative sexual orientations that may be drivers of diseases and new diseases arising thereof. This keeps health communication efforts in a passive position of chasing after arising health issues, rather than leading or driving health agendas, often to the detriment of Africans.

These political influences often can filter into and influence the health practitioner's communication boundaries in their interpersonal experiences with patients. The existent power dynamics of practitioner–patient position the communication of healthcare practitioners as authoritative and not to be questioned. These are often entangled with but are sometimes at odds with the legal limitations imposed in most countries on what a healthcare practitioner may ask of patients, and assured confidentiality in their interpersonal engagement with patients. In South Africa for example there are constitutional legal limitations on how and what a healthcare practitioner may ask a patient and the type of environment in which they may do so (HPCSA 2008).

However, abuse of power or authority of voice in consultation rooms is a reported frequent occurrence, and in these settings public health patients do not always have opportunity to engage practitioners through questions about their conditions, courses of treatment, risks, side effects and alternatives. The regulatory environments provide for patients to be informed in order to be able to have control over their health. Patients, if informed, can be empowered to participate meaningfully in helping practitioners manage and treat them back to health, where thus it becomes a partnership and not simply a reliance on practitioners to be wholly responsible for patients' health statuses.

In addition to systemic regulatory communication burdens, practitioners also have to fight cultural conceptions of them set by traditional healers. They spend a significant amount of time working to earn patient trust before they are able to deliver health communication messages, which may be contradictory of traditional interventions (see case study). There are also challenges of practitioner–patient age gaps, and the manner of overt and covert communication in these interactions.

Patient rights have been globally accepted as involving protection of patients at all costs, in formulation of wording and scope of coverage regarding patient experiences during healthcare provision. The enshrined rights govern the power dynamics in health care, dignity preservation of patients, legal recourse for violation of rights, yet on the ground there are often no concrete mechanisms or resources to enforce them. Health communication campaigns may use language that offends recipients, limits their rights or vilifies alternative methods of treatment they may trust, all which sets conditions for rejection of such health communication. Communication of the patients' rights may empower them to feel more in charge and able to ask pertinent questions regarding their course of treatment, which may threaten the influence of healthcare practitioners' communication. Thus, healthcare practitioners may withhold information from their patients in order to preserve their positions of power that are often reinforced by limited resources available to patients e.g. number of doctors, hospitals, medicines etc.

Global bodies like the WHO are central to the critical process of monitoring health communication effectiveness, what efficiencies have been gained and the coordination of knowledge sharing. International Health Regulations were formulated by the WHO in 2005 to help provide concrete guidelines for countries globally on health, and the communication was simplified to include ten steps towards implementation of the regulations. Such regulations have a direct influence on the formulation of communication surrounding health care, as WHO is the overarching body governing health.

Activism for health

At the individual country level, activist or civil society organisations play a crucial role in creating awareness about and finding solutions to health-related problems globally. Typically, most of the global health organisations, such as Doctors without Borders/Médecins Sans Frontières (MSF), the United Nations International Children's Emergency Fund (UNICEF) and CARE International, have a strong presence in Africa because of the various health needs that prevail.

Activist organisations provide a human face to health problems and create visibility for them in societies by fighting for the health rights of marginalised groups. MSF underscores the importance of civil service organisations in its claim that some West and Central African countries have been neglected in terms of global HIV efforts partly because of the limited support role of these organisations (MSF 2016). As a result of fighting for health-related rights, some activist organisations have changed dominant narratives about health problems in countries or have changed national policy. For example in Uganda in 1987, when the HIV/AIDS pandemic was at its peak, the activist organisation The AIDS Support Organisation (TASO) was founded by Noerine Kaleeba together with a group of friends and colleagues, some of whom had been infected by HIV. At the time, there was great stigma about HIV/AIDS in the country, causing the founders to meet informally in secret in each others' homes or offices to provide one another with mutual psychological and social support. These founder members voluntarily used their time and other resources to visit AIDS patients, carrying them to the hospital for medical attention, while at times they provided basic material and counselling support. These actions paved way for the government to offer stronger support systems for People Living with HIV/AIDS (PLWH) and ultimately lessened societal stigma about the disease.

Benefits to health care as a result of activism by organisations have in some countries been greater than in other countries. In South Africa for instance the HIV/AIDS activist organisation Treatment Action Campaign (TAC), co-founded in 1998 by Zachie Achmat, has been instrumental in campaigning for access for HIV treatment among PLWH. In 2002, the organisation took government to the South African Constitutional Court over provision of treatment and won the case. The South African Constitutional Court ordered the government to provide anti-retroviral drugs to prevent mother-to-child transmission of HIV during birth. The benefits of that achievement were realised long after the case was won. HIV transmission from mother-to-child (MTCT) in South Africa fell to just 1.5 percent in 2015, down from 30 percent in the early 2000s, exceeding the national target of 1.8 percent (AVERT 2015). Today the organisation agitates for various health rights ranging from the provision of better health care by national, provincial and local hospitals and clinics, monitoring national HIV and TB government responses and ongoing provision of access to affordable medicine. In 2017, TAC partnering with over 30 other organisations marched to the national Department of Trade and Industry in Pretoria to hand over a memorandum to the minister asking government to fix the medicine patent laws (#fixthepatentlaws), to enable the use of generic and cheaper medicines for diseases such as cancer in the country.

Activist organisations use various tactics to achieve their goals. For example, the TAC (Yawa 2018) has:

- Engaged in civil disobedience, in which some of members have in the past gone to police stations, to open cases against one-time Minister of Health Manto Tshabalala-Msimang and the Minister of Trade and Industry Alec Erwin in relation to medicine patents.
- Targeted public platforms where a Minister of Health would be addressing people. They would access the meetings with unidentifiable clothing, then would identify themselves during the meeting and pose questions to the minister.
- Mobilised and engaged in protest marches on the streets and to health facilities e.g. to the Department of Trade and Industry.
- Engaged in sit-ins (mobilised about 900 people, gone inside a healthcare facility without interrupting the healthcare services, accessed the administration block and conducted peacefully sit-ins).
- Participated in night vigils and marches against two Provincial Government Health Members of Executive Committee (MECs) in Gauteng and Free State Provinces.
- Arranged pickets, streets marches in which they submitted memoranda to the relevant people.

On the negative side, activism may detract from the actual cause, with society focusing on the tactics employed by organisations rather than communication of the health problems at hand (Lubinga 2020). Health advocacy organisations may also use activism to raise their organisational profile, rendering the activism inauthentic to the cause. Arising from the activities of such organisations as well as growth in computer-mediated communication due to technological advancements, have initiated the growth of online activism, too.

Online health activism

The global growth of the internet has significantly changed the face of activism. People are able to participate in social movements and causes in which they believe in, regardless of their geographic location. The internet has helped surface voices previously not heard (Pal and Dutta 2008) and thus enabled such groups as women, LGBTQI+ communities and young people to surface issues that have previously been silenced, on their health experiences. Online, people can form communities, such as Global Citizen, where people from around the globe may join to contribute towards causes they believe in. These communities use the power of online social communication to pressure governments through coordinated and targeted communication to take action on causes, such as improving health care for women and children, enforcing rights for all with respect to causes such as dignified access to health care, particularly in developing states, including African countries.

These online communities can circumvent controlled media and help highlight on-the-ground issues to global watchdogs and bring them to the attention of other influential bodies. Social activists can use measures to help protect their true identities online to avoid victimisation by authorities and local communities in carrying out their work on issues that may be incommunicable offline. The influence of these online groups is often evidenced in the reactions of governments to social pressures imposed on them by the activities of online social activists, sometimes leading to amendments in policies or the subversion of intended communication. Online health communication activism campaigns have been vibrant. Examples include the drive for provision of free pads for young girls in Africa, better HIV/AIDS medication provision, improved public health systems, male circumcision risks and fat feeding camps for young girls (*leblouh*) in Mauritania. In addition, online activists have campaigned to highlight child marriage health implications for young girls, female genital mutilation and anti-smoking movements, which are just some of the causes that have been fought for vehemently online. These campaigns originate from countries that are far apart on the continent such as Mauritania, South Africa, Malawi and Nigeria, although they have attracted global participation, even though in their countries of origin some activists may suffer limited media access at times.

Whilst social activism online has evolved health communication activist strategies and surfaced issues that may have been suppressed in the past, it is often undertaken at the risk of the lives of leading figureheads of these movements. Online security and access to information has been misused in some countries, like Egypt, by authorities to silence online communities by employing fear tactics, which may include killing the social movement leaders (Acconcia 2018). Often in developing economies, foreign investment or aid can drive motivations in health communication messaging and the execution of underhanded tactics by politicians helping to protect their patrons' industries from threat by social activist communities' causes. The multiplicity of causes being fought online can inadvertently result in audience fatigue (Anderson 2018) and an unfortunate minimisation of the importance of health communication. This has been a concern of the South African Minister of Health regarding the effectiveness of HIV/AIDS communication, his concern is specifically the stubborn infection rate among youth which is still considered to be too high (Sehoai 2018).

Health communication and culture

Communication is culture and culture is communication (Burton and Dimbleby 2006). This statement rings truer when applied to health communication, because people are oft unable to enjoy health without communication. As already discussed in the theory section, culturally based health approaches have evolved based on the fact that in Africa there can be no effective health communication without consideration of culture.

Barriers to health communication that have been discussed in this chapter such as language exclusion or lack of access to messages in the media or during consultation with health practitioners represent cultural aspects. Language is an element of culture and a social representation of socio-cultural groups. Representations come about as a result of social interaction as well as communication between individuals and groups (Hoïjer 2011), using language as an instrument of expression of thought and feeling. It is through social life that individuals exchange ideas and points of view, generating a positive conflict that helps improve knowledge and this leads to the development of cultural and material tools e.g. language, technology etc. (Tateo and Iannaccone 2012). This applies to health communication, too. As cultures interact and societies become more diverse, health communicators have attempted to develop a language that can convey the gravity of the communication messages. Makalela (2015, 16) points out, "the advent of super diverse settings in the 21st century has increasingly required . . . acknowledg[ing] the linguistic fluidities that overlap into one another." In the health communication sphere, this requires communicators to be interculturally competent in order to have the appropriate level of sensitivity when working across different cultures with overlapping messages.

Artificial intelligence, social media, mHealth and eHealth: evolving areas in communicating health

The year 2020 pioneered the use of artificial intelligence and robotics in the fight against COVID-19 for health communication in Africa. For example, Rwanda introduced the use of robots to protect health personnel from the contagion. Five human-sized robots, such as Akazuba, Ikirezi, Mwiza, Ngabo and Urumuri, took over roles by medical personnel, among others communicating with patients by detecting people who were not wearing masks and instructing others to wear masks properly (WHO 2020b). In addition, communication technology has grown exponentially, especially over the last decade, spurred by increased globalisation that has driven significant innovation in ICTs. These computer-mediated technologies have been drivers for growth in health industries and have improved health communication. One of the main drivers for this exponential growth has been the ubiquitous proliferation of the mobile phone, in particular, smartphones (Watson, Pitt, Berthon and Zinkhan 2002).

Individuals in developing countries may use mobile devices (mHealth) to access healthcare information, which is posted online, or be able to connect with a healthcare practitioner, without face-to-face interaction. Through search engine optimisation, patients are able to search for online experts in close proximity to them or by specialty or through mobile applications with information portals on a range of health issues. While ICTs, the internet and the devices that facilitate and enhance online interpersonal communication have many benefits, they do also present health communication with some challenges.

Access to information regarding health may make patients feel that healthcare experts are dispensable, to the point that they may choose DIY health care, leading to probable misdiagnoses and misinformation through channels such as health chat forums from the general public online (eHealth). Because communication technologies facilitate a meeting of people from different cultures online, health communication online is not often uniform. The online opinion environment can greatly differ from an individual's offline world in such a way that opinions they come across online are likely to be more diverse (Schulz and Roessler 2012). These technoscapes, which involve the fluidity of technology that makes tangible and intangible knowledge flows possible across boundaries (Pal and Dutta 2008), are seen as useful for transcending both geographical and social boundaries. They do however still leave out a large cross-section of society who have limited or no access to the internet of the ongoing conversations.

Internet penetration in Africa, as compared to the rest of the world, lags far behind. At the low end of the scale in Africa, Eritrea was reported as having an internet penetration of 1.4 percent at the end of 2017, whilst Kenya was reported as having the highest internet penetration rate in the same period of 85 percent (Internet World Stats 2017). The overall average rate for the continent however is still 20 percent behind the rest of the world. Technoscapes "simultaneously . . . produce an ongoing process of 'othering'" (Edwards 2011, 39), by only giving those with the means to access these channels voice both at global and local levels simultaneously, influencing each other in relation to the power of interpretation, acceptance or rejection of disseminated messages (Pal and Dutta 2008; Edwards 2011). The theoretical phenomena in critical modernism of technoscapes form part of communication infrastructure in globalisation, shaping the speed and flow of discourses as well as how discourses will be taken up (Edwards 2011) for health communication as an example.

These online conversation enablers however more often work to highlight important issues of health, can lead to better-informed patients, help ease the barriers of communications for healthcare practitioners as well as demystify previously incommunicable aspects of health. They can also increase access for patients in rural areas, far from medical assistance, through e-consultations. In order for the computer-mediated health communication messages to be effective and trustworthy, the communication still needs to be integrated and converge with traditional, local and other forms of media, in addition to the various other communication contexts in which health communication takes place.

Language and messaging in health communication

Health and wellness have always been integral to African cultures. In several African cultures, for instance, greeting a person during any time of the day, centres around asking about the wellness of the other. For example in Sesotho, on greeting another person in the morning, one would ask, "*O robetse hantle?*" literally translated into English meaning, "Did you sleep well? or "*O tsohile hantle?*" meaning "Did you wake up well?" In most African cultures, meeting and greeting is not merely phatic communication, a meaningless social function; rather it intends and is expected by the other, to deliberately solicit responses about the other's wellbeing such as whether they actually slept and woke up feeling well. Hence, a discussion of language use in health communication as additional to everyday social interaction is relevant.

The (mis)use of language in health messaging across different contexts presents a barrier to communication. Africa has over 2,000 known languages and dialects spoken, with Nigeria alone having 500 languages (Tran 2012). Thus, health promotion organisations, as well as governments are ill-equipped to present tailor-made health messages that accommodate each of these innumerable languages. Yet the majority of rural-based people in Africa lack comprehension of Western languages' nuance and hidden meaning. The default for most organisations and governments is to communicate in the *lingua francas* of most African countries; English, French, or Portuguese, or target languages for the bigger segments, resulting in linguistic exclusion of minorities in populations. Another setback to possibilities to communicating using indigenous languages is that some of them lack socially acceptable and culturally appropriate terminology. Seidel (1990) found in Uganda that some local languages such as Runyankole lacked socially acceptable terms that healthcare providers could use to demonstrate condom use and sexuality for example.

Translations without Borders Founder, Thicke reveals that in Thange in Eastern Kenya she saw AIDS orphans playing in front of posters with advice on AIDS prevention (Tran 2012). "The posters carried excellent advice, but they were in English, a language that people didn't understand," she said, adding that people do not just die of disease, but from a lack of knowledge on how to avoid getting sick. In South Africa, Levin (2014) found that more parents cited language and cultural barriers as a major barrier to health care than structural and socio-economic ones. This was a result of parents not having access to same-language healthcare practitioners. Only 6 percent of the medical interviews were conducted partly or wholly in the patient's home language.

Use of cryptic health messages

In both mass communication and interpersonal contexts, messages have been communicated cryptically. For public messages, the intention is often achievement of organisational goals, while, at both public and interpersonal levels, communicators, whether organisations or healthcare providers, both attempt to be culturally sensitive by avoiding explicit, possibly taboo words. Researchers argue that many African cultures are conservative and avoid having to directly mention sexually related terms, yet most of them are fundamental to communicating health (Baxen and Breidlid 2009; Kamwendo 2008). In Botswana, a billboard message about HIV infection referred to extra-marital affairs as small houses (Kamwendo 2008), which may be contextually understood among the local people. However, in any given society, there are people who may reside (or even visit), who are not local but may be important target audiences in terms of health-related messages in terms of their behaviour that may miss the high-context meaning of such messages.

Some researchers argue that on the positive side, metaphors enhance health communication by acting as educational tools. Metaphors are also perceived as having the capacity to assist healthcare practitioners such as doctors to simplify terms that would otherwise be difficult for patients to grasp as well as frame and tailor the experience of illness to the patient's needs (Ervas et al. 2017). It should be noted, too, that many of the healthcare providers, especially doctors, in most of the African countries may be foreign (as is the case of South Africa which has a large component of doctors from Cuba working in rural hospitals) or may not speak the language of the patients.

Still, the outcome of using cryptic language is that it is either too complex for people to understand or is rendered too metaphoric that it loses the essence of what is being communicated. In both cases, the message does not achieve the intended goal. In South Africa, for instance although the intention of loveLife in using cryptic messages as a strategy was to get audiences to talk about HIV/AIDS, messages were misinterpreted. For example, a loveLife message with a slogan, "Prove your love, protect me," was interpreted by a member of the target audience to mean, "having sex with him means that you will be proving your love for him" (Lubinga et al. 2010, 43). Various researchers found varying levels of abstraction of messages and corresponding misinterpretation of the cryptic messages (Singer 2005; Thomas 2004).

Loss of meaning in translation

In the interpersonal context it is crucial for the healthcare provider to understand the description of the nature of illness by the patient in order to administer the necessary treatment. Van der Berg (2016) argues that successful provider–patient outcomes are based on rapport between both parties, the patient's control of the dialogue and amount (possibly quality) of information exchanged. Levin (2014) found that in most of the South African healthcare system consultations are held in patients' second or third languages. In these contexts, nurses are relied on to interpret for doctors who are not competent in English or Afrikaans. The problem is exacerbated in the rural areas where nurses work with Cuban doctors, with no knowledge of Spanish, since from 1996, 460 Cuban doctors have been invited to work in rural hospitals (Govender 2011).

Mass media messages for major campaigns are often crafted in the *lingua franca* of the country and are then translated into indigenous African languages in most countries. The detail is at times lost in translation, because African languages are ambiguous, with one word having several meanings, which is not the case with *lingua francas* for instance.

The ethics of communicating health in Africa

The area of ethics is closely correlated to the high regulatory environment which governs health communication. This includes the explicit outlining of the genuineness of the medication issued or provided by public health systems. The formation of the health communication needs to be focussed on the patient, and should not set blame on patients or place the burden of responsibility solely on them.

Sometimes in health communication messages information is hidden from the public/audiences in order to protect the interests of communicators of health communication messages, whether for profit or to gain favour. Such influential people may often be willing to go against international human rights (IHR) and likely violate patients' human rights. Recently the DA Shadow Member of Executive Committee (MEC) of Health in the Gauteng Provincial Legislature in South Africa, Jack Bloom, was taken to task by media and the public in South Africa over his misuse of absolute numbers with respect to the number of patient deaths at Baragwanath Hospital without proportional context in order to curry political favour. A leading health journalist, Katharine Child, went on to explain publicly the challenge with this and how it was unethical (Twitter 2018).

Often during protests accusations emerge with little regard for ethical consideration of communication, particularly if the risks to patients and the general population are discussed in health communication. The risks often seem to be overlooked in health communication, with the benefits overstated, particularly for global interventions, such as contraception (Lubinga and Sitto 2018), HIV/AIDS and lifestyle diseases such as diabetes.

An example of an unethical study was the "Tuskegee Study of Untreated Syphilis in the Negro Male." This US study, which was started in 1932 and lasted 40 years, involved misinformation and human rights violations. The investigators did not adequately inform participants of the objectives of the study, deliberately misled them into participation and did not inform them that they could choose to drop out (CDC 2017b). The absolute and misleading unethical nature of experimentation during the study of health issues is a practice that is ongoing today on the African continent. In Africa, researchers have been reported as having experimented with live subjects without providing adequate communication to them. Studies involving anti-retroviral therapy (ART) in Uganda, Zimbabwe and Côte d'Ivoire continue to be flagged by international bodies as being unethical (Wemos 2008). These studies remain in existence because pharmaceutical companies in Africa often circumvent processes by exploiting vulnerable populations in developing countries, putting their health and human rights at risk (Shah 2013).

The exclusion of rural, less educated recipients of health communication messages through the use of technical language that is full of medical jargon or that is in a *lingua franca* that is not used in rural areas also blurs the lines of ethics. This is not ethical with respect to the rights of those patients to be empowered to make informed medical decisions about their health based on what is communicated to them.

Barriers to health communication

Barriers to digital commication and social media exist, although they may in fact positively impact on health communication. Digital and social media are cost-effective; they can reach wider audiences in geographically disparate places almost simultaneously and without additional cost burdens regardless of the number of people reached. However, one of the biggest barriers to accessing information distributed through these media is access to the internet. While global internet access is on the rise, the gap between those who have access and those who do not is widening, which has implications for health communication development.

Developing countries are much further behind with these media because of their underinvestment in infrastructure such telecommunications infrastructure (Campos 2018). The UN recognises that it is most often vulnerable groups that lack adequate access to use ICTs and the internet, seriously challenging the UN's declaration of access to the internet as a fundamental universal human right (UN News 2015). Coupled with little political will, the digital divide is likely to grow considering that some governments continually use their power to shut off internet access during politically restless times or if online information is considered a threat to power e.g. Zimbabwe, Uganda, Egypt, Libya, Cameroon, Ethiopia (Mukeredzi 2017). The deliberate violation of the UN-declared human right has far reaching consequences, particularly for health, as computer-mediated technologies could be used to improve the delivery of public health communication to remote communities at affordable rates.

Linked to this barrier is that of online security, a growing shadow fed by activities such as hacking, whereby a third party accesses a person's personal information through social media applications (e.g. Facebook's 2018 security breach scandal) and what has been coined by American President Donald Trump as "fake news." A lack of security increases the vulnerability of online users and can have life-threatening consequences with regard to health communication, such as the use of misinformation to make life/death decisions, victimisation of online health activists or even cutting people off from essential health communication.

In terms of health promotion in Africa, governments face budget constraints forcing them to select diseases to prioritise in terms of communication. Prioritisation appears to be driven by the burden of the disease and the measure of its effects on society. Priority in communication is also made on the basis of whether messages will be effective because of the scarcity of resources. As a result, HIV/AIDS has taken the bulk of the resources and has been the subject of several campaigns. However, diseases such as cancer (apart from breast cancer for women and prostate cancer for men) continue to prevail or seem to be on the increase, and then there are other diseases whose target populations are ignorant of the risks, such as with male breast cancer (Motloutsi and Lubinga 2017). Would interventionists consider combining promotion of similar diseases in health messages communicated to target audiences such as female and male breast cancer, rather than focusing on the female version only? Prioritisation of diseases and focussed efforts have resulted in what MSF has termed as the exclusion of millions of Western and Central African people from global HIV efforts (MSF 2016).

In sum, this chapter has mapped key organisational players of healthcare communication in Africa. It has critiqued theories commonly used for researching health in Africa, whose balance is tipped in favour of dominant Western approaches despite criticism that they are ill-fit for African contexts. It presented a case study underscoring the important role of communication in concerted efforts to fight the Ebola virus in some West African countries. It examined the important role of civil society or activist organisations as well as online health activism. It highlighted impediments to languaging in health communication messages, ethics in healthcare communication, and barriers to such communication.

References

Acconcia, G. 2018. *The Murder of Giulio Regeni, Two Years on.* www.fairobserver.com/region/middle_east_north_africa/giulio-regeni-murder-egypt-human-rights-italy-news-23100/ (Accessed 5 October 2018).

Airhihenbuwa, C.O. 1989. Perspectives on AIDS in Africa: Strategies for prevention and control. *AIDS Education and Prevention,* 1(1): 57–69.

Airhihenbuwa, C.O. 1995. *Health and Culture: Beyond the Western Paradigm.* Thousand Oaks, CA: Sage.

allAfrica. 2018. *VIDEO: Museveni – Mouth is for Eating, Not for Oral Sex.* https://allafrica.com/view/group/main/main/id/00060293.html?utm_campaign=allafrica%3Aeditor&utm_medium=social&utm_source=twitter&utm_content=promote%3Agroup%3Aacbllp./ (Accessed 5 October 2018).

Al Jazeera. 2019. *Community Mistrust Worsening DR Congo Ebola Outbreak: Study,* 28 March. www.aljazeera.com/news/2019/03/community-mistrust-worsening-dr-congo-ebola-outbreak-study-190328062938247.html (Accessed 29 March 2019).

Anderson, J. 2018. *10 Signs of Social Media Fatigue in Your Audience – And How to Fix It Quickly.* www.allbusiness.com/10-signs-social-media-fatigue-107625-1.html./ (Accessed 5 October 2018).

AVERT. 2015. *South Africa Exceeds National Mother-to-Child Transmission Target.* www.avert.org/news/south-africa-exceeds-national-mother-child-transmission-target./ (Accessed 5 October 2018).

Baxen, J. and Breidlid, A., eds. 2009. *HIV and AIDS in Sub-Saharan Africa: Understanding the Implications of Culture and Context.* Cape Town: UCT Press.

Burton, G. and Dimbleby, R. 2006. *Between Ourselves – An Introduction to Interpersonal Communication.* London: Hodder Education, 3rd ed.

Campos, Z. 2018. *The Economic Cost of Poor Infrastructure.* www.africanfinanceandtech.com/single-post/2018/02/28/The-Economic-Cost-of-Poor-Infrastructure./ (Accessed 5 October 2018).

CDC. 2017a. *2014–2016 Ebola Outbreak in West Africa.* www.cdc.gov/vhf/ebola/history/2014-2016-outbreak/index.html./ (Accessed 5 October 2018).

CDC. 2017b. *The Tuskegee Timeline.* www.cdc.gov/tuskegee/timeline.htm./ (Accessed 5 October 2018).

The Conversation. 2017. The role of NGOs in Africa: Are they a force for good? *The Conversation.* https://theconversation.com/the-role-of-ngos-in-africa-are-they-a-force-for-good-76227 (Accessed 5 October 2018).

Dionne, K.Y. 2014. *Why West African Governments Are Struggling in Response to Ebola.* www.washingtonpost.com/news/monkey-cage/wp/2014/07/15/why-west-african-governments-are-struggling-in-response-to-ebola/?utm_term=.a8b1c90aea93./ (Accessed 5 October 2018).

Dutta-Bergman, M.J. 2005. Theory and practice in health communication campaigns: A critical interrogation. *Health Communication,* 18(2): 103–122.

Dutta-Bergman, M.J. 2008. *Communicating Health: A Culture-Centred Approach.* Cambridge: Polity Press.

Edwards, L. 2011. Critical perspectives in global public relations: Theorizing power. In Bardhan, N. and Weaver, C.K., eds. *Public Relations in Global Cultural Contexts: Multi-paradigmatic Perspectives.* London: Routledge, 29–50.

Ervas, F., Montibeller, M., Grazia, R.M. and Pietro, S. 2017. Expertise and metaphors in health communication. *Medicina e Storia,* 16(9–10): 91–108.

Fishbein, M.A. 1980. Theory of reasoned action: Some applications and implications. In Howe, H.E. and Page, M.M., eds. *Nebraska Symposium on Motivation.* Lincoln: University of Nebraska Press, vol. 27, 65–116.

Fishbein, M.A. and Ajzen, A. 1975. *Beliefs, Attitudes, Intentions, and Behavior: An Introduction to Theory and Research.* Reading. MA: Addison-Wesley.

Govender, K. 2011. *Cuban Doctors Make a Difference in Rural Areas*. www.sanews.gov.za/world/cuban-doctors-make-difference-rural-areas./ (Accessed 5 October 2018).

Hoïjer, B. 2011. Social representations theory: A new theory for media research. *Nordicom Review: Nordic Research on Media & Communication*, 32(2): 3–16.

Hollemans, E. 2005 Lovelife gets attitude. *Mail and Guardian*, 18 January. www.mg.co.za/article/2005-01-18-lovelife-gets-attitude (Accessed 25 March 2019).

HPCSA. 2008. *Guidelines for Good Practice in the Health Care Professions: National Patients' Rights Charter Booklet 3*. Pretoria: Health Professions Council of South Africa.

Internet World Stats. 2017. *Internet Users Statistics for Africa*. www.internetworldstats.com/stats1.htm./ (Accessed 5 October 2018).

Iwelunmor, J., Newsome, V. and Airinhenbuwa, C.O. 2014. Framing the impact of culture on health: A systematic review of the PEN-3 cultural model and its application in public health research and interventions. *Ethnicity and Health,* 19(1): 20–46.

Janz, N.K. and Becker, M.H. 1984. The health belief model: A decade later. *Health Education Quarterly,* 11(1): 1–47.

Kamwendo, G. 2008. "But Having Small Houses Spreads HIV": Problems of Language and Communication in Health Services in Sub-Saharan Africa. *Globalisation and Languages: Building on Our Rich Heritage*. Proceedings of the UN-UNESCO conference Tokyo Japan. http://archive.unu.edu/globalization/2008/files/UNU-UNESCO_2008_Globalization_and_Languages.pdf (Accessed 5 October 2018).

Kiwuwa, D.E. 2015. *Africa Is Young: Why Are Its Leaders so Old?* https://edition.cnn.com/2015/10/15/africa/africas-old-mens-club-op-ed-david-e-kiwuwa/index.html./ (Accessed 5 October 2018).

Levin, M. 2014. Language and allergy education: Review article. *Current Allergy and Clinical Immunology*, 27(4): 290–291.

loveLife. 2010. *HCT & Youth: Issues, Challenges and Lessons Learned*. https://lovelife.org.za/en/studies-surveys-and-reports/ (Accessed 24 March 2019).

Lubinga, E. 2020. Protest as communication for development and social change in South Africa. In Servaes, J., eds. *Handbook of Communication for Development and Social Change*. Singapore: Springer. doi.org/10.1007/978-981-10-7035-8_133-1.

Lubinga, E., Schulze, M., Jansen, C. and Maes, A. 2010. HIV/AIDS messages as a spur for conversation among young South Africans? *African Journal of AIDS Research,* 9(2): 175–185.

Lubinga, E. and Sitto, K. 2018. *Agency, Access and the Power of Female Voices Online: A Case Study of #depoprovera*. Paper presented to SACOMM Conference, Johannesburg, 12–14 September.

Makalela, L. 2015. Translanguaging as a vehicle for epistemic access: Cases for reading comprehension and multilingual interactions. *Per Linguam*, 31(1): 15–29.

Motloutsi, A. and Lubinga, E. 2017. Communicating male breast cancer: Knowledge and awareness among some South African youth. *Communitas*, 22(1): 87–97.

MSF. 2016. *Out of Focus: How Millions of People in West and Central Africa Are Being Left Out of the Global HIV Response*. www.msf.org.za/system/tdf/publications/out_of_focus_english2.pdf?file=1&type=node&id=3026/ (Accessed 5 October 2018).

Mukeredzi, T. 2017. *Uproar Over Internet Shutdowns*. www.un.org/africarenewal/magazine/august-november-2017/uproar-over-internet-shutdowns./ (Accessed 5 October 2018).

NBC News. 2020. *African Countries that Faced Ebola Outbreaks Use Lessons to Fight COVID-19, Experts Say*. https://www.nbcnews.com/news/world/african-countries-faced-ebola-outbreaks-use-lessons-fight-covid-19-n1181156 (Accessed 5 October 2020).

Pal, M. and Dutta, M.J. 2008. Public relations in a global context: The relevance of critical modernism as a theoretical lens. *Journal of Public Relations Research*, 20(2): 159–179.

Rosenstock, I.M. 1974. The health belief model and preventive health behavior. *Health Education Monographs*, 2(4): 354–386.

Schulz, A. and Roessler, P. 2012. The spiral of silence and the internet: Selection of online content and the perception of the public opinion climate in computer-mediated communication environments. *International Journal of Public Opinion Research*, 24(3): 346–367.

Sehoai, R. 2018. *South Africa Slashes HIV Infection Rate by 44%*. www.health-e.org.za/2018/07/18/sas-hiv-infection-rate-goes-down/ (Accessed 5 October 2018).

Seidel, G. 1990. Thank God I said no to AIDS: On the changing discourse of AIDS in Uganda. *Discourse and Society*, 1(1): 61–84.

Shah, S. 2013. *Unethical Drug Trials Exposed in South Africa and Other Developing Countries.* http://sonia shah.com/unethical-drug-trials-exposed-in-south-africa-and-other-developing-countries/ (Accessed 5 October 2018).

Singer, R. 2005. Is lovelife making them love life? *Mail and Guardian*, 24 August. https://mg.co.za/article/2005-08-24-is-lovelife-making-them-love-life/ (Accessed 5 October 2018).

South African Development Community. 2012. *Health.* www.sadc.int/themes/health/ (Accessed 5 October 2018).

Tateo, L. and Iannaccone, A. 2012. Social representations, individual and collective mind: A study of Wundt, Cattaneo and Moscovici. *Integrative Psychological and Behavioral Science*, 46(1): 57–69.

Thomas, K. 2004. A better life for some: The loveLife campaign and HIV/AIDS in South Africa. *Agenda*, 62: 29–35.

Tobor, N. 2018. *Benin Cancels Social Media Tax.* www.iafrikan.com/2018/10/02/social-media-benin-policy-government/ (Accessed 5 October 2018).

Tran, M. 2012. Translators fight the fatal effects of the language gap. *The Guardian*, 11 April. www.theguardian.com/global-development/poverty-matters/2012/apr/11/volunteers-translation-language-health-messages/ (Accessed 5 October 2018).

Twitter. 2018. https://twitter.com/katjanechild/status/1026461960467034113 (Accessed 5 October 2018).

UN News. 2015. *'Turn Digital Divides into Digital Opportunities,' Ban Tells Annual UN Forum on Internet Governance.* www.un.org/sustainabledevelopment/blog/2015/11/turn-digital-divides-into-digital-opportunities-ban-tells-annual-un-forum-on-internet-governance/ (Accessed 5 October 2018).

USAID. 2018. *Global Health.* www.usaid.gov/south-africa/global-health. (Accessed 5 October 2018).

Van der Berg, V.L. 2016. Still lost in translation: Language barriers in South African health care remain. *South African Family Practice*, 58(6): 229–231.

Vuso, K. 2014. *SAA Goes Global with Ebola Education Social Media Strategy.* www.flowsa.com/blog/entry/saa-goes-global-with-ebola-education-social-media-strategy (Accessed 5 October 2018).

Watson, R.T., Pitt, L.F., Berthon, P. and Zinkhan, G.M. 2002. U-commerce: Expanding the universe of marketing. *Journal of the Academy of Marketing Science*, 30(4): 333–347.

Wemos. 2008. *SOMO Briefing Paper on Ethics in Clinical Trials.* www.eldis.org/document/A24180 (Accessed 5 October 2018).

Whembolua, G.S., Conserve, D.F. and Tshiswaka, D.I. 2015. Cultural identity and health promotion: Assessing a health education program targeting African immigrants in France. *The Journal of Pan African Studies*, 8(2): 23–39.

Witte, K. 1992. Putting the fear back into fear appeals: The extended parallel process model. *Communication Monographs*, 59(4): 329–349.

Witte, K. and Allen, M. 2000. A meta-analysis of fear appeals: Implications for effective public health campaigns. *Health Education Behaviour*, 27(5): 591–615.

World Health Organisation. 2020a. *WHO Director-General's Opening Remarks at the Media Briefing on COVID-19*, 11 March 2020. https://www.who.int/dg/speeches/detail/who-director-general-s-opening-remarks-at-the-media-briefing-on-covid-19---11-march-2020 (Accessed 5 October 2020).

World Health Organisation. 2020b. *Robots Use in Rwanda to Fight Against COVID-19.* https://www.afro.who.int/news/robots-use-rwanda-fight-against-covid-19 (Accessed 5 October 2020).

World Health Organisation. 2020c. *New COVID-19 Law Lab to provide vital legal information and support for the global COVID-19 response.* https://www.who.int/news/item/22-07-2020-new-covid-19-law-lab-to-provide-vital-legal-information-and-support-for-the-global-covid-19-response (Accessed 5 November 2020).

WorldOMeters. 2020. *Africa Population (LIVE).* https://www.worldometers.info/world-population/africa-population/#:~:text=The%20current%20population%20of%20Africa,of%20the%20total%20world%20population./ (Accessed 5 October 2020).

Yawa, A. 2018. Interview with TAC Secretary General, Johannesburg, 14 February.

17

The politics of identity, trauma, memory and decolonisation in Neill Blomkamp's *Chappie* (2015)

Beschara Karam

Introduction

The aim of this research is look at the South African context as represented in the film and to argue that Chappie's "identity" is not only formed from his presentist, experiential context (born into criminal violence) of his individual traumas but also from his inherited trauma. A trauma which Ron Eyerman terms a collective "tear in the social fabric" or a "societal wound" (2004, 4). Which, in this particular case, is that of apartheid and colonial traumas.

With regards to the film itself, *Chappie* (2015) was directed by Neill Blomkamp and set in 2016 in a "near-future" Johannesburg. The city is depicted as dystopic and violent, filled with crime, poverty and melancholy (not dissimilar to South Africa today circa 2020. The film is embedded with motifs and elements from South Africa's past. For example, "Tetravaal" is reminiscent of the "Transvaal", a province named by the colonisers of South Africa. The company provides robotic "peace" enforcers. Tetravaal is itself presented as dictatorial and authoritarian, very much like the previous Nationalist government, the enforcers of the violent apartheid regime. The chapter is relevant as it is an example of endogeneity: that is, African representation that affirms African positions, contexts and subjectivities (Mafeje 2000). It is knowledge creation, from and about, Africa. This is because the film *Chappie* has – through concepts of Othering, marginalisation and intergenerational and historical pain and memory – *questioned African* contexts. In this case, South Africa. It has also questioned positions; subjectivities; agencies, or lack thereof; centralities; and binaries. As such, the film works as an agent of change, by conscientising citizens about post-colonialism, or the myth of post-colonialism (Ndlovu-Gatsheni 2013). After all, can it really be a post-colonial era when South Africa is constantly being re-colonised? The film also reflects on the inherited apartheid and colonial structures/institutions, values, ideologies and, capital/economy. All of which continue to either "haunt" or "ghost" South Africans and South Africa, or continue to link them to colonial power relations, institutions and beliefs. A brief overview of the literature follows.

Multidisciplinary literature: trauma and memory studies, film studies and decolonisation studies

Cathy Caruth, whose work is foundational to the field of trauma studies, refers to trauma as a wound, or wounds, inflicted on the mind, or individual's body (1995; 1996). As such, she does not write of trauma as a social wound, but an individual experience. Her work is predominantly based on the individual traumas of the victims of the Holocaust and of those who survived the nuclear devastations of Hiroshima and Nagasaki. This is in part because her work is almost entirely based on the psychoanalytic work of Sigmund Freud, which in turn deals predominantly with the psychical trauma of the individual. Caruth also argues that textual, psychoanalytical and deconstructive approaches can assist audiences in understanding the cinematic texts that bear witness to traumatic events (1995; 1996; 2003). In doing so, these films make the reprehensible traumata, and the un-representable, accessible. Since her seminal works, other academics have theorised about collective traumas (cf. Bayer 2010; Berger 2010; Brown 1995; Buelens, Durrant and Eaglestone 2014; Craps and Rothberg 2011; Hartman 1996, 2003a and 2003b; Hirsch 2003 and 2012). For instance, Jeffrey Alexander states that this type of collective trauma:

> occurs when members of a collective feel they have been subjected to a horrendous event that leaves indeleble marks upon their group consciousness, marking their memories forever and changing their future identity in fundamental and irrevocable ways.
>
> *(2004, 1)*

Similarly, the American Psychiatric Association writes that trauma presents itself with a group of symptoms that includes nightmares, emotional numbing, flashbacks, somatic reactions, repeated hallucinations and an absence of recall of the traumata (2000, 467–468). While Ron Eyerman has conceptualised collective trauma as a "tear in the social fabric" of a society (2004, 4). Trauma studies itself has focused on "iconic" cultural traumas, which include the Holocaust and other genocides, and the effects of these traumas on the individual. In doing so, trauma studies omitted both historical and/or cultural contexts. Until more recently (circa 1997) with, for example, Marianna Hirsch identifying inter-generational and post-memory/history trauma (2012), Michael Rothberg calling for an acknowledgement of cross-cultural and cross-generalational trauma, or a "multidirectionality of traumas" (2009), that looks not only at "iconic" trauma, but other historical traumatas, for instance, the Atlantic Slave Trade, apartheid, colonisation and capitalism (Rothberg 2009; cf Karam 2012), the emphasis is no longer only on the individual traumas, but also taking cognisance of the historical and cultural contexts in which these traumas occurred. Caruth has acknowledged that "history is a symptom" (1995). By this, she means that traumas are linked to historical contexts and historical eras and that individuals "inherit" these traumas, which are experienced as "ghostings" or "hauntings". Herrero and Allué also argue that history and individual trauma are inextricably bound (2011). While Judith Butler has stated that "isolating the individuals [trauma] absolves us of the necessity of coming up with a broader explanation for events" (2004, 5). This is particularly relevant in understanding historical traumas, such as apartheid and colonisation, and how these traumas have been inherited by the early generations born into South Africa's "democracy". Sabelo Ndlovu-Gatsheni has in fact argued that Africans have suffered trauma twice, though colonisation and for being considered unhuman (2013). Both wounds (re)occur, and both are still prevalent in South Africa.

Arthur Neal has written that that "just as the rape victim becomes permanently changed as a result of the trauma, the nation becomes permanently changed as a result of trauma in the social realm" (1998, 36). As such, psychological or individual trauma and collective trauma are linked. However, this comparison that Neal makes must be treated with caution. Neal seeks out to make the similarities and links between individual psychical trauma and collective trauma. However, this is not to say that a rape of an individual is necessarily the same, or experienced in the same way, as a collective trauma, and vice versa. Rather, he seems to be referring to how individual traumas can be treated, and even "cured". Individuals can go on to live fruitful and successful lives, and even, if they are fortunate enough, have closure at some stage of their lives. This is of course dependent on whether there is treatment available to them. However, and this is the point that I feel Neal is trying to make: cultural traumas are a constant, they are recurring and ongoing, an often daily struggle. I would therefore like to suggest that both the individual trauma as experienced, as well as the historical context in which these traumas occur, are relevant to understanding collective trauma. In addition, I believe that they are inextricably bound (cf. Herrero and Allué 2011).

Returning briefly to Ron Eyerman, who claims that collective representation is needed in order to repair "the tear in the social fabric" (2004, 4). These collective traumas also include, "by extension, cultural and ethnic traumas" (Herrero and Baelo-Allué 2011, i). Furthermore, Herrero and Baelo-Allué argue that collective and individual traumata "in literature has become one of the most common ways of expressing and representing trauma" (2011, i). To which I add filmic texts, as another popular way of representing such traumas. Consider films such as *12 Years a Slave* (McQueen 2013) and *Amistad* which centres on the trans-Atlantic trade (Spielberg 1997) and *Schindler's List* which depicts the Holocaust (Spielberg 1993). *Hotel Rwanda* (George 2004) and *Imbabazi* (*The Pardon*; Karekezi 2013), are both films that focus on the Rwandan genocide. Another film, *The Bang Bang Club* (Silver 2010), about the South African "transitional" era from apartheid to democracy circa 1990s, represents an era of collective trauma. All these films depict both individual and collective traumas. The stories centre around a specific individual (or group of individuals, such as the South African photographers in the *The Bang Bang Club*), within the greater context of a cultural or ethnic trauma. As a result of this long cinematic history of filmic representations of trauma, several groundbreaking studies have similarly emerged within the cinematic scholarly realm. For example, Janet Walker's *Trauma Cinema: Documenting Incest and the Holocaust* (2005), Joshua Hirsch's *After Image, Trauma and the Holocaust* (2004), Raya Morag's *Waltzing with Bashir: Perpetrator Trauma and Cinema* (2013) and E. Anne Kaplan and Ban Wang's *Trauma and Cinema* (2004).

However, the aim of this chapter is not to provide an overview of films that have represented trauma, which is extensive. Neither is it an attempt to cover the already existing scholarly work that focuses on the representation of trauma, which is also well documented. Rather, it is to add to the emerging research that specifically focusses on African films, representing African historical, cultural, collective and individual traumas. African cinema studies have recently (circa 2007–2020) seen a strong emergent sub-field of study emphasising the representation of African trauma. Most specifically: films representing apartheid atrocities (cf. Botha 2007; Rijsdijk 2007) or the films depicting the South African Truth and Reconciliation Commission (cf. Karam 2012; Karam 2019; Mhando and Tomaselli 2009). And, more recently (circa 2017 and 2018), research that focusses on films that cover post-colonial or post-apartheid trauma, such as Lizelle Bisschof and Stephanie van der Peer's *Art and Trauma in Africa* (2017), as well as Claire Scott's article "The truths/fictions/traumas of Marikana: exploring violence and trauma in three films, *The Marikana Massacre: Through the Lens* (2013); *Miners Shot Down* (2014), and *Night Is Coming: A Threnody for the Victims of Marikana* (2014)" (2018). Also, worth mentioning are Mark

Kirby-Hirst and Beschara Karam's *Inexba (The Wound): Sexual, Gender, Cultural and Religious Traumata on the African Screen* (2018) and their co-authored editorial "Traumata on screen: Cinematic views from Africa" (2018). This body of research already situates individual trauma within its historical context and the trauma South Africa has inherited. In trying to better understand the larger situation and position of post-apartheid and post-colonial traumas, I turn to decolonial studies.

Decolonial studies/decolonisation

Like the seminal authors of decoloniality, Walter Mignolo (1995; 2000), Ramón Grosfoguel (2007; 2011), Enrique Dussel (1977) and Aníbal Quijano (1991, 2000), several African authors and scholars are thinking with, and from, "subalternalized racial/ethnic/sexual spaces and bodies" (Grosfoguel 2011, 2; cf. Grosfoguel 2007). In doing so, we have had to acknowledge that South Africa, as a post-colonial country, is still racialised, hierarchical, classist, capitalist, heteropatriarchal, gentrified, imperialist and Westernised (Ndlovu-Gatsheni 2013). South Africa is still embedded with insidious colonial and institutional power relations. It is therefore essential that such authors and scholars, as well as various popular culture texts, challenge the "colonial power matrix" (Quijano 1991, 2000). This matrix includes reified gender hierarchies, international and local racialised divisions of labour and class, aesthetic hierarchies and epistemic hierarchies that preface or privilege "the west over the rest". Quijano elaborates on his concept by stating that it is an "organising principle" involving domination and exploitation (1991, 2000). Furthermore, it is intrinsic socio-culturally, politically, institutionally and epistemologically (Quijano 1991, 2000). This "colonial power matrix" ("*patron de poder colonial*") or "coloniality of power" is still inherent in South Africa. *Chappie* challenges this "colonial power matrix." It does so by providing a reflexive "decolonial critique" that acknowledges the silenced and subalternised, with the central character Chappie representing the marginalised and Othered. The personal traumas that he experiences, represent similar, if not identical traumas experienced by the subalterns in South Africa, most significantly, during both the apartheid and post-apartheid eras. The film questions the "colonial power matrix" that infiltrates South Africa on every level. It does this by cleverly positioning a Western, global company "Tetravaal" as the epicenter of the narrative. This is exemplified by their use of robotic scouts who use violence and terror to restore order to an anarchic South Africa. The West (an international capitalist company) has returned to recolonise South Africa under the guise of "saving it".

The film: *Chappie*

Chappie begins with documentary-style footage and newsreels of violent protests and looting (Blomkamp 2015). The opening sequence is the Minister of Police announcing that it is the "re-birth of the city" with the implementation of a new "police force". These are the robotic "scouts". However, their creator "Deon Wilson" (Dev Patel) has a much higher ambition: making the scouts sentient. The company he works for, "Tetravaal", a weapons manufacturer, headed up by CEO "Michelle Bradley" (Sigourney Weaver) refuses his request to work on such a project. Instead, he works on it at night at home, in secrecy. He decides to test his artificial intelligence (AI) programme on a decommissioned scout. A scout that has been scheduled for recycling (during his lifespan he was crushed by a car, shot at point blank and for all intents and purposes was already "dead"). He "steals" this scout. Just as he is about to "birth" his new creation, he is kidnapped, along with his robot. The criminal gang who highjacks him demand that he take a master key and shut down all scout activity. This will enable them to do a 600 million ZAR transit heist "safely". This gang is headed up by "Ninja" (Watkin Tudor Jones), "Yolandi" (Yolandi Visser) and "Amerika" (Jose Pablo Cantillo). As part of the sub-plot, they owe another criminal, "Hippo" (Brandon Auret), 20 million ZAR. They force Deon to "build" the scout and to upload his consciousness programme into the decommissioned robot. "Chappie" is "born". When the scout is "turned on", he is terrified; he scuttles and hides. The point-of-view camera shows a terrified "being", who is "confused". It takes much coaxing and "baby talk" from Yolandi to get him to come out from his hiding place (behind some boxes). She names him "Chappie" (voiced by Sharlto Copley). Under threat of death, Deon must leave Chappie with the gang and return to work, but he promises to return. Chappie is then confronted by his different caregivers: Yolandi, his "mommy", who tries to teach him about love, and Deon, his "maker", who tries to teach him about science and arts. And lastly, Ninja, his "daddy", who uses tough love to try and teach Chappie to do his criminal bidding. For Ninja, Chappie is a means to an end, to pull off the heist of a lifetime. Ninja often loses his temper with Chappie, who has been coded to "do no harm". In order to teach Chappie a lesson and introduce him to the harsh socio-realities of life, Ninja takes Chappie on "a little road trip". He drops him off in an isolated area of Johannesburg in front of some delinquent youths. They think that the scout is a policeman, and they then attack him, shoot him and set him on fire. As he limps home, he is kidnapped by a jealous colleague of Deon's, "Vincent Moore" (Hugh Jackman) (previously a RECCE during the apartheid era). In the back of a van, Vincent and his accomplices take a chainsaw and start to dismember him. After they saw off his arm, black liquid pours out, not unlike thick textured dark red blood. Chappie manages to escape them and find his way back home where Amerika fixes Chappie by re-attaching an (orange) arm. A remorseful Ninja returns and decides to train Chappie, all to make Chappie "belong". He does this by spray-painting "tattoos" on him, giving him "cool" bling and "gangsta" jewellery to wear. He also teaches him to shoot, speak and swear like himself and their gang. Ninja and Amerika then start Chappie on a life of criminality. Finally, they attempt the heist they had been planning all along. Hippo, Ninja's archnemesis, sees the heist on television and immediately demands all of the 600 million ZAR owed him. Simultaneously, Deon's colleague, Vincent, has taken the master key and switched off all the scouts. The robots simply lie down, except for Chappie who is, of course, no longer a part of this central system. Because of the chaos that ensures, Vincent is given permission to use "the MOOSE". This is a giant robot that is more like a large transformer/tank/helicopter/cannon. He claims it will bring order to the country. Instead, with jealousy his prime motive, he sends it to Ninja and Yolandi's hide out. The result? Yolandi is killed and Deon is fatally wounded. But Chappie manages to "save" Deon by transferring Deon's consciousness into another decommissioned scout. Deon and Chappie manage to escape and go on the run together.

Having briefly discussed the film and its narrative, the chapter now turns to a an in-depth analysis, because, as several authors argue, a "textualist approach" can provide us with a unique access to trauma (Caruth 1995; 1996; 2003; Hirsch 2003; 2012; Hartman 1996; 2003a; 2003b; and, Herrero and Baelo-Allué 2011), thereby attaching us to a history or histories, in this case apartheid, post-colonialism and neo-colonialism.

Individual and collective trauma in *Chappie*

In the film itself, several different types of trauma are represented: individual trauma (Chappie's), collective trauma, inherited historical trauma (post-colonial trauma) and the trauma of neo-colonialism. This is similar to films such as *12 Years a Slave* and *Imbabazi*, with individual trauma linking with other forms of trauma. The "symptoms" of trauma are presented in Chappie and are also present in the way that the film itself unfolds. For instance, there is no direct reference to apartheid or the historical or social traumata or wound. There is no direct recall of this "tear in the social fabric", but there is emotional numbing, "hallucinations" and "flashbacks". There is "ghosting", for example, the documentary footage of the violence shown in the "future" South Africa, could quite easily be taken from the period during the height of apartheid (circa late 1980s). These images include tanks pouring into townships, black youths burning tyres in the roads (reminiscent of "necklace burnings" – a violence well known to South Africans) and black youths throwing stones and rocks at the army and the police. Even when the teenagers petrol-bomb Chappie, all of these scenes are the "ghosting" of the trauma of the wound of apartheid. South Africa's collective trauma has been "buried" or sublimate, and yet its "symptoms" appear and disappear constantly as the ghosts of apartheid and colonialism. In South Africa, post-apartheid, these "symptoms" continue sometimes overtly, as with the Marikana Massacre in 2012 (cf. Desai 2014), and other times covertly, as with the racism that seems embedded in our entire socio-political fabric (institutional, bureaucratic, capitalist economy). But it is Chappie's personal trauma, situated within the context of the collective post-colonial wound that is significant. It is this that underlines his own search for his "identity" and "place" in South Africa. From the outset, Chappie is traumatised, from his "birth", his Othering, even before his human "consciousness" is uploaded onto his hardware. He is Othered not only from his own "species", robots/scouts, in that he is labelled "reject" (stamped on his forehead). During that period, he had to have an ear replaced (bright orange). His outward appearance depicts him as "different". He is also unlike the other scouts in that his exterior, or robotic skeleton, is badly damaged. He is not as shiny, new or polished as his "peers". After he is "sentient", he differs even more significantly from the other scouts. He is of course also Othered in that he is not human. In addition, he is heavily stigmatised and stereotypically labelled a "pig" – all the criminal elements in society hate the law enforcement that he represents.

Throughout the film, Chapple experiences three distinct personal traumas: his first personal trauma is when he is attacked by youths, shot at, beaten and finally lit on fire. His second personal trauma is when he has his arm sawn off by the vindictive and bitter colleague from Tetravaal, Vincent Moore. His "pain", "bewilderment" and "shock" are palpable, despite his being a "machine". The trauma is very much a psychical trauma, because, after all, he cannot himself feel pain in a physiological sense. His third trauma is when he shoots the security guards during the heist. He was told that he is merely making them "sleep". However, the realisation that he assassinated these security guards registers belatedly. This trauma, as with other traumas, are not identifiable at the time of the incident. He cries pathetically at the guards, "Why won't you sleep?". He touches their blood and tries to make sense of what he is seeing, as their life blood drains away from them. This trauma is doubly distressing because he has perpetrated violence without realising or knowing the consequences. All of which only become "real" to him after the fact, much later, when his "mommy" dies, and his "maker" suffers a fatal gunshot wound. It is only then, as a deferred experience, does he realise what he has done. However, most worrying is the violence of the post-colonial society, which despite all intents and purposes, including the establishment of the Truth and Reconciliation Committee in 1996, continues to permeate society's stratifications. Not only an insidious violence, such as racism, heteronormativity, class or gender, which continues to penetrate the fabric of our structures and institutions, but also societal violence, as evidenced by South Africa's high crime rate. Included in this ongoing violence is an economy of violence, or "capitalistic violence", for lack of a better term. This would include labourers, such as miners, being paid far below the subsistence wage for jobs that are incredibly dangerous (cf. Desai 2014). Just as Chappie is trying to find himself and to make sense of the society and family he was "birthed" into, so, too, we find that South

Africans are also trying to make sense of a supposedly democratic society. A country that has ostensibly forgiven all previous apartheid and colonial transgressions and reconciled. "Supposedly" because if we had truly apologised, forgiven and reconciled with one another, we would, as a society, be whole, tolerant and, civil. Instead, we are agonistic, uncivil and intolerant. South Africa is a country where the anger, frustration and discontent are overflowing into the streets, no more so than on our university campuses where the youth are calling for accountability, social and economic change and the removal of colonial icons (Cecil John Rhodes, for instance, #RhodesMustFall) that serve as reminders of their masters and colonisers. These spaces are also where these masters are continuously being reified and (re)mythologised. A "collective shout" is demanding the delinking from everything colonial – industrial, corporate, educational and economic (to mention but a few). Most significant is the call for the delinking from imperialist and colonial ways of thinking – ethics, morals, values, worldviews, mentalities and philosophies.

This call for the decolonisation of campuses is not only for pedagogy (modes of teaching) and curricula (knowledge production, knowledge creation, content of modules), but also infrastructure (a capitalist economy where private universities thrive). "Transformation" is an exclamation for the equitable distribution of wealth, for example, access to higher education (cf. *FeesMustFall,* #FMF), the free education promised to them by the liberation party, and now the ruling party, the African Nationalist Congress.

South Africa is not only full of angry youths, it is also a country that is populated with post-colonisers, or recolonisers; capitalist enterprises; a "new" black elite that serves to re-enforce capitalist ideology, an apartheid of economy. We must look at the Marikana massacre of 2012 as an example of post-colonial recolonialisation. Where, just as in the film *Chappie*, the government and its infrastructures use brute force to subdue "the masses". It is likewise a country that is fraught with other forms of violence: xenophobia; misogyny and gender violence; heteropatriarchy (with corrective rapes and murder of black and coloured lesbians and queers, in the townships).

Geographically, South Africa as a landscape has also suffered trauma. For instance, take Johannesburg, a major city in Gauteng Province. It is worthwhile stepping back into time to "recover" some of the history of Gauteng in order to fully understand the importance of the province and some of its major cities. Gauteng is a Sotho name, with *gauta* meaning "gold"; thus Gauteng means: "place of gold". The term *gauta* itself is derived from the Dutch word for gold, *goud*. It is a reference to the Dutch, who were one of the first colonisers of South Africa in the 1600s. Gauteng is also sometimes referred to *eGoli*, a Zulu term. The city's name acknowledges how the province has been built on gold, as the gold mining industry is predominantly based here. This major province includes Soweto, Johannesburg and Pretoria. During apartheid, many painful, traumatic, devastating and politically significant events occurred here, such as the Rivonia Trial in 1963 and 1964, the Soweto Uprising in 1976 and the Sharpeville Massacre in 1960. Gauteng includes two major townships, Soweto, which borders the mining belt south of Gauteng, and Alexandria, which borders the very high-end suburbs of Sandton and Houghton. The locals often refer to this township as "Gemorrah" (Nkosi 2012), because the land has been raped, violated and irrevocably traumatised, mined until the land is nothing but dry sand (as found along the Highveld and the abandoned Rand mines). Nothing more can be done with those mines. They are filled with toxic sludge that will cost too much to drain. The mines continuously "implode", archaic structures which are no longer able to support themselves, collapsing inward. It is a landscape not only devoid of all nutrients but littered with the "carnage" of abandoned mines and disused technology – rusted electrical pillars and mining machinery, unusable trucks and decrepit on-site "offices". They appear as carcasses, broken, thrown away "bodies". Reminders of not only an insatiable, voracious, capitalist economy, but the violation of the land and people. They serve as a testament to horrific working conditions, and as "ghosts", faded memories of a haunted, dreadful history. Similarly, in the film *Chappie*, Gauteng is depicted as a dystopic site of trauma, replete with dead bodies littering the streets and unemployed vagrants living in the abandoned Johannesburg buildings. South African architectural icons, such as the Hillbrow Ponte Tower and the disused cooling towers and the Soweto Township are shown as hopelessly in disrepair. The past and present are joined but disjointed: both are in the present and half buried in the past. With ongoing violent activities still testifying to a violent legacy, from the colonial apartheid era and, the post-colonial era, such as, xenophobia, it is no accident that the film plays out within the province of Gauteng.

Rather dismally, the film was slated at the box office, with reviewers calling the film a "robotic mess" and "farcical", with an obsession of how the AI conceptualisation was a complete failure (Coyle 2015; Gleiberman 2015). However, one needs to shift from the emphasis of AI and instead focus on Chappie's quest to become "human". Human/humanity, in a country consumed by trauma, violence, capitalism and consumerism. His pursuit can be seen as a metaphorical quest for one's identity in this country filled with unrest and anger. The film itself ends on a "positive" if completely unrealistic note: Deon and his "son" Chappie manage to escape. Later, Chappie uploads his "mommy" (from a saved flashdrive) into a new, beautiful, just created, white robot. The film therefore does end with the possibility of hope. There is the prospect of South Africans transcending our accumulated traumata and post-colonial violence, and being united in a forgiving, but as yet, unrealised future.

Conclusion

In concluding, the relevance of this chapter (and film) is that it is an example of what Archie Mafeje has called "endogeneity", that is, African representation that affirms African context, experiences and subjectivities; African insights; and knowledge from Africa (2000). That which re-centres Africa from the margins to the centre. In other words, the film *Chappie* has, through concepts of trauma, Othering, memory and marginalisation, *questioned African* subjectivities, agencies, or lack thereof, centralities and binaries. As such, it therefore serves to work as a change-agent, by questioning post-colonialism, or the myth of post-colonialism (Ndlovu-Gatsheni 2013). Afterall, it cannot be "post" if the "colonial matrix" still exists and continues to "entangle" us. Thus, the film ultimately does not offer us any answers of how we are to navigate our own identities in a "societal wound" that is unhealed. Neither does it suggest ways in which we can overcome our accumulated traumata and be united in an as yet unrealised, peaceful and unified future. It is, rather, a metaphor, in which to raise some of the very real issues that South Africa and South Africans are constantly grappling with. It is also interesting then, that Chappie, while endowed with human consciousness, empathy and human physical traits (such as his very "gangsta" walk), by the end of the film, he remains Othered, marginalised and assumingly living in the shadows (on the run with his father), a "freak" of sorts. In other words, there is no closure or resolution or happy ending for Chappie. It is also ironic that he chooses a perfect, white robot to insert his mommy's identity into. But, as Caruth has stated, texts are important in understanding and bearing witness to the unrepresentable or reprehensible (1995). As such, the film *Chappie* bears witness to the traumas of South Africa's past *and* the present. In doing so, it challenges us to interrogate our own subjectivities/identities within collective, individual and historical contexts. Even if we are born with a clean *tabula rasa*, or as with Chappie, a completely sterile "mind", how do we avoid inheriting these collective, cultural and historical traumas? How are we to dis-entangle ourselves from the apartheid landscape and apartheid and colonial histories? How can we delink from colonial economics and institutions that continue to be embedded with core colonial philosophies and values? Where racism, patriarchy and heteronormativity thrive? How can we find our own identity in an economy that seeks to repeatedly recolonise us, and South Africa? *Chappie* raises these questions, and as such, it is a thoughtful, reflexive film that asks the audience to take context and positionality into account, and ultimately poses the question: how do we find ourselves in a so-called post-colonial country, an open societal wound that has yet to heal? I would like to suggest that it begins with decolonisation, de-linking, disentangling, engagement, listening and hearing, reflecting and transcending. But as to how, that is also a process that has yet to resolve itself.

I would like to end this chapter by including a poem by Nyasha Mboti, a poet and scholar. The poem can be seen as a metaphorical text, not dissimilar to that of a film. Like film, it conjures up the realities of South Africa and South Africans, using phrases instead of images. It serves to re-emphasise my argument about the world inhabited by Chappie and South African citizens, a heavily politicised one. It points to a country divided by apartheid economics, saturated with both crime and poverty, recolonised by glocal companies, ceaselessly haunted by the trauma and legacies of violence, together with race and class issues. There has, in fact, been no liberation. This is made worse by the denialism, the lies, neo-liberalism, re-enslavement and the corruption, all of which are poignantly captured in a few evocative words by Mboti:

> *Tells me*
> Experience
> Has taught me that poverty
> Is a humungous cage
> A huge horror, of course
> My conscience tells me
> That Africa is a crime scene
> (Open your eyes, lovechild)
> I wish God knew
> How it felt to be poor
> Then we would perhaps
> Take good care of ourselves
> Then the profitmakers
> Would look stupid for once
> But it is not obvious. It is not
> A complete victory at all
> I wonder
> What it is
> Will we, God bless us,
> Dig up
> The golf links?
>   (2011, 118)

References

12 Years a Slave (McQueen). 2013. Film and production. *IMDB*. https://www.imdb.com/title/tt2024544/?ref_=fn_al_tt_1.

Amistad (Spielberg). 1997. Film and production. *IMDB*. https://www.imdb.com/title/tt0118607/?ref_=fn_al_tt_1.

Alexander, J.C. 2004. Toward a theory of cultural trauma. In Alexander et al., eds. *Cultural Trauma and Collective Identity*. Berkeley: University of California Press, 1–30.

APA (American Psychiatric Association). 2000. *Diagnostic and Statistical Manual of Mental Disorders*. Fourth Edition: Text Revision (DSM–IV-TR). Washington, DC: American Psychiatric Publishers, 467-468.

The Bang Bang Club (Silver). 2010. Film and production. IMDB. https://www.imdb.com/title/tt1173687/?ref_=fn_al_tt_1.

Bayer, G. 2010. After postmemory: Holocaust cinema and the third generation. *Shofar: An Interdisciplinary Journal of Jewish Studies*, 28(4): 116–132.

Berger, A.L. 2010. Unclaimed experience: Trauma and identity in third generation writing about the holocaust. *Shofar: An Interdisciplinary Journal of Jewish Studies*, 28(3): 149–158.

Bisschof, L. and van de Peer, S., eds. 2017. *Art and Trauma in Africa: Representations of Reconciliation in Music, Visual Arts, Literature and Film*. London: IB Tauris.

Botha, M. 2007. *Painful Lives and Painful Pasts: South African Cinema After Apartheid*. Parklands: Genugtig!.

Brown, L.S. 1995. Not outside the range: One feminist perspective of psychic traumas. In Caruth, C., ed. *Trauma: Explorations in Memory*. Baltimore: Johns Hopkins University Press, 100–113.

Buelens, G., Durrant, S. and Eaglestone, R. 2014. *The Future of Trauma Theory: Contemporary Literary and Cultural Criticism*. Oxford: Routledge.

Caruth, C., ed. 1995. *Trauma: Explorations in Memory*. Baltimore: Johns Hopkins University Press.

Caruth, C., ed. 1996. *Unclaimed Experience: Trauma, Narrative, and History*. Baltimore: Johns Hopkins University Press.

Caruth, C. 2003. Trauma and experience. In Levi, N. and Rothberg, M., eds. *The Holocaust: Theoretical Readings*. Edinburgh: Edinburgh University Press Ltd., 192–199.

Chappie (Blomkamp). 2015. Film and production. IMDB. www.imdb.com/title/tt1823672/locations.

Coyle, J. 2015. 'Chappie' Movie Review: Neil Blomkamp's Latest Sci-Fi Fable Short-Circuited by Its Own Jumbled Machinery. www.nola.com/movies/2015/03/chappie_movie_review_neill_blo.html (Accessed 25 April 2019).

Desai, R., dir. 2014. *Marikana: Miners Shot Down*. Johannesburg: Desai.

Dussel, E. 1977. *Philosophy of Liberation*, trans. Martínez, A. and Morkovsky, C. New York: Orbis Books.

Eyerman, R. 2004. The past in the present: Culture and the transmission of memory. *Acta Sociologica*, 47(2): 159–169.

George T., 2004. *Hotel Rwanda*. Film and production, IMDB. https://www.imdb.com/title/tt0395169/jEFFREY

Imbabazi/The Pardon (Karekezi). 2013. Film and production. IMDB. https://www.imdb.com/title/tt2180405/?ref_=nv_sr_srsg_0.

Gleiberman, O. 2015. Film review: Neil Blomkamp's "Chappie" is a robotic mess. *BBC Culture*. www.bbc.com/culture/story/20150305-chappie-a-robotic-mess (Accessed 25 April 2019).

Grosfoguel, R. 2007. The epistemic decolonial turn. *Cultural Studies*, 21(2–3): 211–223.

Grosfoguel, R. 2011. Decolonizing post-colonial studies and paradigms of political-economy: Transmodernity, decolonial thinking and global coloniality. *Transmodernity: Journal of Peripheral Cultural Production of the Luso-Hispanic World*, 1(1): 1–38.

Hartman, G.H. 1996. *The Longest Shadow: In the Aftermath of the Holocaust*. Bloomington: Indiana University Press.

Hartman, G.H. 2003a. Language and culture after the holocaust. In Levi, N. and Rothberg, M., eds. *The Holocaust: Theoretical Readings*. Edinburgh: Edinburgh University Press Ltd., 313–317.

Hartman, G.H. 2003b. Holocaust and hope. In Postone, M. and Santner, E.L., eds. *Catastrophe and Meaning: The Holocaust and the 20th Century*. Chicago: Chicago University Press, 232–249.

Hartman, G.H. 2004. Audio and video testimony and Holocaust studies. In Hirsch, M. and Kacandes, I., eds. *Teaching the Representation of the Holocaust*. New York: The Modern Language Association of America, 205–219.

Herrero, D. and Baelo-Allué, S., eds. 2011. *The Splintered Glass: Facets of Trauma in the Post-Colony and Beyond*. New York and Amsterdam: Rodopi.

Hirsch, M. 2003. Mourning and Postmemory. In Levi, N. and Rothberg, M., eds. *The Holocaust: Theoretical Readings*. Edinburgh: Edinburgh University Press Ltd., 416–422.

Hirsch, J. 2004. *After Image, Trauma and the Holocaust*. Philadelphia: Temple University Press.

Hirsch, M. 2012. *The Generation of Postmemory: Writing and Visual Culture After the Holocaust*. Columbia: Columbia University Press.

Imbabazi/The Pardon (Karekezi). 2013. Film and production. *IMDB*. https://www.imdb.com/title/tt2180405/?ref_=nv_sr_srsg_0.

Kaplan, E.A. and Wang, B. 2004. *Trauma and Cinema*. Hong Kong: Hong Kong University Press.

Karam, B. 2012. *Landscapes of the Unconscious Mind: A Dialectic of Self and Memory on a Post-Colonial, South African Landscape in the Hand-Animated, Charcoal-Medium Films of William Kentridge*. Ph. D. thesis, University of South Africa, Pretoria.

Karam, B. 2019. The representation of perpetrator trauma. *Forgiveness Communicatio*, 45(1): 71–86.

Mafeje, A. 2000. Africanity: A combative ontology. *CODESRIA Bulletin*, (1): 66–71.

Mboti, N. 2011. Tells us. In Mbire, M.Z., ed. *Ghetto Diary and Other Poems*. Harare, Zimbabwe: ZPH Publishers (Pvt) Ltd, 118.

Mignolo, W. 1995. *The Darker Side of the Renaissance: Literacy, Territoriality and Colonization*. Ann Arbor: Michigan University Press.

Mignolo, W. 2000. *Local Histories/Global Designs: Coloniality, Subaltern Knowledges, and Border Thinking*. Oxford: Princeton University Press.

Morag, R. 2013. *Waltzing with Bashir: Perpetrator Trauma and Cinema*. London: IBTauris.

Neal, A.G. 1998. *National Trauma and Collective Memory: Major Events in the American Century*. Armonk, NY: Sharpe.

Ndlovu-Gatsheni, S. 2013. *Coloniality of Power in Postcolonial Africa: Myths of Decolonzation*. Dakar; Council for the Development of Social Science Research in Africa. https://codesria.org/IMG/pdf/0-Coloniality_of_Power_Ndlovu_Prelim.pdf?3311/c4053b4df101ba6371f78777ee747f6e74e26679.

Nkosi, L. 2012. South Africa: Running with White people. *The Guardian*. www.theguardian.com/world/2012/oct/23/south-africa-race-run.

Quijano, A. 1991. Coloniality and modernity /rationality. *Indigenous Peru*, 13(29): 11–20.

Quijano, A. 2000. Coloniality of power and social classification. *Journal of World-Systems Research*, VI(2): 342–386.

Rijsdijk, I.M. 2007. The White man's curse: Stander and the last Sumarai. In Botha, M., ed. *Marginal Lives & Painful Pasts*. Cape Town: Genugtig!, 282–317.

Rothberg, M. 2009. *Multidirectional Memory: Remembering the Holocaust in the Age of Decolonization*. Cultural Memory in the Present Series. Stanford, CA: Stanford University Press.

Schindler's List (Spielberg). 1993. Film and production. *IMDB*. https://www.imdb.com/title/tt0108052/?ref_=fn_al_tt_1.

Scott, C. 2018. The truths/fictions/traumas of Marikana: Exploring violence and trauma in three films, the Marikana Massacre: Through the lens (2013), miners shot down (2014), and night is coming: A threnody for the victims of Marikana (2014). *Communicatio*, 44(4): 18–32.

Walker, J. 2005. *Trauma Cinema: Documenting Incest and the Holocaust*. London: University of California Press.

18
Nollywood as decoloniality

Ikechukwu Obiaya

Introduction

Decolonisation, according to Frantz Fanon, is accompanied by violence and, in fact, requires it. As he put it,

> Decolonization, which sets out to change the order of the world, is clearly an agenda for total disorder. . . . You do not disorganize a society, however primitive it may be, with such an agenda if you are not determined from the very start to smash every obstacle encountered.
>
> *(Fanon 2004, p. 2)*

One could say that Nollywood exemplifies this notion of Fanon's. However, Nollywood's upturning of the old order did not take the path of physical violence advocated by Fanon, who noted that "decolonization reeks of red-hot cannonballs and bloody knives" (Fanon 2004, p. 3). But Nollywood, nevertheless, found a way of cutting the colonial umbilical cord by disrupting the established system and attaining real independence. This agency and alternative role of Nollywood at the global scale can be understood in terms of what Ndlovu-Gatsheni (2015, p. 485) terms "decoloniality as an epistemological and political movement" of praxis and "liberatory language" which is crucial for the future for Africa. "Decoloniality speaks to the deepening and widening of decolonization movements in those spaces that experienced the slave trade, imperialism, colonialism, apartheid, neocolonialism, and underdevelopment" (ibid). Nollywood's unrivalled creative power in the global film industry is symbolic of the journey of cinema from colonialism, decolonisation to decoloniality in the Nigerian and African context.

African cinema has to a great extent been a dependent cinema, and the frustrations of colonialism that led to Fanon's incendiary words were truly present in this sector. According to Haynes (2017, p. 3), although Africa was integrated into the international circuits quite early, it "was integrated on the worst possible terms." The continent was placed solely at the receiving end – it could watch but was hindered in the production and distribution of films. "Under the colonial system, the prejudices of the colonisers made it impossible for them to imagine that an African could actually make any sort of film, let alone a feature film" (Armes 2008, p. 3). This view had a subsequent impact on postcolonial Africa since many of the newly independent countries found themselves ill-equipped for filmmaking. Andrade-Watkins (1996, p. 181) notes that the filmmaking difficulties faced by Africans "have been compounded by colonial and postcolonial traditions and policies regarding cinema." The strongest influence in African cinema has been colonialism. This is because it was through colonialism that the initial structures for filmmaking were put in place across the continent, and much of the ideological approach towards the cinema has also been a consequence of this reality.

"Filmmaking in Africa and by Africans has been rather turbulent with, above all, problems of limited funds and a poor production and distribution infrastructure" (Obiaya 2011, p. 129). This led Jean Rouch (2003, p. 47) at some point to refer to Africa as "the most backward continent in the area of film production." Writing in 1994, Ukadike bemoaned this lack of development of African cinema, attributing it to the fact that black Africans were still economically and culturally dependent in spite of having attained political independence. According to him, "This dilemma, created by a colonial past and cemented by a neo-colonial present, has prevented the emergence of a real national cinema capable of speaking for and to Africans" (Ukadike 1994, p. 1).

However, a mere 14 years after these words of Ukadike were written, Barrot (2008, p. xi) points to "9,000 films telling thousands of stories that speak to an audience of millions across the African continent" and which constitute "a social, economic and cultural phenomenon without precedent." Tomaselli (2014, p. 14) describes a film industry that was developed by "a handful of scriptwriters, film-makers and performing arts graduates who endeavoured to offer new cultural products that shrugged off the vestige of colonial influence." Nollywood developed from the grassroots on the basis of shoestring budgets (Paulson 2012), and Krings and Okome (203b, p. 1) note that it "has become the most visible form of cultural machine on the African continent." Its products are consumed both within and outside Africa, and its model of filmmaking has influenced the beginning of film production in other countries.

Nollywood came as the second phase of postcolonial filmmaking in Nigeria. The first phase, which began in the 1970s, was fraught with the same challenges as the rest of African cinema. By the late 1980s, thanks especially to the crash of the Nigerian economy, this phase of filmmaking more or less ground to a halt. The number of films produced in the ten-plus years of this phase did not exceed a hundred. But in the first ten years of its existence, Nollywood produced over 3,000 video films that were enjoyed by a wide audience. This is an indication of the creative freedom that the filmmakers of Nollywood had attained for themselves by overcoming the various filmmaking challenges – or, to use Fanon's terminology, smashing every obstacle encountered. This chapter seeks to identify and analyse three key areas in which Nollywood has caused a disruption, namely distribution, audience acceptance, and funding. This analysis will be carried out from a media economics perspective with the goal of presenting this approach as a viable one for studying this sector. The chapter concludes by making reference to how Nollywood is negotiating its position and role in the digital age, with the entry into the market of players such as Netflix.

The framework for analysis

Media economics serves to capture the impact of the various factors that have facilitated or hindered the development of African cinema. These factors are largely audience preference, funding, access to channels of distribution, and the behaviour of the market. Albarran (2002, p. 5) describes media economics as "the study of how media industries use scarce resources to produce content that is distributed among consumers in a society to satisfy various wants and needs." According to Picard (1989, p. 7), the field of study "deals with the factors influencing production of media goods and services and the allocation of those products for consumption."

An important consideration of media economics is the fact that the business practices of media industries are not carried out in a vacuum. Rather, these practices are shaped by the political system of their host country while being subject to the determining role played by market supply and demand in terms of content, mode, and targeted consumer of production. Along these lines, Picard (2002, p. 69) notes that "Governments play significant political and legal roles in creating the framework in which enterprises can operate by creating and enforcing property contract, corporate, and other rights necessary for markets to function." This function of the state has been largely absent in many African countries, and the filmmakers have had to function at the margin of state support.

Owers, Carveth, and Alexander (2004) draw attention to the important link between the media and capital. Substantial capital investment is required for the survival of any media organisation. Without capital, no viable media firm would be able to survive in a challenging economic context. Hence, information in the media sector is tied to economic means, and the media industry cannot afford to ignore economic principles (Owers et al. 2004). Hence McCall (2012) points out that Nollywood's greatest obstacle for growth is the fact that it remains within the informal economy and is hindered from capitalisation due to the absence of the required institutional mechanisms.

The industrial organisational model, a microeconomic theory, provides a framework for examining these realities. This theory offers the model of market structure-conduct-performance (SCP), which Wirth and Bloch (1995, p. 16) explain by saying that "market (or industry) performance is determined by the conduct of the firms within that market, and that firm conduct is determined by various market structure variables." Wirth and Bloch (1995, p. 16) go on to list "the number of sellers and buyers in a market" and "the degree of product differentiation present in a market" as being two of the important definers of market structure. Product differentiation is tied to the ability of firms to create a brand preference among the consumers.

It is worthwhile noting that the SCP model treats the variables of the market structure as exogenous and assumes that, in general, they remain constant. Such variables are subject to manipulation or change as a result of policy intervention (Wirth and Bloch 1995). Examples of these can be found in those structures that facilitate performance, such as regulation and training, as well as the access to funding, the lack of which, for instance, constitutes a barrier for those wishing to enter the film industry. On the other hand, the variables of conduct and performance are considered endogenous. Examples of variables for conduct and performance, respectively, include pricing as well as the investment in production facilities, and firm profitability and allocative efficiency (Wirth and Bloch 1995).

Distribution and reach

Cubitt (2005, p. 193) describes distribution as "the core process in which economic and political moments of human communication take centre stage." As the meeting ground between production and consumption, it "is the key locus of power and profit" (Garnham 1990, p. 162). Anyone that controls distribution wields a lot of power, and this is especially so in the world of film. Distribution determines what films one sees or does not see, and when and how one sees them (Lobato 2009). This is especially so when distribution is controlled by a limited group. Writing in 1993, Emmanuel Sama noted that distribution was still being controlled by "yesterday's masters who have been ruling over the same 'evening classes' virtually ever since the invention of the cinema" (Sama 1996, p. 148). And according to McCall (2012, p. 16), "Africa's auteur films could not reach their African audience commercially or culturally because they were part and parcel of a mode-of-production and mode-of-consumption that was administered from abroad, and to which few Africans had access."

In Nigeria, the control over the distribution circuits was exercised by AMPEC (the American Motion Picture Export Company [Africa]) and the Lebanese-owned companies, NDO Films and CINE Films. AMPEC was formed by Metro-Goldwyn-Mayer, Paramount Pictures, 20th Century-Fox Film Corporation, RKO Pictures Inc., Warner Bros. Inc., Universal Pictures, United Artists and Columbia Pictures. These were the same major American film production companies that made up the Motion Picture Export Association (MPEA) (Segrave 1997). Created in April 1961, AMPEC's registration under the Webb-Pomerene Export Trade Act enabled the members to form a monopoly in foreign territories, something that was not permitted under the antitrust law in the United States. According to Guback, the power of the cartel enabled it to exploit the supply of films handled by its distributor-members, with the control to determine when the supply should come on or go off (Guback 1985). AMPEC freely exercised this ability, using it to chasten exhibitors that showed films that it did not previously approve. While American and European films were controlled by AMPEC, Indian, Egyptian, and Asian films were under the control of NDO and CINE. None of these distributors carried locally made films due, most likely, to the fact that the films were not considered sufficiently profitable.

Like various other African states at the time, the Nigerian government sought to break the distribution monopoly and establish indigenous control of its cinemas. This push came through the Nigerian Enterprises Promotion Decree, which the government promulgated in 1972. The general aim was to place in the hands of Nigerians the ownership and control of companies operating in Nigeria (Inanga 1978). One of the stipulations of the decree was that the exclusive control over the distribution and exhibition of feature films should lie with Nigerians. But this effort to seize control was unsuccessful due mainly to a lack of enforcement on the part of the government. In addition, as Ukadike (1994) notes, some Nigerians colluded with foreign nationals to undermine the law by agreeing to front for the businesses while the previous ownership remained. Eventually, the government established the National Film Distribution Company (NFDC) in 1981, but this did not improve the fortunes of the filmmakers. This was because NFDC was also not much interested in taking on the distribution of locally produced films, thereby bringing the company's reason for existence into question (Balogun 1987).

With the introduction of a direct-to-DVD video filmmaking, the filmmakers established different channels for distributing their videos. According to Larkin (2004, p. 290), the industry "generated an entirely novel mode of reproduction and distribution that uses the capital, equipment, personnel, and distribution networks of pirate media." The videos were distributed through the distribution outlets for electronic goods. This was largely because the financiers of the video-films were in the main dealers in those goods. These dealers, and consequently the main hubs for video sales, were located in the key commercial nerve centres of Lagos, Aba, Onitsham and Enugu (Okome 2007) Distribution of the videos thus largely bypassed the cinema and went directly for sale to wherever buyers could be found – street stalls, video stores, video-clubs, bars and restaurants, barber shops, in the middle of traffic, etc. The videos were also easy to carry across borders in the baggage of travellers.

The structures for distribution that the filmmakers began with were largely informal. Both Lobato (2012) and Miller (2012) consider the informal networks as viable alternatives to the established formal distribution circuits. And according to McCall (2012, p. 11), "Informal markets have been the key to Nollywood's spectacular success, because they make it possible to get video movies to every remote corner of Africa." Considering the previous inaccessibility of the distribution channels, this has been a major achievement for the filmmakers. However, this informality is also a problem. While it is true that it facilitates easy movement and spread, the very informality also undermines profitability since it does not provide for adequate accountability. In the words of Lobato (2010, p. 346), the market "cannot guarantee the return of revenues to producers."

Audience acceptance

Thanks to their exclusion from the established distribution circuits, films of the first phase of African filmmaking were not accessible to the African audience. The films, in the oft cited words of Sama (1996, p. 148), were "foreigners in their own countries . . . making a bashful entry in exactly the same way as a stranger entering another land." Also, rather than entertainment, the filmmakers of the early postcolonial period considered that African filmmaking should in the first place "be an instrument of social and political transformation" (Tcheuyap 2010, p. 25). Thus, the films tended to be largely didactic and not well suited to commercial cinema. Balogun (2004, p. 176) notes that the long dependence of African film on foreign financial assistance "led to a cinematography geared to Western art houses that was not necessarily well received by African popular audiences." The reverse has been the case with the films of Nollywood, which have enjoyed wide audience acceptance. They are heavily consumed not just in Nigeria but all over Africa and beyond (Okome 2010).

An important reason for this popular appeal is the affinity that the consumers have with the films. According to Haynes (2007, p. 31), the industry's "proximity to popular imagination" is its great strength. The films are seen as presenting a mirror in which those of the audience can see themselves (Ofeimun 2004; Okoye 2007; Green-Simms 2012). The popular appeal stems largely from the fact that consumers of the films see them as portraying the realities of society. Thus, for many consumers, the films have a use-value in that they are a means of learning about the society (Esan 2008). The films acquire greater credence in the eyes of the consumers thanks to their ability to faithfully reflect the various social tensions experienced by the viewers (Obiaya 2017). This self-identification that the consumers are able to have reflects an important characteristic of the films – they stem from grassroots popular culture. For this reason, Dovey (2012) highlights the closeness that exists between the filmmaker as storyteller and the audience. The latter contributes to the telling of the story and determines its nature. Hence, Green-Simms (2012, p. 60) makes reference to the "proximity of Nollywood to everyday stories."

The proximity of Nollywood to its audience is also closely related to the commercial nature of the industry. The filmmakers place a lot of emphasis on winning over their audience by offering them entertainment. And the filmmakers, according to Evuleocha (2008, p. 408), are aware of tapping into "a lucrative and long-neglected market" by offering their consumers stories that reflect their daily lives peopled with characters that they can identify with. And in the face of criticism about the content of their films, the filmmakers have responded that they only give the people what they want. This stance is supported by Zajc (2009, p. 77) who notes that "filmmaking in Nigeria is purely commercial activity, so it is clear that the audience is another determinant of the content of video films." This is an important consideration because filmmaking for these cineastes is a business and, in order for it to be viable, the consumer must be satisfied. It is only through patronage on the part of the consumers that the Nollywood filmmakers can recoup their investments. As Haynes (2017, p. xxv) notes, "it is a popular art form whose perspective must stay close to that of its broad audience of ordinary Nigerians or risk commercial disaster."

It is perhaps here that one must cite the great power of Nollywood as a process of decoloniality. According to Ndlovu-Gatsheni (2015, p. 492), "At the core of decoloniality is the agenda of shifting the geography and biography of knowledge, bringing identity into epistemology – who generates knowledge and from where?" Nollywood, by telling the people their story, is bringing to the fore knowledge that previously did not receive any attention in the mainstream. Thus Okoye (2007, p. 28) notes that the films "invent a progressive African aesthetic which undermines the cultural imperialism of the West and underscores the possibility of formulating an African postcolonial identity."

A major consequence of this proximity to the audience is that the films are enjoyed by the most diverse audiences all over Africa (Krings 2010). The explanation for this is to be found in the similarities that those audiences have found between their cultures and the representations in the films. Speaking about the popularity of the films in Tanzania, for instance, Krings (2010, p. 76) notes that the video films "matched the social and cultural realities of everyday life in Tanzania," where, at some point, the local television was wholly given over to the Nigerian video films (Mwakalinga 2013). Dipio (2014), who writes about a Ugandan audience, points out that the details of Nigerian culture portrayed in the films is identifiable with what is found in Ugandan society. The story is no different in many other countries – even beyond Africa – as can be seen, for instance, in Cartelli (2007), Kerr (2011), Krings and Okome (2013a), Waliaula (2014).

Funding and policy

As already indicated, African cinema has largely been a dependent cinema. This has been most obvious in the area of funding as most film productions in sub-Saharan Africa prior to video filmmaking were dependent on foreign capital. This applied especially to the Francophone African countries, which have benefited a lot from French aid. In the Anglophone African countries, filmmakers have had to be more reliant on their own resources. The process of sourcing funds was quite challenging given the expensive nature of shooting in celluloid. Some funding came from the government, which sponsored about three feature films, but there was no clearly defined policy for supporting filmmaking. Thus, many of the filmmakers of this early period practically went bankrupt in the process of making their films. They had to face "the realities of a depressed economy and stringent lending conditions in financial institutions" (Owens-Ibie 1998, p. 5) financing their projects with loans that they were often unable to repay. Hence Balogun (1987) describes the early history of Nigerian filmmaking as "a painful twenty-year long ordeal."

When they came on the scene, the video film directors were also faced with the same challenge of funding as their counterparts in celluloid film production. However, they had a great advantage in that the costs of producing video films were much lower. Raising local funds, therefore, did not turn out as difficult for them. Unlike the sometimes astronomical budgets of celluloid films, the video film production budgets were rather low. When productions in video first started, the budgets ranged from ₦50,000 [about USD 479.24] to ₦100,000 [USD 958.49] (Adesanya 2000). This, of course, was accompanied by very poor quality. The relatively low cost of production has however meant that the producers are generally able to recoup their investments and earn enough to fund the next video-film. Over the years, the budgets of the films have increased, but the costs remain much lower than what is required for celluloid filmmaking.

The video films "draw on the wealth of the business class. They may be backed by big merchants from Onitsha or Aba or elsewhere" (Haynes and Okome 2000, p. 64). For instance, the first big hit of the industry, *Living in Bondage* (1992), was funded by Kenneth Nnebue, a businessman dealing in electronic goods who financed the film from the proceeds of his business.

Such businessmen did not only finance the films; they also distributed them, hence the reference to them as 'marketers'. According to Haynes and Okome (2000, p. 70), "The marketers are the best organised and most powerful element in the industry. . . . most of the video distributors started as importers of electronics and blank cassettes or pirated foreign videos. Other businessmen, in car parts or more dubious enterprises, may use video deals as a way of laundering money." As suppliers of the funds, they had a say in the productions and were often accused of being dictatorial over what storyline, actors, ideas, etc., should be used in a particular production.

Although the marketers may be criticised for what some considered their stranglehold on the industry, no one can deny that they played a fundamental role in facilitating the growth of the industry. They made it possible for the filmmakers to source local funds for production. This was essential in the light of the reluctance by the banks to get involved due to the lack of structures. The control that the marketers were accused of exercising over storylines and actors is understandable when seen in the light of their concern to protect their investment. However, in spite of such controls, this source of funding allowed the filmmakers sufficient freedom to tell the local stories unmediated by any external forces. Thus, "the Nigerian video films throw into startling relief how much the African cinema that reaches European or American shores is mediated in ways that make it comprehensible to foreign audiences" (Haynes 2000, p. 5).

But much has changed since the initial years. The marketers no longer wield such powers, and this is due to a number of reasons. In the first place, the return of the cinema and the growth in the number of outlets has led filmmakers to turn to cinema exhibitions as a preferable way for releasing their films. The weekly release of data by the Cinema Exhibitors Association of Nigeria (CEAN) on its site (www.ceanigeria.com/box-office) shows the increased spending by Nigerians at the cinema. The filmmakers' preference, thus, is tied to security given that the increased rate of piracy has often denied them of the returns from DVD sales. Also, turning to the cinema has meant a consequent need for higher-budget films to meet cinematic standards. This has in turn led to a diversification of the sources of funds since, with the greater certainty of fund recovery implied in the cinemas, other institutions and individuals have become more willing to invest in the films. Also, the returns being realised in the cinemas are a further proof that local funding can support the industry.

Additionally, the government now shows a greater willingness to support the film industry. The industry developed in Nigeria's huge informal sector without any input whatsoever from the government. The industry took off and boomed as from the early 1990s, but it was only in 2004 that it was officially acknowledged. In that year, the president's budget speech made reference to the significant foreign exchange earning capacity of the industry. In that same year, the government's policy thrust for the industry was laid out in the National Economic Empowerment and Development Strategy (NEEDS) document. The goal was "to facilitate the development of a technologically competitive, private sector – led film industry in Nigeria that will create employment, wealth, and net foreign exchange earnings" (Nigerian National Planning Commission 2004). None of this, however, truly materialised into firm structures for the industry. The government, in various moments, subsequently announced that it was granting some funds to the industry (Xinhua News Agency 2006; Aminu 2006), but no long term impact was achieved.

Conclusion

Thussu (2007) highlights the reality in today's world of a contra-flow of media pointing out that the flow of media is no longer "one way from the media-rich North . . . to the media-poor

South." Rather, new transnational networks are emerging from the periphery. Nollywood, in creating one of such networks, has proven successful in changing the narrative first for Nigeria and then for Africa at large. Going by the SCP model, it is clear that some important ingredients for that success have been various aspects of the market structure. The two important definers of market structure as identified by Wirth and Bloch (1995) are the number of sellers and buyers in the market and the degree of product differentiation. From the number of films being produced, it is clear that Nollywood has a high number of sellers (filmmakers). This is largely due to the democratisation of the filmmaking process permitted by the video technology. With lower costs and easy-to-use equipment, the entry bar for going into filmmaking was lowered, and this led to a greater number of people going into film production.

The danger of such high numbers lies in the possibility of an oversaturation of the market. In this case, however, this danger was mitigated because the high number of sellers was matched by a high number of buyers. Haynes (2017) identifies Nigeria's "enormous internal market" as one of the essential reasons for the growth of Nollywood. With a population estimated at about 200 million, Nollywood had a very large potential audience to tap into. And, as Evuleocha (2008) has noted, this market had been a long neglected one in the sense that they had not previously been provided with stories and characters that they could relate with. The roaring success of the early video films made the audience preference clear to the filmmakers, and this led to the heavy handedness of the marketers who wanted to maintain the winning formula. This, of course, has had its negative side as it has led to a lot of repetition, especially of themes and storyline.

The success of any brand depends a lot on the ability of the brand owners to make it stand out from the noise of other brands. The importance of product differentiation for Nollywood is obvious. The products were different in terms of style and content, and the audience was won over precisely by the elements of that difference. Granted, that very difference has earned the industry a lot of flak, but it has also earned them droves of committed fans. By recognising the thirst of the audience and being able to satisfy it, the filmmakers have created a brand preference among the consumers of their product.

The gaps or absences in the market structure have moulded the conduct of the filmmakers. The quick fix approach that characterises the industry is a response to the many challenges thrown at them by the gaps in market structure. Filmmaking was trimmed down to its bare bones because there was a lack of big funds; people learnt on the job to make up for the lack of formal training; homes and hotels were converted into sets to make up for the absence of sound stages; pirate measures were permitted as a means of promoting distribution; etc. But what stood out, above all, was the sheer grit of the filmmakers. This has enabled them to find solutions to the challenges they faced. The conduct of the filmmakers has had a tremendous impact on the performance of the market, and this can be measured in terms of their achievement – the establishment of a globally recognised industry built on the basis of shoe string budgets and which tells their stories as they want them told.

Looking to the future, there is the question about how Nollywood will survive in the digital era. There are questions about the extent to and ways in which Nollywood ought to be inserted in the global content streaming services. In addition to the resurgence of the cinema, Nollywood's avenues for distribution have been enhanced by increased possibilities for streaming its content. The South African–owned cable television, MultiChoice, has long promoted Nollywood content through a series of dedicated channels labelled Africa Magic. (It has in this way contributed positively to extending the reach of Nollywood across Africa.) iROKOtv, an online VOD company founded by Jason Njoku, has also been in operation since 2010. However, with the entry of Netflix and CanalPlus, there appears to be a growing interest from players beyond the African continent. Netflix tentatively entered the Nigerian market in 2016 (Eboigbe 2020), but it was only as from 2019 that it began purchasing and commissioning Nollywood content. CanalPlus, on the other hand, acquired the production studio of iROKOtv, ROK, in 2019 in what was seen as a move to gain a foothold on the continent (Richford 2019). According to Brown (2019), this "growing interest in Africa reflects a growing market, as more people go online and earn enough disposable income to subscribe." The entry of these global bodies into the Nigerian market has been welcomed by the filmmakers given the increased possibilities of funding and a wider distribution.

However, doubts have been raised as to whether the entry of these global companies is, in the long run, wholly beneficial to Nollywood. Eboigbe (2020), in talking about the Netflix entry for instance, seems to imply that this could undermine decoloniality. She points to the "temptation of developing stories that they think Americans will like but Africans will find difficult to connect with." This echoes the accusation of cultural imperialism that was hurled at Netflix with reference to its role in Canada (Joseph 2019). The entry of well-funded players into the Nollywood space will certainly result in increased capital and more audiences, but at what cost? Crucially, is it a new threat or opportunity to Nollywood's agency and creativity on the global scale? Further research is required to examine whether and how Netflix as well as pay television channels such as iROKOtv and Africa Magic are reshaping Nollywood.

References

Adesanya, A. 2000. From film to video. In Haynes, J., ed. *Nigerian Video Films*. Athens: Ohio University Centre for International Studies, 37–50.

Albarran, A.B. 2002. *Media Economics: Understanding Markets, Industries and Concepts*. Ames: Iowa State Press.

Aminu, A.B. 2006. Censors board focuses on Naija in the movies. *Weekly Trust*, 13 November.

Andrade-Watkins, C. 1996. Portuguese African cinema: Historical and contemporary perspectives, 1969 to 1993. In Bakari, I. and Cham, M.B., eds. *African Experiences of Cinema*. London: BFI Pub, 132–147.

Armes, R. 2008. *Dictionary of African Filmmakers*. Bloomington: Indiana University Press.

Balogun, F. 1987. *The Cinema in Nigeria*. Enugu: Delta Publications.

Balogun, F. 2004. Booming videoeconomy: The case of Nigeria. In Pfaff, F., ed. *Focus on African Films*. Bloomington: Indiana Universtiy Press, 172–181.

Barrot, P., ed. 2008. *Nollywood: The Video Phenomenon in Nigeria*. Oxford, Ibadan, Bloomington and Indianapolis: James Currey, HEBN Publishers, Indiana University Press.

Brown, R.L. 2019. Whose stories get streamed? Netflix tells more Africans: Yours. *The Christian Science Monitor*, March 5. www.csmonitor.com/World/Africa/2019/0305/Whose-stories-get-streamed-Netflix-tells-more-Africans-yours.

Cartelli, P. 2007. Nollywood comes to the Carribean. *Film International*, 28: 112–114.

Cubitt, S. 2005. Distribution and media flows. *Cultural Politics*, 1(2): 193–214.

Dipio, D. 2014. Audience pleasure and Nollywood popularity in Uganda: An assessment. *Journal of African Cinemas*, 6(1): 85–108.

Dovey, L. 2012. Storytelling in contemporary African fiction film and video. In Khatib, L., ed. *Storytelling in World Cinemas*. London: Wallflower Press, vol. I, 89–103.

Eboigbe, A. 2020. Nollywood and Netflix: Why the honeymoon may not last. *PM News*, March 1. www.pmnewsnigeria.com/2020/03/01/nollywood-and-netflix-why-the-honeymoon-may-not-last/.

Esan, O. 2008. Appreciating Nollywood: Audiences and Nigerian 'films'. *Particip@tions*, 5(1), May. www.participations.org/Volume%205/Issue%201%20-%20special/5_01_esan.htm (Accessed 9 June 2009).

Evuleocha, S. 2008. Nollywood and the home video revolution: Implications for maketing videofilm. *International Journal of Emerging Markets*, 3(4): 407–417.

Fanon, F. 2004. *The Wretched of the Earth*, trans. Philcox, R. New York: Groove Press.

Garnham, N. 1990. *Capitalism and Communication*, ed. Inglis, F. London, Newbury Park and Delhi: Sage.

Green-Simms, L. 2012. Hustlers, home-wreckers and homoeroticism: Nollywood's beautiful faces. *Journal of African Cinemas*, 4(1): 59–79.

Guback, T. 1985. American films and the African market. *Critical Arts*, 3(3): 1–14.

Haynes, J., ed. 2000. *Nigerian Video Films*. Athens: Ohio University Centre for International Studies.

Haynes, J. 2007. Nnebue: The anatomy of power. *Film International*, 30–40.

Haynes, J. 2017. *Nollywood: The Creation of Nigerian Film Genres*. Ibadan: Bookcraft.

Haynes, J. and Okome, O. 2000. Evolving popular media: Nigerian video films. In Haynes, J., ed. *Nigerian Video Films*. Ohio: Ohio University Centre for International Studies, 51–88.

Inanga, E.L. 1978. The first 'indigenisation decree' and the dividend policy of Nigerian quoted companies. *The Journal of Modern African Studies*, 16(2): 319–328.

Joseph, D. 2019. Platforms for people not profit: Digital platforms boast that they've "democratized" cultural production. But what would truly democratic platforms look like in Canada? *Briarpatch*, December. https://briarpatchmagazine.com/articles/view/platforms-for-people-not-profit.

Kerr, D. 2011. The reception of Nigerian video drama in a multicultural female community in Botswana. *Journal of African Cinemas*, 3(1): 65–79. DOI:10.1386/jac.3.1.65_1.

Krings, M. 2010. Nollywood goes East: The localization of Nigerian video films in Tanzania. In Şaul, M. and Austen, R.A., eds. *Viewing African Cinema in the Twenty-First Century*. Athens: Ohio University Press, 74–91.

Krings, M. and Okome, O. 2013a. *Global Nollywood: The Transnational Dimensions of an African Video Film Industry*. Bloomington: Indiana University Press.

Krings, M. and Okome, O. 2013b. Nollywood and its diaspora: An introduction. In Krings, M. and Okome, O., eds. *Global Nollywood: The Transnational Dimensions of an African Video Film Industry*. Bloomington: Indiana University Press, 1–22.

Larkin, B. 2004. Degraded images, distorted sounds: Nigerian video and the infrastructure of piracy. *Public Culture*, 16: 289–314.

Lobato, R. 2009. *Subcinema: Mapping Informal Film Distribution*. Unpublished doctoral thesis, School of Culture and Communication, The University of Melbourne, Melbourne.

Lobato, R. 2010. Creative industries and informal economies. *International Journal of Cultural Studies*, 13(4): 337–354.

Lobato, R. 2012. *Shadow Economies of Cinema: Mapping Informal Film Distribution*. London: Palgrave Macmillan.

McCall, J.C. 2012. The capital gap: Nollywood and the limits of informal trade. *Journal of African Cinemas*, 4(1): 9–23.

Miller, J. 2012. Global nollywood: The Nigerian movie industry and alternative global networks in production and distribution. *Global Media and Communication*, 8(2): 117–133.

Mwakalinga, M. 2013. The political economy of cinema (video film) in Tanzania. *African Review*, 40(1): 203–217.

Ndlovu-Gatsheni, S.J. 2015. Decoloniality as the future of Africa. *History Compass*, 13(10): 485–496.

Nigerian National Planning Commission. 2004. *Meeting Everyone's Needs: National Economic Empowerment and Development Strategy*. Abuja: Nigerian National Planning Commission.

Obiaya, I. 2011. A break with the past: The Nigerian video-film industry in the context of colonial filmmaking. *Film History*, 23(2): 129–146.

Obiaya, I. 2017. Nollywood, female audience and the negotiating of pleasure. In Hole, K., Jelaca, D., Kaplan, A.E. and Petro, P., eds. *The Routledge Companion to Cinema and Gender*. London: Routledge, 342–351.

Ofeimun, O. 2004. In defence of the films we have made. *West Africa Review*, 5.

Okome, O. 2007. Nollywood: Spectatorship, Audience and the Sites of Consumption. *Postcolonial Text*, November. http://journals.sfu.ca/pocol/index.php/pct/article/view/763/425.

Okoye, C. 2007. Looking at ourselves in our mirror: Agency, counter-discourse, and the Nigerian video film. *Film International*, 28: 20–29.

Okome, O. 2010. Nollywood and Its critics. In M. Saul and Austen, R.A., eds. *Viewing African Cinema in the Twenty-First Century*. Athens: Ohio University Press, 26–41.

Owens-Ibie, N. 1998. *How Video Films Developed in Nigeria*. World Association for Christian Communication. www.wacc.org.uk/wacc/publications/media_development/archive/1998_1/how_video_films_developed_in_nigeria (Accessed 28 April 2008).

Owers, J., Carveth, R. and Alexander, A. 2004. An introduction to media economics theory and practice. In Alexander, A., Owers, J., Carveth, R., Hollifield, A.C. and Greco, A.N., eds. *Media Economics: Theory and Practice*. Mahwah and London: Lawrence Erlbaum Associates, 3–47.

Paulson, C. 2012. Marketers and pirates, businessmen and villains: The blurred lines of nollywood distribution networks. *St Antony's International Review*, 7(2): 51–68. www.jstor.org/stable/26228582 (Accessed 21 February 2020).

Picard, R.G. 1989. *Media Economics: Concepts and Issues*. Newbury Park, London and New Delhi: Sage.

Picard, R.G. 2002. *The Economics and Financing of Media Companies*. New York: Fordham University Press.

Richford, R. 2019. Vivendi's canalplus acquires leading Nigerian studio ROK. *The Hollywood Reporter*, July 15. www.hollywoodreporter.com/news/vivendis-canalplus-acquires-leading-nollywood-studio-rok-1224283.

Rouch, J. 2003. Situation and tendencies of the cinema in Africa. In Rouch, J., ed. *Cine-Ethnography*. Minneapolis: University of Minnesota Press.

Sama, E. 1996. African films are foreigners in their own country. In Bakari, I. and Cham, M.B., eds. *African Experiences of Cinema*. London: BFI Pub, 148–156, 2nd Quarter.

Segrave, K. 1997. *American Films Abroad: Hollywood's Domination of the World's Movie Screens*. Jefferson, NC: McFarland & Company Inc.

Tcheuyap, A. 2010. Comedy of power, power of comedy: Strategic transformations in African cinemas. *Journal of African Cultural Studies*, 22(1), 25–40.

Thussu, D.K. 2007. Introduction. In Thussu, D.K., ed. *Media on the Move: Global Flow and Contra-Flow*. Oxon: Routledge, 1–7.

Tomaselli, K. 2014. Nollywood production, distribution and reception. *Journal of African Cinemas*, 6(1): 11–19. DOI:10.1386/jac.6.1.11_1.

Ukadike, N.F. 1994. *Black African Cinema*. Berkeley: University of California Press.

Waliaula, S. 2014. Active audiences of nollywood video-films: An experience with a Bukusu audience community in Chwele market of Western Kenya. *Journal of African Cinema*, 6(1): 71–83. DOI:10.1386/jac.6.1.71_1.

Wirth, M.O. and Bloch, H. 1995. Industrial organisation theory and media industry analysis. *The Journal of Media Economics*, 8(2): 15–26.

Xinhua News Agency. 2006. Nigerian sets up film fund to promote film industry. *Xinhua News Agency*, 12 July.

Zajc, M. 2009. Nigerian video film cultures. *Anthropological Notebooks*, 15(1): 65–85.

19
Afrokology as a transdisciplinary approach to media and communication studies

viola c. milton and Winston Mano

> Education in Africa and for Africans continues to be like a pilgrimage to the Kilimanjaro of metropolitan intellectual ideals, but also to the tortuous route to Calvary for alternative ways of life.
>
> (Nyamnjoh 2012, 37)

The study of media and communications in the global South is limited by uncritical overreliance on theories and methodologies from the global North and, as Nyamnjoh observes above, a struggle to find viable alternatives. In the African context, the problem is exacerbated by the stubborn resilience of coloniality and its concomitant ignorance of contributions from within Africa and the global South in general. This has arguably created gaps in critical conversations needed to deepen and complicate insights in the discipline. The necessary corrective, we argue, is a transdisciplinary approach that centers and takes seriously African "schools of thought" and how these relate to our alternative understanding of media and communications from an African perspective. In the African context, research in media and communication tends to highlight philosophical and empirical differences related to key concepts that connect to African lived experiences, including for example, participation, justice and transformation which remain important for Africa (cf. Frassinelli 2019; milton 2019; Sesanti 2019; Mutsvairo 2018; Mutsvairo and Karam 2018; Mabweazara 2015; 2018; Chasi and Rodny-Gumede 2016; Mano, and Meribe 2017; wa Thiong'o 2009, 2016; Ngomba 2012; Skjerdal 2012; Obonyo 2011; Mano 2010; Banda 2009; Ansu-Kyeremeh 2005; Nyamnjoh 2005; 2011; Kasoma 1996; Karikari 1996). We draw on these insights as well as the contributions to the current volume to center Afrokology as a *transdisciplinary* heuristic toolkit that can anchor self-standing African media and communication which resonates with conditions on the continent. This chapter, therefore, considers the necessary philosophical principles or values as well as methodologies integral to Afrokology as a transdisciplinary heuristic toolkit. As argued in Chapter 1, an African-centered approach is related but different from Asante's (1980) Afrocentrism and more informed by Afrokology and decoloniality:

> It should be possible, however, in what concerns Africa, to have an Africa-centred approach to knowledge production that is driven neither by Eurocentrism nor Afrocentrism, but

> instead invites scholars, in their critical consciousness, to use whatever concepts and research tools they deem most appropriate in studying Africa and the rest of the world. . . . Context, after all, does matter.
>
> (Nyamnjoh 2020, 29)

For this reason, the starting point remains African concerns and epistemologies.

Afrokology, we have argued in Mano and milton, (2021, also Chapter 2 in this volume), is an attempt to re-imagine media and communication studies and to reunite its practice and theory with philosophical roots in Africa. We argue that Afrokology can awaken relational accountability that promotes respectful representation, reciprocity and rights of both the researcher and the researched. Afrokology is presented in this chapter as an innovative heuristic and analytical toolkit that could enhance the academic positioning of media and communication debates and one which is important for connecting critiques of existing and past theories, policies and practices. It is a way of seeing, knowing and doing media and communication that is facilitative. In this sense, Afrokology could be the basis for a deliberate push for more effective epistemological inclusivity. As pointed out in Chapter 2, Afrokology recognises other sources of knowledge as important but puts a premium on relevance and dialogue between and among them. It arrives at this by for example recognising knowledge previously ignored under colonialism which considered it to be

> too savage and primitive to share a table with European colonial enlightenment and often misrepresented in the postcolonial era by ill-adapted curricula, epistemologies, and theories, and by many an academic and scholar whose intellectual clocks are set to the rhythm of transatlantic scholarly cannons, practices, and standards of value in knowledge production and consumption.
>
> (Nyamnjoh 2019, 3)

In doing so, we wish to move away from the idea that knowledge from the global South – particularly Africa – can serve primarily an instrumental function (i.e. mainly as a feature in case studies on disease, violent conflict, aid and development). In the words of Comaroff and Comaroff (2012, 114):

> These other worlds . . . are treated less as sources of refined knowledge than as reservoirs of raw fact: of the minutiae from which Euromodernity might fashion its testable theories and transcendent truths. Just as it has long capitalized on non-Western "raw materials" by ostensibly adding value and refinement to them. In some measure, this continues to be the case.

What is clear from the above is systematic sidelining of knowledge from Africa and other previously colonised contexts in the global South. In Chapters 1 and 2, we mounted a summative critique of the Euro-American bias of media and communication theory and practice. In this final chapter, we will now set out the challenges to be met in constructing an unequivocal decolonised African media and communication studies. This is certainly not the first effort towards decolonising media and communication studies. Yet, as has been argued throughout this volume, despite its laudable ethical origins, which sought to foster cross-cultural and intercultural solidarity, international communication and its concomitant 'de-Westernning' communication studies's efforts to bring everyone and everything into the fray, are, ironically, still largely failing to recognise the perspectives from the global South. First, by their sustained push for internationalisation, scholars in this tradition tend to neglect or misunderstand problems and inequalities that do not have their roots in the unhelpful demarcations andse categories of for example. In the context of education for example, internationalisation has thus far meant large numbers of students from the global South studying in the global North without concomitant internationalisation of philosophical contributions from the global South. Satellite academic institutions from the global North have been set up in the global South to project and engender Northern academic ideas and models. As such, the categories and concepts espoused by internationalisation, such as Thussu's (2009) "counterflows" and/or "contraflows", themselves become inflated in their reach, sometimes even reinforcing the ethnic essentialisms that internationalisation and/or de-Westernisation in fact intend to deconstruct. This can be seen for example in the ways that Netflix engages with African film and soap operas which has involved "sanitising" African production templates for global audiences in a manner that undermines African input and underplays connections to African lived realities. Presenting this as "counterflows", in our view, inflates the contributions from African approaches to storytelling. Merely setting a story in Africa does not constitute a meaningful disruption of the cultural imperialism enforced under colonialism. As is argued by Ndlela (2013, 59) such a "franchising approach, into the sub-Saharan thus can be conceived as one of a variety of internationalisation strategies of media conglomerates" which perpetuates media and cultural imperialism. Netflix, for example, has a huge demand for new shows and has actually provided opportunity for a wider range of voices, but questions should be asked about mediated counterflows, global/local dynamics and audiovisual diversity in relation to its in-house productions. At stake in raising these questions is whether concepts associated with internationalisation, de-Westernisation or even decoloniality have dissolved into mere buzzwords, i.e. free-floating signifiers, devoid of meaning and content. We argue that Afrokology, through its transdisciplinary focus and radical reconnection with relevant African philosophical constructs, can help add more meaning to concepts such as internationalisation, de-Westernisation or even decoloniality.

Afrokology recognises that there is a need for media and communication studies to redress the marginalisation and misrecognition of African scholarship and lived experiences. Moreover, it notes that media and communication as well as related individual disciplines such as history, anthropology, sociology, literature, philosophy and geography are incapable of addressing emerging contemporary problems on their own. In particular, "addressing emerging contemporary problems involves decisions on values that require civic participation and the building of social legitimacy for proposed transition pathways to sustainable societies" (Popa et al. 2015, 45). Afrokology's radicalism thus rejects established agendas and accustomed ways of representation and seeing. First, Afrokology challenges the supposed universal validity of Western definitions of media and communication through what Mignolo and Walsh (2018) calls "re-existence". This is understood to mean the "redefining and re-signifying of life in conditions of dignity" (location 185 of 7946 Kindle). It does so through making visible the underexplored relationship between lived experiences in the global South and global North. Re-existence, therefore, strongly implies that the global South ought to be understood within "its historical antecedents, the historical legacy of colonialisms, and the ensuing period of decolonization" (Shome 2019, 198). Afrokology thus problematises the ways in which the world is known, challenging the unacknowledged and unexamined assumptions at the heart of Western disciplines that are insensitive to the meanings, values and practices of other cultures. We have stated from the onset that recognising the importance of African insight and knowledge in thinking about media and communication in no way constitutes a value judgement concerning the superiority of such knowledge compared to existing media and communication frameworks/approaches. On the contrary, views from Africa open up the field and offer new ways of thinking about issues that tend to be overlooked or conceptualised differently in dominant academic circles. In addition to the foregoing, Afrokology goes beyond interdisciplinarity – which entails a coordination of disciplines in a common cause – arguing instead for a transdisciplinary approach. This requires a mindful repositioning of media and communication theory and practice within, across and beyond disciplines.

This approach, we argue, is best suited towards the goal of re-existence as it encourages collaboration that transcends disciplines and their usual ways of working together in interdisciplinary teams to transform problems in media and communication. Disciplines, according to Nyamnjoh (2017), tend to encourage introversion and emphasise the exclusionary fundamentalism of the heartland rather than the inclusionary overtures of the borderland. As we will show, although some of the content of Africa's media and communication studies is similar to that in the global North, and particularly in the rest of the global South, it is perceived and made sense of differently. Afrokology can, in this sense, address the representational deficiency that is evident in how dominant scholarship in media and communication studies situates itself vis-à-vis the margins. One could argue in this respect that the rhetoric of "diversity" has failed at its job of creating a community and environment that is conscious of the needs and experiences of marginalised academic communities. The chapters in this volume argue for new frames of understanding within media and communication that are better informed by the experiences of Africans within the context of global South, using our marginality as a vantage point. The collective focus constitutes an effort towards recovering the lost historical and contemporary voices of the marginalised, the oppressed and the dominated, through a radical reconstruction of knowledge production. As such, the approach contests the notion of a single path to understanding history and the production of knowledge, arguing instead for the acknowledgement of a diversity of perspectives and priorities. Nyamnjoh rightly suggest that such an approach entails "conviviality in knowledge production [that goes beyond] just seeking conversations and collaboration across disciplines in the conventional sense but also, and even more importantly, the integration of sidestepped popular epistemologies informed by popular universes and ideas of reality" (ibid, 269). It should manifest in new levels of collaboration that unlocks new insights, methods and theories beyond narrow prescriptions of individual academic disciplines, including media and communication.

Thus, we argue that transdisciplinarity is particularly apropos to Afrokology, as the transdisciplinary approach to curriculum integration dissolves the boundaries between conventional disciplines and organises teaching and learning around the construction of meaning in the context of real-world problems or themes (UNESCO International Bureau of Education n.d.). Transdisciplinarity goes further than interdisciplinarity. Whereas interdisciplinary approaches seek to generate "an understanding of themes and ideas that cut across disciplines and of the connections between different disciplines and their relationship to the real world," transdisciplinary approaches embrace what Nyamnjoh (2012, 148) refers to as epistemological interconnectedness and conviviality. Unlike interdisciplinary approaches, transdisciplinary approaches do not merely combine contents, theories, methodologies and perspectives from two or more disciplines, instead, they are

> characterized by integration and overriding of subject boundaries. As a "scientific utopia", it stands out as an intellectual category requiring a wide range of disciplinary, scientific, and epistemological potential. It is different from the multi- and interdisciplinary approach in a way that, on one hand, it transcends the subject boundaries, and, on the other, it is not part of any specific subject research. Thus, the transdisciplinary approach allows for the

understanding of the complexities of the modern world which is a primary feature of its scientific legitimacy.

(Todorova n.d., https://files.eric.ed.gov/fulltext/ED567177.pdf)

In essence then, the attractiveness of a transdisciplinary approach is enabling inputs and scoping across scientific and non-scientific stakeholder communities and facilitating a systemic way of addressing a challenge. Creating transdisciplinary objectives is not an easy task. It needs to include multiple disciplines with a human centered goal or global issue. All these pieces need to connect for the objective to make sense. Thinking the global in terms of many worlds and many worldviews is not just about taking a critical stand against mainstream theories, it is to assume a politically emancipatory position that includes processes of knowing and also defending other possible ways of being in the world (Smith 2005). This entails that African researchers need to move from the margins and participate in the production and articulation of mainstream ideas, from the vantage point of their ontological positions. As is stated by Querajazu (2016, 5),

> The world each being inhabits is populated by entities (persons, objects, theories, practices) that are ontologically configured in processes of choosing and decisions that produce the establishment of reference frameworks that people use to situate themselves in the world. Accordingly, these reference frameworks are very different to a person in the Amazon than to a person raised in a Western city, those frameworks are historically contingent, not natural, neutral or universal.

In this respect, Afrokology as social and theoretical perspective, encourages methodological approaches that embraces the African experience together with an understanding that knowledge produced "must be liberating" (cf. Mazama 2003). At issue is the fact that African ways of knowing and existence must be at the center of approaches to research and practice so that the implementation of principles, methods, concepts and ideas from African cultural experiences shape our understandings of communication theory and practice. The emancipatory approach is intrinsic to Afrokology. It builds on the call by Mignolo (2009) and other academic activists throughout Latin America for scholars to embrace a pluriverse of Southern values, perspectives and societies to understand the coexisting epistemologies and practices of the different worlds and problems we inhabit and encounter. Yet, as Querajazu (2016) notes, in the pluriverse, although those many worlds exist on their own, they are interrelated. Conway and Singh (2011, 701) add that:

> Notions of the pluriverse imply multiple ontologies, multiple worlds to be known – not simply multiple perspectives on one world. Universalist discourses and globalist projects are grounded in a unitary ontology and imperialist epistemologies which assume that the world is one, that it is knowable on a global scale within single modes of thought and is thus manageable and governable in those terms.

It is precisely in these interrelations and intersections that we can find our answers, at least some of them, to the question of ontological difference. Afrokology moves from the viewpoint that the work that we do must contribute to unlocking marginalised ontological and epistemological nuances that can help inform being African in the world. Its transdisciplinary goal is thus geared towards relexicalising our own world to fundamentally disrupt conventional hierarchies of knowledge production, including *who* decides on the questions to ask, *how to ask* them and *how to theorise* the world. In this sense, Afrokology aligns with transdisciplinarity in creating new knowledge that can contribute to societal progress through incorporating both scientific knowledge and societal perspectives (Schramm et al. 2012).

Transdisciplinarity is an approach for research on the complex real-world problems our societies are facing. In their book, Schramm et al. (2012) illustrate how transdisciplinarity contributes to societal and scientific progress through integrating perceptions of problems and knowledge from scientific disciplines and societal practice. Through this process, new knowledge emerges. As has been noted, the mainstream scientific methodologies are often poorly equipped to deal with emerging contemporary problems, hence, "both scientists and policy makers have called for re-conceptualizing the role of experts, practitioners and citizens in the production and use of scientific knowledge" (Popa et al. 2015, 45). Afrokology thus favors approaches that bring researchers from different fields together with society stakeholders to develop solutions valued by the stakeholders. Afrokology as a transdisciplinary toolkit, we argue, have potential to engage with real-world problems and to overcome some of the barriers to implementing change and transformation in African contexts. Transdisciplinarity in this sense presents a fundamental shift in terms of how we perceive disciplines. The prefix 'trans' in transdisciplinarity can be understood to indicate that "which is at the same time across disciplines, and inside different disciplines, and beyond all disciplines" (Niculescu 2014, 19). Transdisciplinarity's goal is therefore "the understanding of the present world, one of its imperatives is the unity of knowledge" (ibid). Crucially, transdisciplinarity goes beyond the mere application of theories, concepts or methods across disciplines with the intent of developing an overarching synthesis (Lattuca 2001). Instead, it focuses on dissolving disciplinary boundaries by focusing on questions that see disciplines as irrelevant. While interdisciplinarity explicitly *critiques* the disciplines, transdisciplinarity *de-emphasises* disciplines (ibid, our emphasis).

Afrokology as a heuristic transdisciplinary toolkit, we argue, can coalesce disciplines' theories and methods into novel approaches that engage with African lived realities. Media and communication currently exist within universities that are not as convivial in practice as one would expect (Nyamnjoh 2017, 269). On the one hand, universities have degenerated into markets producing subjects/disciplines to meet demands that the market can accommodate. On the other hand, "The scarcity of conviviality in universities and among the disciplines and scholars suggests, and rightly so, that the production, positioning and consumption of knowledge are far from a neutral, objective and disinterested process" (ibid). One could argue that the real problem herein is the idea of the disciplines themselves as isolated and predetermined categories. For Nabudere (2006, 25) "The real question for African scholars is whether it is possible and rewarding to adopt such a 'tired' methodology to the innovative and revolutionary work of the African regeneration in research about our societies?" Nyamnjoh (2020, 16) adds that an investment in answering these questions would help address the admission that disciplines might wish to achieve universal knowledge, but often fails to do so. In a rapidly changing Africa, one should question whether dividing universities by academic departments across disciplinary lines creates barriers rather than benefits. There is urgent need to disrupt the neat disciplinary boundaries and the in-built biases it engenders. We argue here that there is a need to transcend the barriers of disciplines, which, in our view, stifles collaboration and misrecognises "the deep power of collective imagination and the importance of interconnections and nuanced complexities" (Nyamnjoh 2017, 267). In other words, the epistemological and methodological approaches based on disciplinary knowledge must be undermined in order to make media and communication more effective (Nabudere 2006, 2). "A 21st century debate of Africa and the Disciplines should do more than target those with power in the academy in the North – non-Africanists and Africanists alike – by focusing on similar dynamics within the African continent" (Nyamnjoh 2020, 16). The need for convivial scholarship in African contexts was recognised by postcolonial scholars and departments in African universities for whom saw cross-disciplinarity and interdisciplinarity provided a gateway for more context specific media and communication programmes.

The efforts towards multidisciplinary and interdisciplinary teaching is perhaps best illustrated by how some English Departments in postcolonial African universities have attempted to transform by incorporating areas such as film, theatre, cultural and media studies. In the 1960s for example, Ngũgĩ wa Thiong'o and Kimani Gecau, amongst others, established community theatre in the context of decolonisation and social change in the English Department at the University of Nairobi. At the University of Zimbabwe (UZ) there has similarly been a deliberate push to rethink and center the teaching of English within African democratic aspirations and social change, following a multidisciplinary approach. The department recognised that, under colonialism, English departments served to confine teaching and learning to the traditions of England, in ways that benefitted England more than it did the students and researchers in these programmes (Department of English and Media Studies, n.d.). Thus, after independence in 1980, the department repositioned itself towards Zimbabwe and Africa, rather than England. Amongst others, in the 1980s and 1990s the Department of English adamantly centered African literature as part of a radical comparative approach to world literatures. The approach foregrounded intersectional social change focussing on the politics of race, gender and class. In 1993, the Department of English at UZ introduced a postgraduate diploma in Media and Communication Studies as part of their curriculum. Multidisciplinary curriculum changes intensified between the 1990s and early 2000s, with attempts at introducing Africa-facing syllabi for both media and communication studies and English literature. Departmental changes during this phase included a new MA programme in Communication and Media Studies which prioritised original research on Zimbabwe and the broader African context. Amongst other areas, there was a strong focus on theatre, music, orature, indigeneity, African languages and African history as key components in media and communication studies. The teaching pioneered innovative arrangements involving a wide range of local, regional and international guest speakers. In addition, the department organised internships and work placement programmes within and outside media, state and civil society organisations in Zimbabwe and regionally. Insisting on a multidisciplinary approach, lecturers teaching on the postgraduate media and communication programme were recruited from amongst others law, sociology, political science, education and English, and were both local and international. The students were similarly recruited from a wide range of disciplines.

In addition to this strong national and regional focus, a mutually beneficial partnership between the UZ Department of English and the Department of Media and Communication at Oslo helped deepen and widen the teaching and learning for researchers and students at both universities. On the one hand, the University of Zimbabwe benefited from collaborative research and teaching which opened the windows on international approaches to media studies and helped to consolidate an international profile for Zimbabwean researchers. On the other hand, staff and students from the University of Oslo equally benefited from studying alongside Zimbabweans as they gained unique insights into African epistemologies which informed their scholarly engagements with African media and journalism. UZ's approach to teaching and learning can be seen as a frontrunner for Afrokology of Media and Communication especially in terms of how its research and teaching deepened and broadened the African focus. Meanwhile in neighbouring South Africa, the Centre for Communication, Media and Society (CCMS) at the University of KwaZulu-Natal (UKZN) similarly pursued an interdisciplinary approach focused on social justice issues. From its inception in 1985, the CCMS, modelled after the Birmingham Cultural Studies Centre, mobilised lecturers and students around issues of domination and resistance (Tomaselli, Mboti and Ronning 2013, 37). The graduate programme was focussed on research that would serve the anti-apartheid struggle, enable interdisciplinarity; and work with civil society and oppositional movements. The CCMS's interdisciplinary approach was borne from the anti-apartheid struggle and infomed by a social justice ethos (ibid). In this sense, the CCMS is a frontrunner of the transdisciplinary approach we outline here. Yet, we argue that the approach did not go far enough as it did not, unfortunately, relixicalise the field in a way that centers African knowledges.

By way of explanation, it can be noted that two approaches, outlined in the Table 19.1, guided postcolonial teaching at African universities committed to changing the locus of power

However, we argue that for epistemological transformation to happen, *trans*disciplinarity is needed. This would mean a move from narrowly focused interdisciplinarity, to an embrace of multiple understandings of disciplinary combinations informing work in media and communication. The transdisciplinary research process entails co-production or systematic integration of knowledge from various scientific and societal bodies of knowledge (Table 19.2).

From Table 19.2, it can be ascertained that transdisciplinarity engenders a new culture based on convergence between disciplines that generates new knowledge, methods and approaches. In our view, the aforementioned examples of disciplinary interventions from Zimbabwe and South Africa speaks to multi- and interdisciplinary innovation which points to inadequacy or incompleteness of disciplinary specific knowledge. These institutional changes were notable initiatives

Table 19.1 Characteristics of multidisciplinary, interdisciplinary and transdisciplinary research

	Participants/ Discipline	Problem Definition	Research Style	Presentation of Findings
Multidisciplinary	Two or more disciplines	Same question but different paradigm *or* different but related questions	"Parallel play" by individuals	*Separate* publications by participants from each discipline
Interdisciplinary	Two or more distinct academic fields	Described/defined in language of at least two fields, using *multiple models* or intersecting models	Drawn from more than one, with *multiple* data sources and varying analysis of same data	*Shared* publications, with language intelligible to all involved fields

Source: Aboelela et al. (2007, p. 340).

Table 19.2 Characteristics of multidisciplinary, interdisciplinary, and transdisciplinary research

Transdisciplinary	Two or more distinct academic fields	Stated in *new* language or *theory* that is broader than any one discipline	Fully *synthesized* methods, may result in new field	*Shared* publications, probably using at least some new language developed for *translation* across traditional lines

Source: Aboelela et al. (2007, p. 340).

to integrate disciplinary perspectives in ways that attempted to plug gaps or incompleteness in existing disciplinary knowledge. The point is that the transformations in the postcolonial education institutions saw individuals with different and diverging interests, philosophies, methodological backgrounds and epistemological systems, and thus potential grounds for conflict, rally around a shared objective. This exemplifies convivial scholarship.

The examples from UZ and CCMS show that potentially transformative research depends on the quest for new knowledge and the existence of a significant shared problem to which participants can contribute in salient ways. It also depends on human and material foundations within disciplines, collaborative mutualism across disciplines, and a transformative learning process that enables knowledge integration across diverse perspectives. We argue that the multidisciplinary initiatives of Departments of English and the interdisciplinary work by the Centre for Communication, Media and Society was a productive and transformative turn that enriched the disciplines. A move towards transdisciplinarity can build on these initiatives and result in a new intimacy with other disciplines that could richly address the current incompleteness in the purely disciplinary approaches of the past. For Nyamnjoh (2020) and Harrison (2016), theorisation inspired by experiences in and of the global South, are instructive in this regard as it amplifies agency and resilience, disavows notions of intellectual inferiority and affirms constructive creativity. The in-built collaboration that such creativity and agency inspire acknowledges incompleteness in knowledge-creation and draws on new cross-fertilisation among disciplinary academic collaborators that could lead to the production of new knowledge. Escalating the disciplinary connections to a transdisciplinary level using Afokology as a heuristic tool can augment African media and communication.

To test the usefulness of the above hypothesis, we proceed by operationalising the concept through outlining the key characteristics that in our view, underpin Afrokology as a transdisciplinary heuristic toolkit for African media and communication studies. In Table 19.3, we operationalise and illustrate Afrokology as a transdisciplinary heuristic toolkit that informs a new relational ontological, axiological and epistemological approach.

Thus, it can be inferred that an Afrokological transdisciplinary approach can help overcome the current intellectual poverty and narrowness of academic disciplines. It implies acknowledging differences between current intellectual traditions in media and communication in terms of their relevance, relational and comparative aspects. The challenge here is to wrest theory from lived realities and feelings in order to connect human responses and feelings to dominant systems of meaning and social action. In other words, Afrokology as a transdisciplinary heuristic toolkit argues for knowledge and experience from all contexts to be respected and valued in their own terms. African knowledge producers are already increasingly aware of this need to be cognisant of the predicaments of those they research, teach and publish. The key, as Nyamnjoh (2020, 15) argues, is not to be bound by disciplines or geography, but to understand that doing justice to the lived realities "requires . . . working in teams, within institutions and in local and global networks of cooperation, as well as with stakeholders beyond the ivory tower". As such, an Afrokological transdisciplinary toolkit values informal knowledge and therefore considers formal education and research to be but one actor in a connected and open teaching, learning and research environment. In this sense, it challenges the supposed universal validity of established theories and concepts while providing alternatives to dominant frameworks and approaches. In Nabudere's (2006, 25) words, "Scholars must be ideologically transformed to see through the conceptual and theoretical frameworks they use and to create different meanings that can sometimes be, not only linguistically translatable, but even epistemologically consistent with the new concepts found within the traditions themselves".

Table 19.3 Afrokology as a transdisciplinary approach to media and communication

		Ontology	Axiology	Epistemology		Research Design	
Reason for doing research	Philosophical underpinnings	Assumptions about the nature of reality	Place of values in the research process	Nature of knowledge	What counts as truth	Methodology	Techniques of gathering data
To undo the misrepresentation and historical marginalisation of African worldviews, thought, knowledge and aesthetics and to relexicalise their own world.	An emancipatory approach, informed by oppositional consciousness which places emphasis on a transdisciplinary approach that encourages amongst others the inclusion of scientific and non-scientific stakeholders.	Ostensibly universal concepts are viewed from multiple perspectives to engage with diverse socially constructed realities that impact on social justice. Emphasis is on pluriversality rather than universality	Enfolding research with praxis is important for empowerment of marginalised/ silenced communities to challenge their oppression.	Knowledge is political and relational. It can amplify human freedom and promote social justice.	That which contributes to unlocking marginalised ontological and epistemological nuances that can help inform being African in the world. It is therefore informed by the set of multiple relations that one has with the pluriverse.	Methodology of the oppressed which is not driven by a particular method but rather by questions that emerge from larger social context. Relational and comparative approaches may provide answers to problems previously outside the scope of the field.	A commitment to public engagement and collaboration as a mode of intellectual production. Researchers construct emic-etic participatory methodological techniques that also engage with lived experience.

To this end, and in order to understand the world, Afrokology draws on critical theory, postcolonial theory, decoloniality, indigenous knowledge, social justice and human rights as frameworks that can assist in decolonising the mind (wa Thiong'o 2009). Researchers adopting an Afrokological stance prioritise the value of furthering social justice and human rights. An understanding that research should be influential in bringing about social change is key. Developing oppositional consciousness rests on researchers being ethically, intellectually and curiosity-wise attuned to the lived realities and feelings of the researched. Afrokology as a transdisciplinary heuristic toolkit foregrounds relational accountability that promotes respectful representation, reciprocity, and rights of the researched. The real-world goal, in this sense, becomes the most important aspect of research. This demands respect for knowledge and experience from all contexts in their own terms. It does not privilege one method or philosophical tradition, but rather different traditions are deployed in a reflexive manner to examine changing contexts. Here, it is useful to turn to transformative learning theory that suggests that "new, integrated conceptual understanding is initiated by disorienting dilemmas" (Pennington et al. 2013, 564). Disorienting dilemmas refer to a trigger that potentially challenges one's taken for granted assumptions, as the initial catalyst for transformative learning.

Transformative learning is a key aspect of the Afrokological toolkit and is the process "by which we transform our taken-for-granted frames of reference (meaning perspectives, habits of mind, mind-sets) to make them more inclusive, discriminating, open, emotionally capable of change, and reflective so that they may generate beliefs and opinions that will prove more true or justified to guide action" (Mezirow 2000, 8). Engaging with others whose life experiences have been significantly different from the lifeworlds of researchers is becoming an increasingly important pre-requisite for impactful research. This calls for "convivial scholarship" that acknowledges incompleteness in existing disciplinary knowledge, and therefore champions integrating and perhaps even overriding disciplinary boundaries in favour of research informed by and catering to social action as a prerequisite for effective praxis. Epistemological interconnectedness and conviviality may lead to insights otherwise not accessible. Under Afrokology, collaborative work across disciplines and with societal actors within a creative transdisciplinary context can profoundly alter the prior research and perspectives of all involved. In addition, these efforts can produce new transdisciplinary connections that can certainly be transformative for how we approach media and communication.

Methodologically, it is argued that innovative linkages of theory and practice fostering mutually beneficial relationships between researchers and the communities they study, can initiate transformative learning. It places a premium on reflexivity on the assumptions and values that underlie the understanding of lived experiences by scientists, practitioners, policy makers and citizens. Researchers therefore employ methods and techniques that are fit to transdisciplinarity, taking into account the contemporary changes and developments in human knowledge. Several authors in this volume pointed to the asymmetrie in how knowledge is valued in both scientific and non-scientific spaces. Empirical evidence has been provided to illustrate how knowledge from the global South has been silenced and misrecognised. This misrecognition has resulted in a situation that fosters a global North–imported, formulaic approach to the research and praxis of media and communication. Yet, standardised evidence and theoretical approaches, when juxtaposed with the current pulsating realities on the ground, have rendered such templates of narrowly defined global North approaches irrelevant (cf. Mano and milton 2020; milton and Mano 2020).

The African setting has cases which show that media models from the global North cannot easily be translated in specific contexts owing to political, cultural and economic differences. A simplistic example of this would be the adoption of a license fee model for public service broadcasting funding in countries such as South Africa and Zimbabwe (Mano and milton 2020). International models of PSB posit that this funding model allows public broadcasters to invest in programming or operational improvements, because they can be confident about their revenue for the term of the license agreement. This, however, is not the experience in these two countries. South Africa and Zimbabwe's particular socio-cultural and economic contexts have made it difficult for any systematic collection of License Fee Revenue as evidenced from annual reports for their respective public broadcasters (ibid). Although compulsory for all broadcasting gadget owners, licence fees in South Africa bring less than a third of the revenue, with close to two thirds coming from advertising and other commercial sources (milton 2018). In addition, in Zimbabwe, it has proved uneconomic to send licence fee inspectors to collect over sparse geographic areas as it is often more expensive to do so (Mano 2016). Since colonial days audiences have also developed a culture of withholding payment of television license fees as a sign of protest against what was widely considered to be colonial institutions. These examples, while simplistic, are demonstrative of the need to develop models and theories in tandem with the lived realities in African contexts. It demonstrates, amongst others, how our theorisation about media, culture and communication does not stay in the theoretical dimension but has enormous consequences for the ways we enact reality and in the creation of socio-political arrangements that end up affecting our daily lives. Writing about the value of excellence theory and activism in the mining industry in South Africa for example, Greeff (2015, 235) concludes that

> organisational communication practitioners would need to be more interpretative in their communicative efforts, as the modernist and mechanistic normativity of the excellence theory hinders appropriate corollaries to organisational activism situations. It is within these interpretative, contextually and situationally driven understandings that organisational communicators will charter and sustain the 'pragmatic value' in democracy.

It can also be noted that power relations in Africa impact media and communication production, representation and consumption in ways that have favored vested interests at the expense of ordinary people. Duncan (2013) asks in this respect why journalists in a 'free press' end up being aligned, often unwittingly, with authority? She concludes that sociology of news perspectives holds limited explanatory value as "they ascribe particular journalistic choices to organisational and institutional dynamics only, to the exclusion of broader power-dynamics outside newsrooms". Duncan (ibid, n.pag.) argues that the South African journalism space does not adequately cater for forms of journalism that expose how power actually works in society:

> Political economy concerns itself broadly with the relationship between the structures of control in capitalist society and the production of wealth needed to reproduce that society, including the power relations in the production and consumption of media. . . . There is no evidence to suggest that South Africa's press owners brought pressure to bear directly on their newsrooms to prevent workers' voices from coming to the fore in the early press reporting of Marikana, as the mining houses do not own significant stakes in the press. Rather, what was in operation was a set of journalistic rituals that have become all too familiar in commodified newsrooms, and ones that do little to give voice, much less agency, to the most powerless in society. In South Africa, unfortunately, these rituals will do little to confront the most serious national challenge of the post-apartheid period, namely to prevent the descent, once again, into a police state.

The foregoing scenarios demonstrate the critical need for research and teaching praxis to include approaches that meet people where they live and thrive. Media and communication studies as such has not only marginalised difference by ignoring other epistemologies, but by neglecting other ontologies, particularly those that belong to indigenous peoples, it relegates them to the realm of myths, legends and beliefs. This constitutes a damaging epistemological position where Africans and others in the global South are silenced or at most incorporated as add-ons. In fact, Elabor-Idemudia (2002) reminds us that the social sciences [and humanities] are founded on the culture, history and philosophies of Euro-Western thought and are either antagonistic to the history and cultures of non-Western societies or have no strategy to give voice to their cultures (Smith 1999, 2005). Consider for example how the communication models in Africa have had to include popular culture, rumours, pavement radio, street theatre. In his work on popular music as journalism in Zimbabwe, Mano (2007, 61) argues that

> Where mass media are weak, and opposition political parties are frail, music can serve as the voice of the voiceless by offering subtle avenues of expression. Popular music can perform the journalistic function of communicating daily issues in ways that challenge the powerful and give a voice to the disadvantaged. Popular music competes and rivals mainstream journalism in the ways it addresses political, social and economic realities in repressive contexts.

This innovative understanding of the nuances of power relations in African cultural contexts gives voice to the culture of the oppressed. Crucially, Mano's argument centers not only on what the songs say, as lyrics are not the only characteristic of songs, but more importantly on how these are interpreted and textured into particular political and economic contexts (75). This is what Sandoval refers to as "coalitional consciousness". Sandoval (2000) argues that a mixture in the appropriation of ideas, knowledge, and theories is necessary as it reflects the reality of surviving as a minority or Other, which entails using every and any aspect of dominant power. Mixing, she argues, is the methodology of survival for the oppressed. Drawing on South African consciousness, Chasi and Rodny-Gumede (2016, 2) refer to this coalitional consciousness/mixing as "legitimating the 'smashing and grabbing' of usable and valuable insights from anywhere while viably calling for the construction and elaboration of conceptual schema that are locally relevant". In *Borders, Media Crossings and the Politics of Translation: The gaze from Southern Africa* (2019), Pier Paolo Frassinelli challenges the reader to take the outside in. Drawing on cultural theory, decoloniality and lived experiences within the South African context, he pushes the boundaries of borders, and our perceptions thereof in politics, in life and also in our discipline. This is reminiscent of Nyamnjoh's argument that [in Africa] we have this capacity for presence and simultaneous multiplicities because when you take others in and you are able to take yourself out, you would be out x number of things you take in and create more impact. Frassinelli (2019) argues for a transdisciplinary approach to media and communication, where the idea of convergence is utilised to revisit the concepts of the border and translation to explore possibilities for constituting and imagining forms of collectivity grounded on difference and forged in struggle against bordering regimes, devices and institutions. This for him is useful for rethinking disciplinary divisions in the humanities and move beyond what has been called the two humanities: "literature, history, and philosophy on one side and communication and media studies on the other" (ibid). We agree with Frassinelli's argument that this task begins with dealing with a plurality of forms, genres and traditions of written, oral, aural, visual and multimodal expression, as well as with their social life and significance. Through our transdisciplinary emphasis we also advocate co-production and synergies beyond disciplinary focus. For us, what is needed is a methodological and theoretical orientation that speak to current social, political and cultural conflicts and dislocations and in so doing, engenders alternative ways of seeing and experiencing media and communication as well as sociocultural experiences across multiple platforms.

What should be evident by now, is that an Afrokology of media and communication studies arises from an understanding that communication is about real people and their interactions with each other and their environments and as such, they ought to matter very much in the research and teaching of our discipline. But the roots of ontological marginalisation are so deep that they are present not only in the theory of media and communication but also impact practice. We have provided examples above which illustrate how the recycling of Western cannons can influence individual and institutional practitioners whose work, from language to formats, fails to adequately connect with contemporary Africanity. Here, Afrokology argues that Afro sensing and a consideration of the context of people become critical in taking forward the study and practice of communication today. Chilisa (2012, 191) highlights seven cardinal African virtues, including truth, justice, rightness, propriety, harmony, reciprocity and order and balance. These virtues, in her opinion, underpin what Reviere (2006) unpacks as the five canons of Afrocentric research enquiry, i.e. *Ukweli* [truth], *Kujitolea* [commitment], *Utulivu* [calmness and peaceful], *Uhaki* [justice] and *Ujamaa* [community]. However, these so-called virtues or canons do not necessarily translate easily from country to country across Africa.

Chasi's chapter in this volume for example takes issue with the notion of Africans as inherently harmonious, noting that this perception has led to a reading of *ubuntu* by many Bantu-language speaking Africans who live in sub-Saharan Africa that emphasises "community, calmness and harmony" without taking into account the inevitability of violence in human reactions. Chasi therefore offers an alternative reading that recognises violence as an integral element in the lived experiences of Africans and from a strategic communication perspective illustrates ways in which the "warrior ubuntu" actor exists as an agent to advance African development and democracy. Chasi's intention is not to refute the idea that Africans value harmony but rather to present an African-facing rereading thereof. His account of *ubuntu* illustrates that, in as much as one cannot apply models and theories from the global North wholesale, one should also be cautious in assuming the mobility of African ideas and values within the continent. Mboti (2015, 144) similarly cautions that African persons are "complex, expressive *doing* beings whose actions are never easily reducible to the limiting duality of 'individual freedom' versus 'interdependent freedom'". Writing about the perception that *ubuntu* necessarily translates to "harmony", he asks "What is it about trying to force Africans to fit, at every turn, these neat conceptual cages?" Mboti (ibid) then argues that

> There is no justification to limiting the categories one can posit nor to the memberships one can hold in these groups. It is not expressly clear, anyway, why one needs to clarify the problem through categories at all. We should be prepared to admit that there may even be other different kinds of ethical relations that may not be necessarily or roughly generalized under the catch-all category of ubuntu. . . . It occurs to me that the question of collisions, and, of course, the other questions that follow from it, would need to be adequately and sufficiently answered first before one assumes what an African morality or African ethics is.

Mboti's provocative argument emphasises the need for a media and communication studies approach that broadens, rather than flattens the scope and breadth of research, coursework and praxis. For this reason, the approach we wish to advance is generative rather than prescriptive. We should broaden the scope of our own literature reviews for example to those literatures and forms of expression that have not yet found their way into the global communities of knowledge and practice. milton (2019) paraphrases Homi Bhabha to argue that scholars of communication need to become familiar with the performative narratives of Africa's diverse contexts as reference points for their pedagogical and philosophical narratives. This will allow an entry-point for Mboti's call to desist limiting our sense-making of African lived experiences, as citizens' particular performances of identity both draw on and disrupt the reference points established in established national and so-called universal pedagogical narratives (cf milton 2019, Bhabha 1994). This then, is one way in which to disrupt the universe and practice the pluriverse. Another is through for example assembling different methods with which we make sense of reality and produce it in different manifestations (Law 2004). This undoubtedly helps make sense and contextualise many of the actions and reactions of different actors in the world. Identity, citizenship, spirituality, culture, power, concepts which are of ordinary use in the communication lexicon, could be analysed and understood in a radically different way just by first accepting the existence of other worlds and their entities, and then by trying to see what these concepts look like or refer to from distinct ontologies.

An example of the above is Africans' engagement with the digital which has been shaped by local and global supervening social necessities. Africans have undoubtedly led the way in developing technologies and services that have been adopted across the world. Africans without adequate internet technology and banking have been innovative in establishing for example M-Pesa, a leading mobile money service, with millions of active customers and thousands of active agents operating across seven African countries. Similarly, and equally exemplary, is Ushahidi, which started as an ad-hoc group of Kenyan bloggers developing a code in a couple of days from various locations in order to try to figure out a way to gather and manage information about the 2008 post-election violence in Kenya. Today, Ushahidi is a nonprofit, open-source software company that develops a web platform that makes it easy for people in any part of the world to disseminate and collect information about a crisis. The innovation allows users to submit reports by text message, email, or web postings, and the software aggregates and organises the data into a map and timeline. Its mission is to build and use technology to help marginalised people raise their voice, and those who serve them to listen and respond better – both crucial aspects of African digital innovations. The African digital innovations have developed in spite of disruption, marginalisation and government sanctioned chaos to become rare success stories in global contraflows. So for example, at the time of writing this, Ushahidi is now the primary incident reporting and situational software for the United Nations Department of Field Services (Ushahidi 2018, n.pag). In addition, the platform has been used in several countries and in different projects, in Africa and elsewhere – from monitoring sexual harassment in Egypt to responding to diverse needs during the Haiti earthquake in 2012. Many innovative African digital startups demonstrate a unique coming together of social, economic and technological thinking – in other words, they already embody aspects of a transdisciplinary turn in knowledge creation. These examples of African conditionalities illustrate the necessity for theoretical explication of the conditions and social relations in which they are produced. As a heuristic tool, Afrokology can inform building new theoretical lenses from Africa that can explicate the immersion of marginalised voices in communication – especially the evolving digital space. This should be done not only to document African experiences, but also as a way to illustrate Africa's role in mothering solutions fit for global citizenship.

Conclusion

Afrokology, in the ultimate, anchors agency to an African-centered approach to media and communication. It is about acknowledging the power of Africans to determine and contribute original transformative thinking in the field, through decoloniality and lived experiences, in ways that are relevant to their context. Afrokology, we have argued in this chapter, is a transdisciplinary heuristic tool, i.e. a way of doing media and communication that is more responsive to the pressing issues of our time. It is not a method per se, but rather a mode of producing knowledge that speaks to content, practice and theory, from specific and historical African realities. As substantiated in Mano and milton (2021), operationalised Afrokology can be the necessary resource for overcoming intellectual stasis in the discipline as it is inclusive of varied African-facing perspectives that inform media and communication. Afrokology as a heuristic tool will require research methods that are developed and adapted to its own specific ontology and epistemology. Having done the aforementioned in this chapter, we argue that identifying, describing and ordering these methods should be the next critical step in operationalising an Afrokology of media and communication. Afrokology allows researchers to redefine their concepts, data, methods, and tools with reference to the emerging requirements from a new context that integrates and synthesises knowledge systems across disciplines and philosophical underpinnings. The chapter has articulated and provided the basis of a transdisciplinary approach that can underpin Afrokology of media and communication. It goes beyond a multidisciplinary and interdisciplinary focus to coalesce disciplines, theories and methodologies together with relevant non-scientific experiences and proficiency. Afrokology therefore encourages critical reflection, relational accountability and epistemological interconnectedness with collaborators. Such reflexivity, we believe, can lead to radical new conceptualisations through which collaborators can revise their mental models and which would allow for the broadening of the conceptual and technical foundations of media and communication. Convivial scholarship, in this sense, is potentially transformative and may provide answers to problems previously outside the scope of the discipline. In other words, the departure from the disciplinary comfort zones enables innovative thinking, which could lead to a radically new vision and innovation for media and communication. The chapter and the book therefore privileges Afrokology as a convivial approach that is inclusive, innovative and transformative.

Afrokology draws from decoloniality as a transformative move. Decolonising research is therefore part of its effort towards "thinking, creating, and acting with the goal of creating a different world" (Maldonado-Torres 2016, 28). In this regard, milton (2019, 33) notes that

> The work we do, the discourses we engage in and the curricula we develop need to take cognisance of, and focus their attention on, problems that are more public and pressing in terms of their relevance to address important social issues. They need to do so without using the tools of the very systems and paradigms that arguably are implicated in creating the problems in the first place. . . . Moreover, we need to examine how power is exercised in and through the very institutions, cultural relations and practices of the systems of which we are critical.

At issue is a need to avoid tools that only cater for narrow parameters of change, which tend to lock us into the very systems of power we are attempting to get out of (Lorde 1984). This is related to Nyamnjoh's (2020, 30) questioning of how and when to deploy disciplinary approaches:

> When and for whom is discipline and conformity needed, desirable, liberating, productive, rational, and an instrument of power and privilege? When and for whom is discipline and conformity needless, undesirable, repressive, unproductive, punishing, irrational, and an instrument of control and delegitimation?

These questions are expressions of the need to develop theory reflective of the freedom, emancipation and development interests of Africans. An express interest is to address the ongoing legacies of colonialism and apartheid. We have shown throughout this volume that there is promise that one or more new conceptual and methodological formulations for communication and media studies are in the works. Given the global marginalisation of our scholars and of our scholarship, it is worth discussing how best these and other new directions should be curated for greater local and global impact.

We have offered Afrokology as a transdisciplinary heuristic toolkit which holds promise for challenging the boundaries of our disciplines and in fact challenge how the humanities are framed. As argued by Pohl (2011, 618) transdisciplinarity involves "a comprehensive, multi-perspective, common-good oriented and useful approach to a socially relevant issue. It is research that does not just try to understand the world, but also aspires to help changing it". As a transdisciplinary heuristic tool, Afrokology would thus have to account for the ever-changing and developing nature of its objects of study, thus in the process redefining both itself and that which it studies. It inevitably involves cross-fertilising various other "disciplined" ideas and influences and is therefore, we submit, deliberately impure, contingent and dynamic. Based on our explication of Afrokology in Mano and milton (2021) and our unpacking of the concept as transdisciplinary toolkit in this concluding chapter, we suggest possible building blocks for an Afrokology of media and communication (1) developing a common vocabulary informed by African history and lived experience for collaborators who need to share information; (2) engaging with epistemologies of knowledge based on African lived experiences and exploring their global implications (Nabudere 2006); (3) establishing a "methodology of the oppressed", including especially speaking to, against and through power and taking seriously oppositional consciousness in postcolonial Africa and the African diaspora cf. Mano and miton (2021, p. 36); (4) developing an ethics of relational accountability that promotes respectful representation, reciprocity, and rights of the researched; and (5) relexicalising the field, including for example reinterpretation of the work of major Euro-American theorists in relation to the insights of those African experiences that insist on international solidarity and resistance to racism, gender and class bias (cf. Chapter 1).

In the final analysis, Afrokology of media and communication will need to go beyond (discipline-based) scientific questions to widen its scope and scale for tackling emerging challenges. The chapter and the volume have so far demonstrated that, while disciplines have been good at providing essential knowledge, methods and tools, they lack capability to handle more complex challenges that demand cross-disciplinary collaboration. For this reason, Afrokology embraces convivial scholarship and epistemological conviviality which allows Africans, "in all their nimble-footedness" to engage with and be engaged by "mobile" disciplines (Nyamnjoh 2020). This we believe, can weigh in on media and communication studies in ways that transcend a mere fixation with superficial indicators of representation and accommodation (cf Nyamnjoh 2020). It is part of what we see as a necessary step in overcoming the discipline's complicitness in historic absences which amongst others has precluded engagement with epistemologies of knowledge based on African lived experiences and their global implications. It is but a vital start of a convivial dialogue which can inform differential consciousness, derived from African self-understanding and the alliance-building strategies it demands for media and communication.

References

Aboelela, S.W., Larson, E., Bakken, S., Carrasquillo, O., Formicola, A., Haas, G.J. and Gebbi, K.M. 2007. Defining interdisciplinary research: Conclusions from a critical review of the literature. *Health Services Research*, 42(1): 329–346, Part 1.

Ansu-Kyeremeh, K. 2005. *Indigenous Communication in Africa: Concept, Applications, and Prospects.* Accra: Ghana Universities Press.

Asante, K.M. 1980. *Afrocentricity, the Theory of Social Change.* Buffalo, NY: Amulefi Pub.

Banda, F. 2009. Kasoma Afriethics: A reappraisal. *The International Communication Gazette,* 71(4): 227–242.

Bhabha, H.K. 1994 [2004]. Dissemination: Time narrative and the margins of the modern nation. In Bhabha, H. K., ed. *The Location of Culture.* London: Routledge, 199–244.

Chasi, C. and Rodny-Gumede, Y. 2016. Smash-and-grab, truth and dare. . . *The International Communication Gazette,* 78(7): 694–700.

Chilisa, B. 2012. *Indigenous Research Methodologies.* Thousand Oaks: Sage.

Comaroff, J. and Comaroff, J.L. 2012. Theory from the South: Or, how Euro-America is evolving toward Africa. *Anthropological Forum,* 22(2): 113–131.

Conway, J. and Singh, J. 2011. Radical democracy in global perspective: Notes from the pluriverse. *Third World Quarterly,* 32(4): 689–706.

Department of English and Media Studies. n.d. *Background.* University of Zimbabwe. www.uz.ac.zw/index.php/about-the-department-english.

Duncan, J. 2013. South African journalism and the Marikana massacre: A case study of an editorial failure. *The Political Economy of Communication,* 1(2). www.polecom.org/index.php/polecom/article/view/22/198.

Elabor-Idemudia, P. 2002. Participatory research: A tool in the production of knowledge in development discourse. In Saunders, K., ed. *Feminist Post-Development Thought.* London: Zed Books, 227–242.

Frassinelli, P. 2019. *Borders, Media Crossings and the Politics of Translation: The Gaze from Southern Africa.* London: Routledge.

Greeff, W.J. 2015. The proof is in the pudding: (Re)considering the excellence of activism in the South African mining industry. *Communicatio: South African Journal for Communication Theory and Research,* 41(2): 220–237.

Harrison, F.V. 2016. Theorizing in ex-centric sites. *Anthropological Theory,* 16(2–3): 160–176.

Karikari, K., ed. 1996. *Ethics in Journalism: Case Studies of Practice in West Africa.* Accra: Panos Institute and Ghana Universities Press.

Kasoma, F.P. 1996. The foundations of African ethics (Afriethics) and the professional practice of journalism: The case of society-centered media morality. *Africa Media Review,* 10(3): 93–116.

Lattuca, L. 2001. *Creating Interdisciplinarity: Interdisciplinary Research and Teaching Among College and University Faculty.* Nashville, TN: Vanderbilt University Press.

Law, J. 2004. *After Method: Mess in Social Science Research.* New York: Routledge.

Lorde, A. 1984 [2007]. The master's tools will never dismantle the master's house. In Lorde, A., ed. *Sister Outsider: Essays and Speeches.* Berkeley: Crossing Press, 110–114.

Mabweazara, H. 2015. Mainstreaming African digital cultures, practices and emerging forms of citizen engagement. *African Journalism Studies,* 36(4): 1–11.

Mabweazara, H., ed. 2018. *Newsmaking Cultures in Africa: Normative Trends in the Dynamics of Socio-Political and Economic Struggles.* London: Palgrave Macmillan.

Maldonado-Torres, N. 2016. *Outline of Ten Theses on Coloniality and Decoloniality,* 1–37. https://fondation-frantzfanon.com/wp-content/uploads/2018/10/maldonado-torres_outline_of_ten_theses-10.23.16.pdf.

Mano, W. 2007. Popular music as journalism in Zimbabwe. *Journalism Studies,* 8(1): 61–78.

Mano, W. 2010. Communication: An African perspective. In Allan, S., ed. *Rethinking Communication: Keywords in Communication Research.* Cresskill, NJ: Hampton Press.

Mano, W. 2016. The state and public broadcasting: Continuity and change in Zimbabwe. In Flew, T., Iosifides, P. and Steemers, J., eds. *Global Media and National Policies: The Return of the State.* London Springer, 190–205.

Mano, W. and Meribe, N. 2017. African communication modes. *The International Encyclopedia of Intercultural Communication* Wiley, 1–10.

Mano, W. and milton, v.c. 2020. Civil society coalitions as pathways to PSB reform in Southern Africa. *Interactions,* 11(2).

Mano W. and milton v.c. (2021). *Routledge Handbook of African Media and Communication Studies*. London and New York: Routledge. pp. 19–42.

Mazama, A. 2003. *The Afrocentric Paradigm*. Trenton: Africa World Press, Inc.

Mboti, N. 2015. May the real Ubuntu please stand up? *Journal of Media Ethics*, 30(2): 125–147.

Mezirow, J. 2000. Learning to think like an adult: Core concepts of transformation theory. In Mezirow, J., ed. *Associates, Learning as Transformation: Critical Perspectives on a Theory in Progress*. San Francisco: Jossey-Bass, 3–34.

Mignolo, W.D. 2009. Epistemic disobedience, independent thought and decolonial freedom. *Theory, Culture & Society*, 26(7–8): 159–181.

Mignolo, W.D. and Walsh, C.E. 2018. *On Decoloniality: Concepts. Analytics. Praxis*. Durham: Duke University Press. www.amazon.co.uk/kindlestore.

milton, v.c. 2018. South Africa: Funding the South African broadcasting corporation. In Herzog, C., Heiko, H., Novy, L. and Torun, O., eds. *Transparency and Funding of Public Service Media – Die deutsche Debatte im internationalen Kontext*. Wiesbaden: Springer VS, 181–202.

milton, v.c. 2019. Kind of blue: Can communication research matter? *Critical Arts*, 33(3): 30–45.

milton, v.c. and Mano, W. 2020. South Africa: Beyond democratic deficit in public service broadcasting (PSB). In Thussu, D.K. and Nordenstreng, K., eds. *BRICS Media: Reshaping the Global Communication Order?* London: Routledge.

Mutsvairo, B., ed. 2018. *The Palgrave Handbook of Media and Communication Research in Africa*. Cham, Switzerland: Palgrave Macmillan.

Mutsvairo, B. and Karam, B.S., eds. 2018. *Perspectives on Political Communication in Africa*. Cham, Switzerland: Palgrave Macmillan.

Nabudere, D.W. 2006. Towards an Afrokology of knowledge production and African regeneration. *International Journal of African Renaissance Studies*, 1(1): 7–32. DOI:10.1080/18186870608529704.

Ndlela, M.N. 2013. Television across boundaries: Localisation of big brother Africa. *Critical Studies in Television: The International Journal of Television*, 8(2): 57–72.

Ngomba, T. 2012. Circumnavigating de-Westernisation: Theoretical reflexivities in researching political communication in Africa. *Communicatio: South African Journal for Communication Theory and Research*, 36(2): 164–180.

Niculescu, B. 2014. Multidisciplinarity, interdisciplinarity, indisciplinarity, and transdisciplinarity: Similarities and difference, RCC perspectives no. 2. *Minding the Gap: Working Across Disciplines in Environmental Studies*, 19–26.

Nyamnjoh, F. 2005. *Africa's Media: Democracy and the Politics of Belonging*. London, New York and Pretoria: Zed Books and UNISA Press.

Nyamnjoh, F. 2011. De-Westernizing media theory to make room for African experience. In Wasserman, H., ed. *Popular Media, Democracy and Development in Africa*. London: Routledge, 19–31.

Nyamnjoh, F.B. 2012. 'Potted plants in greenhouses': A critical reflection on the resilience of colonial education in Africa. *Journal of Asian and African Studies*, 47(2): 129–154.

Nyamnjoh, F.B. 2017. Incompleteness: Frontier Africa and the currency of conviviality. *Journal of Asian and African Studies*, 52(3): 253–270.

Nyamnjoh, F.B. 2019. ICTs as Juju: African inspiration for understanding the compositeness of being human through digital technologies. *Journal of African Media Studies*, 11(3): 279–291.

Nyamnjoh, F.B. 2020. *Decolonising the Academy: A Case for Convial scholarship*. Basel: Basler Afrika Bibliographien (Namibia Resource Centre & Southern Africa), ISBN 9783906927251.

Obonyo, L. 2011. Towards a theory of communication for Africa: The challenges of emerging democracies. *Communicatio*, 37(1): 1–20.

Pohl, C. 2011. What is progress in transdisciplinary research? *Futures*, 43(6): 618–626.

Popa, F., Guillermin, M. and Dedeurwaerdere, T. 2015. A pragmatist approach to transdisciplinarity in sustainability research: From complex systems theory to reflexive science. *Futures*, 65: 45–56.

Pennington, D.D., Simpson, G.L., McConnell, M.S., Fair, J.M. and Baker, R.J. 2013. Transdisciplinary research, transformative learning, and transformative science. *BioScience*, 63(7): 564–573.

Querajazu, A. 2016. Encountering the pluriverse: Looking for alternatives in other worlds. *Revista Brasileira de Política Internacional*, 59(2): e007. www.scielo.br/pdf/rbpi/v59n2/1983-3121-rbpi-59-02-e007.pdf.

Reviere, R. 2006. The Canons of Afrocentric Research. In Asante, M.K. and Karenga, M., eds. *Handbook of Black Studies*. Thousand Oaks: Sage, 261–274.

Sandoval, C. 2000. *Methodology of the Oppressed*. Minnesota: University of Minnesota Press. www.amazon.co.uk/kindlestore.

Schramm, E., Bergmann, M., Jan, T., Knobloch, T., Krohn, W. and Pohl, C. 2012. *Methods for Transdisciplinary Research: A Primer for Practice*. Frankfurt: Campus Verlag.

Sesanti, S. 2019. Decolonized and Afrocentric education: For centering African women in remembering, re-membering, and the African renaissance. *Journal of Black Studies*, 50(5): 431–449.

Shome, R. 2019. Thinking culture and cultural studies – from/of the global South. *Communication and Critical/Cultural Studies*, 16(3): 196–218.

Skjerdal, T.S. 2012. The three alternative journalisms of Africa. *International Communication Gazette*, 74(7): 636–654.

Smith, L.T. 1999. *Decolonizing Methodologies: Research and Indigenous Peoples*. London: Zed Books.

Smith, L.T. 2005. On tricky ground: Researching the native in the age of uncertainty. In Denzin, N.K. and Lincoln, Y.S., eds. *The Sage Handbook of Qualitative Research*. London: Sage, 85–107.

Thussu, D.K., ed. 2009. *Internationalizing Media Studies*. London: Routledge.

Todorova, P. n.d. *The Contemporary Transdisciplinary Approach as a Methodology to Aid Students of Humanities and Social Sciences*. https://files.eric.ed.gov/fulltext/ED567177.pdf.

Tomaselli, K., Mboti, N. and Ronning, H. 2013. South – North perspectives: The development of cultural and media studies in Southern Africa. *Media, Culture & Society*, 35(1): 36–43. DOI:10.1177/0163443712464556.

UNESCO International Bureau of Education. n.d. *Transdisciplinary Approach*. www.ibe.unesco.org/en/glossary-curriculum-terminology/t/transdisciplinary-approach.

Ushahidi. 2018. *10 Years of Innovation: 10 Years of Global Impact. This Is Ushahidi*. www.ushahidi.com/uploads/case-studies/ImpactReport_2018.pdf.

wa Thiong'o, N. 2009. *Re-membering Africa*. Nairobi, Kenya: East African Educational.

wa Thiong'o, N. 2016. *Secure the Base: Making Africa Visible in the Globe*. London: Seagull Books.

Index

Note: Page numbers in *italic* indicate a figure and page numbers in **bold** indicate a table on the corresponding page. Page numbers followed by 'n' indicate a note.

12 Years a Slave (film) 236, 238
20th Century-Fox Film Corporation 248

abolitionism 14, 181
academic marginalisation 8
academic peripheries 6
academic revisionism 6
Access to Information and Protection of Privacy Act and the Public Order (AIPPA) 170–171
Achebe, Chinua 85–86, 126, 142–143, 145
Achmat, Zachie 224
activism for health 223–224
Adejubmobi, M. 7
Adichie, Chimamanda Ngozi 126, 144, 146–148
Afracanah (Kenyan podcast) 133
Africa/African: civilisational achievements 24; cosmology 58–59, 62; epistemologies 19; filmmaking 249; human culture 61; international policy and investments in 4; literary works 13; moral philosophy 54, 61; notions of governance 167–168; religious cosmology 59; rural–urban dichotomy 166; scholarship 3, 7; strategist 58–62
Africa Magic 253
African-centred studies 26–29, 83, 256
African cinemas: African trauma 236; and colonialism 245–246; development 246; distinctiveness 25
African Communication Research 3
African-derived theories 10
Africanisation 7, 10, 12, 15, 21, 22, 26–27, 30–31, 35, 37, 112, 122, 198
Africanity 24, 26, 29, 31, 38, 201–202
African media and communication 2, 23; *in* Africa, *from* Africa and *by* Africans 2, 23; counterhegemonic graffiti in Zimbabwe 167; Frantz Fanon 23, 43–48; Ngũgĩ wa Thiong'o 2, 12, 48–52; ontological pluralism 2; organisations 82; politics of polemicising 2; self-contained theorisation 11

African Media Review 3
African News Agency (ANA) 83
African novel and global communicative potential 13, 141; African woman and international pop-culture influencer 146–148; Africa's soft power 149–152; *Chinua Achebe* 144–146; historical overview 141–142; language choice in modern African literature 142–143; pan-African notion of African literature 144; Wole Yoyinka 148–149
African Tech Round-Up (podcast) 134
African Union and African languages 86
African Writers of English Expression Conference 142
Africa's Media: Democracy and the Politics of Belonging (Nyamnjoh) 6
Africology, American 29
Afriethic 3
Afrikaans broadcasting stations 96
Afrikology see Afrokology
Afrikology, Philosophy and Wholeness (Nabudere) 3
Afrikology and Transdisciplinary (Nabudere) 3
Afrocentricity 16n2, 28–30, 83, 87
Afrocentrism 11, 24, 28, 256
Afroes 13
Afroes Haki 2 online peace game 161
Afroganisations 69
Afrokology 11–12, 15, 16n2, 19–25; African media and communication studies 25–28; convivial Afrokological heuristic tool 34–37; defined 30; endogenous institutional communication 76; explicating and positioning an African approach 28–34; explication of 19; heuristic tool 24–25, 30, 36–37, 256; Nabudere's explication of 31; ontology 69; radicalism 258; as transdisciplinary approach 256–270, **265**
Afrokology and organisational culture 68–69; Afroganisations 69; artefacts 72–73; artefacts as ontological objects 70–72; culture 69–70;

276

Index

empirical exploration 74–78; language as artefact and ontological object 74–77; nature of culture and ontology 77–78
Afro-sensed approach 24
After image, trauma and the Holocaust (Hirsch) 236
agency 59
Ahmida, Ali Abdullatif 183
Airhihenbuwa, C.O. 219–220
airwaves as centre of cultural memory 199–201
Alexander, A. 247
Algerian war of liberation 44–47
Alibi (podcast) 133–134
Al Jazeera 151
Alonso, A. 169
altruism 61
Amabookabooka (podcast) 134
Amazon 82
American Motion Picture Export Company (AMPEC) 248
American Psychiatric Association 235
Amharic 82, 86
Amistad (film) 236
amplification 101
ANC 96
Anderson, J. 127
Anglophone regions of Africa 9
Anglo-Saxon parochialism 22
Ansu-Kyeremeh, Kwasi 6
Anthills of the Savannah (Achebe) 142
anti-retroviral therapy (ART) 229
anti-slavery Facebook groups 181–186, **185**
Appiah, K. 33
Apple 82
Arab Spring 13, 173, 181–190
artefacts 72–73; language and ontological object 74–77; as ontological objects 70–72
artificial intelligence 226
Asante, Molefi Kete 10, 24, 28, 83, 87–88, 256
Association of Community Television, South Africa (ACT-SA) 212
AT&T 82
audio archive 127
authoritarianism 13
autonomy 151
Awachie, Ifeanyi 132
Azikiwe, Namdi 88

Banda, Fackson 156, 194
Bang Bang Club, The (film) 236
Banks, S. 60
Bantu language–speaking Africans 54
Barnett, J. 169
Benchwamerz, The (podcast) 133
Berg, V.L van der 228
Berger, G. 6
Berlin Conference of 1884–1885 9
Berry, Richard 128

Bhabha, Homi 270
Biko, Steve 2
bilingual media gurus, recruitment 86–87
Birgit, B. 84
Birmingham Cultural Studies Centre 262
Bitsch, Rasmus 133, 135
Black Atlantic: Modernity and Double Consciousness, The (Gilroy) 35
black experience, global 29
black identity, interconnectedness of 30
Black Lives Matter (BLM) protests 22
Black Panther (film) 152
Black Skin, White Masks (Peau noire, masques blancs) (Fanon) 44–46
Blankenberg, N. 6
Blomkamp, Neill 14, 234
Bodunrin, I. 169
Borders, Media Crossings and the Politics of Translation: The Gaze from Southern Africa (Frassinelli) 268
Bourgault, Louise M. 5
Brighenti, A.M. 169
Brinkley, John 130
Britz, J.J. 85
broadcasting *see* South Africa, developments in broadcasting policy
Broadcasting Act, 1999 208
Broadcasting Services Regulation Act (2007) 170
Broadcasting White Paper, 1998 208
Brown, Matt 133
Buntu, B.A. 77–78
Burawoy, M. 7
business scholarship 56
Butler, Judith 235
Bvuma 176
Bvuma kuchembera Mugabe 176

Cable News Network (CNN) 181
Cabral, Amilcar 85
Caitaani mũtharaba-inĩ (Devil on the cross) (Thiong'o) 48
Cala 193
Cala University Students Association (CALUSA) 193
Cameroon 81
CARE International 223
Carey, J.W. 58
Cartesianism 31
Caruth, Cathy 235
Carveth, R. 247
Castro-Gómez, S. 192
centralisation, privatisation and 103
centrism 11
Chappie (Blomkamp) 14, 234, 237–238; decolonisation 237; film studies 235–237; individual and collective trauma 238–241; trauma and memory studies 235–237

Index

Chasi, Colin 12–13, 23, 102
Chiwome, E.M. 168
CINE Films 248
Cinema Exhibitors Association of Nigeria (CEAN) 251
citizen journalism 155–156; Afroes Haki 2 online peace game 161; conflict transformation, Kenyan netizens 163; Map Kibera project 160; Mindset education 161; Mzalendo 160–161; Sisi Ni Amani, work of 161–162; Twitter Chief 162–163; Ushahidi in Kenya's 2008 PEV 156–159
civic nationalism 98, 104
coalitional consciousness 268
CODESRIA 3
codification of rules 167
colonialism/colonial 10, 47, 110; epistemes 117; importation 34; languages 9; power matrix 102; scholarship 2
coloniality 93–95, 97, 100, 104
Coloniality, Subaltern Knowledges and Border Thinking (Mignolo) 99
Coloniality of Power in Postcolonial Africa: Myths of Decolonization (Ndlovu-Gatsheni) 3
colonisation 33, 56, 68, 82, 128
Columbia Pictures 248
Comaroff, J. 36, 256
Comaroff, J. L. 36, 256
commercialisation 71
commercial radio 129
Communicare: Journal for Communication Sciences in Southern Africa 3
communication: functions in corporations 57; organisational 267; in racist world 48; ritual view of 127; technological innovations 95; transmission view of 127; *see also* strategic communication, violence of
communication curricula 123; colonial epistemes, defragmenting 117; decolonisation agenda 119–122; decolonised curricula 118–119; employability of university graduates 117–118; gamesmanship, zero-sum 114; recognise context 116; transformation, global 107–122; 'Western' bias 114–116
Communication in Africa: A Search for Boundaries (Doobs) 5
Communication Manifesto, The (Waisbord) 6
Communicatio: South African Journal for Communication Theory and Research 3
Communitas: Journal for Community Communication and Information Impact 3
community radio 129, 193–194
competition literature 71
complex ambivalence 35
Concerning Violence (documentary film, Olsson) 47
conflict transformation 13, 163–164
consent, manufacturing of 58

content diversity 206, 208
conviviality 11, 20, 29
convivial scholarship 11, 32, 261, 266, 271–272
cooperative action, human capacity for 55
corporate communication 68, 72, 77
corruption 120
co-substantiation 55
Couldry, Nick 126
counterflow 258
counterhegemonic graffiti in Zimbabwe 166–167; African media and communication 167; African notions of governance 167–168; anti-Mugabe hate speech 176–178; Mugabe to step down, call for 172–176; political graffiti as cultural medium 168–169; political identity, expression of 170–172; public space and political discourses 169–170
courses in communications and journalism 86
COVID-19 218, 220
Crisis Coalition 176
Critical Arts: A Journal of South-North Cultural and Media Studies 3
critical discourse analysis (CDA) 183
critical political economy 206–207
cryptic health messages 228
Cubitt, S. 247
culture, construct in organisational setting 68–69; Afroganisations 69; artefacts 70–73; culture 69–70; empirical exploration 74–78; language as artefact and ontological object 74–77; nature of culture and ontology 77–78
culture/cultural 69–70; collectivism 78; communication barriers 14; curriculum redesign 86 expression 52; hybridisation 33; imperialism, French 45; nature of 77–78; and ontology 77–78; responsive theories 220; traumas 235; violence 47
curriculum *see* communication curricula

Damned of the Earth, The (Fanon) 44
De Agostini, Enrico 183
Death of a King's Horseman (Yoyinka) 148–149
De Beer, A.S. 102
decoder 211
decoloniality 2, 22, 32, 38, 93, 103
decolonisation/decolonial 6–7, 10, 13, 21, 43, 47–48, 112, 120–122, 128, 192, 198, 237; in Africa 14, 21; of curriculum 13, 109, 118, 121; educators 112; hermeneutic tool 34; of higher education 108; media and communication 111; nollywood as 245–253; project 202; theories contextualised 196–197
decolonising African media 34, 81–83, 107–108; African Union and African languages 86; communication curricula 114–122; curriculum redesign 86; debate 109–112; de-Europeanise mentality 85–87; literature 83–85; media

Index

and Afrocentricity 87–88; media content and adaptations 87–88; recruit bilingual media gurus 86–87; survey 112–114
Decolonising the Mind: The Politics of African Language and Literature (wa Thiong'o) 49–50, 143
deculturation programme 26
de-Europeanise mentality 85–87; African Union and African languages 86; bilingual media gurus, recruitment 86–87; curriculum redesign 86
demarcation 29
democratisation 128
Department of Kiswahili 85
de-provincialisation 23–24
deprovincialisation 85
de-racialisation 102–103
Derricourt, Robin 99
de-Westernisation 37, 108–110, 257, 258
Diamond, Larry 152
digital migration 14, 206, 210–214
digital terrestrial television (DTT) 14, 206; migration 207; restructuring process 210; terrestrial television technologies 210
digitisation 128
Dijk, T.A. van 193
Diop, Cheikh Anta 81, 85, 87
directional intimacy 132
disalienation 44, 48
discipline, African media and communication as academic 1–3, 5–7, 8–12, 15, 19–21, 23, 28–29, 32, 33, 36, 68, 82, 107–112, 123, 258–266, 271–272
discourse analysis 13, 181, 189
disembededdness 101
diversification 109
diversity 206
Doctors without Borders 223
Doobs, Leonard W. 5
Downing, J. 5
DSTV 209–210, 212
du Plooy, G. 111
Dussel, Enrique 237
Dutta-Bergman, M.J. 220
DVB-T2 211
Dying Colonialism, A (L'an V de la revolution algerienne) (Fanon) 44–46

East African Regional Broadcasting Service (EARBS) 85
Ebo, E. 6
Eboigbe, A. 253
Ebola in West Africa 220–221
Economic Community of West African States (ECOWAS) 218
economism 101
Ecquid Novi: African Journalism Studies 3

eGoli 240
eHealth 226–227
Elias, N. 61
emancipation 4
empirical exploration 74–78
Encore 213
encryption 211–213
endogenous institutional communication 76
enforcement of human rights 118
enlightenment 4
epistemology/epistemological 24; conviviality 24; interconnectedness 29, 259, 271; justice 30; totalitarianism 31
ethnic-driven languages 87
eTV 209, 212
Eurocentrism 33, 99
Euro-North-America–centric perspectives 5
Evuleocha, S. 249
Extended Parallel Process Model (EPPM) 219

Facebook: anti-slavery groups 181–186, **185**; Swahili 81
Faculty of Informatics and Virtual Education 85
faith-based organisations (FBOs) 218
familiars 59
Fanagalo 68, 73, 76, 78
Fanon, Frantz 2, 12, 43–48, 85, 96, 111, 129, 197; a author 44; birth 44; early life 44; *El Moudjahid* 44; *Front de Liberation Nationale* (FLN) 44; power of postcolonial elites 43; socioeconomic inequalities 43; theory of disalienation 44
#FeesMustFall protest 43, 240
Feuilles d'Afrique: Etude de la presse de l'Afrique subsaharienne (Tudesq) 5
Figuoera, Y. 193
film: funding and policy 250–251; studies 235–237
filmmaking, direct-to-DVD video 248
First Person (podcast) 134
fixed-line infrastructure 131
#fixthepatentlaws 224
Flamholtz, E. 72
Fonlon, Bernard Nsokika 85
formalisation 167
Frassinelli, Pier Paolo 12, 268
free-to-air environment 209, 211–212, 214
Freire, P. 97

Gathoni, Mwai 161
Gaynor, T.S. 169
Gecau, Kimani 262
general public online (eHealth) 226
geopolitics 3, 10
ghetto 167
Gidden, A. 59–60
Gilroy, Paul 20

Index

Global Citizen 225
Globalectic approach to curricula 111
Globalectics: Theory and the Politics of Knowing (Thiong'o) 49, 51
global information networks 152
globalisation 83
global North 5–7, 9, 14
global South 35, 108
global village 82
Goffman, E. 55
Google 82
Goro, Wangũi wa 49
graffiti 166, 168–169, 177–178
Grain of Wheat, A (Thiong'o) 50
Greeff, W.J. 12, 267
Grosfoguel, Ramon 101, 237
Group of 77 (G77) 16n1
Grunwald Declaration on Media Education, 1982 110

Habermas, J. 5
Habermas' theory of public sphere 189
Half of a Yellow Sun (Adichie) 146–148
Hall, Stuart 35, 46, 48
Hallin, D.C. 5, 95
Halvorsen, T.A. 84
Haraway, Donna 104
harmony 25, 54–55, 58, 60, 269
Harrison, F.V. 264
Hausa 81–82, 86, 147
Health Belief Model (HBM) 219
health communication 14, 192, 217–218; activism for health 223–224; artificial intelligence 226; barriers 230–231; contextualising 218–219; cryptic health messages 228; and culture 225–226; Ebola in West Africa 220–221; eHealth 226–227; ethics 229–230; health theories 219–220; language and messaging 227–229; loss of meaning in translation 228–229; mHealth 226; online conversation enablers 226–227; online health activism 225; regulatory environment 221–223; social media 226
health theories 219–220
Hersman, Erik 157
heterogeneity 102
heuristic toolkit 24–25, 30, 36–37, 256
hip-hop movement, American 169
Hirsch, Joshua 236
HIV/AIDS campaigns 218
Holocaust 235
Hotel Rwanda (film) 236
human beings 60; communication, violent 55–56; co-substantiality 60; substances 55
humanism 24
humanitarian crisis 156
human rights 103, 118–119, 156, 158

human trafficking 182–183
hybridity 35

identity, self-conscious flexibility of 36
Imbabazi (film) 236
imperialism 45
imperial Manichean misanthropic scepticism 94
incommensurability 32
incompleteness 20, 23, 25–26, 33, 266
independence 15, 34, 44, 48, 82, 84
Independent Broadcasting Authority (IBA) 129, 205
Independent Broadcasting Authority Act, 1993 207
Independent Communications Authority of South Africa (ICASA) 205
Independent Electoral and Boundaries Committee (IEBC) 159
indigenisation 26
Indigenous Communication in Africa: Concept, Application, and Prospects (Ansu-Kyeremeh) 6
indigenous knowledge 21, 28, 266
Inexba (The Wound): Sexual, Gender, Cultural and Religious Traumata on the African Screen (Kirby-Hirst and Karam) 237
information and communication technologies (ICTs) 218
institutional communication 69, 76
institutionalised violence 91–92
Integrated Information Communication Technology (ICT) policy 207
intellectual–political approaches 29
intellectual violence 37
interconnectedness 24, 30, 32
interdisciplinary research, characteristics of **263**
International Association for Media and Communication Research (IAMCR) 37, 112
International Criminal Court (ICC) 157
International human rights (IHR) 229
internationalisation 37, 108–110, 119, 258
Internet 126–127, 155
Invention of Africa: Gnosis, Philosophy and the Order of Knowledge, The (Mudimbe) 2
iOS 11 135
iPod 127
iROKOtv 253
isiXhosa 82, 84, 86
iSiZulu 96
isiZulu aphorism 59
iTunes 128, 133, 135

Jalada Africa 52
Jena, N. 169
journalism: education 114; ethics 3
Journal of African Media Studies (JAMS) 3, 25
Junne, G. 156
jural community 168

Index

Kamiriithu Community Education and Cultural Centre 50
Kamwangamulu, N. 54
Kanu, I.A. 167
Kaplan, E. Anne 236
Karam, Beschara 14, 237
Karenga, M. 29
Kariuki, Francis 162
Kasoma, Fancis 3
Keesing, R.M. 69
Kenya Human Rights Commission (KHRC) 158
Kenyan new media platforms 155; *see also* citizen journalism
Kenyan Queer Questions (podcast) 133
Kenyatta, Jomo 81, 89
Kershaw, T. 29
Kibaki, Mwai 156
Kim, W. 56
Kirby-Hirst, Mark 236–237
Kiswahili 82–83, 85–87
knowledge production 2–3, 23–24, 101, 108, 259–260
Kobia, David 157
#KOT 157
kuwanda kwakanaka 62
Kwakangoshatira pupedza muto 62

Lang, G.E. 167
Lang, K. 167
language 24; choice in modern African literature 142–143; and culture 51; and messaging 227–229; overestimating power 75; underestimating power 75–76
Larkin, B. 127
Latour, Bruno 59
Lederach, J.P. 163–164
Leon Commission report 73–74
Lerner, Daniel 99
L'Etang, J. 68
Levi, M. 29
LGBTQI+ communities 225
liberal democracy 6
liberalism 24, 151
liberation struggle 4
linear broadcast model 128
linguistic exclusion 227
linguistic pluralism 143
literary fiction 145
literature 83–85
lived realities 3, 23, 35, 264, 266–267
Livingston, S. 109
Lobato, R. 248
locus of enunciation 100
Lor, P.J. 84
Louw, E.P. 92
Lubinga, Elizabeth 14
Lumumba, Patrice 89

maat 24, 32
Ma'at 7
Machaya, C. 170–171
Madala 76
Madhubuti, H.K. 30
Mafolo, Thomas 144
Magubane, Bernard 98
Maldonado-Torres, Nelson 94
Mamdani, Mahmood 98–99
Mancini, P. 5, 95
Mandela, Nelson 102
Mangeya, Hugh 13, 166
Manichaean zero-sum fashion 113
Mano, Winston 3, 69
Manzella, Joseph 102
Map Kibera 13, 158, 160
marginalisation 1–2, 11, 19, 234, 241, 270, 272
Marikana Massacre: Through the Lens, The (film) 236
market-led economies 206
Martin, A. 72
Marxism 91
Masoga, M.A. 24
Mass Communication in Africa (Mytton) 5
mass media broadcaster 135
Mass Media in Sub-Saharan Africa (Bourgault) 5
Matigari 49
Matt Brown Media 133
Mauburgne, R. 56
Maxwell, J.A. 35
Mazama, A. 87
Mazrui, Ali 81–82, 84–85, 190
Mbeki, T. 152n1
Mbembe, A. 177–178
Mbigi, L. 6
Mbinjama, A. 83–84
McCall, J.C. 247
McKinsey, 207
McLuhan, Marshall 82, 92
McPhee, R. 60
Médecins Sans Frontières (MSF) 223
media: and Afrocentricity 87–88; and colonial project 194–195; and communication studies 21; content and adaptations 87–88; dissemination 81; economics 15; and memory 195–196; in post-apartheid South Africa 95; programme **198**; systems 5, 95; theories, normative 5
media decolonisation in Africa 81–83; African Union and African languages 86; curriculum redesign 86; de-Europeanise mentality 85–87; literature 83–85; media and Afrocentricity 87–88; media content and adaptations 87–88; recruit bilingual media gurus 86–87
media institutions 10, 14, 192–198, 201–203, 207
media in South Africa 91–92; configurations, in post-apartheid South Africa 95–99; locus

Index

of enunciation, of media theory and 99–104; power, modernity/coloniality and 92–95
media studies 3, 4, 7, 11–12, 20, 21, 26, 107, 110, 112, 118, 119, 120, 123, 167, 262, 272
Member of Executive Committee (MEC) 229
memory 235–237
mental slavery in Africa 86–87
Meribe, N. 69
Merwe, Lara van der 13
meta-ontology 71
Methodology of the Oppressed (Sandoval) 36
Metz, T. 54
mHealth 226
Mhudi (Plaatjie) 142
Michuki, John 155
microeconomic theory 247
Mignolo, Walter D. 35, 91, 95, 99, 237, 258
Miller, J. 248
milton, v.c. 92
mindset education 161
Miners Shot Down (film) 236
Mining Qualifications Authority (MQA) 73–74
MISA 194
Misra, A. 38
misrecognition 4, 258, 266
mixing 131
M-Net 209–210
Mobutu, Joseph-Desire 26
Mochama, Tony 157
modernisation 6, 97
modernity 2, 100, 104
Modisane, Bloke 143
Moeti oa Bochabela (Mafolo) 144
monolith metaphor 72
Morag, Raya 236
moral philosophy 12, 22, 54–56, 58, 60, 131
More, Mabogo 98, 100
Motale, Steve 103
Motion Picture Export Association (MPEA) 248
Movement for Democratic Change (MDC) 171, 171–172
Moving the Centre: The Struggle for Cultural Freedoms (Thiong'o) 49
Moyo, L. 108
Mpofu, Shepherd 102
Mudimbe, Valentine 91, 98–99
Mugabe, Robert 27, 173; anti-Mugabe hate speech 176–178; anti-Mugabe sentiments 172–177, 172–177; call to step down 172–176
MultiChoice 205–206, 210–214
multidisciplinary research, characteristics of **263**
multiplicity 69
Mutsvairo, B. 108
mystification 101
Mytton, Graham 5
Mzalendo 13, 160–161

Nabudere, Dani 28–29, 32, 68, 77, 264
Nabudere, D.W. 10–11, 16n2, 24
Najam, A. 16n1
Nakamura, Lisa 126
Napoli, P.M. 206
narrative 126
Naspers 205, 209–210
National Cohesion and Integration Committee (NCIC) 159
National Economic Empowerment and Development Strategy (NEEDS) 251
National Film Distribution Company (NFDC) 248
national liberation movements 48
National Party (NP) 96
National Steering Committee (NSE) 159
Nativism 31
NATO 187
Ndlovu, Morgan 102
Ndlovu-Gatsheni, S.J. 20, 85, 91, 101, 235, 250
NDO Films 248
Neal, Arthur 236
neologisms 22
Netflix 253, 258
new media 155
Ngcaweni, B. 29
Niehaus, I. 59
Nigeria: films (cinemas) 14, 250; media 81; stories 145
Night Is Coming: A Threnody for the Victims of Marikana (film) 236
Nkrumah, Kwame 26
Nkrumah, Osagefo Kwame 88–89
Nnebue, Kenneth 250
Nollywood as decoloniality 14, 245–246; audience acceptance 249–250; distribution and reach 247–249; framework for analysis 246–247; funding and policy 250–251
non-governmental organisations (NGOs) 218
nongovernment radio broadcasters 129
non individuality 26
non-profit organisations (NPOs) 218
Nordenstreng, K. 6
North, global 5–7, 9, 14
nostalgia and belonging 201–202
Nothias, T. 4
Not Your African Cliche 132
Nwosu, P.O. 26
Nyamnjoh, Francis B. 3, 6, 11, 20, 25, 33, 61, 86, 111, 256–257, 259, 264
Nye, Joseph 149–152
Nyerere, Julius Kambarage 26, 88

Obeng-Quaidoo, I. 26
Odinga, Raila 156
Okigbo, Christopher 143
Okolloh, Ory 157

Olsson, Goran Hugo 47
on-air conversations 132
Ong, Walter 130–131
online community 155
online conversation enablers 226–227
online health activism 225
On the Postcolony (Mbembe) 2
ontology 24, 71, *71*, 77–78
openness 170
oral storytelling 130–131; affordability 131; community-building 131–132
organisational capacity 57
organisational communication 267
organisational culture *70*, 75
organisational goals 56
organisational languages 73
organisational ontology 71, *71*
Organisation for Economic Co-operation and Development (OECD) 16n1, 146
Organisation of African Unity 141
Osha, Sanya 31–32
otherness 24
Otherwise? (podcast) 133
Owers, J. 247

Palm-Wine Drinkard, The (Tutuola) 142
pan-Africanism: notion of African literature 144; writing 9
Pare, A. 169
particularism, theoretical 7
particularity 6–7, 15, 21, 34, 201
Peace in Our Pockets 161–162
PeaceNet 159
Pedagogy of the Oppressed (Freire) 97
PEN-3 Cultural Model 219
People Living with HIV/AIDS (PLWH) 224
performativities 97
peripheries 8
Peteet, J. 170
Picard, R.G. 247
Picarelli, J.T. 182
Pithouse, Richard 43
Plaatjie, Sol T. 142
pluralism 25, 69, 151
pluriversality 25, 32
pluriverse 1–2, 6, 15, 260, 265
podcast in Africa 13, 126–127; definition 127–128; infrastructure 134–135; mass media model 132; oral storytelling 128–129; reality 132–134; theoretical benefits 130–132; theorising media and cultural formation 127
polarisation 9
political economy 169
political graffiti as cultural medium 168–169
political identity 170–172
political victimisation 168
positionality 32, 46, 242

post-apartheid South Africa 91–92, 95–99
postcolonialism/postcolonial 10; filmmaking 246; forms of communication 9; transformation of public media 207; universities 122
post-election violence (PEV) 155
power 1–4, 9, 12–13; African media 43, 45–47, 49, 50; African podcasting and 126, 136; African strategic communication 59; Afrokology and 19, 21, 33, 36–37, 72, 75, 79, 261, 263, 267–268, 270–272; in *Chappie* 234, 237; citizen journalism and 155, 162; community radio and 194, 196; decolonisation and 87–89, 91–104, 110–111; graffiti 161–168, 170–171, 173–174; health communication and 221–223, 225, 227, 230; modern slavery and 182–183, 188–190; Nollywood and 245, 247, 248, 250; private sector media 206, 209, 213; soft 141–153
precolonialism 10
President's Emergency Plan for AIDS Relief (PEPFAR) 218
private sector media on sustainability of SABC 205–206; broadcast restructuring 207–210; compromise over encryption 213–214; digital migration policy 210–214; DSTV 209–210; encryption 211–213; free-to-air television and the SABC 214; M-Net 209–210; Naspers 209–210; political economy approach 206–207; qualitative research methods 207; South Africa's broadcasting policy 207–214
privatisation and centralisation 103
provincialising 23–24
public media institutions 207
Public Order and Security Act (POSA) 170
public-service broadcaster 205
public space and political discourses 169–170
Public Wi-Fi 135

Querajazu, A. 260
Quijano, Anibal 94, 197, 237

Race and the Construction of the Dispensable Other (Magubane) 99
racism 119–120
radical reorientation 19
Radio-Alger 195
Radiolab 131
rainbowism 98
Randal, Y. 72
Rao, S. 36
reconceptualisation 87
re-existence 4, 258–259
Refilwe Africa 219
reflexivity 266, 271
Reghellin, M. 169
regional resource-sharing schemes 85
regulatory environment 221–223

Index

relative obscurity 61
Renan, Ernest 98
renovate 34
resource dependence theory 71
#RhodesMustFall protest 43, 85, 240
Riley, P. 60
ritual view of communication 127
River Between, The (Thiong'o) 48
RKO Pictures Inc. 248
Rodney, Water 85
Rotich, Juilana 157
Rouch, Jean 246

SABC-run Zulu radio station 129
Said, E.W. 5, 127
Sama, Emmanuel 247
Sandoval, C. 36, 268
Sankara, Thomas 89
sankofa 24, 32
Santos, Boaventura 91
Schein, E.H. 69, 71
Schein's typology (elements of organisational culture) 70
Schiller, H.I. 102
Schindler's List (film) 236
Schramm, E. 261
Schutz, Elna 135
scientific racialism 58
Scott, M. 4
Selassie, Haile 141
self-actualisation 149
self-congratulatory representations 97
SemioCode 183–184
Sesotho 144
set-top box control 211
sexism 120
Sharperville Massacre, 1960 169
Shona 62
Shortell, Timothy 184
Siebert, S.F. 5
signal-scrambling system 211
single story 4, 7, 146–147
Sisi Ni Amani, work of 13, 161–162
Sisi Ni Amani Kenya (SNA-K) 156, 161–163
Sitto, Karabo 14
Skjerdal, T.S. 26
slavery: American 189; anti-slavery Facebook groups 181–186, **185**; mental, in Africa 86–87
slave trade in Libya 181–183; data analysis 184–185; discussion and conclusion 187–190; findings 185–187; methodology 183–184; new global trade 182
Smart 157–158
smart box/decoder 211
smartphones 131
Smith, L.T. 198
Sobering, The (podcast) 134

social conflict 163
social justice in education 111
social media 14, 226; *see also* Facebook
social media abolitionism 14
socio-cultural groups 226
sociogeny 44
soft-coercion 98
soft power 149–152
Sound Africa (podcast) 134
Soundcloud 135
South, global 35, 108
South Africa, developments in broadcasting policy 207; broadcast restructuring 207–209; DSTV 209–210; M-Net 209–210; Naspers 209–210
South Africa, media in 91–92; configurations, in post-apartheid South Africa 95–99; locus of enunciation, of media theory and 99–104; power, modernity/coloniality and 92–95
South African Broadcasting Corporation (SABC) 92–93, 205–206; *see also* private sector media on sustainability of SABC
South African Communications Association (SACOMM) 112
South African Communications Forum (SACF) 212
South African Human Rights Commission (SAHRC) 103
South African mining industry 68–78
South African Truth and Reconciliation Commission 236
Southern African Development Community (SADC) 218
Southern African Institute for Mining and Metallurgy (SAIMM) 74
Southernising 108
Soweto Uprising, 1976 169
Soyinka, Wole 143–144
spectrum 108, 166, 209–210, 214, 221
Spread, The (podcast) 133
state-run broadcasting companies 129
strategic communication, violence of 54–55; human communication 55–56; management of risks 57; strategy 56–58; Ubuntu and vital force of the African strategist 58–62
strategic organisation 58
strategy 56–58
structural adjustment policies (SAPs) 146
structural inequalities 4
structuration approach 59
subscriptions to access 206, 209–210
sustainability 14, 23, 211
Swahili 9
syncretism 26

Taylor, D.S. 26
technical instrument 46

Index

Teer-Tomaselli, R.E. 194, 209
Tempels, P. 60
Texeira, R.P. 178
The AIDS Support Organisation (TASO) 223
Theory of Reasoned Action 219
Things Fall Apart (Achebe) 145
Thompson, J.B. 95
Thussu, D.K. 251, 258
Tomasello, M. 60
Torres-Maldonado, N. 93, 103, 197
Toward the African revolution (Fanon) 44
trans-Atlantic trade 236
transdisciplinarity 20, 32, 261, **263**
transformative learning 264, 266
transformative power 21
translanguages 86
transliteration 86
transmission view of communication 127
trauma: cross-generalational 235; individual and collective 238–241; and memory studies 235–237; multidirectionality of 235
Trauma and Cinema (Kaplan and Wang) 236
Trauma Cinema: Documenting Incest and the Holocaust (Walker) 236
Treatment Action Campaign (TAC) 224
Trump, Donald 4
Tsedu, Mathata 103
Tsvangirai 177
Tuck, E. 192
Tudesq, Andre-Jean 5
Tutuola, Amos 142
Twitter Chief 162–163
Tyali, Siyasanga M. 14

ubuntu 7, 24, 26, 32, 54; African strategist, force of 58–62; moral philosophy 54
ujaama 24
Ukadike, N.F. 248
UKhozi FM 129
UNESCO-funded McBride Report 3
UNESCO International Commission 109
United Artists 248
United Nations 187
United Nations Development Programme (UNDP) 159
United Nations Economic Commission for Africa 83
United Nations International Children's Emergency Fund (UNICEF) 223
United States Agency for International Development (USAID) 218
universal humanism 44
universality 6–7, 15, 21, 25, 32, 34, 78, 94, 108
universal pedagogical narratives 270
Universal Pictures 248
University of KwaZulu-Natal (UKZN) 262
University of Zimbabwe (UZ) 262, 264

Ushahidi 13; crisis 161; crisis mapping 156; in Kenya's 2008 PEV 156–159; platform 155–156
'*ushe madzoro hunoravanwa*' 172
Uzong, E. 16n2, 28

Vambe, M. 30
Van Horne, Winston 10, 28
Verizon 82
violence of strategic communication 54–55; human communication 55–56; strategy 56–58; Ubuntu and vital force of the African strategist 58–62
visual media 128
Voice of Free Algeria 46–47
Vukani Community Radio (VCR) 14, 192–193; airwaves as centre of cultural memory 199–201; broadcasting 201; community radio station 193–194; decolonial theories contextualised 196–197; decolonisation project 202; media and colonial project 194–195; media and memory 195–196; nostalgia and belonging 201–202; on-air content 201; research methods 198–199

Wadhwa, K. 155
Waisbord, S. 6, 110
Walker, Janet 236
Walsh, C.E. 258
Waltzing with Bashir: Perpetrator Trauma and Cinema (Morag) 236
Wang, Ban 236
warfare 12, 54–58
Warner Bros. Inc. 248
Wasserman, H. 36, 102
wa Thiong'o, Ngũgĩ 2, 12, 48–52, 85, 91, 98, 100, 111, 126, 262; birth 48; career 48; cyborature 52; education 48; *Globalectics: Theory and the Politics of Knowing* 51; linguistic diversity 50; novels 48–49
Watson, H. 155
Watson, T. 68
Weep Not, Child (Thiong'o) 48
Western colonialism 109
Western/Euro-American ideologies in African contexts 68–69
Wi-Fi hotspots 131
Wilderson, B. Frank 100
Willems, Wendy 102
William, J. Wilson 182
Wilson, William J. 167–168
Wiredu, K. 26
witches 59
Wits Radio Academy 135
Wizard of the Crow (Thiong'o) 49
Wolf, Eric 98–99
Wolof 81–83, 86–87
World Health Organisation (WHO) 218, 223
World Summit on Information Society (WSIS) 83
Woza 169

Index

Wretched of the Earth, The (Fanon) 47–48
Writers in Politics: A Re-engagement with Issues of Literature and Society (Thiong'o) 49

Xhosa 144, 152
Xhosa speakers 200

Yang, K.W. 192
Year Five of the Algerian Revolution; The Wretched of the Earth (*Les damnés de la terre*) (Fanon) 44

Yoruba 81–83, 86–87
Yoyinka, Wole 148–149

ZANU (PF) 170–172
Zegeye, A. 30
Zeleza, P. 33
Zimbabwe 54, 166, 168–169, 176–177, 267
Zulu 82–83, 87, 144
Zuma, Jacob 101, 103